The Home Pattern Book of Needlecraft

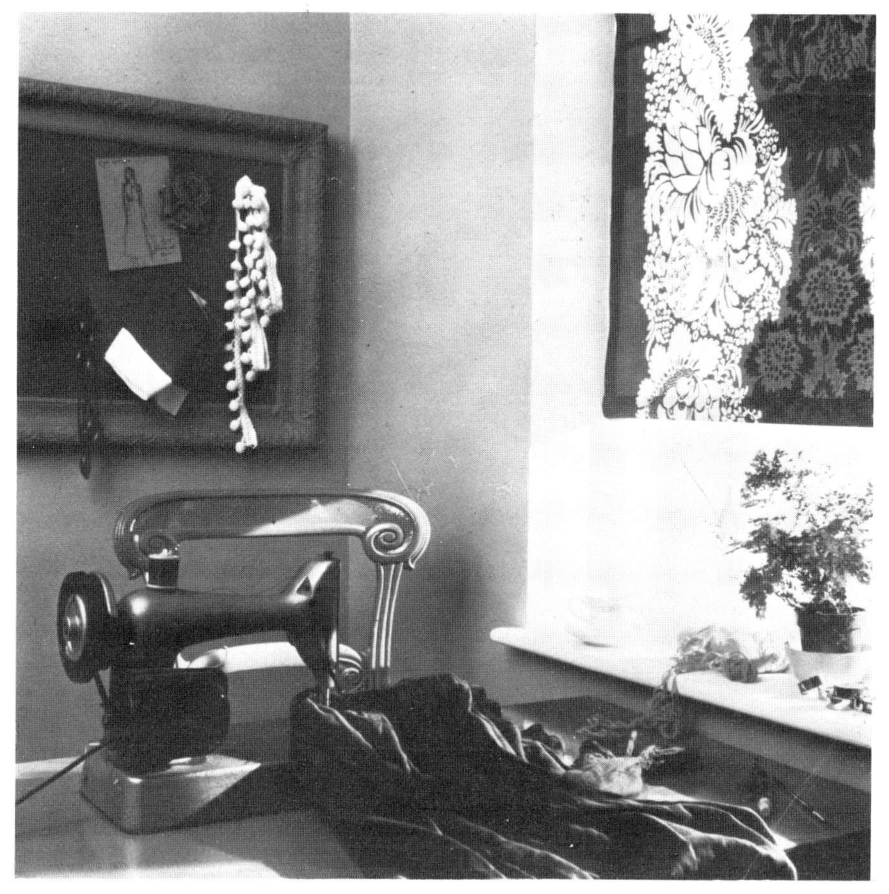

The Home Pattern Book of Needlecraft is adapted from *Joan Fisher's Guide to Needlecraft*, *Joan Fisher's Guide to Knitting*, *Joan Fisher's Guide to Embroidery*, and *Joan Fisher's Guide to Crochet*.

This edition published in 1979 by
New English Library Limited,
Barnard's Inn,
Holborn,
London EC1N 2JR,
England

Created, designed and produced by
Trewin Copplestone Publishing Ltd, London

Printed in Italy by New Interlitho, Milan

SBN 450 04437 8

The Home Pattern Book of Needlecraft

Joan Fisher

NEW ENGLISH LIBRARY
TIMES MIRROR

CONTENTS

INTRODUCTION

A needle and a length of yarn . . . basic materials perhaps, but to the needlewoman they can be as expressive and as individual as palette and brush are to an artist, pen and paper to a writer.

And the results can be as fascinating and as wide-ranging. A child's simple embroidery worked in a single stitch, an ambitious and intricate tapestry wall hanging, a cobwebby lace edging, a multicoloured Fair Isle pullover . . . each is achieved with just needle and thread.

To be skilled with a needle has long been a hallmark of accomplishment for young ladies. In the 17th century, when the King of Siam asked King James I to provide him with an English wife, he was offered a young lady described as being of excellent parts for 'music, her needle and good discourse'.

Perhaps a skill in needlecraft is no longer a prerequisite of wifely prowess, but the attraction of making things to wear or to decorate our homes has never really changed. There is still, and no doubt always will be, a great satisfaction in producing fine traditional embroideries. On the other hand, an ability to knit, crochet or dressmake can bring instant fashion right to your fingertips, and give you the pleasure of making and wearing low-cost garments in colours and styles tailormade to suit you perfectly. And, on a practical level, an understanding of sewing techniques will help you to make elegant soft furnishings to enhance your home.

This book offers an introduction to the basic needlecraft subjects: sewing, knitting, crochet, embroidery and macramé. The age-old craft of macramé involves no needles and no stitches . . . just yarn and knots. But almost every trade and profession boasts its own range of knots: the surgeon has his knots, so has the gardener, and so has the seaman . . . The decorative macramé knot is the needlewoman's knot, and for this reason justifies its place here.

This book should inspire you to create with needle and thread many beautiful things, and should open doors to a world of creative satisfaction and rewarding self-expression.

JOAN FISHER

Chief photographer:
Rex Bamber

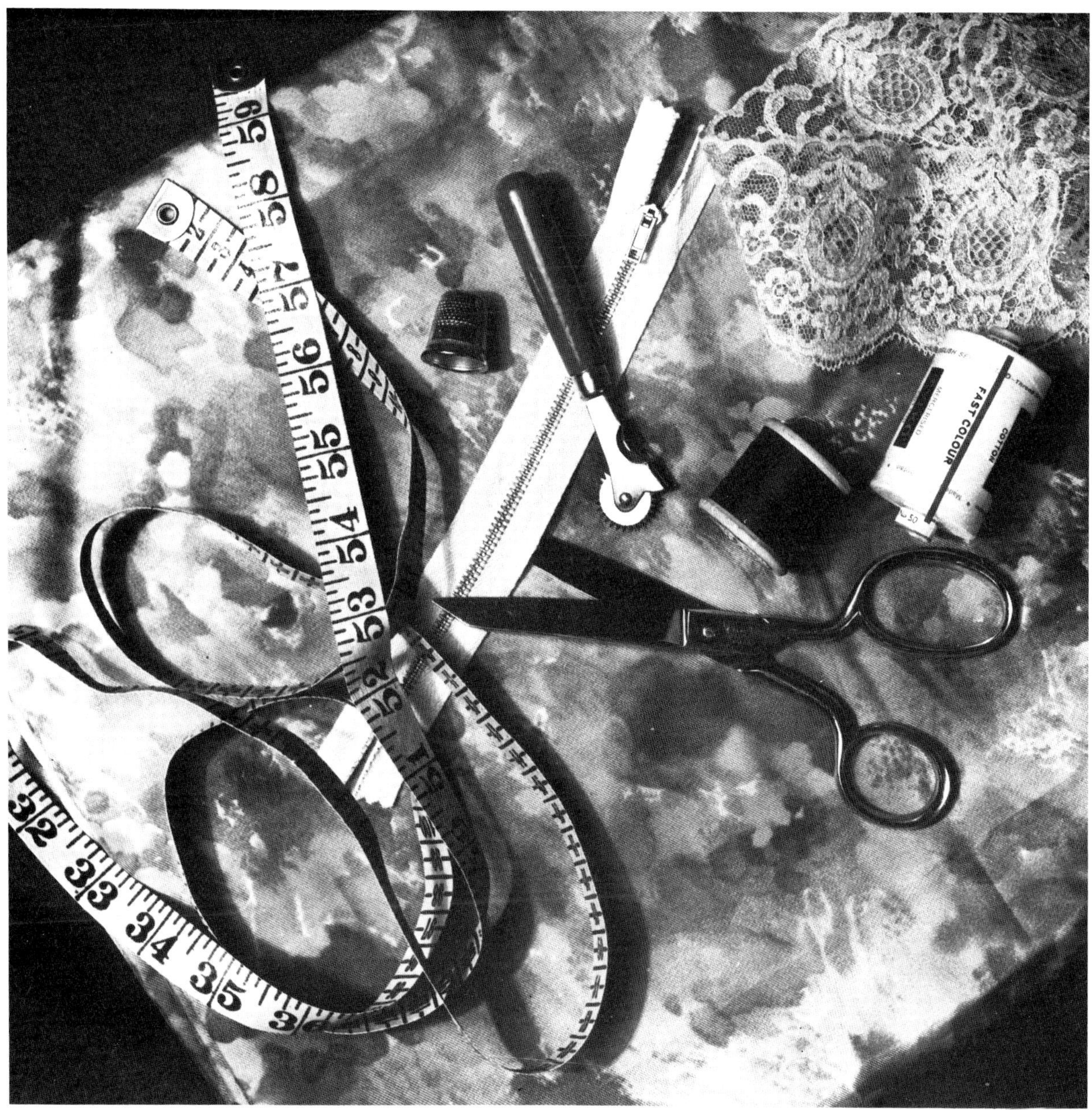

Section One
SEWING

Anyone can make a dress! That is, anyone can buy a length of fabric, cut out a pattern and stitch the pieces together. But unless care and attention are paid to the details of sewing, and trouble taken to learn the 'tricks of the trade', the result may well be an ill-fitting, unflattering garment which does not justify the time and effort spent in the making.

Sewing like any other form of handicraft, is an art. With practice and patience, it is an art which can be learned. When the reward is a ward-robe of beautiful, perfectly-fitting clothes, time spent in initial study is well repaid.

Our instructions here will introduce you to the basic elements of the craft of sewing and, starting on page 9, there are five easy-to-make patterns for simple but attractive classic garments.

Part 1—General

EQUIPMENT
Needles

For hand sewing, have a selection of mixed sizes, including No. 7 darners for basting, and No. 9 sharps or straws for fine work. For machine sewing, use No. 11 for fine fabrics, No. 14 for general purposes, No. 16 for heavy fabrics.

Pins

Use good-quality steel pins, as these will not leave rust marks or holes in your fabric.

Scissors

Three pairs are required: shears for cutting fabrics, a medium sized sharp pair for cutting paper, and a small pointed pair for clipping seams. Pinking shears are also useful.

Sewing threads

Again a varied selection is best. For general use, a 60 cotton or 50 or 60 mercerised cotton (ordinary mercerised) is best. For heavy fabrics, such as tweed or corduroy, use a 40 cotton or 40 mercerised cotton (heavy duty mercerised). For fine and sheer fabrics, use a fine nylon or Terylene thread, or a fine mercerised. There are good-quality multi-purpose threads also available which can be used with all fabric types and weights.

Also useful

Tape measure; yard stick; iron; ironing board and sleeve board; pressing cloth; tailor's chalk; dressmaker's carbon paper and tracing wheel; thimble; hem marker; stitch unpicker; paper and pencil.

FABRICS

If you already make your own clothes you will know how exciting fabric shops and departments can be! In fact the selection of a suitable fabric can sometimes be difficult because there is such a wonderful range of designs and fabric types to choose from. However, if you are a beginner, then it is best to limit your choice to an easy-to-handle fabric. Slippery materials and ones that fray easily can try the patience of the most experienced dressmaker. Cotton fabrics are good for beginners; so are the cotton and wool mixtures, and fine wools.

A plain fabric which will not need lining is a good choice. If you choose a pattern, then make sure it is a small irregular one. Checks, stripes and prints with a large or regular pattern repeat are tricky, as they need careful matching at seams and edges. The fabric chart below will serve as a guide to the basic fabrics generally available, and any special treatment these fabrics require.

Fabric Guide

Fabric	Description	Thread, Needle & Tension	Pressing	Special Care
Brocade	Heavy fabric, with raised patterns. Made from silk, cotton or synthetics.	Ordinary mercerised cotton or silk; medium machine needle; 12-14 sts. per in.	Moderate iron.	Neaten seams to prevent fraying.
Cotton	A natural fibre, available in different patterns and weights.	Lightweight fabrics: ordinary mercerised cotton; fine machine needle; 16-20 sts. per in. Heavy fabrics: medium machine needle; 12-14 sts. per in.	Hot iron.	Starch lightly for a crisp finish.
Corduroy	Cotton pile fabric in narrow or wide ribs.	Heavy-duty mercerised cotton; medium-coarse needle; 10-12 sts. per in.	As for velvet.	Cut pattern with pile of fabric running up.
Linen	A natural fabric. Light or heavy weight.	As for cotton.	A hot iron over a damp cotton cloth.	—
Silk	Various types available — e.g. tussah, shantung, tulle.	Sheers: fine machine needle; 16-20 sts. per in. Heavier weights: same needle; 8-10 sts. per in. Use silk thread.	Moderate iron.	—
Synthetics	Various types usually sold under trade names — Dacron, Courtelle, Crimplene, Tricel etc. All strong, hard-wearing man-made fabrics.	Terylene, nylon or multi-purpose thread; fine machine needle. Fine fabrics: 15-20 sts. per in. Heavier fabrics: 10-12 sts. per in.	Cool iron, if pressing is necessary.	Do not spin dry.
Velvet	Pile fabric made from cotton, nylon, silk or rayon.	Heavy-duty mercerised cotton for cotton, silk or wool; nylon or Terylene for synthetics; medium needle; 10-12 sts. per in.	Use a velvet pressing board or stand dry iron upright. Place a damp cloth over wrong side of fabric, pass back and forth over iron.	Cut pattern with pile of fabric running up and baste seams before sewing to prevent slipping.
Wool	Many different types and weights, from fine light-weight qualities for dresses to heavy qualities for coats.	Light and medium weights: ordinary mercerised cotton, medium needle; 12-14 sts. per in Heavy weights: medium-coarse needle; 10-12 sts. per in.; heavy-duty mercerised cotton.	Warm iron over a damp wool cloth.	Place strips of paper between seam and dress when pressing to stop seams showing through.

YOUR SEWING MACHINE

It is worth spending time getting to know your sewing machine. Study the instruction book which is usually supplied with a machine and learn exactly what your machine is capable of doing. The instruction book should also tell you how to thread the machine, fit the needle and alter the tension or length of stitch to suit different fabrics. As a general rule, the finer the fabric the shorter the stitches should be. Heavy, thicker fabrics need longer stitches.

If you have never used a sewing machine before, have several practice sessions on odd scraps of material before you embark on making a finished garment. Begin by sewing straight lines of stitches. Use a soft pencil to draw lines on your fabric scraps then stitch along these guide lines. Then try square, zigzags and curved lines, working at different speeds. Then do the same exercises without pencil guide lines.

Once you are proficient on one layer of fabric, do the same stitches on two layers, pinning the layers together with the pins at right angles to the line of machining, and stitching $\frac{1}{2}$ in. from edge of fabric. If your machine has a hinged foot you can machine over the pins, but with a fixed or rigid foot you must take them out as they reach the presser foot otherwise you could damage the needle.

It is always a good idea before making up any garment to take two scraps of the fabric you are using, pin them together and machine a few lines — curved, straight and zigzag. Look carefully at the fabric and see if it has puckered, on one or both sides. If both sides are puckered, the tension is too tight and the stitch probably too small. Loosen the tension, lengthen the stitch (i.e. a lower number of stitches per inch) and try again. If only the under layer is puckered your fabric is 'travelling'. It must be basted before you machine any seams; otherwise, without basting, the under layer will always end up shorter.

BASIC TECHNIQUES

Note. Other important sewing techniques, such as putting in a zip, making pockets, and lining a garment, are included in the patterns to make, starting on page 9.

Seam finishes

If you intend to line a garment, then it is not necessary to finish the seams. Merely press the seams open before stitching lining in place. All unlined garments should have their seams finished by any of the following methods. Neatening seams prevents unravelling of fabrics which are inclined to fray easily, and also strengthens the seam and gives a 'professional' look to your finished garment.

Pinking. This is one of the easiest and quickest methods of all seam finishes, and is ideal for inexpensive, closely woven fabrics such as cotton. All you have to do is to cut along seam edges with pinking shears.

Machine stitching. This is a good strong finish for thinner fabrics like fine wool, linen, light-weight cotton and synthetics. Turn under raw edge for about $\frac{1}{4}$ in. and machine stitch close to fold.

Zigzag edging. If you have a swing needle or zigzag attachment on your machine, all fabrics can be neatened in this way. Just stitch along edges of turnings, adjusting width of zigzag and length of stitch to suit fabric. A loosely woven material needs a deep zigzag, a finer fabric can take a smaller, narrower one.

Bound edges. Excellent for loosely woven tweeds or unlined jackets. Take a 1 in. wide bias strip of fine linen or silk to match fabric, and stitch, right sides together, to the raw seam edges about $\frac{1}{4}$ in. from edge. Fold the strip over raw edge and machine stitch again along seam, close to fold.

Oversewing. This is the only method of seam finishing which should be left until garment is complete. Trim the seams neatly, cutting away any loose threads, and then work small slanting stitches by hand over the raw edges. Work from left to right.

French seam. This seam should be used for all sheer and very fine fabrics. With wrong sides of fabric together baste along seam line. Stitch $\frac{1}{4}$ in. above basting. Trim seam close to stitching, remove basting, press seam to one side. Turn seam to inside so right sides of fabric are together. Stitch along seamline, press and open. First seam should have been trimmed enough to prevent any raw edges showing.

Layering and clipping turnings

The seam allowance on the curved edges on any part of a garment should always be layered and clipped so they will lie flat and even, with no unsightly bumps.

Layering. When two or more layers of fabric are seamed and pressed together — round a collar edge, neckline or armhole — the turnings should be 'layered'. This means each turning should be trimmed (after seam has been stitched) slightly narrower than the previous one to give a series of 'steps'. When pressed, the edges will taper off smoothly into the garment without leaving a ridge.

Clipping. Except on very loosely woven fabrics the turnings of curved edges should be clipped as well as layered. This will prevent unnecessary bulk or lumpiness in the finished garment, and help seams to stretch and lie flat.
In the case of an inward curving seam, such as

an armhole, all you have to do is to snip at intervals with small, sharp-pointed scissors into the seam allowance at right angles to the stitching line, but being careful of course not to snip the stitches. For outward curving seams, such as collars, small notches should be cut at intervals from seam allowance. Again, be careful not to snip stitches.

Hems

There are various ways in which hems can be finished and stitched in place, but the following method is simple and quick to do, the stitching is virtually invisible on the right side of work, and it is suitable for most fabrics and garments.
Turn up hem to length required. Trim loose threads from raw edge, and neaten edge. Press the hem well, then run the tip of iron under neatened edge to take away any impression of stitching on the dress. Roll back ¼ in. round neatened edge on to right side. Very lightly catch the hem to the dress, using a single thread and sewing by hand. Pick up just a few threads of the hem fabric along the edge you have rolled back and a single thread of the dress fabric. Space the stitches so they are about ½ in. apart, and leave thread loose between. This is called catch-stitching. As each stitch is worked, let hem fall back into position. Remove pins and basting. This method of stitching hems can also be used for stitching armhole and neck facings in position.

Buttonholes

Worked buttonholes. These may be made by machine or by hand. In both cases the buttonholes are worked after the garment is completed. To work by hand, first mark the buttonhole on the straight grain of fabric. Stitch around the mark, as shown in diagram below, circling at end nearer garment edge. Cut buttonhole on centre mark and overcast the edges. Now work buttonhole stitches over the edges working from right to left. At end towards garment edge, form a 'fan', as shown in the diagram. Make a bar at the end opposite the fan by taking several stitches across the end and working buttonhole stitches over the threads and through the garment cloth.

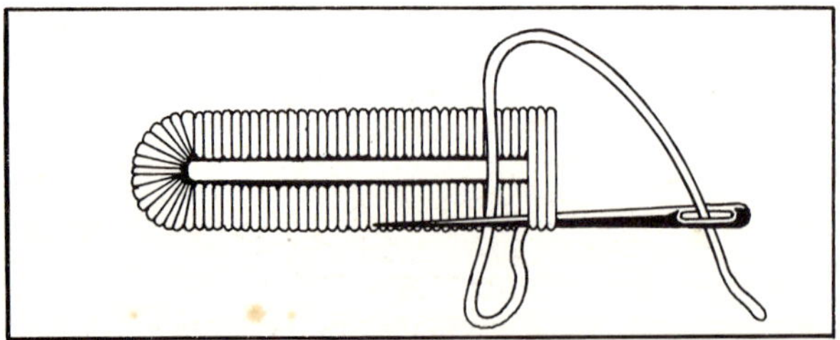

Bound buttonholes (tucked strip method). Cut a straight grain lengthwise strip of fabric 1½ in. wide and the total length of all buttonholes plus 1 in. for each buttonhole. Set seam gauge

on machine ½ in. from needle. With edge of fabric strip against gauge, baste stitch the length of the strip. Repeat on opposite edge.
Fold strip to wrong side on stitched lines. Press. Baste-stitch ⅛ in. from folds. Remove stitching on fold edges and cut strip into separate pieces the buttonhole length plus 1 in. With right sides together, place one folded edge exactly ¼ in. either above or below marked buttonhole line. Stitch through each fold the exact length of buttonhole. Fasten thread at both ends.

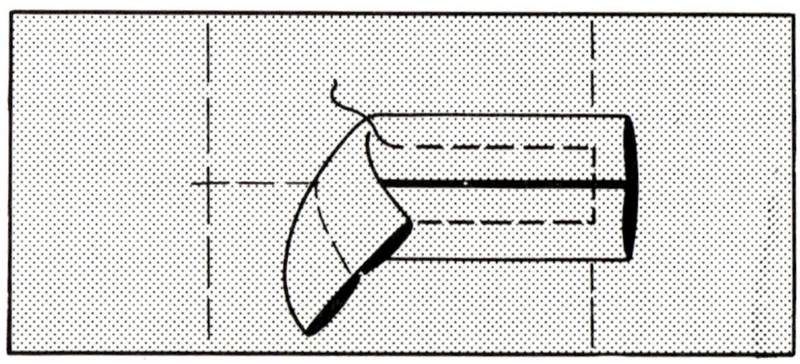

From wrong side, start at centre on marked line and slash through garment and strip to ⅜ in. or ¼ in. from ends. Clip diagonally into corners. Turn strip to wrong side through slash, pulling the ends to straighten. On right side of garment, catch stitch together the bound edges.

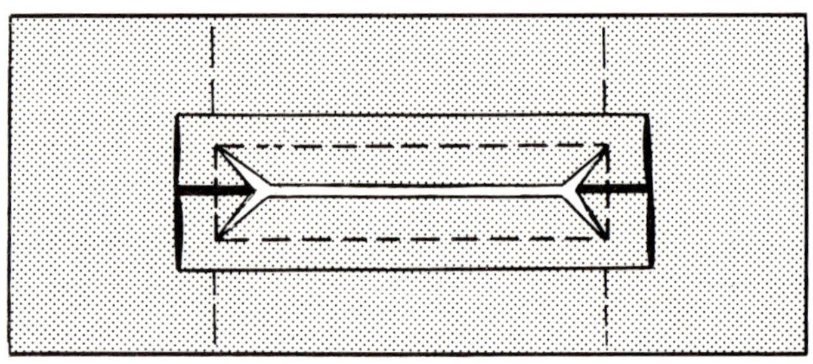

Place garment right side up on machine and fold material back so the end of strip and the triangular slashed piece can be put under needle. Back stitch across strips, ends and base of triangular piece. Repeat stitching several times.

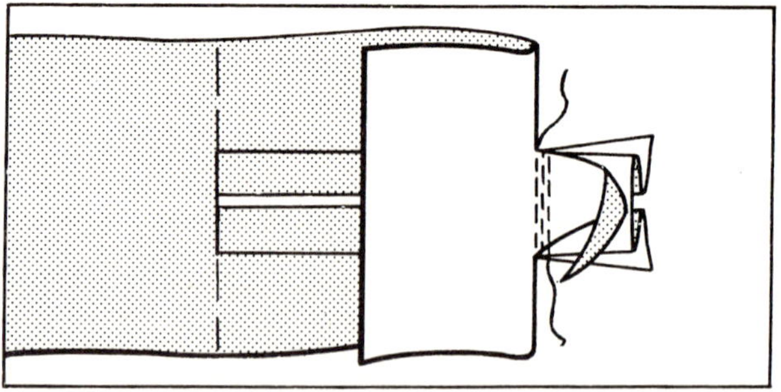

PAPER PATTERNS

Commercial paper patterns are ready for use. Normally they include full-size paper pattern pieces for the garment you are to make, full instructions for making up the garment, and a layout diagram showing how to place the pattern pieces on your fabric for cutting out. Follow the instructions and diagrams carefully — and you cannot go wrong!

Our garments to make, starting this page, are presented in the form of diagram patterns. This type of pattern is a replica in miniature of a full-sized pattern; you have to scale-up from the miniature diagram and prepare a pattern to the correct finished size, and then use this to cut out your fabric. Obviously this pattern preparation takes a little longer than if you are working from a commercial paper pattern, but it is not difficult to do.

The first step is to mark out a large sheet of strong brown or white paper into squares. If the diagram pattern you are following is given on a 1-in. grid, then mark out your paper into 1-in. squares. However if the pattern is on a 2-in. grid, or even a $\frac{1}{2}$-in. one, then you must mark out your paper to correspond.

When your paper is clearly marked out in squares, copy the pattern as given on the miniature diagram on to your grid. Each of the squares on the miniature diagram represents one square on your paper. Copy the outlines and positions of lines, curves and angles in relation to the squares as accurately as possible. If you want to adjust the fitting of the pattern pieces, this the time to do it. For instance, if the diagram is given for a size 34 in. bust, and you are size 36 in., then add $\frac{1}{2}$ in. to all side edges of both back and front. If you are a size smaller, then reduce the side edges by the appropriate amount.

If there are facings involved, these may be marked on the miniature diagram as shaded areas. Mark in the shaded area to your full-size diagram, then trace over these with tracing or greaseproof paper. Cut out all pattern pieces, labelling them if necessary so you know which part of the garment each pattern piece is for. Any markings or instructions on the miniature diagram should be transferred to the full-size pattern. A lengthwise arrow on the miniature diagram shows the direction of the lengthwise grain of the fabric. and indicates that the pattern piece should be placed in this direction on the fabric.

Part 2—Patterns

Three-piece beach outfit
Also illustrated in colour on page 20

MATERIALS
For complete outfit (if made up in same fabric throughout): 4½ yd. of fabric, 45 in. wide. **For wrap and suntop only:** 4 yd. of fabric, 36 in. wide. **For shorts and belt** (in contrast fabric): 1⅝ yd. fabric, 36 in. wide. 2 buttons, each ⅝ in. in diameter. An 8-in. zip fastener. Petersham for waist band. Hook and eye.

FABRIC SUGGESTIONS
Our outfit is made up in Cepea printed cotton (wrap and suntop) and Tootals plain cotton poplin (shorts). Any cotton, plain or patterned, would be suitable.

SIZE NOTE
The pattern as given will comfortably fit bust size 34 in., hip size 36 in. To adapt pattern to fit your size, add to or subtract from the side seams of pattern pieces (see note on left); centre back length of wrap is 33 in.

TO MAKE YOUR PATTERN

The diagram opposite gives the pattern pieces you need. One square on the diagram equals 1 in. Prepare your full-size pattern on squared paper, following instructions opposite.

TO MAKE

Cut out fabric pieces, following cutting-out layouts below. Place pieces on fold of fabric where indicated on layouts (to avoid a seam at this point in the garment). All seams should be stitched $\frac{5}{8}$ in. from the edge of fabric. Unless otherwise stated, press all seams open after stitching.

Shorts

Stitch darts in back and front pieces, as indicated by guide lines. With right sides together, stitch centre front edges, then stitch centre back edges, matching notches.

Right sides together stitch shorts back to shorts front at side seams, leaving left-hand side seam unstitched for 8 in. from waist edge. Stitch zip in position to this unstitched section of seam (see detailed instructions for stitching zips on page 18). Stitch inside leg seam. Trim and clip seam, layering if necessary. Cut a length of petersham your waist measurement plus 2 in. Right sides together, stitch this round waist edge of shorts. Press petersham to wrong side and secure with neat slip-stitches on inside of seams. Turn in ends of petersham level with side (zip) edges of shorts, and slipstitch neatly. Sew on hook and eye to fasten. Turn up hem round leg edges to length required, and catchstitch in place (see page 8).

Suntop

Stitch darts in back bodice, as indicated by guide lines. Stitch back bodice sections together at centre back edges, right sides together.

Stitch darts in bodice front sections, then stitch bodice front sections to bodice back, right sides together, at side and shoulder seams.

Stitch front facings to back neck facing at shoulder edge. With right sides together, stitch complete facing section to bodice, matching notches. Layer and clip seam, and turn facing to inside. Press well. Neaten raw edges of facings.

Stitch one armhole front facing to one armhole back facing at shoulder and underarm edges. With right sides together, stitch in place to one armhole edge of bodice, matching shoulder and underarm seams. Layer and clip seam, and press facing to wrong side. Press well. Neaten raw edge of facing. Stitch facings for other armhole in a similar way. Catchstitch facings lightly to inside of garment on seams to hold in place.

Stitch 2 lower band sections together along straight short edges, press seam open, then fold entire band in half lengthwise, right side together. Stitch each pointed short end, following shape of point. Trim seams and turn band right side out. Right sides together, stitch band in position to lower edge of suntop, stitching through one layer of band only. Turn in seam allowance on remaining raw edge, and slipstitch neatly inside suntop, over seam just worked.

Make 2 worked buttonholes (see page 8) in the lower band, making the first buttonhole $\frac{1}{2}$ in. from centre front pointed edge on bodice right front, the second one 7 in. along. Make each buttonhole $\frac{7}{8}$ in. long. Sew buttons to lower band of bodice left front to correspond.

Wrap

Note. This pattern can be used to make an attractive light-weight summer dressing-gown.

Stitch darts in each front section, as indicated by guide lines. Stitch front sections to back section at side and shoulder seams, right sides together.

Stitch front facings to back neck facing, right sides together, at shoulder edges.

With right sides together, stitch entire facing section to centre front and back neck edges of wrap. Layer and clip seam, and press facing to wrong side. Neaten raw edges. Catchstitch facing to shoulder seams of wrap.

Stitch underarm seams of each sleeve. Right sides together, stitch each sleeve in position to wrap, matching notches and underarm seams, and easing sleeve as you stitch the seam as indicated on the pattern. Layer and clip seam.

Turn up hem at lower edge and sleeves to length required, and catchstitch neatly in place (see page 8). Open up centre front facings to stitch lower hem, then fold facings back in place over hem. Catchstitch facings to hem.

To make belt, stitch 2 sections together, right sides facing, along one short edge to form one long strip. Fold this strip in half lengthwise, right sides together. Stitch short edges at each end, then stitch long seam, leaving an opening to turn belt right side out. Trim seam. Turn right side out, press well, turn in seam allowance on remaining raw edges and slipstitch neatly to close.

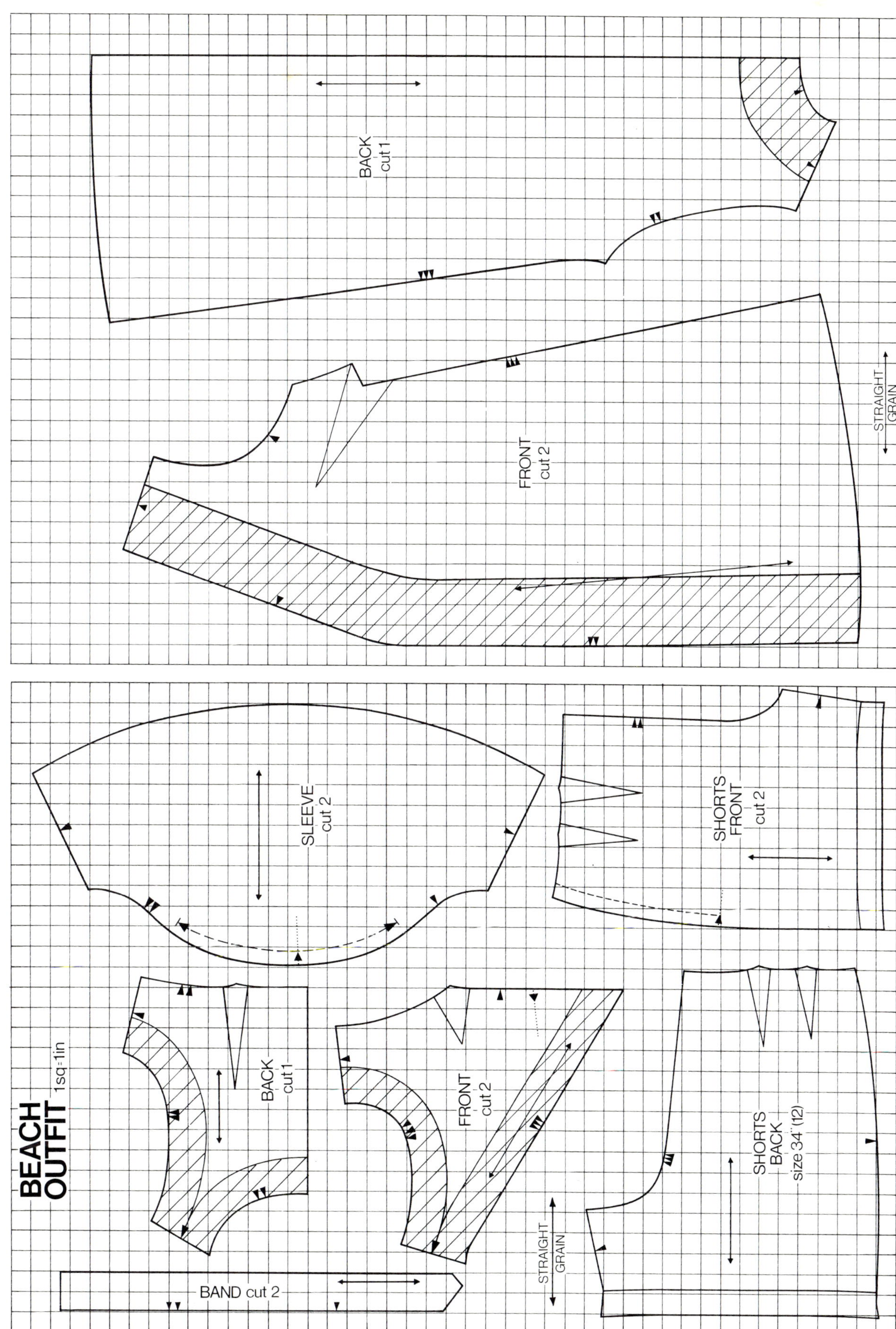

BACK
cut 1
FRONT
cut 2
STRAIGHT GRAIN
BEACH OUTFIT
1 sq = 1 in
SLEEVE
cut 2
BACK
cut 1
FRONT
cut 2
BAND cut 2
SHORTS FRONT
cut 2
SHORTS BACK
size 34'' (12)
STRAIGHT GRAIN

Girl's cape and pinafore dress

MATERIALS

For cape: 2 yd. of fabric, 45 in. wide, or $1\frac{5}{8}$ yd. of fabric, 54 in. wide; 2 yd. of lining fabric, 36 in. wide; 4 round metal buttons; 1 hook and eye. **For pinafore dress:** $\frac{7}{8}$ yd. of fabric, 54 in. wide, or $1\frac{1}{8}$ yd. of fabric, 45 in. wide; $1\frac{1}{4}$ yd. of wide ric-rac braid, and $1\frac{1}{4}$ yd. of narrow ric-rac braid; a 9-in. zip fastener.

FABRIC NOTE

Our cape is made in Digoloom wool velour in red, with the pinafore dress in Digoloom washable wool in purple, trimmed with red ric-rac braid. Any good-quality wool fabric would be suitable.

SIZE NOTE

Dress and cape should comfortably fit a girl aged 5-7 years. To adapt the pattern add to or subtract from the side seams of the pattern pieces (see note on page 9); if necessary adjust the length as well; centre back length of cape is $23\frac{1}{2}$ in.; centre back length of pinafore dress is $22\frac{1}{2}$ in.

TO MAKE YOUR PATTERN

The diagram opposite gives the pattern pieces you need. One square on the diagram equals 1 in. Prepare your full-size pattern on squared paper, following instructions on page 9.

TO MAKE

Cut out fabric pieces, following cutting-out layouts below. Place pieces on fold of fabric where indicated on layouts (to avoid a seam at this point in the finished garment). For lining for cape cut side front and back sections and hood, following cutting line marked on pattern. All seams should be stitched $\frac{5}{8}$ in. from the edge of fabric. Unless otherwise stated, press all seams open after stitching.

Cape

Stitch shoulder darts in back, as indicated by guide lines. Stitch one centre front section to one side front, right sides facing, matching notches and leaving seams unstitched where marked on pattern. Stitch other centre front and side front sections in a similar way.

Stitch cape back to cape front at side edges, right sides facing. Fold each centre front edge back on to right side, so curved neck edges line up. Stitch from fold along neck edge for $1\frac{1}{4}$ in. Layer and clip seam, and turn right side out. Press.

Place hood sections together, right sides facing, and stitch right round curved edges (back and top of head). Clip seam and press open. Fold $1\frac{1}{4}$ in. round front (face) edges to wrong side. Baste to hold in place, then machine stitch on right side of work round entire edge $\frac{1}{4}$ in. from fold.

Stitch back shoulder darts in lining, and stitch lining back section to lining side sections, with right sides together. Stitch lining hood sections together, right sides facing, round curved (back and top of head) edges. Place hood lining inside hood, wrong sides together, and back seams matching. Turn in raw edges of lining round front (face) edges and slipstitch neatly in place. Baste neck edges together.

With right sides facing, stitch hood and lining in position to neck edge of cape. Do not catch centre front facing into the stitching. Press seam down. Place cape lining in position inside cape, wrong sides together. Turn in raw edges round centre front facings and lining, and slipstitch neatly to inside of hood. Turn in remaining raw edges of lining and slipstitch to inside of cape centre front facings. Turn up hems at lower edge to required length (open out facing sections) and catchstitch neatly (see page 8). Oversew facings in place along lower edge.

Place 2 tab sections together, right sides facing, and stitch right round edges, leaving a gap in seam to turn right side out.

continued on page 14

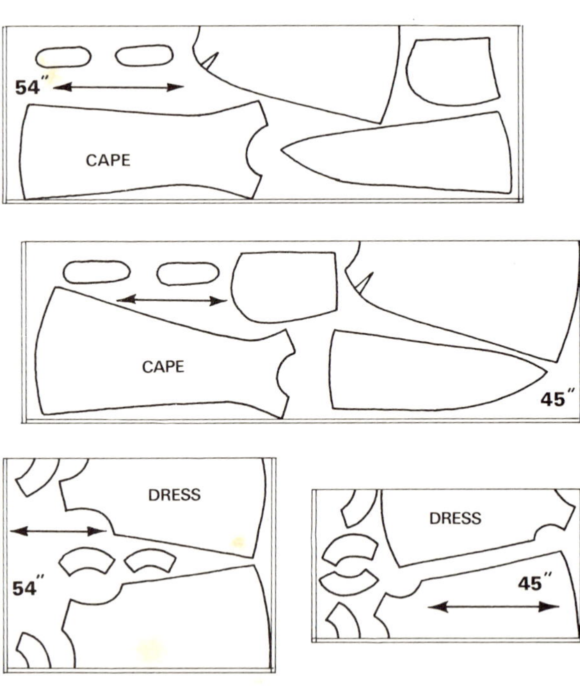

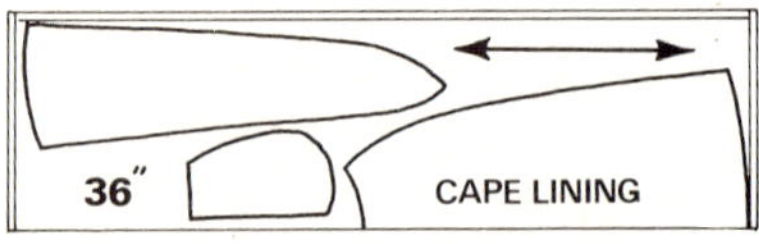

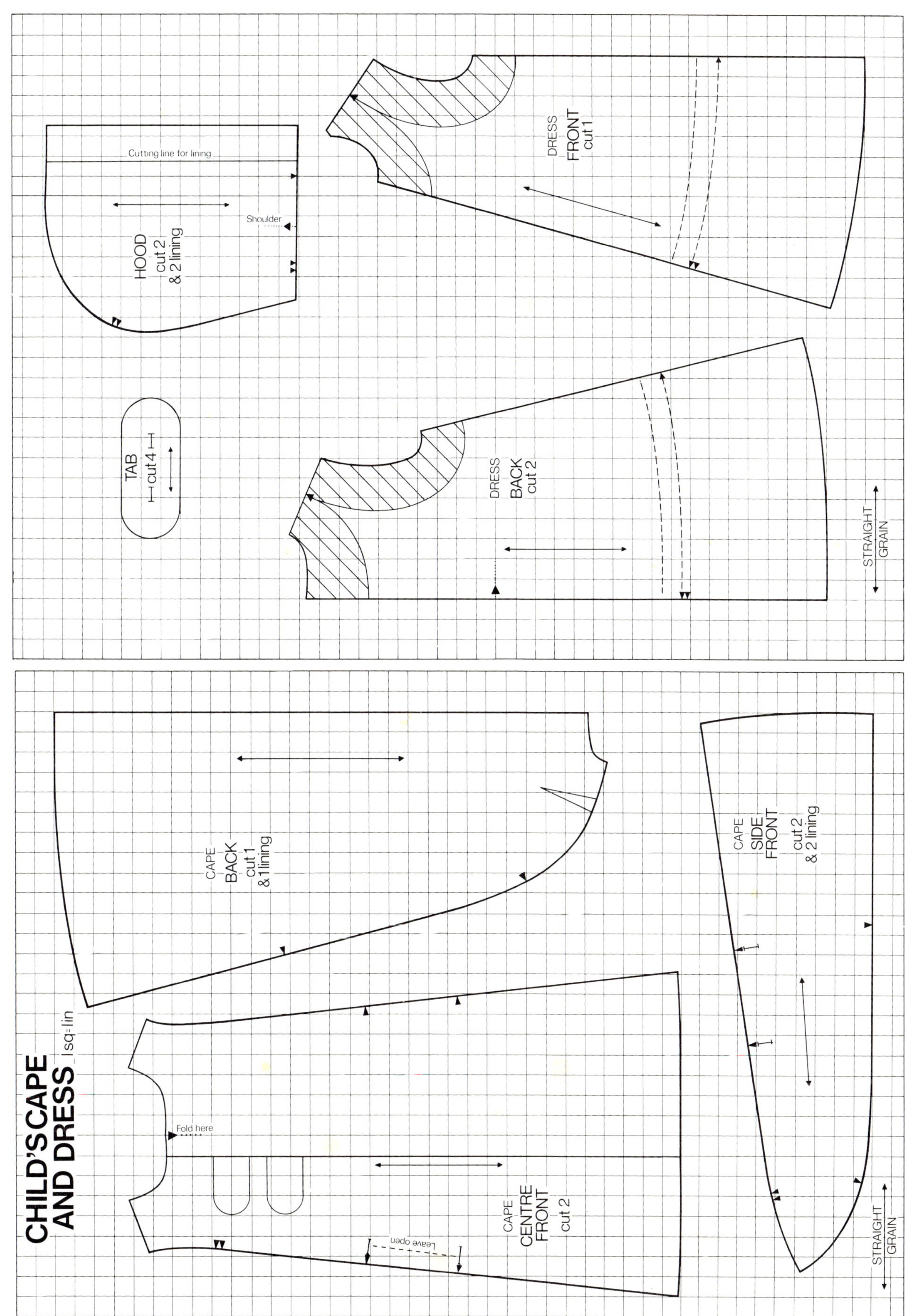

CHILD'S CAPE AND DRESS
1 sq = 1 in
Cutting line for lining
HOOD
cut 2
& 2 lining
Shoulder
TAB
cut 4
DRESS
FRONT
cut 1
DRESS
BACK
cut 2
STRAIGHT
GRAIN
CAPE
BACK
cut 1
& 1 lining
CAPE
SIDE
FRONT
cut 2
& 2 lining
CAPE
CENTRE
FRONT
cut 2
Fold here
Leave open
STRAIGHT
GRAIN

The cape has a decorative double tab fastening.

Layer and clip seam and turn right side out. Turn in seam allowance on remaining open edges and slipstitch closed. On right side of work, machine stitch right round edges, $\frac{1}{4}$ in. from edges. Repeat with other pair of tabs.

Make 2 worked buttonholes on each tab, as indicated on pattern. Sew 2 buttons to cape right front, and 2 to left front to fasten tabs (see pattern for position). Sew hook and eye at centre front neck edges to fasten.

Pinafore dress

Right sides together, stitch centre back edges together, leaving 9 in. unstitched from neck edge down. Stitch zip into this opening, following instructions on page 18.

Stitch dress back to dress front, right sides together, at side and shoulder edges.

Right sides together, stitch front neck facing to back neck facings. Stitch facing section to neck edge of dress, right sides facing. Layer and clip seams. Press to wrong side. Neaten raw edges of facing. Turn in raw edges at centre back and slipstitch neatly to zip tapes. Catchstitch facing to inside of dress on seams.

Right sides facing, stitch one front armhole facing to one back armhole facing at shoulder and underarm edges. Stitch in place to one armhole of dress, right sides facing, and matching shoulder and underarm seams. Layer and clip seams. Turn facing to wrong side. Press well. Neaten raw edges and catchstitch lightly to inside of dress on seams. Stitch other armhole facings in place in a similar way.

Turn up hem at lower edge to length required and catchstitch neatly (see page 8).

On right side of dress stitch ric-rac braids in position, as marked on pattern.

Coat

illustrated in colour on page 21

MATERIALS

3 yd. of fabric, 54 in. wide, or $3\frac{1}{2}$ yd. of fabric, 45 in. wide. $3\frac{1}{4}$ yd. of lining fabric, 36 in. wide. $1\frac{1}{4}$ yd. of interfacing, 27 in. or 36 in. wide. 2 metal buttons, each $1\frac{1}{8}$ in. in diameter. 1 press stud. 1 hook and eye.

FABRIC NOTE

Our coat is made up in Digoloom wool velour. Any good-quality coat-weight woollen fabric would be suitable.

SIZE NOTE

Coat should comfortably fit bust size 34/36 in., hip size 36/38 in. To adapt the pattern to fit your size, add to or subtract from the side seams of pattern pieces (see note on page 9); centre back length $39\frac{1}{2}$ in.

TO MAKE YOUR PATTERN

The diagram opposite gives the pattern pieces you need. One square on the diagram equals 1 in. Prepare your full-size pattern on squared paper, following instructions on page 9.

continued on page 16

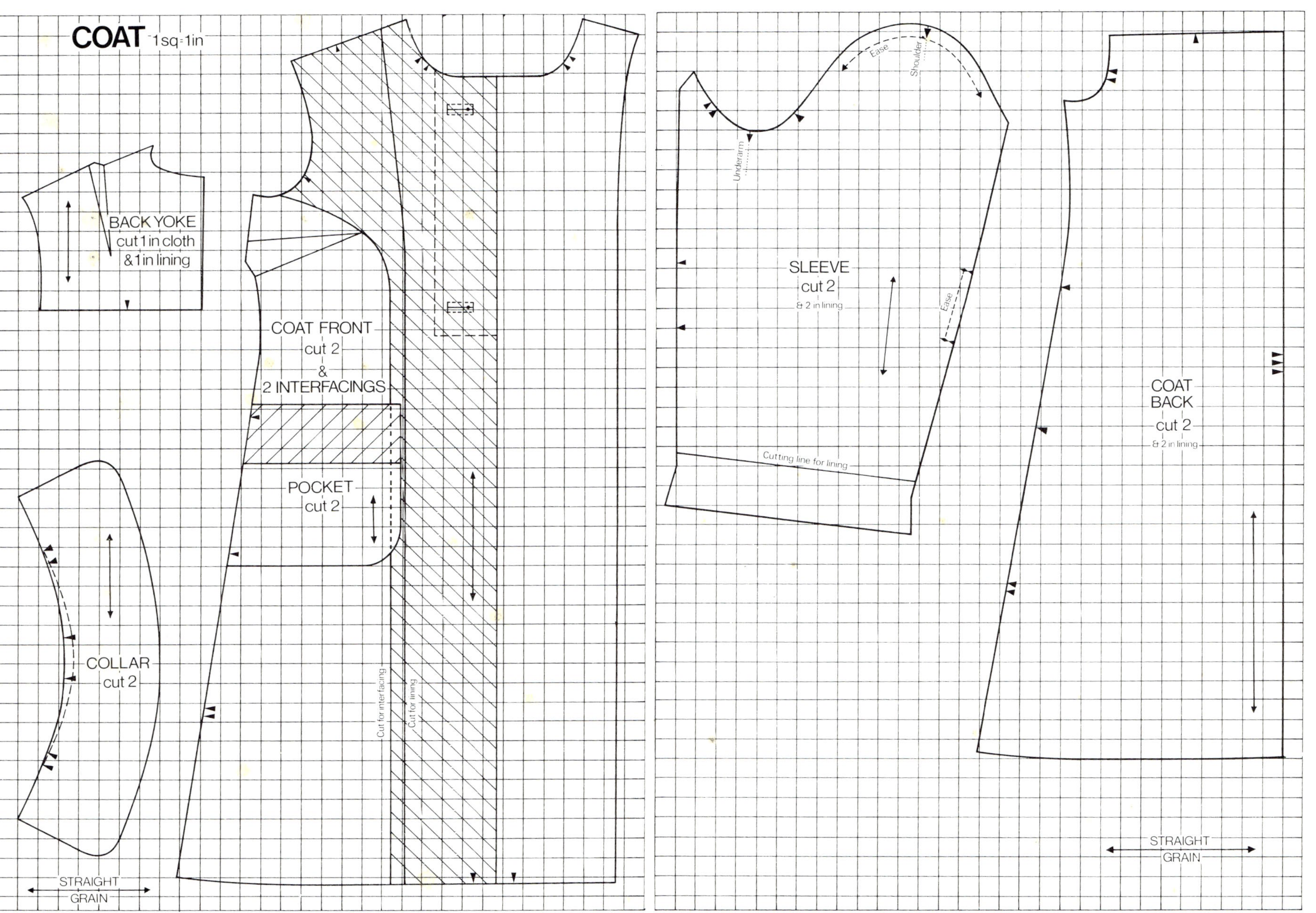

COAT 1 sq = 1 in
BACK YOKE
cut 1 in cloth
& 1 in lining
COAT FRONT
cut 2
&
2 INTERFACINGS
POCKET
cut 2
COLLAR
cut 2
Cut for interfacing
Cut for lining
STRAIGHT GRAIN
SLEEVE
cut 2
& 2 in lining
Underarm
Ease
Shoulder
Ease
Cutting line for lining
COAT BACK
cut 2
& 2 in lining
STRAIGHT GRAIN
15

TO MAKE

Cut out fabric pieces, following cutting-out layouts below. Place pieces on fold of fabric where indicated on layouts (to avoid a seam at this point in the finished garment). Cut interfacing sections as shown, and cut lining sections as shown. All seams should be stitched $\frac{5}{8}$ in. from the edge of fabric. Unless otherwise stated, press all seams open after stitching. Stitch bust darts in coat front sections. Stitch back shoulder darts in back yoke section. Right sides facing, stitch centre back seam in coat back sections.

Stitch coat back to back yoke, right sides facing. Place right pocket facing in position on right pocket. Baste along top edge. Neaten opposite edge of facing. Place pocket lining in position on top of pocket, again right sides together. Stitch round top, right-hand side and lower edge. Layer and clip seams, and turn right side out. Press well. Catchstitch facing to lining on inside of pocket. Stitch left pocket in a similar way. Now place pockets in position on coat front, wrong sides of pocket to right side of coat. Line up side edges and baste. Slipstitch pockets to coat down inner side edge and lower edge. Fold each centre front edge back on to the right side, along fold line marked. On wrong side of coat, baste interfacing for centre fronts in position. Stitch neck edge from fold for $1\frac{3}{4}$ in. Layer and clip seam. Turn right side out. Press well.

Right sides together, stitch coat front section to coat back at shoulder and side edges, enclosing pockets in the side seams as you stitch, and enclosing interfacing in shoulder seams. Pin collar interfacing to one collar section, wrong sides together (this will be the undercollar). Stitch round all edges $\frac{1}{2}$ in. from edge of fabric. Layer and clip seam. Right sides together, stitch upper collar to undercollar round outside edges (leave neck edge unstitched). Layer and clip seams and turn right side out.

Stitch collar to neck edge of coat, with undercollar against right side of coat. Stitch through undercollar and coat only — do not catch upper collar into the seam. Press seam down, and baste unstitched edge of upper collar over the seam.

On right front of coat, make 2 bound buttonholes (see page 8), positioning the first 1 in. down from neck edge, the second 10 in. below. Begin the buttonholes 1 in. from centre front edge, and make each $1\frac{1}{4}$ in. long.

Turn in seam allowance along neck edges of centre front facings and slipstitch neatly to basted edge of upper collar. If wished, work a line of machine stitching on right side of coat to enclose the buttonhole section on right front.

Stitch seam in each sleeve, right sides together, then stitch each sleeve in place to coat, right sides facing, and matching underarm and shoulder points as marked on sleeve pattern with underarm and shoulder seams of coat. Ease top of sleeve to fit, where marked on pattern. Layer and clip seam. Turn up sleeve hems, and hem round lower edge to length required and catchstitch neatly (see page 8).

To make lining: stitch darts as for coat, then stitch back sections together, stitch side and shoulder seams. Stitch sleeve seams, then stitch sleeves into lining armholes. Stitch hems round sleeves and lower edge.

Press well. layering and clipping any seams as necessary. Place inside coat, wrong sides together, and slipstitch in place round neck edge, to centre front facings, to sleeve hems and to lower hem. Stitch also round armhole seams.

Stitch hook and eye to fasten centre front neck edge, and stitch press stud to fasten front edges, midway between the 2 buttonholes. Stitch buttons to left front to correspond with buttonholes.

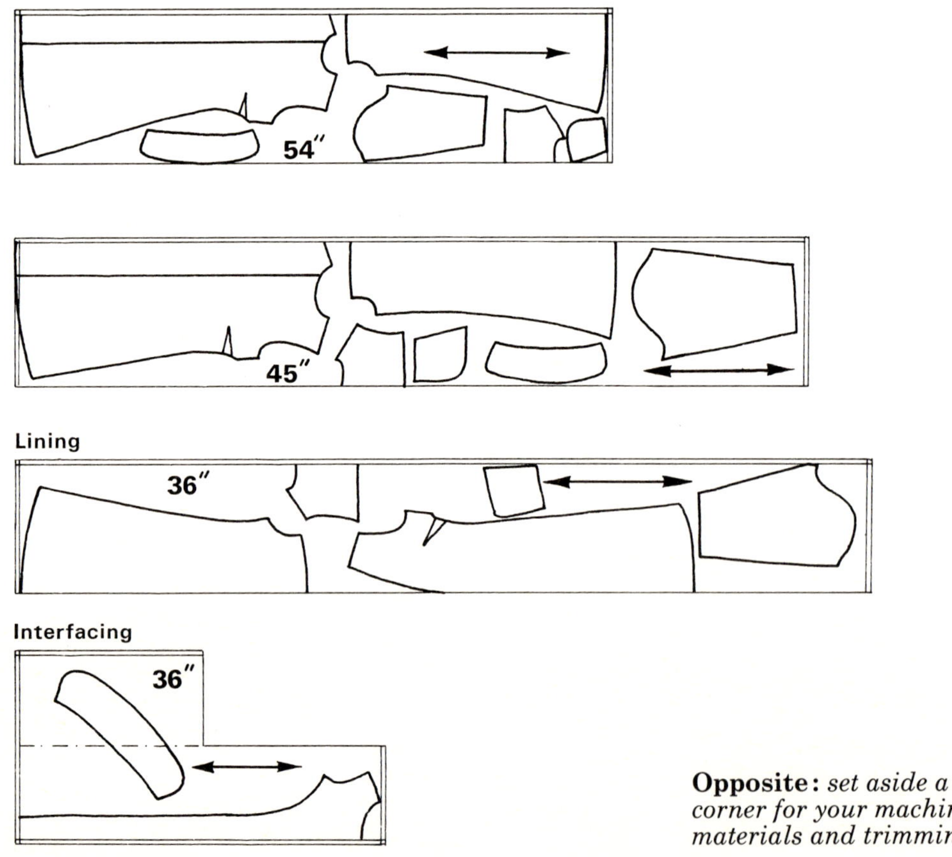

Two-way classic dress

This dress may be made either in normal length for everyday wear, or full-length for an evening or party dress. The everyday version is shown right, in black and white. The full-length version is illustrated in colour on page 24.

MATERIALS

For short dress: $2\frac{7}{8}$ yd. of fabric, 36 in. wide, or $2\frac{1}{8}$ yd. of fabric, 45 in. wide. **For long dress:** $3\frac{5}{8}$ yd. of fabric, 45 in. wide, or $4\frac{3}{4}$ yd. of fabric, 36 in. wide; 4 yd. of lining fabric, 36 in. wide (optional); $\frac{3}{4}$ yd. of contrasting fabric for sash. **For both dresses:** a 20-in. zip fastener; a hook and eye.

FABRIC SUGGESTIONS

Our short dress is made up in Tootals printed Dicel, the long dress in Tootals printed Terylene voile. Any similar fabrics would be suitable.

SIZE NOTE

The pattern as given will comfortably fit bust size 34 in., hip size 36 in. To adapt the pattern to fit your size, add to or subtract from the side seams of pattern pieces (see note on page 9); centre back length of short dress 40 in.; centre back length of long dress $56\frac{1}{2}$ in.

TO MAKE YOUR PATTERN

The diagram on page 22 gives the pattern pieces you need. One square on the diagram equals 2 in. Prepare your full-size pattern on squared paper, following instructions on page 9. If you only wish to make short dress then follow hemline as marked on pattern, and omit sleeves, bow and contrast sash. The back neck facing is the same for both dress versions, but the front neckline and its facings are different. Follow appropriate line for the style you are making (i.e. high round neckline for short dress, low V neckline for long dress). For long dress, omit armhole facing section and tie belt, and use full length of the pattern.

TO MAKE

Cut out fabric, following cutting-out layouts opposite. Place pieces on fold of fabric where indicated on layouts (to avoid a seam at this point in the finished garment). Cut 2 straight pieces of fabric, each 5 in. by 36 in., to make tie belt for short dress. Cut 2 sash sections for long dress from contrast fabric. All seams are stitched $\frac{5}{8}$ in. from the edge of fabric. Unless otherwise stated, press all seams open after stitching.

Short dress

Stitch bust darts in dress front, and back shoulder darts in each back section, as indicated by guide lines on pattern. Stitch centre back edges, right sides together, leaving seam open for 20 in. from neck edge.

Stitch zip fastener in position to this seam: baste edges together along seam line; press seam open.

Place fabric on working surface, so pressed seam is facing you. Place zip, right side down, over open seam with the slider 1 in. below the raw neck edge. Make sure teeth of zip are exactly in centre of tacked seam, then pin zip in place. Baste and remove pins. You can either machine the zip in position if you have a special zipper foot, stitching $\frac{1}{4}$ in. from teeth of zip all the way round. Or you can sew the zip in by hand. Use a single thread and work from right to left on right side of work, taking small back stitches and leaving a $\frac{1}{4}$-in. space between each stitch. Remove basting when zip is stitched in position. Press well. **

Right sides together, stitch front neck facing to back neck facings, at shoulder edges. Stitch facings in position to dress neck edge, right sides together. Layer and clip turnings, and press facing to wrong side. Press well. Neaten raw edges, turn in seam allowance on centre back edges and catchstitch lightly in place to tape of zip.

Right sides facing, stitch one front armhole facing to one back armhole facing at shoulder and underarm edges. Stitch to one armhole of dress, right sides facing and matching notches, and shoulder and underarm seams. Layer and clip turnings. Press facing to wrong side. Neaten raw edge and catchstitch lightly to inside of dress at seams. Stitch other armhole facings in place in a similar way. Try on dress and turn up hem to length required. Catchstitch neatly in place (see page 8). Sew hook and eye to fasten centre back neck edges.

To make belt, sew strips together at one short edge to make one long strip. Fold this strip in half lengthwise, right sides together. Stitch short edges at each end, and stitch the long seam, leaving an opening to turn belt right side out. Trim seams, turn belt right side out. Press well. Turn in seam allowance on remaining open edges and slipstitch neatly.

Long dress

If a lining is required follow cutting-out layout as marked, and cut out dress front and back sections only.

Make up dress, following making instructions for short dress as far as **.

Make up lining sections, if used, in a similar way. Place inside dress, wrong sides together. Turn in seam allowance on open edges above centre back seam in lining, and slipstitch neatly to zipper tape. Oversew lining to dress round armhole edges. Baste neck edges together.

With right sides facing, stitch front neck facing to back neck facings at shoulder edge. Stitch entire facing section in position to dress neck edge, right sides together. Layer and clip seam, and press facing to wrong side, over lining. Press well. Neaten raw edges, turn in seam allowance on centre back edges and catchstitch lightly to tape of zip. Catchstitch neatened edge of facing to lining to hold in place.

Right sides facing, stitch underarm seam in each sleeve. Run a gathering thread round top of each sleeve, as marked on pattern. Pin each sleeve in place to dress, right sides facing, and matching notches and underarm seams. Adjust gathers to fit. Stitch seam. Layer and clip seam. Turn up hems round lower edges of dress and of lining, also of sleeves. Catchstitch

neatly in place (see page 8). Sew hook and eye to fasten centre back neck edges above zip.

To make sash, fold one section in half lengthwise, right sides facing, and stitch long edges together, and the straight diagonal edges. Turn strip right side out. Pleat at unstitched edges as marked on pattern, and baste to hold in place. Stitch other sash section and pleat in a similar way. Now, with right sides together, stitch sash sections together at pleated edges. Stitch sash to right side of dress, stitching centre seam of sash to centre front of dress immediately below neckline, so sash forms an inverted 'V'. The ends are then taken under the bust and round to the back where they can be tied in a bow.

To make bow, fold fabric in half lengthwise and stitch down long side and one short side. Clip seams and turn right side out. Press well, turn in seam allowance on remaining open edges and slipstitch closed. Run 2 rows of gathering stitches down centre of bow, as marked on pattern, and draw up to measure 2 in. at this point. Stitch bow to dress front over stitched point of sash. Position bow so lower edge is the widest edge.

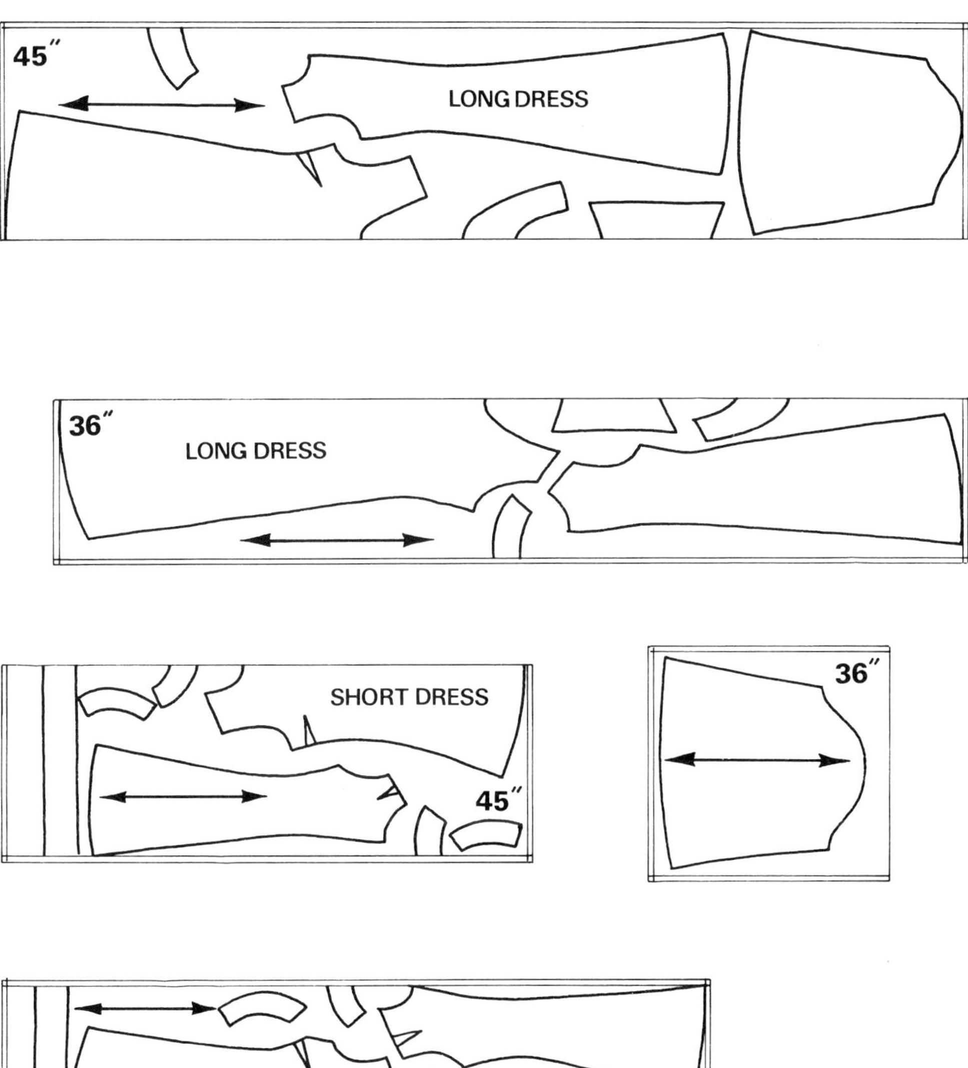

Three-piece beach set, consisting of wide-sleeved wrap, suntop and shorts—see page 9.

20

Classic coat—right for every occasion.
See page 14 for instructions to make.

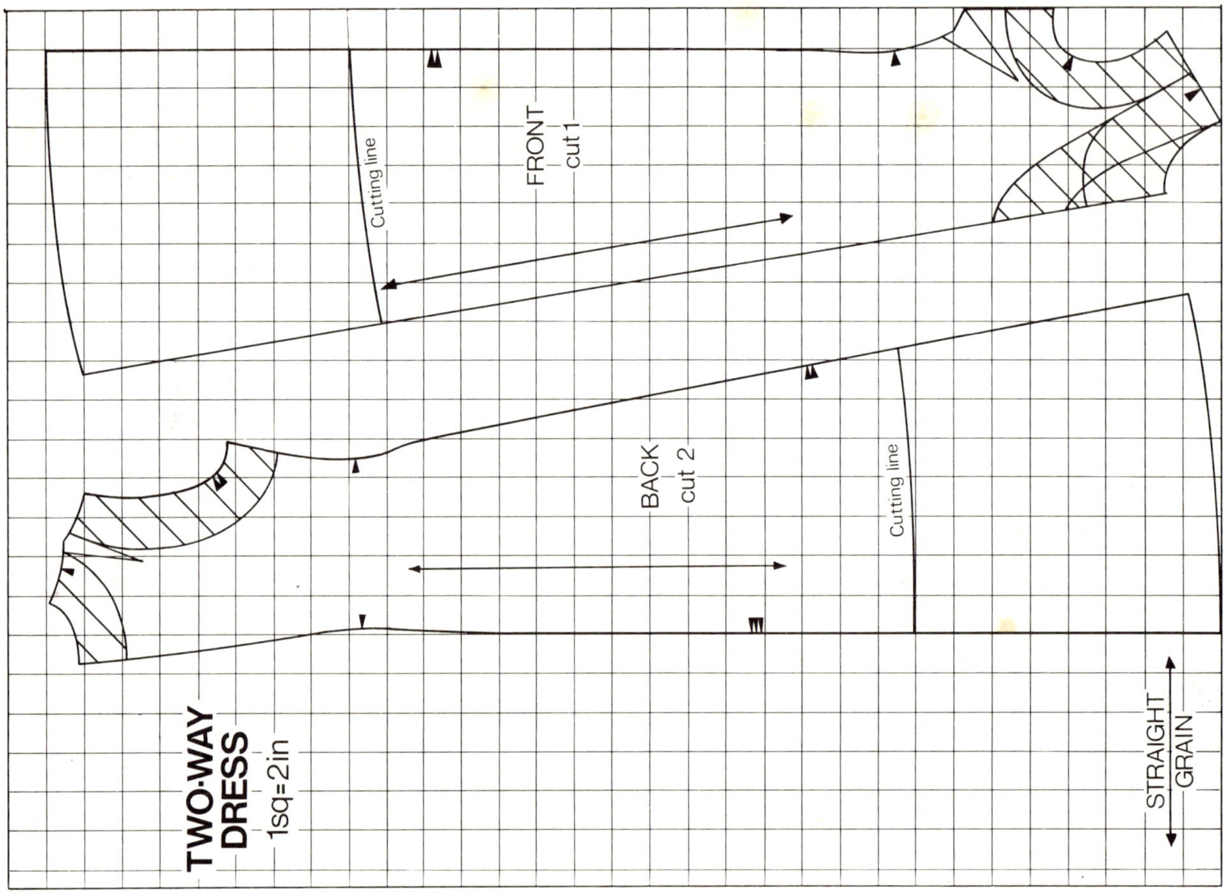

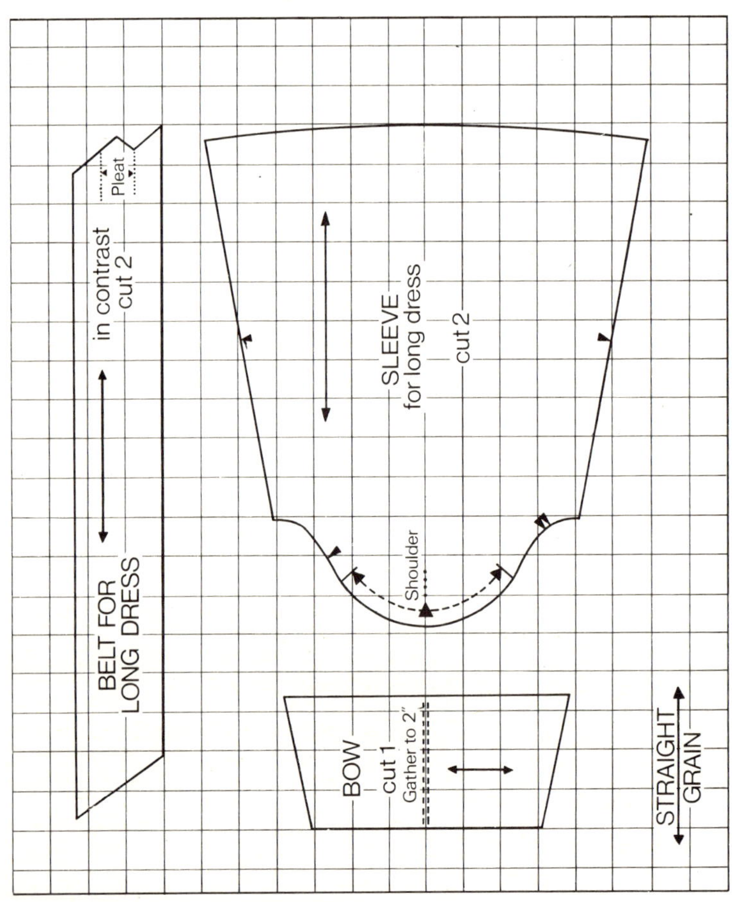

TWO-WAY DRESS
1sq=2in
Cutting line
FRONT
cut 1
BACK
cut 2
Cutting line
STRAIGHT GRAIN
BELT FOR LONG DRESS
in contrast
cut 2
Pleat
SLEEVE
for long dress
cut 2
Shoulder
BOW
cut 1
Gather to 2"
STRAIGHT GRAIN

Boy's shirt and shorts

MATERIALS
For short and shirts in the same fabric: 1¾ yd. of fabric, 36 in. wide. **For shorts only:** ¾ yd. of fabric, 36 in. wide. **For shirt only:** 1⅜ yd. of fabric, 36 in. wide. A waist length of ½-in. elastic. 4 small buttons.

FABRIC NOTE
Our shirt and shorts are made up in Tootals cotton denim. Any mediumweight cotton would be suitable.

SIZE NOTE
Shirt and shorts should comfortably fit a boy aged 6-8 years. To adapt the pattern to fit a different size, add to or subtract from the side seams of the pattern pieces (see note on page 9); if necessary adjust the length as well; centre back length of shirt 17½ in.

TO MAKE YOUR PATTERN
The diagram on page 26 gives the pattern pieces you will need. One square on the diagram equals 1 in. Prepare your full-size pattern on squared paper, following instructions on page 9.

TO MAKE
Cut out fabric pieces, following cutting-out layouts below. Place pieces on fold of fabric where indicated on layouts (to avoid a seam at this point in the finished garment). Cut one pocket section only.
All seams should be stitched ⅝ in. from the edge of fabric. Unless otherwise stated, press all seams open after stitching.

Shirt
Stitch back to front sections at shoulder and side edges, right sides facing.
Fold collar section in half lengthwise, right sides facing. Stitch along short edges at each end. Trim seams. Turn collar right side out and press well.
On each front section of shirt, fold centre front edge back on to the right side, lining up curved neck edges. Stitch along neck edge from the fold for ¾ in. Trim seam. Turn facing to wrong side and press well. Now place collar in position to neck edge of shirt, right sides facing. Stitch in place, only stitching through one thickness of collar, and being sure not to catch centre front facings into the stitching.

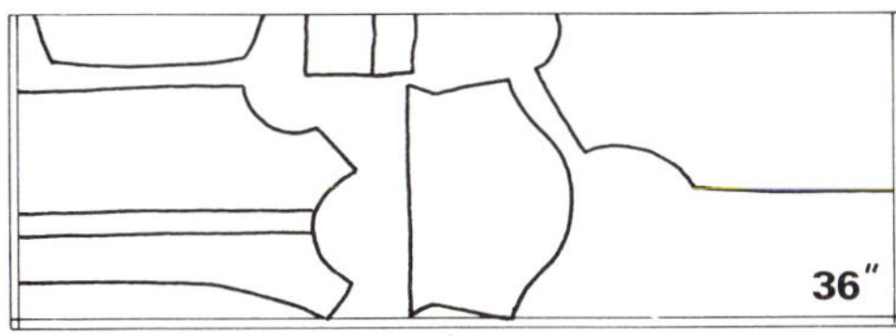

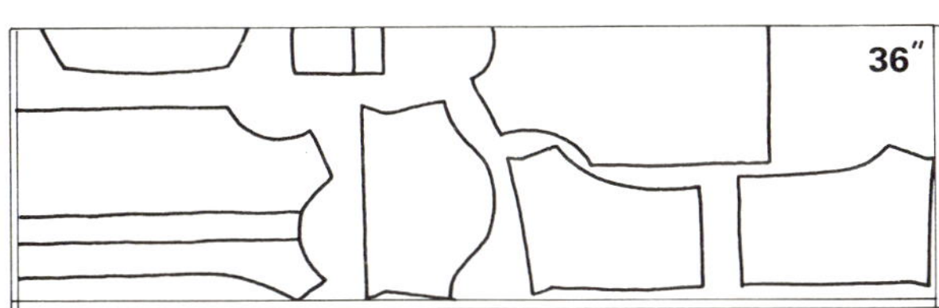

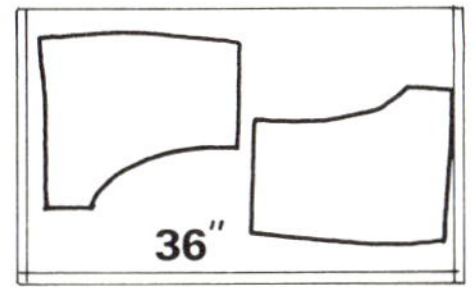

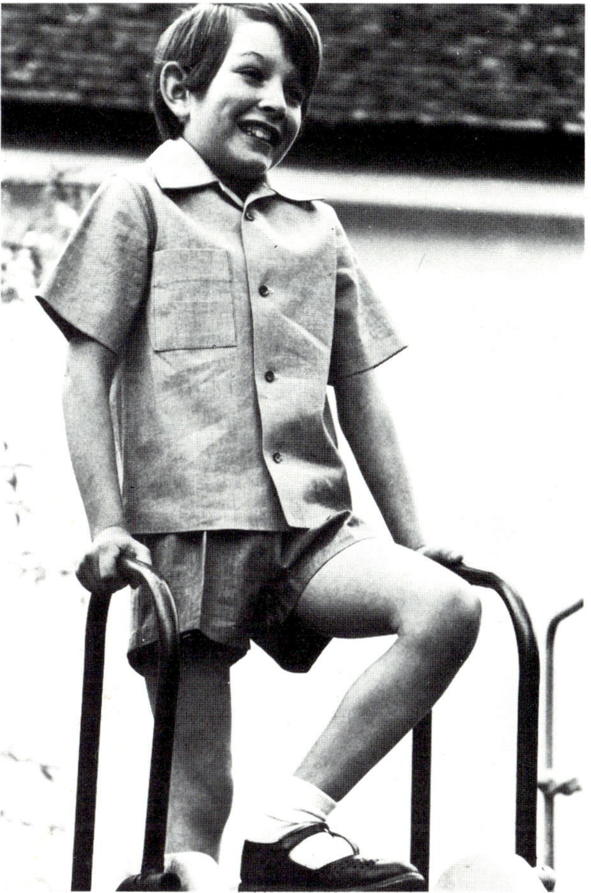

Turn in seam allowance along remaining raw edges of collar and slipstitch neatly to inside of shirt, along back of seam just worked. Turn in raw edges on centre front facings at neck edge and slipstitch also to back of collar seam. Neaten raw edges of centre front facings, and slipstitch shoulder edge to inside of shirt along seam.
Stitch underarm seam in each sleeve, right sides facing, then stitch each sleeve into shirt, right sides facing. Layer and clip seam. Turn up hems at sleeve ends, and lower edge of shirt (open out facings) and catchstitch neatly (see page 8). Fold back centre front facings and slipstitch in place to lower edge. Neaten all edges of pocket piece. Fold back one short end to wrong side, as marked on pattern. Position pocket on right front of shirt, as indicated on pattern. Machine stitch in place with a contrasting thread round side edges and lower edge. On left front (or right front if making the shirt for a girl) make 4 worked buttonholes (see page 8) positioning one 3½ in. up from lower edge, the other 3 at 3½ in. intervals. Begin each buttonhole ½ in. from centre front edge, and make each ½ in. long. Sew buttons to right front to correspond.
If wished work machine stitching in a contrasting colour thread round shoulder, armhole and side seams.

Shorts
With right sides facing, join centre front edges. With right sides facing, join centre back edges.
Join shorts front to shorts back, with right sides facing, at side edges, and at inside leg edges.
Neaten raw edges at waist, then fold to inside of shorts to form a 1-in. casing. Stitch, leaving an opening at one side seam to thread elastic through. Thread elastic through casing, and stitch ends of elastic together. Slipstitch opening in casing closed.
Turn up hems at lower leg edges to length required. Catchstitch neatly (see page 8).

The graceful evening version of the two-way dress (see page 18).

Leisure clothing can be functional and fun.

BOY'S SHIRT AND SHORTS 1sq=1in

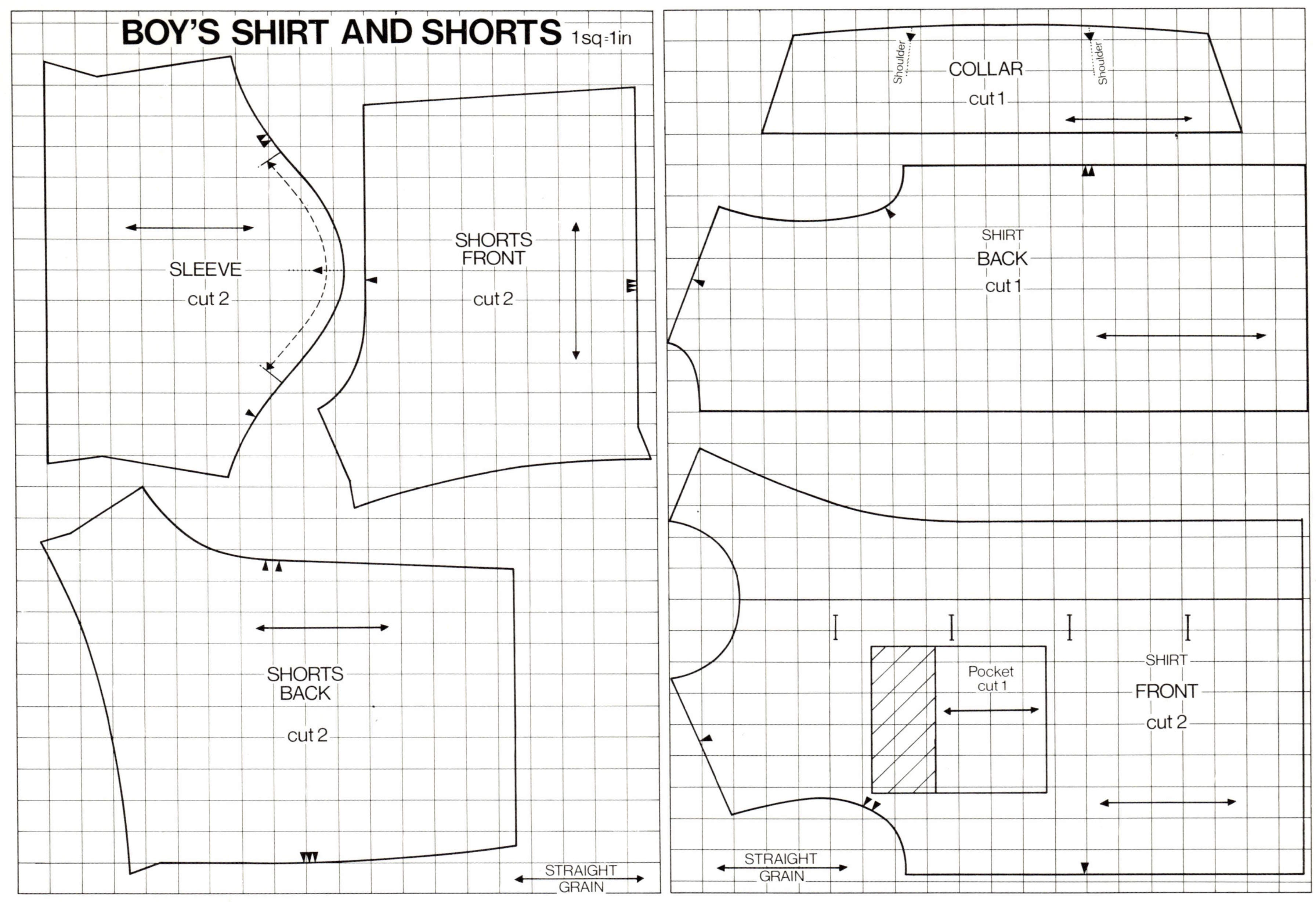

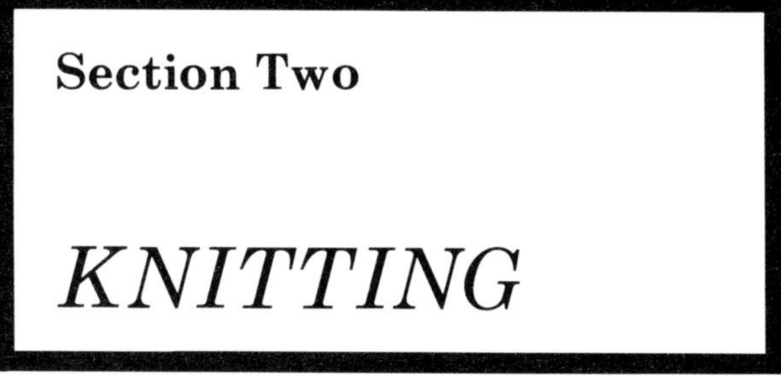

GUIDE TO KNITTING NEEDLE SIZES

British Sizes	Continental Sizes	USA Sizes
14	2	0
13	—	—
12	2.50	1
11	3.00	2
10	3.25	3
—	3.50	4
9	4.00	5
8	4.50	6
7	4.75	7
6	5.00	8
5	5.50	9
4	6.00	10
3	7.00	$10\frac{1}{2}$
2	8.00	11
1	9.25	13

Throughout the centuries attempts have been made to knit most items of personal and household adornment – in England in the 16th century, the boy king Edward was presented with a pair of knitted silk stockings from Spain. In Turkey it is reputed the scarlet fez hats were at one time knitted. During the Victorian era when needlework of all kinds was so universally popular, every conceivable item was knitted – from sofa rugs, counterpanes and antimacassars to fine lacy insertions and edgings, collars and shawls. Today knitting is as popular – if not more so – as it has ever been. But just as fashions in dress, furnishings and art change, so have fashions in knitting. The stitches, techniques and traditional patterns remain the same, but the way we use them, and the new exciting yarns and colours available to us, mean that knitting has taken on a completely new look: a look of today, reflecting modern trends in fashion and design.

Part 1—General

BASIC EQUIPMENT

The only two essentials for knitting are a pair of knitting needles and a ball of yarn, although a few additional items will help to make life easier.

Needles

Knitting needles are available in various thicknesses, the sizes being denoted by a series of numbers (see chart below). In the British range of sizes, the lower numbers indicate the thickest needles, the high numbers the fine needles. In the USA the system is reversed, with the high numbers used for thick needles, low numbers for fine ones. Needles may be of metal, nylon, plastic or wood, and each size is usually available in a choice of lengths. Which length you choose is a matter of personal preference, although a pattern involving a great number of stitches will be more comfortably worked on long needles.

Needles should always be clean, smooth and rigid – never use needles which show an inclination to bend easily. It is well worth while always buying the best-quality needles.

Cable needles

These are very short needles with points at both ends used for taking stitches to the front or back of the knitting when working a cable pattern. Choose a cable needle as near as possible to the size of the needles being used for the main pattern.

Stitch holder

Frequently a pattern will instruct you to leave a number of stitches aside while others are knitted, then the first stitches are returned to later. Some patterns suggest keeping these stitches on a spare needle until required, but a stitch holder is more satisfactory as there is then no danger of any stitches slipping off and unravelling. Small numbers of stitches can be kept on a safety pin.

Also useful

A **tape measure** – to measure the garment as you knit it. Always measure your work on a flat surface, taking care not to pull at the edges. Measure along the straight line of the work.

A **row counter** – this is a small tube placed on the end of the knitting needle; it has numbers which are turned after each row in order to keep count of the number of rows worked.

A **crochet hook** – to work a crochet border round a finished knitted garment; it is also useful for picking up dropped stitches.

For finishing garments you will need pins for pinning out to the right size, an iron, ironing board and cloth for pressing, and sewing needles for joining seams.

YARNS

Wool is the traditional yarn for knitting, but there are excellent synthetic yarns available now, and also mixtures of wool and synthetics which combine the advantages of each. Cotton yarns are good for knitting summer clothes and babies' wear. Most yarns are available in different thicknesses – 2, 3 or 4-ply, double knitting and so on – your pattern will tell you which to use. As

Left and above: *same basic pattern, made up in different fabrics, with different trimmings (see Sewing Section).*

Knitted playclothes keep toddlers warm and comfortable.

the colour of yarn may vary slightly between dye lots, it is important to buy all the yarn you need for a particular design from the same dye lot (a dye lot number is usually marked on the label of each ball). Most shops will put the yarn aside for you for a period of time so you can buy it a few balls at a time if you do not want to buy the whole amount at the beginning.

HOLDING YOUR NEEDLES AND YARN

English method

Pass the yarn round the little finger of the right hand, then take it under the third and middle fingers and then over the first finger. The right-hand needle rests between the thumb and the first finger (like holding a pencil) and the finger stays close to the work. The left-hand needle is held with the fingers and thumb above it and the needle firmly against the palm. During work the left hand pushes the stitches along the needle towards the point, and the right first finger moves the yarn to work each stitch.

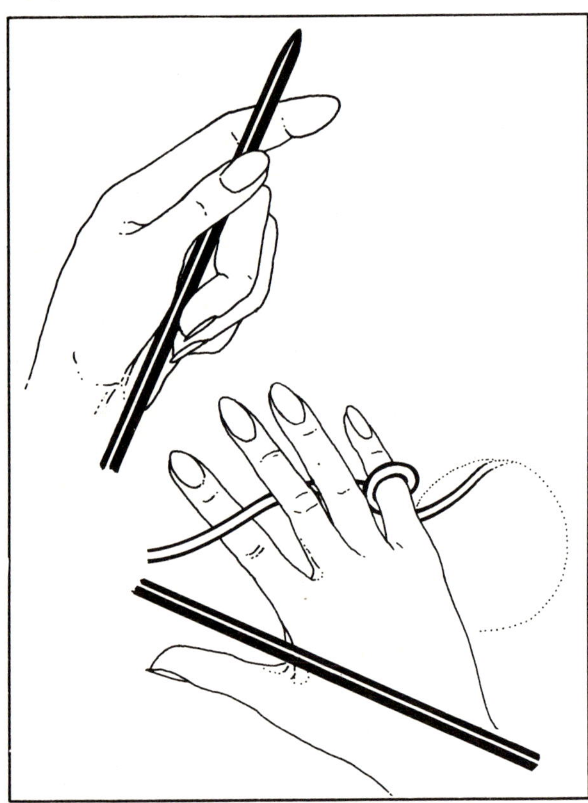

Continental methods

In the French method both hands hold the needles from on top. The yarn goes round the little finger, then over the two middle fingers and the first finger. The first finger moves the yarn as in the English method. Another method used on the continent has the yarn held by the first finger of the left hand. The needles are held as in the French method, but the yarn goes over the little finger of the left hand, under the middle two fingers then round the first finger.

Left-handed workers

If you are left-handed, then the above procedures are merely reversed – i.e. for the English method, the left hand controls the yarn, and the right hand controls the stitches.

CASTING ON

Thumb method

Undo a length of yarn from the ball – about three times the finished length required.
Make a slip loop: hold yarn between thumb and

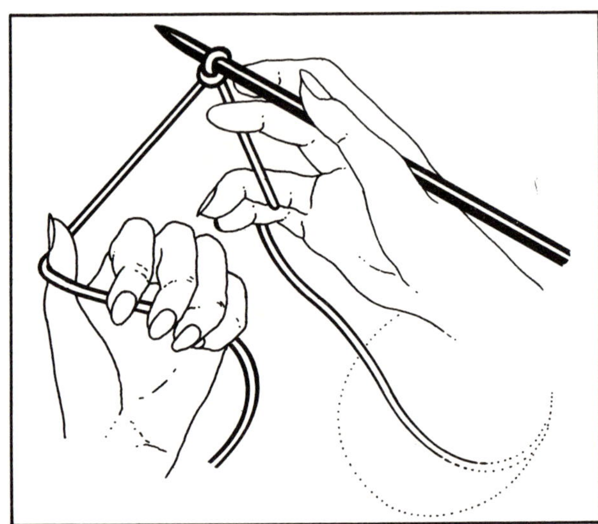

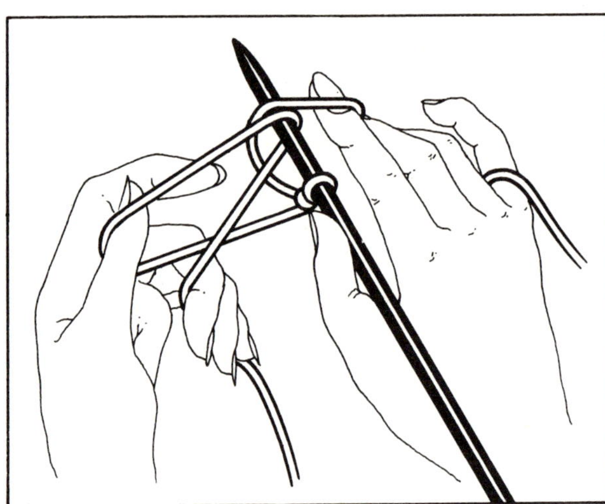

first finger of left hand; take yarn from ball in right hand and make a loop by taking main yarn over other yarn and hold loop in left hand.
Now take a needle in your right hand, put it through the loop and with it draw through the main yarn from the ball, thus making a loop on the needle. Pull yarn end to draw loop tight.

Hold the needle with the loop on it in the right hand with the main yarn coming from the ball at the back; hold other yarn in left hand under all four fingers. Take this yarn round left thumb clockwise close to the needle. Insert needle into loop on thumb, pass main yarn from ball under needle point, then with needle draw yarn through loop and let loop on thumb slip off. Pull yarn to draw stitch tight. Continue making stitches in this way until the required number is reached.

Two-needle method

Draw a short length of yarn from ball then make a slip loop as described in the thumb method above. Put needle with slip loop on it into left hand with main yarn at front. Taking second needle in right hand, insert this needle into loop

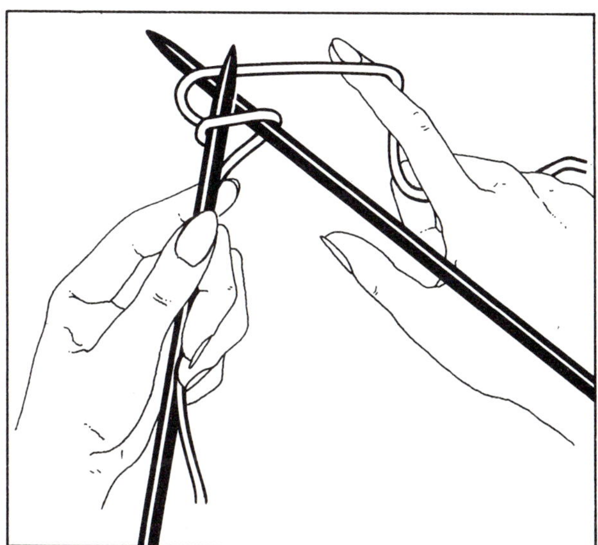

from left to right, pass main yarn under point of right-hand needle and then with this needle draw main yarn through loop to form a new loop on needle. Transfer this new loop to left-hand needle which now holds two stitches. Continue in this way until required number of stitches are formed. This method gives a 'looped' edge and if a firm edge is required the first row of knitting must be worked into the backs of the stitches.

Between-stitch method

Begin by making a slip loop and first stitch in a similar way as for the two-needle method above. Now, instead of inserting right-hand needle into stitch on left-hand needle, insert it between the two stitches, complete stitch as two-needle

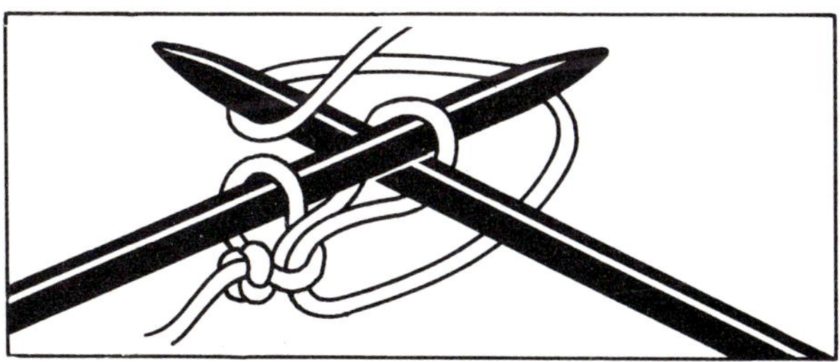

method. Continue in this way for length required. This method gives a twisted edge.

STITCHES
Knit stitch

Hold the needle with your cast-on stitches in your left hand and the empty needle and main yarn in your right hand (or vice versa if you are left-handed). Insert right-hand needle into first stitch on left-hand needle from left to right, main yarn at back of work, then take yarn under point of right-hand needle (diagram 1). With right-hand needle pull main yarn through stitch to form a loop on right-hand needle (diagram 2) and let loop on left-hand needle slip off. One stitch has been knitted on to right-hand needle. Continue along row in this way.

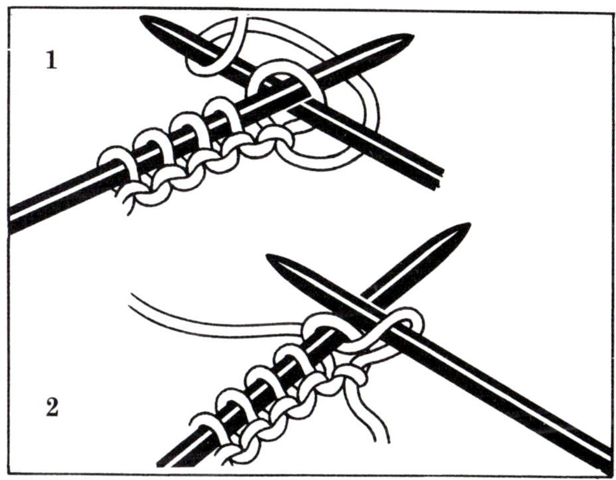

Purl stitch

Hold the needle with your cast-on stitches in your left hand and the empty needle and main yarn in right hand. Insert right-hand needle into first stitch from right to left, main yarn at front

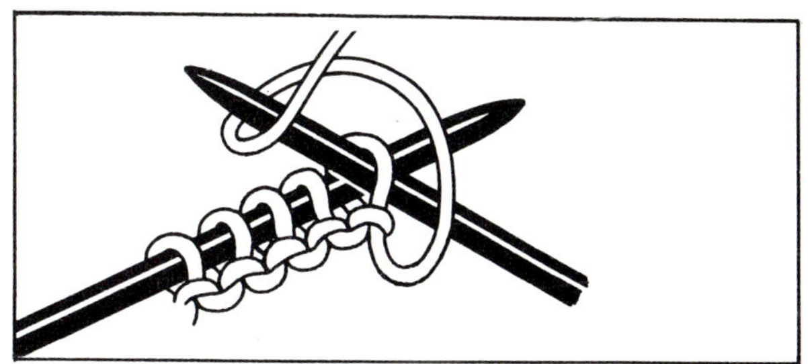

of work. Take yarn over and then under point of right-hand needle. Turn right-hand needle away from you to draw loop through on to needle and then drop loop from left-hand needle. Continue along row in this way.

INCREASING

At the beginning or end of a row increases of several stitches can be made by casting on.

Once you've mastered the basic skills, you can knit a vast range of items—not just clothing like the pretty sweater pictured on the **right** but also soft furnishings such as the three-colour cushions **above**.

Increases of a single stitch made by one of the following methods are usually worked within the main body of the work, and not at the end of a row.

Work twice into one stitch

This is the most usual method. Start to knit or purl the stitch in the usual way but do not drop the loop from the left-hand needle; now insert

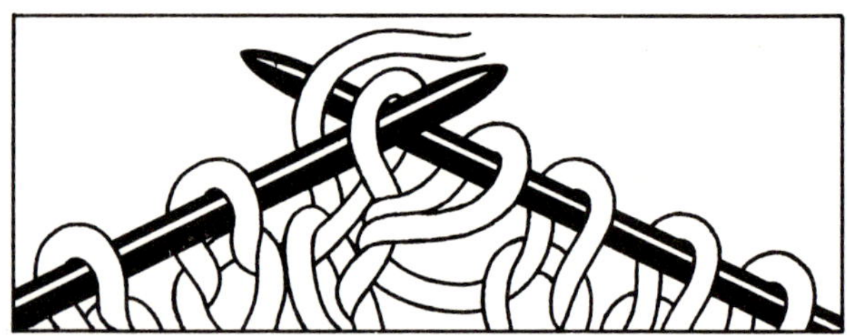

right-hand needle into back of loop from right to left for a knit stitch or from left to right for a purl stitch, and work into it again. The diagram above shows a knit stitch being worked into for the second time.

Yarn round needle or yarn over needle

This method of increasing leaves a small hole in the knitting so is usually used in lacy patterns (see opposite). In every case the strand which goes over the needle is worked as a stitch on the next row. In lacy patterns where a hole in the work is required but no increase in the number of stitches, then two stitches are usually worked together either just before or just after the 'made' stitch. Where an increase is required then the yarn is simply taken over or round the needle at the point where you want to increase the width of your work. See full instructions on page 38.

Lifting loop from previous row

Another method of making an extra stitch is to lift the loop lying between the last stitch and the next stitch on to the left-hand needle and then to knit it through the back of the loop.

DECREASING

At the beginning of a row decreases of several stitches can be made by casting off (see below). Decreases of one or two stitches made by any of the following methods are usually worked within the main body of the work and not at the end of a row.

Working two stitches together

Two stitches, sometimes three, are knitted or purled together as one stitch. When two stitches are knitted together the decreased stitch slopes to the right, so if lines of decreases are being worked at each end of the work – such as on a skirt – decreases at the end of the row are often worked by knitting two stitches together through the backs of the loops as this makes the decreased stitch slope to the left. The reverse happens when two stitches are purled together.

Pass slipped stitch over

This is worked by slipping one stitch on to the right-hand needle without working into it, then knitting the next stitch; the slipped stitch is then passed over the knitted stitch and dropped off the needle.

CASTING OFF

Never cast off too tightly, unless the pattern specifically instructs you to do so, as there is much less 'give' in this last row than in ordinary knitting.

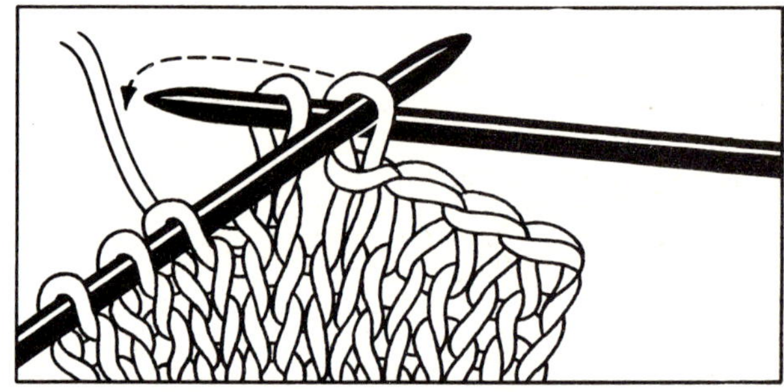

Work the first two stitches of the row in the usual way, keeping pattern correct. With the point of the left-hand needle lift the first stitch worked over the second stitch and let it fall. Work another stitch on to the right-hand needle then lift the first stitch over the second again. Work all along the row until only one stitch remains. Draw up this stitch to make it a long one, remove needle, break yarn and thread yarn end through stitch. Draw up tightly.

TENSION

Every pattern gives a tension measurement which refers to the number of stitches and rows and should be equal to one square inch for that particular pattern. Different sizes of needles will give different tension measurements with the same yarn. To achieve the correct size of finished article it is essential to work to the tension given in the pattern. Before starting work on any garment test your tension by working a small square, of 3 or 4 in., using the yarn and needle size recommended by the pattern, and the correct stitch pattern. Press this square then mark off with pins a 2-in. square in the middle of it. Count the number of stitches and rows in this square and check them with the tension given in the pattern. If the stitches and rows are fewer than those given, try again with needles a size smaller; if they are too many, try again with needles a size larger. Only start to knit the garment when you have found the right needles to achieve the correct tension.

BASIC STITCH PATTERNS

Garter stitch

Every row is a knit row. An elastic, ridged piece of work results. If every row is worked in purl stitches a similar fabric is produced.

Stocking stitch

This consists of one row of all knit stitches, and one row of all purl stitches worked alternately. It gives a smooth surface on the right (knit) side. Sometimes the reverse side is used as the right side and this is called reversed stocking stitch.

Ribbing

In single ribbing each row consists of one stitch knit followed by one stitch purl all along; in double ribbing two knit stitches are alternated with two purl. On the second row stitches which were knitted on the first row are purled and vice versa.

Example of single rib (k.1, p.1) pattern.

Example of double rib (k.2, p.2) pattern.

Example of wide rib (k.6, p.2) pattern.

Moss stitch

This is worked in a similar way to single rib, but stitches which were knitted on the first row are again knitted on the second row, and the purl stitches are purled. Double moss stitch is two stitches knitted followed by two stitches purled.

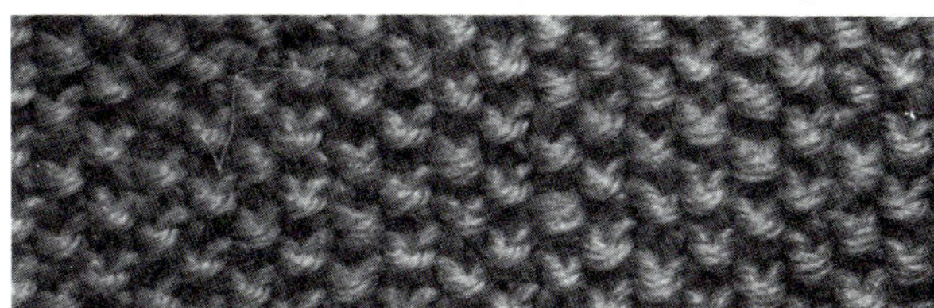

FANCY STITCH PATTERNS

Lacy patterns

The principle of working lacy patterns is that holes, or open stitches, are set at regular intervals into a solid fabric. These holes are created by taking the yarn round the needle between two stitches to form an extra stitch. The extra stitch is usually compensated for by working two stitches together either before or after the extra stitch. Sometimes however stitches will be added in one row, and taken off in the next. The way in which the yarn is taken round the needle to form the new stitch will depend on the stitch pattern you are using.

Example of a lacy pattern

Classic sweater with centre lacy panel

The feminine touch: a bolero made of soft mohair yarn

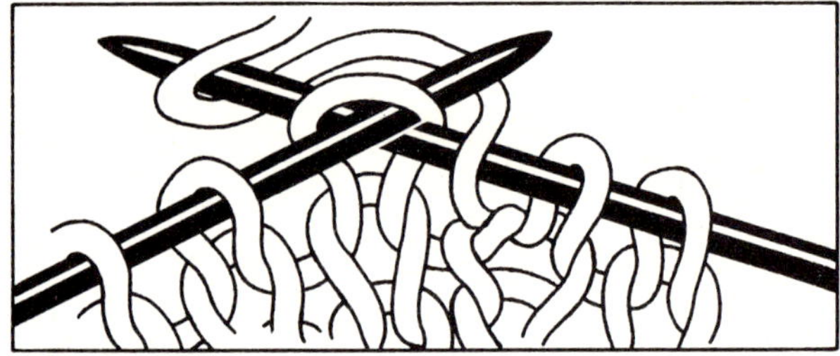

If you want to make the new stitch between two knit stitches, then bring the yarn forward between the needles and take it back over the top of the right-hand needle so the yarn is then in the correct position for knitting the next stitch on the left-hand needle. This is usually called 'yarn forward' (y.fwd.).

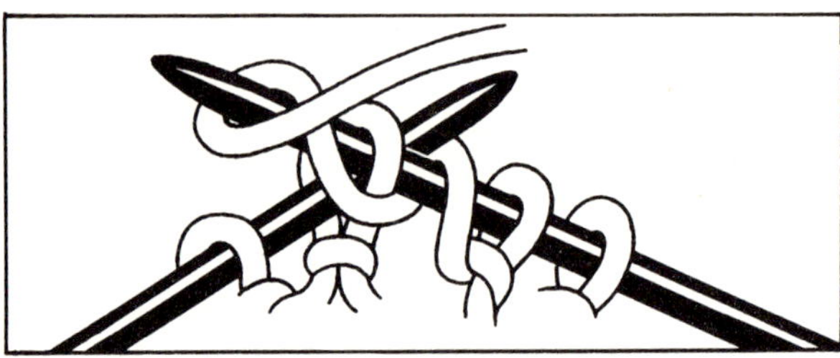

If you want to make the new stitch between two purl stitches, then take the yarn over the top of the right-hand needle, then bring it back under it to the front of the work again ready to purl the next stitch on the left-hand needle. This is usually called 'yarn round needle' (y.r.n.).

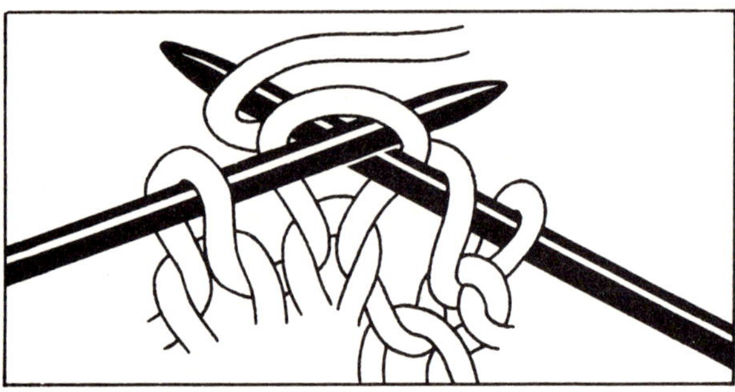

If you want to make the new stitch between a purl and a knit stitch, take the yarn over the top of the right-hand needle ready to knit the next stitch on the left-hand needle. This is usually called 'yarn on needle' (y.o.n.).

If you want to make the new stitch between a knit and a purl stitch, then first bring the yarn forward between the needles, then take it over the top of the right-hand needle and bring it back under it to the front of the work again, as for 'yarn round needle'. The yarn is then in position ready to work the next purl stitch on the left-hand needle. This is also usually called 'yarn on needle' (y.o.n.).

Cable patterns

Simple 'twisted' stitch patterns can be achieved by working in the backs of stitches, instead of into the fronts as usual. Diagram 1 shows a stitch being knitted through the back loop.

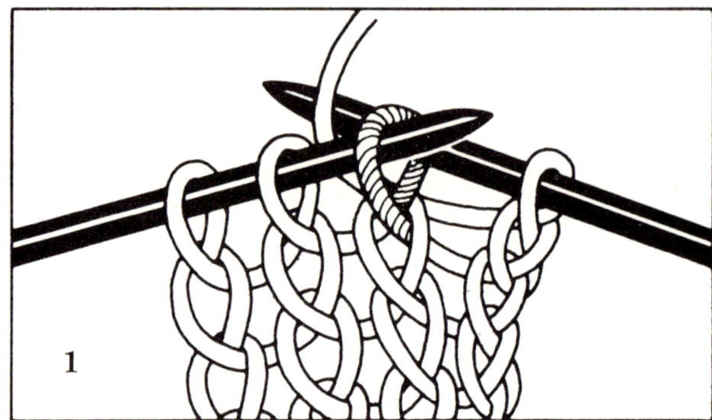

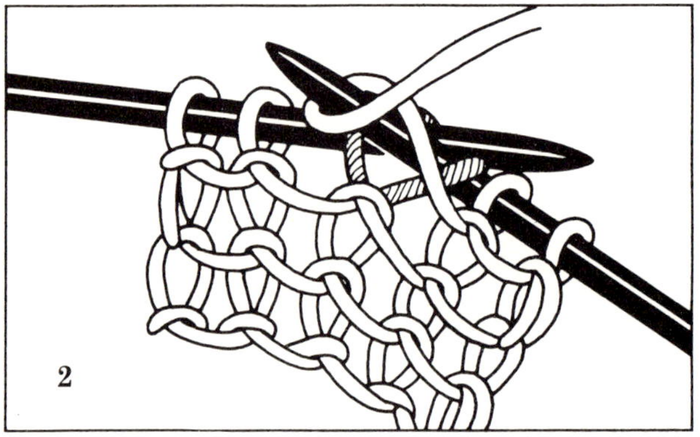

Diagram 2 shows a stitch being purled through the back loop.

Alternatively, a 'mock' cable effect can be achieved by knitting the second or third stitch on the left-hand needle before the first one or two. To produce a proper cable pattern however, with the traditional twisted rope-like rib, it is necessary to use a cable needle (see page 27). Two, three or more stitches are slipped from the left-hand needle on to the cable needle before being worked and then the cable needle is held either at the front of the work or the back, depending on which direction you wish the cable to twist. The corresponding number of stitches are then worked from the left-hand needle in the usual way, and then the stitches are knitted from the cable needle.

Blarney Kiss, a traditional cable pattern used in Aran knitting.

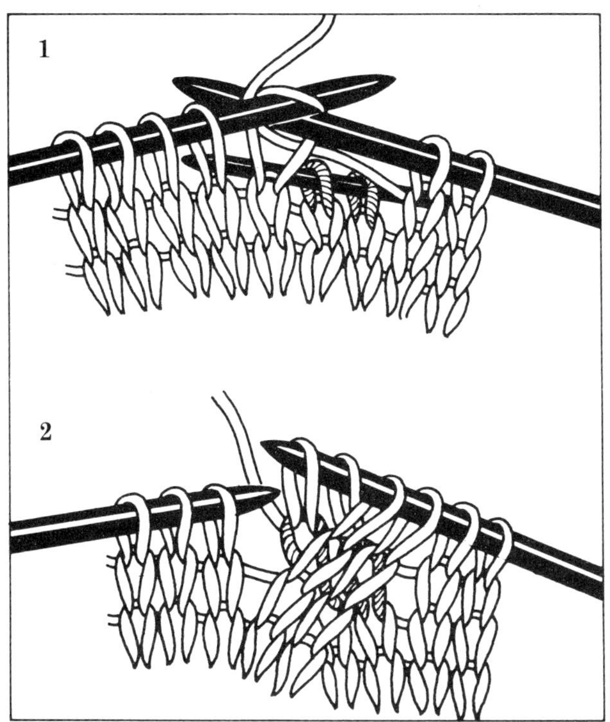

Diagrams 1 and 2 show a 'cable 4 back' pattern being worked: i.e. two stitches are slipped on to the cable needle and held at the back of the work while the next two stitches on the left-hand needle are worked, then the stitches on the cable needle are worked.

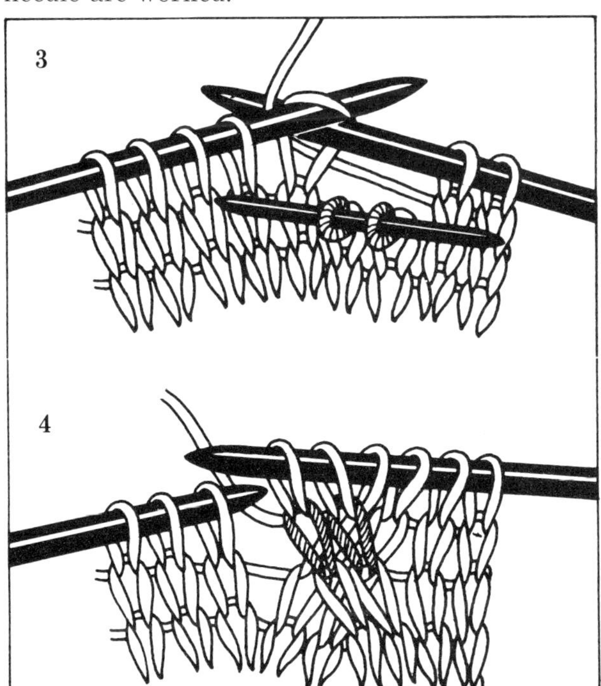

Diagrams 3 and 4 show a 'cable 4 front' pattern being worked: i.e. two stitches are slipped on to the cable needle and held at the front of the work while the next two stitches on the left-hand needle are worked, then the stitches on the cable needle are knitted.

Colour work

Any type of knitting using more than one colour of yarn, from a simple regular stripe pattern to a complex Fair Isle design, is termed colour knitting. Normally colour patterns are worked in stocking stitch, and although a particular design may use several different colours, as a general rule no more than two colours are ever in use at the same time. The easiest way to manipulate the two yarns is to hold one colour in your left hand, the other in your right. When yarn is not in use it is carried across the back of your work by one of the following methods:

Stranding. This method is suitable if each colour is used for only a few stitches. Take the yarn not in use across the back of work and pick it up when required. Cross the yarns at each colour change, and take care neither to pull the yarns too tightly, nor to leave them hanging too slackly.

Weaving. This method is suitable for patterns where each colour is used over a fairly large area. The yarn not in use should be woven under the colour in use.

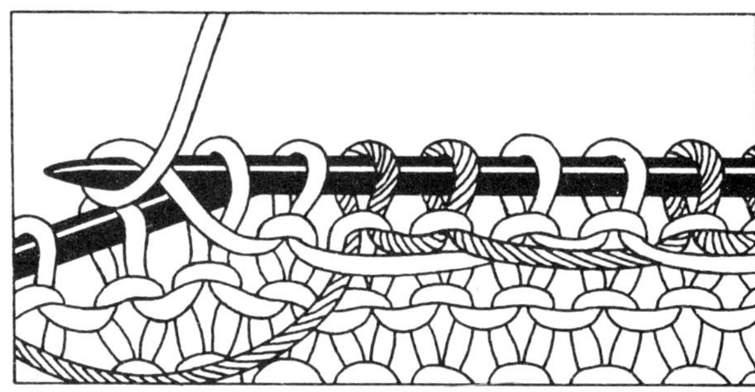

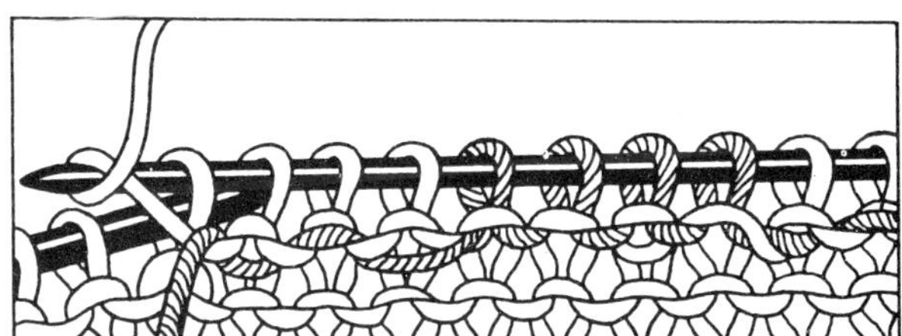

Sometimes, where large areas of colour are required, it is possible to combine these two methods to give a really professional finish to your work – i.e. strand over not more than three or four stitches then weave in the colour not in use when working the next stitch.

All things bright and beautiful—traditional sweater or contemporary tunic. The choice is yours.

When joining vertical sections of colour (in a checked pattern, for instance) the colours must be twisted on the wrong side of the work where they meet, the colour to be used being twisted round the colour to be dropped.

Working from a chart. Colour knitting patterns are often given in chart form. The chart is usually set out on tiny squares similar to graph paper, and each of these squares represents one knitted stitch: the squares reading across represent the number of stitches in the row (or one repeat of the pattern); the squares reading vertically represent the number of rows in the pattern. The odd-numbered (knitted) rows are worked from right to left, the even-numbered (purl) rows from left to right.

CIRCULAR KNITTING

Sometimes it is wished to knit a continuous seamless tube – for a sock or polo collar, for example. This can be done either by using a set of four needles with points at both ends or one long flexible circular needle with points at both ends. With four needles, it is best to cast all stitches on to one needle, and then divide them among three needles – the fourth is used for the knitting.

Four traditional stitch patterns: top line, left to right—lattice rib (see page 54) and alternating cables (see page 47); bottom line, left to right—classic basketweave (see page 50) and fancy trellis (see page 51).

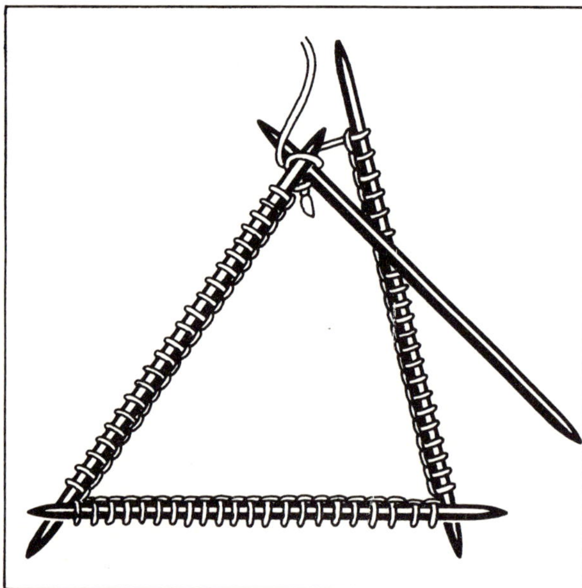

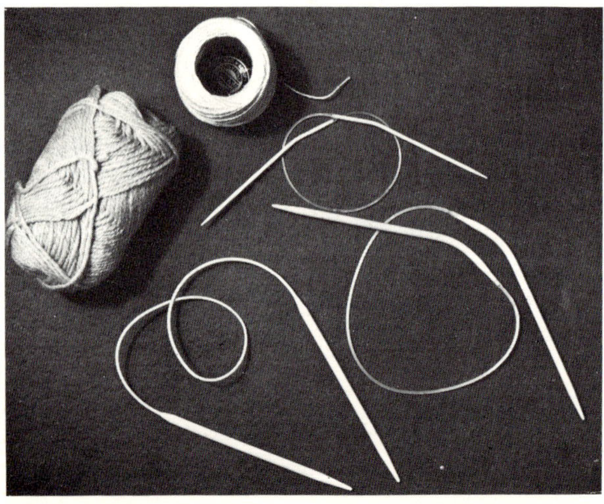

Work the first and last stitches of each needle tightly to avoid a gap. When working in rounds in this way the right side will be facing on every round.

When working with a circular needle, it is important to choose the correct length of needle for the pattern you are working. Stitches should reach from point to point without stretching.

USEFUL TECHNIQUES

Joining yarn

A knot should not be used as it will make an ugly lump in your work. Instead splice the yarn in the following way: unravel the yarn for a few inches at the end of the old ball and at the beginning of the new one and cut away a few strands of each. Twist the two ends together (by rubbing them between your palms). You should now have a join that is no thicker than the original basic yarn. Any loose ends should be carefully run into the back of the fabric when the garment is finished, using a darning needle.

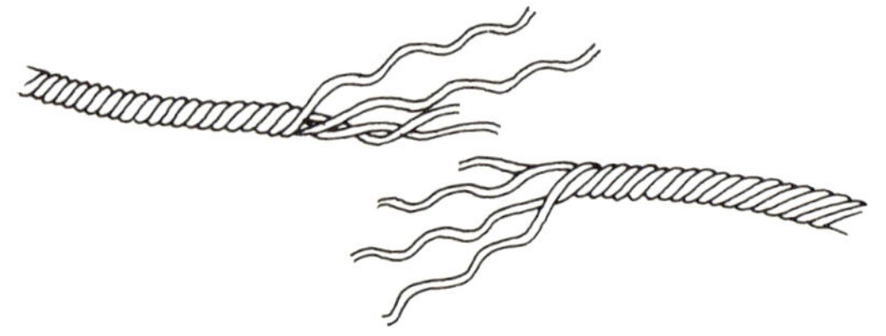

Pressing and blocking

Pressing is a very important part of the finishing process when you have made a knitted garment. Properly done, it can be slow work, but should not be skimped on this account. A good press can not only make sewing up much easier, it also makes a difference to the look of the finished garment. Pressing should be done to the individual knitted pieces, before sewing them together. Read any pressing instructions on your pattern, or on the label of the balls of yarn, since some yarns (especially synthetics) should not be pressed at all. If pressing is recommended, this is the way to do it: thread any loose ends on to a large-eyed darning needle and run them into the wrong side of the knitted fabric. Lay each piece right side down on a thick blanket, and carefully pull it out to the correct size and shape (check against measurements given in the pattern). Be sure to keep the fabric straight all the time. Do not stretch ribbed sections such as welts and cuffs.

Now pin the piece to the blanket, putting pins close together all round the edges of the garment, working from the outer edge inwards. This process is called blocking.

Lay a damp cloth across the piece and press lightly with a moderately hot iron. Too heavy a press can spoil a fancy pattern; far better to press lightly twice. A completely ribbed garment should be only very lightly pressed once. When pressing once, remove the damp cloth and allow the steam to evaporate. Remove pins. If you are using a yarn that requires no pressing, block the garment pieces as described above, then lay a damp cloth over the fabric and leave it until the fabric is quite dry. The pieces are now ready to be sewn together.

Dropped stitches

There is no need to panic if you drop a stitch. An experienced knitter can use a spare needle to repair a 'ladder', but you will probably find the job easier if you use a fine crochet hook. Slip the hook into the dropped stitch and take it up the knitting, looping through each row as if it had been knitted (remember to reverse the action if you have to pick up across knitted and purled rows).

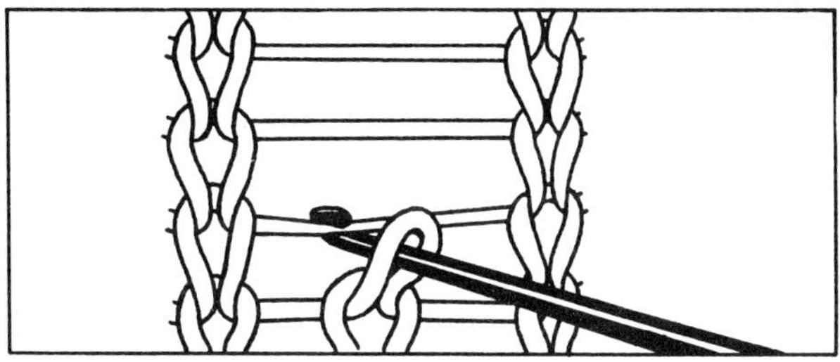

SEWING UP GARMENTS

If possible, when sewing pieces together, use the yarn which was used for knitting up the garment. If the yarn is very thick, it may be possible to strand it (i.e. to pull out a single strand of the yarn) and use this. If not, then a carefully matched yarn should be used.

There are two seams to choose from when sewing up edges: flatstitched seam and backstitched seam.

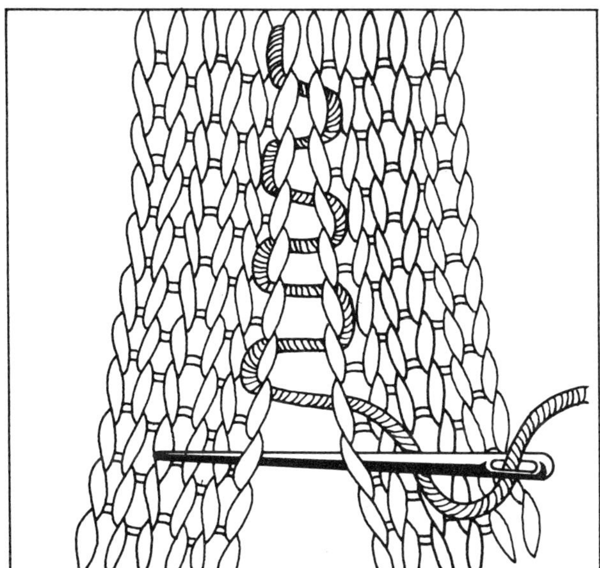

Flatstitched seam. This is used for putting on an edging, or joining ribbed sections. With right sides of work facing each other, place the two pieces edge to edge. Using an overcasting stitch, draw the edges together, but do not draw the thread too tightly or it may snap (especially as this stitch is used for parts of garments such as welts and cuffs which have to take considerable strain).

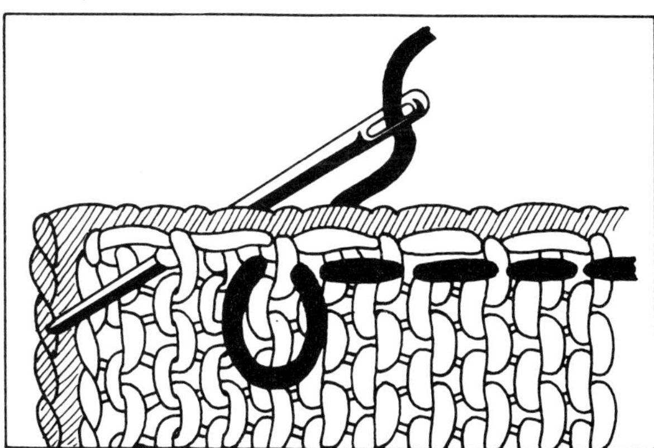

Backstitched seam. This should be used for all main seams. With right sides of work together, backstitch with small stitches as close to the edge as possible.

Seams should be pressed again lightly when they are finished. The normal order of seam stitching is as follows: shoulder seams, sew in sleeves, then sew sleeve and side seams as one long continuous seam. Edgings and pockets should be stitched in place last.

If you are working with an exceptionally heavy yarn, or making a very big garment (a car coat, for instance, or a man's thick sweater), it is sometimes wise to tape shoulder and armhole seams. This prevents sagging and stretching. When the seam is complete, enclose it with binding tape and stitch through. Heavy garments should never be hung up, but always stored flat.

Waistbands. The waistbands on skirts, trousers and shorts can be finished with rows of shirring elastic. On the wrong side of work, run the elastic through every knit stitch on every alternate row to depth of waistband required.

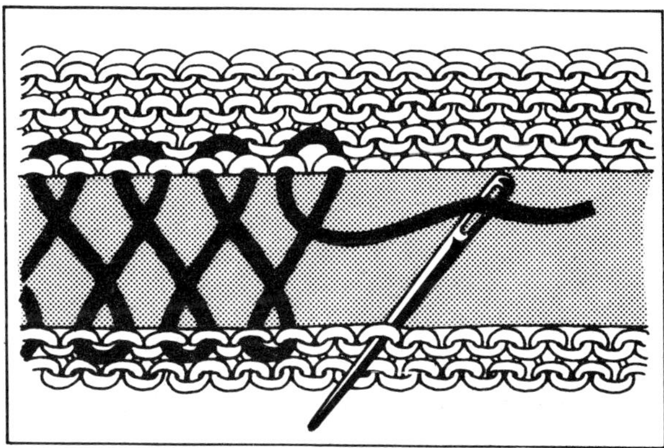

Alternatively a casing can be made on the wrong side of work and elastic, usually 1 in. wide, threaded through this casing. The casing can be formed by working herringbone stitches to depth of waistband, as shown in the diagram above.

44 *Roll-collar pullover is worked mainly in rib, with*
a honeycomb-patterned yoke section.

Fair Isle designs are delightful for children.

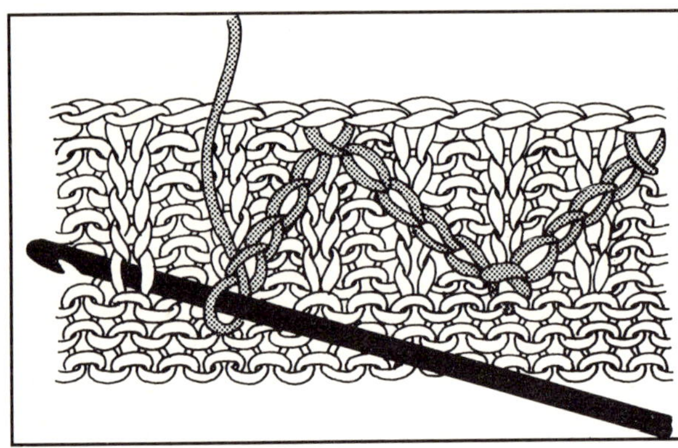

If preferred, a crochet casing can be made: insert hook into the top of one ribbed section on the knitted fabric, work one slip stitch, then work chain to depth of casing required, miss one ribbed section, and work one slip stitch into bottom of next rib. Work number of chain as before, then one slip stitch, miss one ribbed section, and one slip stitch into top of next rib. Continue in this way to form a zigzag casing of crocheted chains.

Grafting

This is a process by which two pieces of knitting can be joined without casting off and without making a seam. Place the two needles with the stitches on them together and then using a tapestry needle and length of yarn, 'sew' a new row of knitted stitches between the two groups. The diagram below shows how this is done, and how two stitches are slipped off each needle alternately. This diagram shows grafting being worked in a stocking stitch pattern, but grafting may be worked in any stitch pattern.

Picking up stitches

After the main parts of a garment have been worked and stitched together, stitches sometimes have to be picked up round a neckline or armhole edge and a collar, neckband or edging worked on these.

To pick up stitches, have the right side of work towards you and put the point of the needle through a whole loop at the edge or through both loops of a cast-off stitch. Put the yarn round the needle and draw a loop through, thus making a loop on the needle. Continue in this way across the edge until the required number of stitches are picked up. Work collar or edging on these stitches. Always make sure stitches are spaced

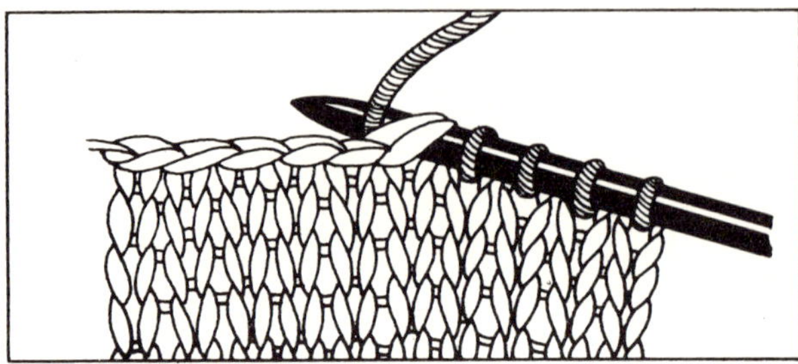

out evenly. If necessary measure across the edge first and use pins to mark the correct positions for picking up the stitches.

It is sometimes easier to use a fine needle or a crochet hook to pick up stitches and then to slip them on to the correct size needle for the edging.

Buttonholes

Small buttonholes, suitable for ball-type buttons and baby garments, can be made simply by taking the yarn over or round the needle and then knitting together the next two stitches (see lacy patterns, page 35). Larger buttonholes are usually made by casting off a number of stitches on one row and replacing them by casting on a similar number on the following row immediately over the cast-off stitches. The exact number of stitches cast off will depend on the size of button being used.

CROCHET STITCHES

A crochet edging worked round neck, sleeve and hem edges of a completed garment will give a decorative and neat finish to almost any knitted garment. A row of single crochet (slip stitch) worked all round the edge of a garment will be virtually invisible but will give a firm neat finish to edges which might otherwise droop or look uneven.

If a decorative border or edging is required, then further rows of crochet in any pattern are worked into the foundation row of single crochet.

Crochet and knitting can also be effectively combined in the same design – for instance, by using inset crochet motifs in a knitted fabric. It is as well therefore to be familiar with a few basic crochet stitches—see Section Two of this book.

ABBREVIATIONS

The following are the abbreviations formally used in knitting patterns:

alt.	alternate
beg.	beginning
cont.	continue
dec.	decreas(e)(ed)(ing)
foll.	following
g.st.	garter stitch
in.	inch(es)
inc.	increas(e)(ed)(ing)
k.	knit
m.1	make one stitch (usually by taking yarn over or round the needle – see lacy patterns, page 35)
m.st.	moss stitch

p.	purl
patt.	pattern
p.s.s.o.	pass slipped stitch over
rem.	remain(ing)(der)
rep.	repeat
sl.	slip
st(s).	stitch(es)
st.st.	stocking stitch
t.b.l.	through back of loop
tog.	together
y.b.	yarn back
y.fwd. (or y.f.)	yarn forward
y.o.n.	yarn over needle
y.r.n.	yarn round needle

Crochet abbreviations

ch.	chain
d.c.	double crochet
sl.st.	slip stitch
tr.	treble

Pattern sizes

If a pattern gives a range of different sizes, then normally instructions are given in size order, with the different instructions relating to larger sizes in brackets. Where only one set of figures occurs this refers to all sizes.

Part 2—Dictionary of Stitch Patterns

Alternating cables
also illustrated in colour on page 41

This is a flat version of cable rib, similar to a traditional cable but without the rope-like effect.

Cast on a multiple of 9 sts. plus 3 (e.g. 30).
1st row: * p.3, k.6; rep. from * to last 3 sts., p.3.
2nd and alt. rows: * k.3, p.6; rep. from * to last 3 sts., k.3.
3rd row: * p.3, C4 back (see Wheatear Cable pattern, page 58), k.2; rep. from * to last 3 sts., p.3.
5th row: * p.3, k.2, C4 front (see Wheatear Cable pattern, page 58); rep. from * to last 3 sts., p.3.
6th row: as 2nd row.
Rows 3-6 form pattern.

Blue, green and white Fair Isle stitch pattern
illustrated in colour on page 56

This is a decorative three-colour Fair Isle which can be used as an all-over pattern, or in bands of Fair Isle alternated with bands of plain background colour.

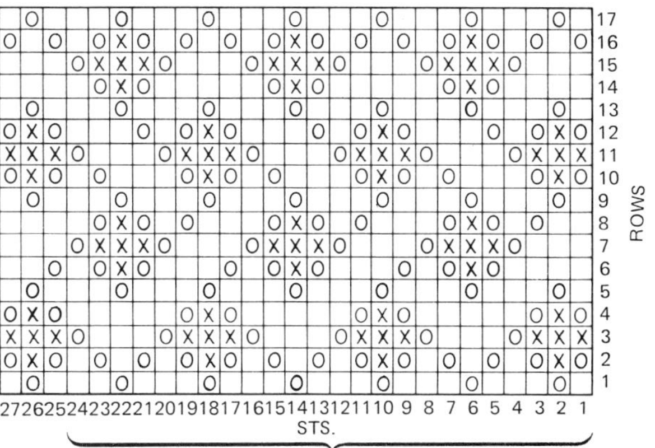

☐ WHITE
☒ GREEN
◯ BLUE   1 SQUARE = 1 STITCH

The pattern is repeated over 24 sts., so cast on a multiple of 24 plus 1 st. to give extra st. at end of row.
Work 4 rows of st.st. in white (or number of rows wished to give band of plain colour), then cont. in st.st., work from the chart below to form the colour pattern. Each square on the chart represents one stitch, and each horizontal row of squares represents one row in the pattern.
The colour motif repeats across work from stitch 1–24 inclusive. Work the final st. in the row to correspond with the first st. in the repeat.
Work may continue in alternate bands of plain colour and Fair Isle pattern as wished.

Butterfly stitch

Small open motifs are set in stocking stitch to give lightness of texture; ideal for baby wear and summer tops.

Cast on a multiple of 10 sts. (e.g. 20).
1st row: * k.2 tog., y.fwd., k.1, y.fwd., sl.1, k.1, p.s.s.o., k.5; rep. from * to end.
2nd row: * p.7, sl.1 purlwise, p.2; rep. from * to end.
3rd and 4th rows: as first and 2nd rows.
5th row: k.
6th row: p.
7th row: * k.5, k.2 tog., y.fwd., k.1, y.fwd., sl.1, k.1, p.s.s.o.; rep. from * to end.
8th row: * p.2, sl.1 purlwise, p.7; rep. from * to end.
9th row: as 7th row.
10th row: as 8th row.
11th row: as 5th row.
12th row: as 6th row.
These 12 rows form pattern.

A teenager demonstrates her individuality in her knitting **(above)** *while the little ones enjoy dressing like Mother* **(opposite).**

Classic basketweave stitch
also illustrated in colour on page 41

This gives a firm texture with an interesting surface; good for coats, jackets, skirts and trousers.

Cast on a multiple of 10 plus 7 (e.g. 27).
1st row: * p.7, k.3; rep. from * to last 7 sts., p.7.
2nd row: * k.7, p.3; rep. from * to last 7 sts., k.7.
3rd and 4th rows: as first and 2nd rows.
5th row: p.2, * k.7, p.3; rep. from * to last 5 sts., k.3, p.2.
6th row: k.2, * p.3, k.7; rep. from * to last 5 sts., p.3, k.2.
7th and 8th rows: as 5th and 6th rows.
These 8 rows form pattern.

Diagonal rib

A closely-textured stitch which is used most effectively with a heavy yarn where it gives a three-dimensional effect.

Cast on a multiple of 5 sts. (e.g. 30).
1st row (wrong side): * p. 2, (k. into front and back of next st.) 3 times; rep. from * to end.
2nd row: * (k.2 tog. t.b.l..) 3 times, k.2; rep. from * to end.
3rd row: * p.1, (k. into front and back of next st.) 3 times, p.1; rep. from * to end.
4th row: * k.1, (k.2 tog. t.b.l.) 3 times, k.1; rep. from * to end.
Continue in this way, moving the pattern one stitch along on every alt. row.

Diamond lattice

This is a firm yet open stitch which can be used with yarns of all weights, but it is probably at its best in fine yarn for a delicate design, such as an evening top or baby dress.

(Note. The extra stitch is an edging stitch but is needed in the 15th row; edging stitches at each end of the needle are recommended on all open-work designs as this makes sewing up easier.)
Cast on a multiple of 10 sts. plus 1 (e.g. 21).
1st row: k.1, * y.fwd., sl.1, k.1, p.s.s.o., k.5, k.2 tog., y.fwd., k.1; rep. from * to end.
2nd row and alt. rows: p.
3rd row: k.1, * k.1, y.fwd., sl.1, k.1, p.s.s.o., k.3, k.2 tog., y.fwd., k.2; rep. from * to end.
5th row: k.1, * k.2, y.fwd., sl.1, k.1, p.s.s.o., k.1, k.2 tog., y.fwd., k.3; rep. from * to end.
7th row: k.1, * k.3, y.fwd., sl.1, k.2 tog., p.s.s.o., y.fwd., k.4; rep. from * to end.
9th row: k.1, * k.2, k.2 tog., y.fwd., k.1, y.fwd., sl.1, k.1, p.s.s.o., k.3; rep. from * to end.
11th row: k.1, * k.1, k.2 tog., y.fwd., k.3, y.fwd., sl.1, k.1, p.s.s.o., k.2; rep. from * to end.
13th row: k.1, * k.2 tog., y.fwd., k.5, y.fwd., sl.1, k.1, p.s.s.o., k.1; rep. from * to end.
15th row: k.2 tog., * y.fwd., k.7, y.fwd., sl.1, k.2 tog., p.s.s.o.; rep. from * ending with sl.1, k.1, p.s.s.o.
16th row: p.
These 16 rows form pattern.

Embossed leaves

A shaped motif which stands away from the ground fabric. It is easier to work than it looks and is effective used in horizontal bands as well as in all-over patterns.

Cast on a multiple of 7 sts. plus 6 (e.g. 34).
1st row: p.6, * y.o.n., k.1, y.o.n., p.6; rep. from * to end.
2nd row: * k.6, p.3; rep. from * to last 6 sts., k.6.
3rd row: p.6, * k.1, y.fwd., k.1, y.fwd., k.1, p.6; rep. from * to end.
4th row: * k.6, p.5; rep. from * to last 6 sts., k.6.
5th row: p.6, * k.2, y.fwd., k.1, y.fwd., k.2, p.6; rep. from * to end.
6th row: * k.6, p.7; rep. from * to last 6 sts., k.6.
7th row: p.6, * k.3, y.fwd., k.1, y.fwd., k.3, p.6; rep. from * to end.
8th row: * k.6, p.9; rep. from * to last 6 sts., k.6.
9th row: p.6, * sl.1, k.1, p.s.s.o., k.5, k.2 tog., p.6; rep. from * to end.
10th row: * k.6, p.7; rep. from * to last 6 sts., k.6.
11th row: p.6, * sl.1, k.1, p.s.s.o., k.3, k.2 tog., p.6; rep. from * to end.
12th row: * k.6, p.5; rep. from * to last 6 sts., k.6.
13th row: p.6, * sl.1, k.1, p.s.s.o., k.1, k.2 tog., p.6; rep. from * to end.
14th row: * k.6, p.3; rep. from * to last 6 sts., k.6.
15th row: p.6, * sl.1, k.2 tog., p.s.s.o., p.6; rep. from * to end.
16th row: k.
17th row: p.
18th row: k.
19th and 20th rows: as 17th and 18th rows.
These 20 rows form pattern.

Fancy trellis
also illustrated in colour on page 41

A favourite open-work stitch for children's clothes or evening wear. It gives a regular, interesting surface with enough firmness even for outerwear if the yarn used is heavyweight.

Cast on a multiple of 7 sts. (e.g. 28).
(Note. An edge st. at each end is recommended.)
1st row: * k.2, k.2 tog., y.fwd., k.3; rep. from * to end.
2nd row: * p.1, p.2 tog. t.b.l., y.r.n., p.1, y.r.n., p.2 tog., p.1; rep. from * to end.
3rd row: * k.2 tog., y.fwd., k.3, y.fwd., sl.1, k.1, p.s.s.o.; rep. from * to end.
4th row: p.
5th row: * y.r.n., sl.1, k.1, p.s.s.o., k.5; rep. from * to end.
6th row: * y.r.n., p.2 tog., p.2, p.2 tog. t.b.l., y.r.n., p.1; rep. from * to end.
7th row: * k.2, y.fwd., sl.1, k.1, p.s.s.o., k.2 tog., y.fwd., k.1; rep. from * to end.
8th row: p.
These 8 rows form pattern.

Fleur de lis

This is one of the classic two-colour patterns which can be used for evening tops or husky sweaters, depending on the weight and type of yarn used.

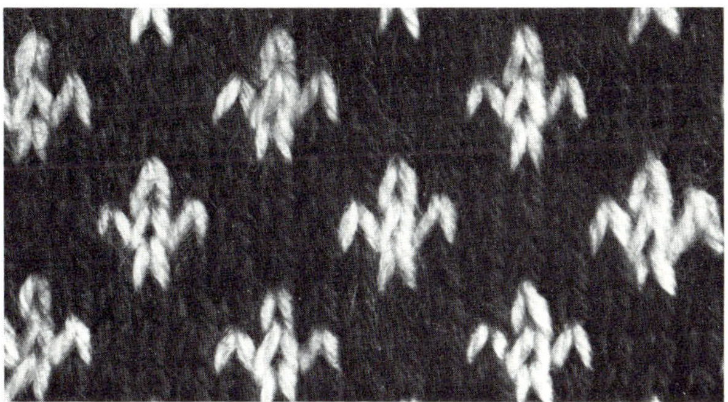

(Note. The pattern has to be reversed on completion to give the fleur de lis shape.)
Use two colours of yarn, one dark, one light (D., dark; L., light).
Cast on a multiple of 6 sts. plus 3 (e.g. 21).
1st row: k.3 D., * 1 L., 5 D.; rep. from * to end.
2nd row: p.1 L., * 3 D., 3 L.; rep. from * to last 2 sts., p.2 D.
3rd row: as first row.
4th row: p.2 D., * 1 L., 5 D.; rep. from * to last st., p.1 L.
5th row: k.2 L., * 3 D., 3 L.; rep. from * to last st., k.1 D.
6th row: as 4th row.
These 6 rows form pattern.

Houndstooth

Another favourite two-colour design which is usually associated with sporty designs – try it for the fronts of a cardigan or on a suit. Almost any colour combination looks good.

Use two colours of yarn, one dark, one light (D., dark, L., light).
Cast on a multiple of 4 sts. (e.g. 32).
1st row: k.2 L., * 1 D., 3 L.; rep. from * to last 2 sts., k.1 D., 1 L.
2nd row: p., * 1 L., 3 D.; rep. from * to end.
3rd row: k., * 1 L., 3 D.; rep. from * to end.
4th row: p.2 L., * 1 D., 3 L.; rep. from * to last 2 sts., 1 D., 1 L.
These 4 rows form pattern.

52   *Striking cabled sweater*

*For high days and holidays—gaily-striped sweater
and teaming knickerbockers*

Lacy chevron

This stitch gives a V-shaped patterning of open-work set between open ribs. It is ideal for a light jumper or child's dress.

Cast on a multiple of 12 sts. (e.g. 48).
1st row: * k.3, y.fwd., sl.1, k.1, p.s.s.o., k.2, k.2 tog., y.fwd., k.1, y.fwd., sl.1, k.1, p.s.s.o.; rep. from * to end.
2nd and alt. rows: p.
3rd row: * k.1, k.2 tog., y.fwd., k.1, y.fwd., sl.1, k.1, p.s.s.o., k.1, k.2 tog., y.fwd., k.1, y.fwd., sl.1, k.1, p.s.s.o.; rep. from * to end.
5th row: * k.2 tog., y.fwd., k.3, y.fwd., sl.1, k.1, p.s.s.o., k.2 tog., y.fwd., k.1, y.fwd., sl.1, k.1, p.s.s.o.; rep. from * to end.
6th row: p.
These 6 rows form pattern.

Lacy rib

A firm yet open stitch which can be used by itself or as vertical bars inset between ribs of plain knitting or a different open-work stitch.

Cast on a multiple of 4 sts. (e.g. 20).
1st row: * k.2, y.fwd., sl.1, k.1, p.s.s.o; rep. from * to end.
2nd row: * p.2, y.r.n., p.2 tog.; rep. from * to end.
These 2 rows form pattern.

Lattice rib
also illustrated in colour on page 41

A raised chain on a reversed stocking stitch ground, effective in fine yarns or heavy ones.

Cast on a multiple of 8 sts. plus 4 (e.g. 28).
1st row: * p.4, cross 2 L. (i.e. with right-hand needle behind first st., k. the 2nd st. through the front loop then k. the first st. in usual way and take both off needle together), cross 2 R. (i.e. passing in front of first st. k. 2nd st. through front loop then k. first st. in usual way and take both off needle together); rep. from * to last 4 sts., p.4.
2nd row: * k.4, p.4; rep. from * to last 4 sts., k.4.
3rd row: * p.4, k.1, p.2, k.1; rep. from * to last 4 sts., p.4.
4th row: * k.4, p.1, k.2, p.1; rep. from * to last 4 sts., k.4.
5th and 6th rows: as 3rd and 4th rows.
These 6 rows form pattern.

Linked lozenges
also illustrated in colour on page 56

A two-colour pattern which has an all-over squared shape. In pastels it looks pretty for baby wear, but in solid colours and thick wool it will make a handsome sports sweater. Use two colours of yarn, one dark, one light (D., dark, L., light).

Cast on a multiple of 8 sts. plus 1 (e.g. 33).
1st row: k., * 2 D., 5 L., 1 D.; rep. from * to last st., k.1 D.
2nd row: p., * 1 L., 1 D., (2 L., 1 D.) twice; rep. from * to last st., p.1 L. **3rd row**: as first row.
4th row: p., * 2 L., 1 D., 3 L., 1 D., 1 L.; rep. from * to last st., p.1 L.
5th row: k., * 3 L., 3 D., 2 L.; rep. from * to last st., k.1 L.
6th row: p., * 1 D., 2 L., 1 D., 1 L., 1 D., 2 L.; rep. from * to last st., p.1 D.
7th row: as 5th row.
8th row: p., * 2 L., 1 D., 3 L., 1 D., 1 L.; rep. from * to last st., p. 1 L.
These 8 rows form pattern.

Medallion cables

This gives an attractive alternative to the conventional cable. The rib is kept open after each set of cabling; very effective in extremely thick yarns. A cable needle will be required.

Cast on a multiple of 11 sts. plus 3 (e.g. 36).
1st row: * p.3, k.8; rep. from * to last 3 sts., p.3.
2nd row: * k.3, p.8; rep. from * to last 3 sts., k.3.
3rd and 4th rows: as first and 2nd rows.
5th row: * p.3, C4 back (i.e. slip 2 sts. on cable needle then put to back of work, k.2, then k. sts. from cable needle), C4 front (i.e. slip 2 sts. on cable needle then put to front of work, k.2 then k. sts. from cable needle); rep. from * to last 3 sts., p.3.
6th row: as 2nd row.
These 6 rows form pattern.

Mock cable

A twisted rib which gives the effect of a narrow cabling without having to use a cable needle.

Cast on a multiple of 5 sts. plus 3 (e.g. 23).
1st row: * p.3, k.2; rep. from * to last 3 sts., p.3.
2nd row: * k.3, p.2; rep. from * to last 3 sts., k.3.
3rd and 4th rows: as first and 2nd rows.
5th row: * p.3, cross 2R (see Lattice Rib pattern, opposite); rep. from * to last 3 sts., p.3.
6th row: as 2nd row.
These 6 rows form pattern.

Open arches

A lacy stitch with pointed shapes. It is fairly firm when worked in a double knitting yarn.

Cast on a multiple of 4 sts. plus 1 (e.g. 25).
1st row: k.1, * y.fwd., k.3, y.fwd., k.1; rep. from * to end.
2nd and alt. rows: p.
3rd row: k.1, * k.1, sl.1, k.2 tog., p.s.s.o., k.2; rep. from * to end.
4th row: p.
These 4 rows form pattern.

Pink and white Fair Isle stitch pattern
illustrated in colour on page 56

This is an open diamond-shape motif which can be used in a decorative band above ribbing at welt and cuffs on a sweater or cardigan, or to form an all-over pattern, if preferred.

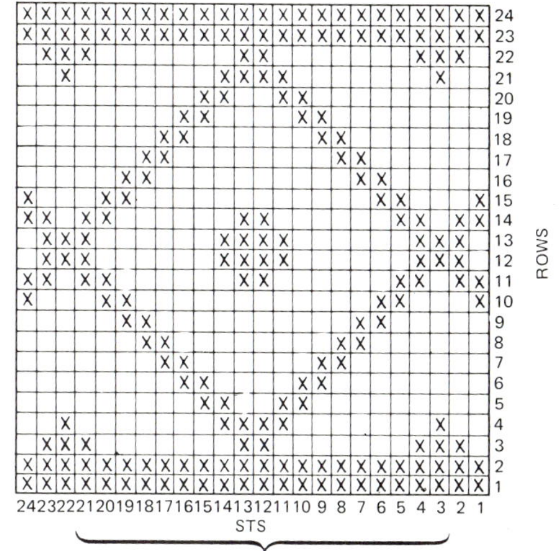

The pattern is repeated over 19 sts., so cast on a multiple of 19 plus 5 sts. to give 2 extra sts. at beg. of row, 3 extra sts. at end of row.
Work 6 rows of st.st. in white, then cont. in st.st., work from the chart above to form colour pattern. Each square on the chart represents one stitch, and each horizontal row of squares represent one row in the pattern. The colour motif is repeated from stitch 3–21 inclusive across work. Work the final 3 sts. in the row to correspond with the 3 sts. at beg. of row (i.e. sts. 3, 2 and 1 on chart).
Work may continue in alternate bands of plain colour and Fair Isle pattern as wished.

Raised diamonds

A firm stitch with a raised surface which is interesting without being obtrusive, and is a pleasant variant on any garment where stocking stitch is appropriate.

Cast on a multiple of 8 sts. (e.g. 32).
1st row: * p.1, k.7; rep. from * to end.
2nd row: * k.1, p.5, k.1, p.1; rep. from * to end.
3rd row: * k.2, p.1, k.3, p.1, k.1; rep. from * to end.
4th row: * p.2, k.1, p.1, k.1, p.3; rep. from * to end.
5th row: * k.4, p.1, k.3; rep. from * to end.
6th, 7th and 8th rows: as 4th, 3rd and 2nd rows.
These 8 rows form pattern.

Red, white and blue Fair Isle stitch pattern

This is a geometric pattern of squares which is
equally effective repeated across work, or used
as a single motif set in a plain background.

The pattern is repeated over 26 sts., so cast on a multiple
of 26 plus 1 st. to give extra st. at end of row.
Work 2 rows of st.st. in white (or number of rows
wished to give band of plain colour), then cont. in
st.st., work from the chart, right, to form the colour
pattern. Each square on the chart represents one stitch
and each horizontal row of squares represents one row
in the pattern. The colour motif repeats across work
from stitch 1–26 inclusive. Work the final st. in the row
to correspond with the first st. in the repeat. Work may
continue in alternate bands of plain colour and Fair
Isle pattern as wished.

ROWS

Row	26	25	24	23	22	21	20	19	18	17	16	15	14	13	12	11	10	9	8	7	6	5	4	3	2	1
15	X	X			X		X				X	X	X	X	X				X		X			X	X	
14	X	X			X		X				X	X		X	X				X		X			X	X	X
13					X		X							X					X		X					X
12			X		X						X	X		X	X						X		X			
11		X		X							X	X	X	X	X							X		X		
10		O				O	O	O	O	O						O	O	O	O	O				O		O
9	O				O	O			O	O			O			O	O			O	O				O	
8						O				O		O	O	O		O				O						O
7		O				O	O		O	O			O			O	O		O	O				O		
6		O				O	O	O	O	O						O	O	O	O	O				O		O
5		X		X							X	X	X	X	X							X		X		
4			X		X						X	X		X	X						X		X			
3					X		X							X					X		X					X
2	X	X			X		X				X	X		X	X				X		X			X	X	X
1	X	X			X		X				X	X	X	X	X				X		X			X	X	

STS.

☐ WHITE
☒ RED
⊡ BLUE   1 SQUARE = 1 STITCH

56

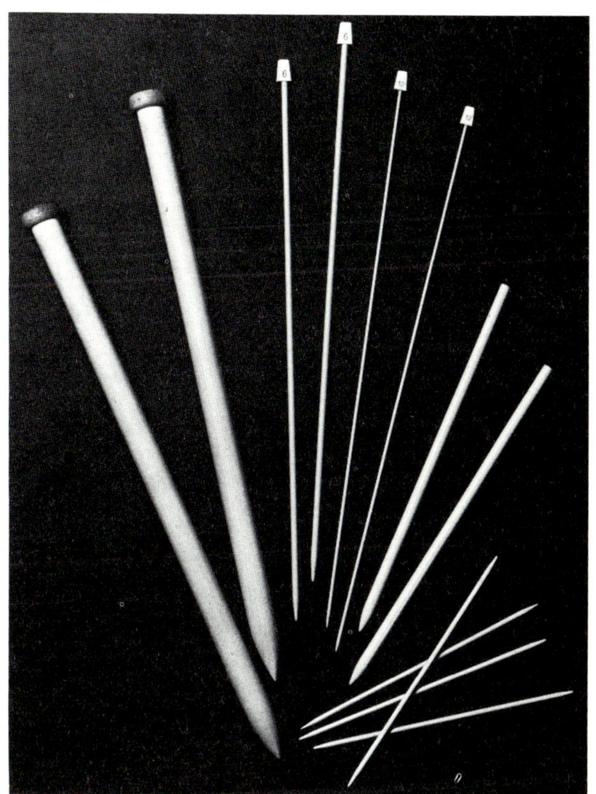

The tools of the trade

*A cape, dress and jersey set like this is easy to knit—
but hard to buy off-the-peg.*

Rib and eyelet

A fancy rib with regularly-spaced open-work, suitable for men's or women's garments, as it has a tailored look.

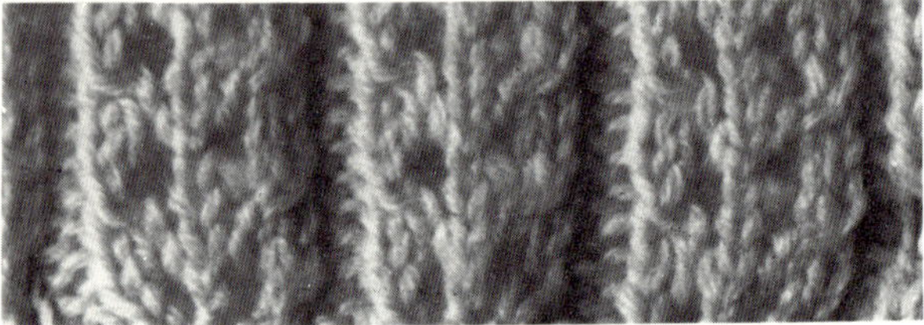

Cast on a multiple of 7 sts. plus 6 (e.g. 27).
1st row: k.2, * p.2, k.2 tog., y.fwd., k.1, y.fwd., k.2 tog. t.b.l.; rep. from * to last 4 sts., p.2, k.2.
2nd row: p.2, * k.2, p.5; rep. from * to last 4 sts., k.2, p.2.
3rd row: k.2, * p.2, k.5; rep. from * to last 4 sts., p.2, k.2.
4th row: as 2nd row.
These 4 rows form the pattern.

Two-tone tweed

A textured stitch which employs a second colour discreetly to give a tweedy effect; excellent for sporty, tailored garments.

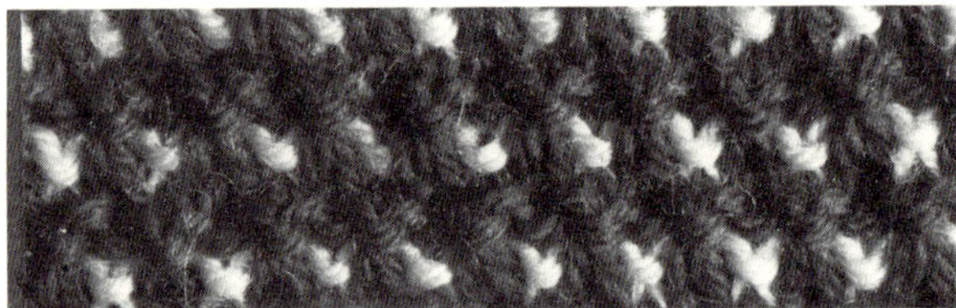

Cast on a multiple of 2 sts. plus 1 (e.g. 21).
1st row: using dark shade, k. **2nd row**: as first row.
3rd row: using light shade, * k.1, sl.1 purlwise; rep. from * to last st., k.1.
4th row: using light shade, * k.1, y.fwd., sl.1 purlwise, y.b.; rep. from * to last st., k.1.
5th and 6th rows: as first and 2nd rows.
7th row: using light shade, * sl.1 purlwise, k.1; rep. from * to last st., sl.1.
8th row: using light shade, * sl.1 purlwise, y.b., k.1, y.fwd.; rep. from * to last st., sl.1.
These 8 rows form pattern.

Vandyke stitch

A simple but effective open stitch which gives a scalloped edge (shown here with a border of garter st.). This stitch is suitable for skirts, as the width of the panels can be adjusted to give graduated shaping.

Cast on a multiple of 12 sts. plus 1 (e.g. 25).
1st row: * k.1, y.fwd., k.4, sl.1, k.2 tog., p.s.s.o., k.4, y.fwd.; rep. from * to last st., k.1.
2nd row: p.
These 2 rows form pattern.

Wheatear cable

A narrow fanning band which is worked on the cable principle and which 'grows' in a repeating design. A cable needle will be required.

Cast on a multiple of 15 sts. (e.g. 45).
1st row: * p.1, k.13, p.1; rep. from * to end.
2nd row: * k.1, p.13, k.1; rep. from * to end.
3rd row: * p.1, C6 back (i.e. slip 3 sts. on cable needle, put to back of work, k.3, then k. sts. from cable needle), k.1, C6 front (i.e. slip 3 sts. on cable needle, put to front of work, k.3, then k. sts. from cable needle), p.1; rep. from * to end.
4th row: as 2nd row.
These 4 rows form pattern.

Wide plait

An intricate-looking piece of multiple cabling which would be an excellent centre band on a plain heavy sweater or down the sides of trousers.

Cast on a multiple of 23 sts. plus 5 (e.g. 51).
1st row: * p.5, k.18; rep. from * to last 5 sts., p.5.
2nd and alt. rows: * k.5, p.18; rep. from * to last 5 sts., k.5.
3rd row: * p.5, (C6 back—see Wheatear Cable pattern, above) 3 times; rep. from * to last 5 sts., p.5.
5th row: as first row.
7th row: * p.5, k.3, (C6 front—see Wheatear Cable pattern, above) twice, k.3; rep. from * to last 5 sts., p.5.
8th row: as 2nd row.
These 8 rows form pattern.

Part 3—Patterns

CHILDREN

Pram set
illustrated in colour on page 60

MATERIALS
For pram cover: 12 balls ($\frac{3}{4}$ oz. each) Hayfield Courtier Super Crimp Bri-Nylon 3-ply. One pair No. 3 knitting needles (USA size $10\frac{1}{2}$). **For dress and jacket:** 7 balls ($\frac{3}{4}$ oz. each) Hayfield Courtier Super Crimp Bri-Nylon 3-ply. One pair each Nos. 12, 11 and 10 knitting needles (USA sizes 1, 2 and 3). Three-buttons. 2 yards baby ribbon.

MEASUREMENTS
Pram cover: approx. 24 in. by 36 in.
Dress and jacket: to fit chest size 18 (20, 22) in.; length of dress 12 ($13\frac{1}{2}$, 15) in. (adjustable); length of dress sleeve seam 1 in.; length of jacket 8 ($9\frac{1}{2}$, 11) in. (adjustable); length of jacket sleeve seam 5 ($6\frac{1}{2}$, 8) in. (adjustable).

TENSION
5 sts. to 1 in. with No. 3 needles and yarn double over patt.; $7\frac{1}{2}$ sts. and 11 rows to 1 in. with No. 11 needles and yarn single over st.st.

ABBREVIATIONS
See page 46.

PRAM COVER
With No. 3 needles and 2 strands yarn cast on 113 sts. and, using 2 strands tog. throughout, k. 8 rows. Now beg. patt.
1st row: k.
2nd row: p.
3rd row: k.1, * y.o.n., k.2, k.3 tog., k.2, y.o.n., k.1; rep. from * to end.
4th row: p.1, * p.1, y.r.n., p.1, p.3 tog., p.1, y.r.n., p.2; rep. from * to end.
5th row: k.1, * k.2, y.o.n., k.3 tog., y.o.n., k.3; rep. from * to end.
6th row: p.
7th, 8th, 9th and 10th rows: k.
These 10 rows form patt. Cont. in patt. until work measures about 35 in. from cast-on edge, ending with a 10th patt. row. K. 3 rows. Cast off.

Edging
With right side facing, pick up along one side edge 3 sts. from each garter st. part and 7 sts. from each rep. of the 10-row patt. K. 7 rows. Cast off.
Rep. along other side edge.
Cast off.

DRESS
FRONT
With No. 10 needles and 1 strand yarn, cast on 81 (89, 97) sts. and k. 8 rows.
Cont. in 10-row patt. as given for Pram Cover until work measures approx. 7 ($7\frac{1}{2}$, 8) in. (or slightly more) from cast-on edge, ending with a 5th patt. row. Change to No. 12 needles.
Next row: p.1, * p.2 tog., p.6; rep. from * to end: 71 (78, 85) sts.

K. 4 rows. Change to No. 11 needles.
Beg. with a k. row, cont. straight in st.st. until work measures $8\frac{1}{2}$ ($9\frac{1}{2}$, $10\frac{1}{2}$) in. from cast-on edge, ending with a p. row (if necessary adjust length here).

Shape Armholes
Cont. in st.st., cast off 3 sts. at beg. of next 2 rows, then dec. 1 st. at each end of next 4 (5, 6) rows and of foll. 2 alt. rows.
Work straight in st.st. on rem. 53 (58, 63) sts. until armholes measure $2\frac{1}{2}$ (3, $3\frac{1}{2}$) in., ending with a p. row.

Shape Front Neck
Next row: k.20 (21, 22); turn.
Work another 5 rows on these sts. only, dec. 1 st. at neck edge on next and every foll. alt. row: 17 (18, 19) sts.

Shape Shoulder
Next row: cast off 5, k. to end.
Next row: p.2 tog., p. to end.
Rep. last 2 rows once. Cast off rem. 5 (6, 7) sts. Return to sts. still on needle, slip first 13 (16, 19) sts. on to a st. holder, then complete second side of neck to match first, reversing shapings.

BACK
Work as Front to beg. of armholes.
Shape Armholes and Buttonbands
1st row: cast off 3, k. to end.
2nd row: cast off 3, p.29 (32, 36), cast on 5 (6, 5); turn: 35 (39, 42) sts.
Keeping the 5 (6, 5) sts. at centre edge in garter st., cont. in st.st. dec. 1 st. at side edge on next 4 (5, 6) rows and on foll. 2 alt. rows: 29 (32, 34) sts. Work straight in st.st. with garter st. border until Back matches Front to beg. of shoulder shaping, ending at side edge.

Shape Shoulder
Cast off 5 sts. at beg. of next row and next alt. row, then 5 (6, 7) sts. at beg. of next alt. row.
Leave rem. 14 (16, 17) sts. on st. holder.
Using pins, mark position of 2 buttons on the garter st. buttonband allowing for a 3rd button on 2nd row of neckband.
With wrong side facing rejoin yarn to 35 (39, 42) sts. still on needle.
1st row: k.5 (6, 5), p. to end.
Cont. and complete this side of Back to match first, reversing shapings and working buttonholes to correspond with button marks as follows, beg. first buttonhole rows at side edge.
1st buttonhole row: k. to last 4 sts., cast off 2, k.1.
2nd buttonhole row: k.2, cast on 2, patt. to end.

SLEEVES (make 2 alike)
With No. 12 needles cast on 41 (49, 57) sts. and k. 4 rows.
Change to No. 11 needles and work the 10-row patt. once. (For a longer Sleeve, add extra st.st. rows here.)

Shape Top
Cont. in st.st., cast off 3 sts. at beg. of next 2 rows, 1 st. at beg. of next 6 rows and 2 sts. at beg. of foll. 8 (10, 12) rows. ** Cast off.

TO COMPLETE
Sew shoulder seams.

Neckband
With right side facing and No. 12 needles, beg. at centre edge of left side of Back and pick up all sts. from holders round neck, and also 10 sts. from one side of

front neck and 10 (11, 11) sts. from other side: 61 (69, 74) sts.

1st row: k.5 (6, 5), p. to last 5 (6, 5) sts., k. to end.

2nd row: k.7 (7, 5), * y.o.n., k.2, k.3 tog., k.2, y.o.n., k.1; rep. from * to last 6 (6, 5) sts., k.2 (2, 1), cast off 2, k.1.

Casting on 2 sts. over those cast off on previous row, and always keeping the 5 (6, 5) sts. at each end of needle in garter st., work the 4th to 9th rows of the 10-row patt. Cast off loosely.

To Make Up

Sew side seams. Set in Sleeves and sew sleeve seams. Catch in place lower edge of button band. Press seams. Sew on buttons to correspond with buttonholes.

JACKET
MAIN PIECE

With No. 10 needles cast on 181 (197, 213) sts. and k. 6 rows.

Next 2 rows: k.6 and leave these sts. on safety pin, k. to end: 169 (185, 201) sts.

continued on page 62

Three-piece pram set of dress, jacket and pram cover (see page 59).

Coat and leggings with smocked effect yoke (see page 62).

Cont. in the 10-row patt. as given for Pram Cover until work measures approx. 3½ (4½, 5½) in. from cast-on edge, ending with a 5th patt. row.
Next row: p.1, * p.2, p.2 tog., k.4; rep. from * to end: 148 (162, 176) sts.
K. 2 rows.
Next (eyelet) row: k.3 (2, 5), * y.o.n., k.2 tog., k.2: rep. from * to last 1 (0, 3) sts., k. to end.
K. 1 row. Change to No. 11 needles.
Beg. with a k. row, work straight in st.st. until work measures 4 (5, 6) in. from cast-on edge, ending with a p. row (if necessary adjust length here).

Right Front
1st row (armhole shaping): k.36 (39, 43); turn.
2nd row: cast off 3, p. to end.
Dec. 1 st. at armhole edge on next 4 (5, 6) rows and on foll. 2 alt. rows. Work straight on rem. 27 (29, 32) sts. until armhole measures 3 (3½, 4) in. ending at centre edge.

Shape Front Neck
Next row: k.7 (8, 10) and leave these sts. on safety pin, k.20 (21, 22).
Work another 6 rows in st.st., dec. 1 st. at neck edge on every p. row: 17 (18, 19) sts.

Shape Shoulder
Next row: cast off 5, p. to last 2 sts., p.2 tog.
Next row: k.
Rep. last 2 rows once. Cast off rem. 5 (6, 7) sts.

Back
Rejoin yarn to sts. still on needle at back armhole edge.
1st row: cast off 3, k.72 (80, 86); turn: 73 (81, 87) sts.
2nd row: cast off 3, p. to end.
Complete back armhole shaping by dec. 1 st. at each end of next 4 (5, 6) rows and of foll. 2 alt. rows. Work straight on rem. 58 (64, 68) sts. until Back matches Front to beg. of shoulder shaping. Cast off 5 sts. at beg. of next 4 rows and 5 (6, 7) sts. at beg. of foll. 2 rows. Leave rem. 28 (32, 34) sts. on st. holder.

Left Front
Rejoin yarn to armhole edge of rem. 36 (39, 43) sts. then complete to match Right Front, reversing shapings.
Buttonbands
With No. 11 needles, pick up one set of 6 sts. from safety pin near lower edge and cont. in garter st. until band will fit comfortably as far as beg. of front neck. Put the 6 sts. with the 7 (8, 10) sts. on safety pin at neck and sew band in position.
Work on other set of 6 sts. in same way.

Neckband
Sew shoulder seams. With right side facing and No. 12 needles, beg. at centre edge of right front and pick up sts. from safety pin, pick up 10 sts. round front neck, pick up sts. from back st. holder, pick up 10 sts. round front neck, then sts. from safety pin: 74 (80, 86) sts.
K. 1 row.
Next (eyelet) row: k.2, * y.o.n., k.2 tog., k.1; rep. from * to end.
K. 3 rows. Cast off.

SLEEVES (make 2 alike)
With No. 12 needles cast on 41 (49, 57) sts. and k. 4 rows. Change to No. 10 needles and work first 6 rows of the 10-row patt.
Next (ridge) row: p.
Change to No. 11 needles and, beg. with a p. row, cont. in st.st., inc. 1 st. at each end of 11th row from ridge row and of every foll. 8th row until there are 49 (57, 63) sts.

Work straight until sleeve measures 5 (6½, 8) in. from ridge row, ending with a p. row (if necessary, adjust length here).

Shape Top
Work as top of Dress Sleeve to **. Cast off 3 sts. at beg. of next 2 rows. Cast off.

TO COMPLETE
Sew sleeve seams and set in sleeves. Press on wrong side. Thread ribbon through eyelet holes at neckband and waist, and tie ends in bows.

Coat and leggings
illustrated in colour on page 61

MATERIALS
9 (11, 12) balls (1 oz. each) Peter Pan Baby Quick Courtelle Double Knitting. One pair each Nos. 9 and 10 knitting needles (USA sizes 5 and 3). One crochet hook International Standard Size 3.50. One cable needle. Four small buttons.

MEASUREMENTS
To fit chest size 18 (20, 22) in.; length of coat 10½ (11, 11½) in.; length of coat sleeve seam 5 (5½, 6) in.; leggings front seam 8½ (9, 9) in.

TENSION
6 sts. to 1 in. with No. 9 needles.

ABBREVIATIONS
See page 46; cr. L. st., cross long st. (slip next 2 sts. on to cable needle and leave at back of work, k. tog. long st. and first st. on cable needle, k. into front and back of 2nd st. on cable needle, pick up left-hand side of long st. purlwise across front of work, k. tog. t.b.l. this left-hand side of long st. and next st.).

COAT BACK
With No. 9 needles cast on 81 (85, 93) sts.
Work 6 rows in garter st. (every row k.).
7th row: sl.1, k.2 (4, 3), y.r.n. twice, * k.5, y.r.n. twice; rep. from * to last 3 (5, 4) sts., k.3 (5, 4).

8th row: sl.1, p.1 (3, 2), sl.1, drop 2 y.r.n. loops of 7th row (long st. made), * p.4, sl.1, drop 2 y.r.n. loops of 7th row; rep. from * to last 3 (5, 4) sts., p.2 (4, 3), k.1.
9th row: sl.1, k.2 (4, 3), sl.1, * k.4, sl.1; rep. from * to last 2 (4, 3) sts., k.2 (4, 3).
10th row: sl.1, p.1 (3, 2), sl.1, * p.4, sl.1; rep. from * to last 3 (5, 4) sts., p.2 (4, 3), k.1.
11th row: sl.1, k.0 (2, 1), * cr. L st., k.1; rep. from * to last 0 (2, 1) sts., k.0 (2, 1).
12th to 16th rows: k.
Rep. 7th to 16th rows once. Cont. in st.st. until work measures 6¼ (6½, 6¾) in. from cast-on edge, ending with a p. row.

Shape Yoke
1st row: sl.1, k.1 (k.3, k.2 tog.), k.2 tog., * k.2, k.2 tog.; rep. from * to last 1 (3, 4) sts., k.1 (k.3, k.2 tog. twice): 61 (65, 68) sts.

Change to No. 10 needles. K. 5 rows.
Change to No. 9 needles.

Shape Armholes

1st row: cast off 3 sts., k.5 (7, 6), y.r.n. twice, * k.5, y.r.n. twice; rep. from * to last 8 (10, 9) sts., k.8 (10, 9).
2nd row: cast off 3 sts., p.4 (6, 5), sl.1, drop 2 y.r.n. loops, * p.4, sl.1, drop 2 y.r.n. loops; rep. from * to last 5 (7, 6) sts., p.4 (6, 5), k.1.
Working 3rd to 10th rows as 9th to 16th rows of Back, k.2 tog. at each end of 3rd and 5th rows, working extra sts. in st.st. Rep. 7th to 16th rows of Back twice more. Cont. in garter st. until armholes measure 4 (4¼, 4½) in.

Shape Shoulders

Cast off 10 sts. at beg. of next 2 rows, 8 (9, 10) sts. at beg. of next 2 rows. Cast off rem. sts.

LEFT FRONT

With No. 9 needles cast on 49 (51, 55) sts.
Work 6 rows in garter st.
7th row: sl.1, k.2 (3, 3), y.r.n. twice, * k.5, y.r.n. twice; rep. from * to last 11 (12, 11) sts., k.11 (12, 11).
8th row: k.8, p.2 (3, 2), sl.1, drop 2 y.r.n. loops, * p.4, sl.1, drop 2 y.r.n. loops; rep. from * to last 3 (4, 4) sts., p.2 (3, 3), k.1.
Cont. in patt. as now set with 8 sts. at front edge in garter st. until the 26 patt. rows have been worked as for Back. Cont. in st.st. with 8 sts. at front edge in garter st. until work matches Back to yoke, ending with a wrong-side row.

Shape Yoke

For size 18 only. 1st row: k.2 tog. 4 times, * k.1, k.2 tog; rep. from * to last 11 sts., k.2 tog., k.9: 34 sts.
For size 20 only. 1st row: k.2 tog. 3 times, * k.1, k.2 tog.; rep. from * to last 9 sts., k.9: 36 sts.
For size 22 only. 1st row: sl.1, k.1, k.2 tog., * k.1, k.2 tog.; rep. from * to last 9 sts., k.9: 40 sts.
For all sizes. Change to No. 10 needles.
2nd to 6th rows: k.
Change to No. 9 needles.

Shape Armhole

Next row: cast off 3 sts., k.5 (6, 6), y.r.n. twice, * k.5, y.r.n. twice; rep. from * to last 11 (12, 11) sts., k.11 (12, 11).
Cont. in patt. as now set, with front border still in garter st., dec. 1 st. at beg. of 3rd and 5th rows. to match Back (10 rows of patt. worked 3 times), then work in garter st. and at the same time when armhole measures 2¾ (3, 3) in. end at front edge.

Shape Neck

Cast off 8 (8, 9) sts. at beg. of next row, 2 (2, 3) sts. at beg. of next alt. row, then dec. 1 st. at neck edge on alt. rows until 18 (19, 20) sts. remain.
Cont. straight until Front measures same as Back to shoulder, ending at side edge.

Shape Shoulder

Cast off 10 sts. at beg. of next row. K. 1 row. Cast off rem. sts.

RIGHT FRONT

Work as Left Front, reversing patt. and all shapings. 7th row will read sl.1, k.10 (11, 10), y.r.n. twice, * k.5, y.r.n. twice; rep. from * to last 3 (4, 4) sts., k.3 (4, 4).
Mark position for 4 buttons on garter-st. border of Left Front, the first 5 in. from cast-on edge, the last at top of garter-st. border, the other two evenly spaced between, then work buttonholes on Right Front to correspond with marked positions in foll. way.

Buttonhole row (right side): sl.1, k.2, k.2 tog., y.f., k.6 (7, 6), patt. to end.

SLEEVES (make 2 alike)

With No. 9 needles cast on 33 (35, 38) sts.
Work 6 rows in garter st.
7th row: sl.1, k.3 (4, 3), y.r.n. twice, * k.5, y.r.n. twice; rep. from * to last 4 (5, 4) sts., k.4 (5, 4).
Now work in patt. as set, until 16th row has been worked.
Next row: k. twice into first st., k.6 (4, 6), k. twice into next st., * k.5, k. twice into next st.; rep. from * to last 7 (5, 6) sts., k.6 (4, 5), k. twice into last st.: 39 (42, 45) sts.
Cont. in st.st., inc. 1 st. at each end of 3rd and every foll. 6th row until there are 47 (50, 53) sts. Cont. straight in st.st. until work measures 5 (5½, 6) in. from cast-on edge.

Shape Top

Cast off 3 sts. at beg. of next 2 rows. Dec. 1 st. at each end of every k. row until 23 (24, 25) sts. remain. Cast off 4 sts. at beg. of next 2 rows.
Work 1 row.
Cast off rem. sts.

COLLAR

With No. 10 needles cast on 78 (83, 85) sts.
Work 6 rows in garter st.
7th row: sl.1, k.8 (8, 9), y.r.n. twice, * k.5, y.r.n. twice; rep. from * to last 9 (9, 10) sts., k.9 (9, 10).
Keeping first and last 6 (6, 7) sts. in garter st. for borders, work 5 rows in patt. as now set.
13th row: sl.1, k.6 (9, 10), k.2 tog., * k.8, k.2 tog; rep. from * to last 9 (11, 12) sts., k.9 (11, 12).
14th row: k.
15th row: sl.1, k.6 (9, 10), k.2 tog., * k.7, k.2 tog.; rep. from * to last 8 (10, 11) sts., k.8 (10, 11).
K. 1 row. Work 1 more dec. row. K. 1 row. Cast off.

TO COMPLETE

Sew shoulder, side and sleeve seams.
Set Sleeves into armholes. Sew Collar round neck. Sew buttons on to Left Front to correspond with buttonholes.

LEGGINGS
RIGHT LEG

With No. 10 needles cast on 65 (73, 77) sts.
Work 4 rows in k.1, p.1 rib, beg. first and alt. rows sl.1, k.1, p.1.
5th (eyelet) row: sl.1, k.1, y.f., k.2 tog., * p.1, k.1, y.f., k.2 tog.; rep. from * to last st., k.1.
Work 5 more rows in rib.
Change to No. 9 needles.

Shape Back

1st row: k.
2nd row: p.
3rd row: sl.1, k.5 (6, 7); turn.
4th and every alt. row: sl.1, p. to last st., k.1.
5th row: sl.1, k.11 (13, 15); turn.
Cont. working 6 (7, 8) more sts. before each turn until the row 'sl.1, k.29 (34, 39); turn' and the foll. row have been worked.
Next row: sl.1, k.64 (72, 76).
Cont. in st.st. inc. 1 st. at beg. of next k. row and every foll 6th row until there are 75 (83, 87) sts.
Cont. straight until work measures 8½ (9, 9) in. from cast-on edge, measuring along front seams, ending with a p. row.

Shape Leg

Cast off 3 (4, 4) sts. at beg. of next 2 rows.
Cont. in st.st. dec. 1 st. at each end of next and every

foll. 4th row 1 (2, 3) times, then on every k. row until 33 (37, 41) sts. remain.

Cont. straight until leg measures 5½ (5½, 6) in., ending with a p. row.

Change to No. 10 needles. Work 6 rows in k.1, p.1 rib as for beg. of Leggings, working eyelet row as at waist on 3rd row.

Change to No. 9 needles.

Shape Foot

Next row: sl.1, k.21 (24, 26); turn and leave rem. sts. on st. holder.

2nd row: sl.1, k.10 (11, 12); turn.

Cont. in garter st. on these centre (instep) sts. for 2¼ (2½, 2½) in. Leave instep sts. on safety pin. Break yarn. Starting at beg. of instep pick up 12 (13, 13) sts. along side of instep, k. instep sts., pick up 12 (13, 13) sts. along 2nd side of instep, k. 11 (12, 14) sts. from st. holder.

Next row: sl.1, k.56 (62, 66).

Work 4 (6, 6) more rows in garter st.

Next row: k.2 tog., k.20 (22, 24), k.2 tog., k.9 (11, 11), k.2 tog., k.20 (22, 24), k.2 tog.

K. 1 row.

Next row: k.2 tog., k.19 (21, 23), k.2 tog., k.7 (9, 9), k.2 tog., k.19 (21, 23), k.2 tog.

Work 1 row, then another dec. row. Rep. last 2 rows. Cast off.

LEFT LEG

Work as Right Leg, but reverse back shaping by reading k. for p. and p. for k. and inc. at end of k. rows instead of at beg.

TO COMPLETE

Sew front, back, leg, and foot seams.

With crochet hook make ch. lengths to thread through eyelet holes at waist and ankles. Make a tassel for each end of each ch. length and attach.

Pretty smock dress with lacy-patterned yoke (see page 66)

Bonnet and muff worked in a looped pattern (see page 66)

Smock dress

illustrated in colour on page 64

MATERIALS
6 (7, 8) balls (25 gr. each) Hayfield Diane in main shade and 1 (1, 2) balls in a contrasting shade. One pair each Nos. 10, 8 and 7 knitting needles (USA sizes 3, 6 and 7).

MEASUREMENTS
To fit chest size 22 (24, 26) in.; length 16 (18, 21) in. (adjustable); length of sleeve seam 2 in. (adjustable).

TENSION
6½ sts. and 8 rows to 1 in. over st.st. with No. 8 needles.

ABBREVIATIONS
See page 46; M., main shade; C., contrasting shade.

FRONT AND BACK (make 2 alike)
With No. 10 needles and M. cast on 88 (98, 108) sts. and, beg. with a k. row, work 8 rows in st.st.
9th (picot) row: k.2, * y.f., k.2 tog.; rep. from * to end.
Change to No. 8 needles and, beg. with a p. row, cont. in st.st., dec. 1 st. at each end of 10th row from picot edge and every foll. 8th row until 78 (84, 90) sts.

Cont. straight until work measures 11½ (13, 15½) in. from picot edge, ending with a p. row. (adjust length here, if necessary).

Shape Armholes
Cast off 4 sts. at beg. of next 2 rows.
Next row: k.2 tog., k. to last 2 sts., k.2 tog.
Next row: p.
Rep. last 2 rows once. Leave rem. 66 (72, 78) sts. on st. holder.

SLEEVES (make 2 alike)
With No. 10 needles and M. cast on 45 (50, 55) sts. and, beg. with a k. row, work 4 rows in st.st.
5th row: k.1 (2, 3), * y.f., k.2 tog.; rep. from * to end.
Change to No. 8 needles and, beg. with a p. row, work 5 rows in st.st.
11th (eyelet) row: as 5th row.
12th row: * p.4, p. twice into next st.; rep. from * to end: 54 (60, 66) sts.
Beg. with a k. row, cont. straight in st.st. until work measures 2 in. (or required length) from 5th row, ending with a p. row.

Shape Top
Work as Front and Back armholes.
Leave rem. 42 (48, 54) sts. on st. holder.

TO COMPLETE
Yoke
Sew raglan seams, leaving seam between Back and left sleeve unsewn. Then, with right side facing, No. 7 needles and C., k. across sts. of left sleeve, sts. of Front, sts. of right sleeve and Back sts.: 216 (240, 264) sts.
2nd row: * k.2, p.2, k.2; rep. from * to end.
3rd row: * p.1, k.2 tog., y.f., sl.1, k.1, p.s.s.o., p.1; rep. from * to end: 180 (200, 220) sts.
4th row: * k.1, p.3, k.1; rep. from * to end.
5th row: * p.1, k.3, p.1; rep. from * to end.
6th row: as 4th row.
Rep. last 2 rows 1 (2, 3) times.
Next row: p.1, * k.2 tog., y.f., k.1, p.2 tog.; rep. from * to last 4 sts., k.2 tog., y.f., k.1, p.1: 145 (161, 177) sts.
Next row: k.1, * p.3, k.1; rep. from * to end.
Work another 4 (6, 8) rows straight in rib patt. as set.

Next row: k.1, * k.2 tog., y.f., sl.1, k.1, p.s.s.o.; rep. from * to end: 109 (121, 133) sts.
Cont. in st.st. until work measures 4½ (5, 5½) in. from beg. of armholes, ending with a p. row.

Neck Ribbing
Change to No. 10 needles and M.
1st row: k.1, * k.2 tog., k.1; rep. from * to end.
Work 5 rows in k.1, p.1 rib.
With No. 8 needles cast off very loosely in rib.

To Make Up
Press dry, using a cool iron. Sew seam between Back and left sleeve, joining sides of neck ribbing as well. Sew side and sleeve seams. Turn up hems at lower edge and on Sleeve on the picot rows and catch lightly in position on wrong side. Press seams. With C. make 2 twisted cords each 22 in. long and thread one through each sleeve eyelet row, tying ends in bows.

Bonnet and muff

illustrated in colour on page 65

MATERIALS
2 balls (50 gr. each) Patons Promise for bonnet, 1 ball for muff. One pair each Nos. 8 and 10 knitting needles (USA sizes 6 and 3). 2½ yd. ribbon, 1 in. wide.

MEASUREMENTS
Face edge of bonnet approx. 14 in.; length of muff 6½ in.; width of muff 5½ in.

TENSION
10 sts. and 16 rows to 2 in. over pattern on No. 8 needles.

ABBREVIATIONS
See page 46; m.l., make loops by knitting next st., winding yarn 3 times over needle and round first and second fingers of left hand, then over needle again, draw 4 loops through, then place loops back on left needle and knit them together with st. through back of loops.

BONNET
With No. 10 needles, cast on 65 sts. and work 4 rows st.st., starting with a k. row.
Next row: k.1, * y.fwd., k.2 tog.; rep. from * to end.
Starting with a p. row, work 5 rows in st.st.
Next row: make hem by knitting tog. 1 st. from needle and 1 loop from cast-on edge all across row.
Next row: k.
Change to No. 8 needles and work in main patt. as follows:
1st row (right side): p.
2nd row: k.1, * m.l., k.1; rep. from * to end.
3rd and 5th rows: p.
4th row: k.
6th row: m.l., * k.1, m.l.; rep. from * to end.
7th row: p.
8th row: k.
These 8 rows form patt.
Continue straight in patt. until Bonnet measures 5½ in., ending with right side facing.
Next row: cast off 21, patt. to last 21 sts., cast off 21.
Break off yarn.
Rejoin yarn to remaining group of 23 sts. and continue in patt. for 4½ in. ending with right side facing.
Cast off.

TO COMPLETE

Using a cool iron and dry cloth, press parts lightly on wrong side, taking care not to spoil pattern.
Using a fine backstitch seam, join cast-off sts. to sides of Bonnet.
With No. 10 needles and right side facing, pick up 57 sts. along lower edge of Bonnet leaving sides of hem free.
** Work 3 rows in st.st., starting with a p. row.
Next row: k.1, * y.fwd., k.2 tog.; rep. from * to end.
Work 3 rows in st.st., starting with a p. row. Cast off.
Fold band in half to wrong side and slip-stitch neatly in position. **
Join side of hems together. Press seams. Cut two lengths of ribbon, each 2 ft. 3 in. Make rosettes with ribbon leaving ends to tie, and stitch to sides of Bonnet.

MUFF

With No. 8 needles, cast on 29 sts. and work in patt. as for main patt. of Bonnet until piece measures 9 in. ending with right side facing. Cast off.

TO COMPLETE

Press as for Bonnet.
With No. 10 needles, pick up 51 sts. along side edges and work as for Bonnet from ** to **.
Join seam. Press seam. Attach remaining ribbon to each side of Muff.

Dressing-gown (for boy or girl)

illustrated on page 68

MATERIALS

10 balls (25 gr. each) Sirdar Courtelle Random. One pair each Nos. 10 and 9 knitting needles (USA sizes 3 and 5). Six buttons $\frac{1}{2}$ in. in diameter.

MEASUREMENTS

To fit chest size 22 in.; length 24 in.; sleeve seam 8 in.

TENSION

7 sts. to 1 in. with No. 9 needles.

ABBREVIATIONS

See page 46.

MAIN PIECE

With No. 10 needles cast on 182 sts. and k. 8 rows.
Change to No. 9 needles and cont. in st.st. with a garter-st. border (every row k.) at each end of 8 sts.
Work 8 rows (adjust length here).
For Girl's Dressing-Gown
Next (buttonhole) row: k.3, cast off 2, k. to end.
Next row: k.8, p. to last 8 sts., k.3, cast on 2, k.3.
For Boy's Dressing-Gown
Next (buttonhole) row: k. to last 5 sts., cast off 2, k. to end.
Next row: k.3, cast on 2, k.3, p. to last 8 sts., k.8.
For Girl's or Boy's Dressing-Gown
Cont. in st.st. keeping borders correct for 148 rows, making 4 more buttonholes in same way as before with 34 rows between each buttonhole.

Shape Armholes

Next row: k.47, cast off 8, k.72 (including st. on needle used in casting off), cast off 8, k. to end.

Left Front

Working on last set of 47 sts. only, work 1 row.
1st row: k.1, k.2 tog. t.b.l., k. to end.
2nd row: k.8, p. to last 3 sts., p.2 tog., k.1.
3rd row: as first row.
4th row: k.8, p. to last st., k.1.
Rep. last 4 rows twice.

Next row: k.1, k.2 tog. t.b.l., k. to end.
Next row: k.8, p. to last st., k.1.
Next row: k.1, k.2 tog. t.b.l., k. to end.
For Girl's Dressing-Gown
Rep. last 2 rows until 24 sts. remain.
For Boy's Dressing-Gown
Rep. last 2 rows, making a buttonhole on 6th and 7th rows, until 24 sts. remain.
For Girl's or Boy's Dressing-Gown
Shape Neck
Next row: cast off 8 sts., p. to last st., k.1.
** Cont. to dec. at armhole edge as before on foll. 5 alt. rows and **at the same time** cast off 4 sts. at neck edge at beg. of foll. alt. row, 2 sts. on next alt. row, and 1 st. on next alt. row.
Work 1 row. K. rem. sts. tog. Fasten off.

Back

Rejoin yarn to centre sts. with wrong side facing and work to end.
1st row: k.1, k.2 tog. t.b.l., k. to last 3 sts., k.2 tog., k.1.
2nd row: k.1, p.2 tog., p. to last 3 sts., p.2 tog. t.b.l., k.1.
3rd row: as first row.
4th row: k.1, p. to last st., k.1.
Rep. last 4 rows twice, then rep. last 2 rows until 30 sts. remain. Cast off.

Right Front

Rejoin yarn to rem. sts. with wrong side facing and work to end.
1st row: k. to last 3 sts., k.2 tog., k.1.
2nd row: k.1, p.2 tog., p. to last 8 sts., k.8.
3rd row: as first row.
4th row: k.1, p. to last 8 sts., k.8.
Rep. last 4 rows twice.
Next row: k. to last 3 sts., k.2 tog., k.1.
Next row: k.1, p. to last 8 sts., k.8.
For Girl's Dressing-Gown
Rep. last 2 rows making a buttonhole on 7th and 8th rows, until 24 sts. remain.
For Boy's Dressing Gown.
Rep. last 2 rows until 24 sts. remain.
For Girl's or Boy's Dressing-Gown
Shape Neck
Next row: cast off 8 sts., work to last 3 sts., k.2 tog., k.1.
Work as left front from ** to end, reversing all shapings.

SLEEVES (make 2 alike)

With No. 10 needles cast on 37 sts. and k. 6 rows.
Next row: k.3, * k. twice into next st., k.4; rep. from * 5 times, k. twice into next st., k.3: 44 sts.
Change to No. 9 needles and work in st.st., inc. 1 st. at each end of 5th row and every foll. 6th row until there are 58 sts.
Cont. straight until work measures 8 in. (or required length).
Shape Top
Cast off 4 sts. at beg. of next 2 rows.
Next row: k.1, k.2 tog. t.b.l., k. to last 3 sts., k.2 tog., k.1.
Next row: k.1, p. to last st., k.1.
Rep. last 2 rows until 8 sts. remain. Cast off.

COLLAR

With No. 9 needles, cast on 8 sts.
1st row: k. twice into first st., k. to end.
2nd row: k.
3rd to 6th rows: rep. first and 2nd rows twice: 11 sts.
7th row: k.8; turn.
8th row: k. to end.
9th to 12th rows: k. all sts.

continued on page 70

Dressing gown (see page 67)

68

Roll-collared dress with a Fair Isle border pattern
(see page 70)

Rep. 7th to 12th rows 22 times, then 7th and 8th rows once.
Next row: k. 2 tog., k. to end.
Next row: k.
Rep. last 2 rows once.
Next row: k.2 tog., k. to end.
Cast off.

TO COMPLETE

Do not press. Sew in Sleeves. Sew on Collar. Sew on buttons to correspond with buttonholes.
Make a 60 in. long twisted cord with tassels and st. to sides at waist level.

Pink, brown and white dress
illustrated in colour on page 69

MATERIALS
5 (5, 6) oz. Lister Lavenda Double Knitting in pink, 2 oz. in brown and 1 oz. in white. One pair each Nos. 9 and 11 knitting needles (USA sizes 5 and 2).

MEASUREMENTS
To fit chest size 22 (24, 26) in.; length 16 (18, 21) in.; sleeve seam 2 in.

TENSION
6 sts. and 8 rows to 1 in. over st.st.

ABBREVIATIONS
See page 46; P., pink; W., white; B., brown.

FRONT
With B. and No. 11 needles cast on 84 (92, 102) sts. and work 7 rows in st.st.
8th row: k. (to mark hemline).
Change to No. 9 needles and beg. with a k. row work 5 rows in st.st.
6th row: join in W. and p. in W.
With B. k. 1 row, p. 1 row (size 26 in. only: dec. 1 st. at both ends of row): 84 (92, 100) sts.
9th row: * k.1 W., k.3 B; rep. from * to end.
10th row: * (p.1 W., p.2 B.) twice, p.2 W.; rep. from * to last 4 sts., p.1 W., p.2 B., p.1 W.
11th row: k.2 B., k.2 W., * k.1 B., k.2 W., k.3 B., k.2 W.; rep. from * to end.
12th row: * p.3 W., p.1 B.; rep. from * to end.
With W., k. 1 row, p. 1 row. With B., k. 1 row.
Change to P. and beg. with a p. row, cont. in P. in st.st., dec. 1 st. at both ends of 19th row from hemline and of every foll. 10th row until you have 72 (78, 84) sts.
Work straight to complete 11 (12½, 15) in. (or length required) from hemline, ending after a p. row.

Shape Raglan Armholes
Cast off 4 sts. at beg. of next 2 rows.
Next row: k.2, k.2 tog. t.b.l., k. until 4 sts. rem., k.2 tog., k.2.
Next row: p.
Rep. these last 2 rows until 36 (38, 40) sts. rem., ending after a p. row.

Shape Front Neck
Next row: k.2, k.2 tog. t.b.l., k.6; turn.
Dec. 1 st. at neck edge on next and foll. alt. rows, cont. to shape armhole by dec. 1 st. every right-side row until 1 st. rem. Fasten off.
Returning to sts. still on needle, slip first 16 (18, 20) sts. on to a spare needle and complete second front point to match first, reversing shapings.

BACK
Work as for Front, omitting front neck opening and working dec. on every right-side row for armhole shaping until 26 (28, 30) sts. rem. Leave sts. on a spare needle.

SLEEVES (make 2 alike)
With B. and No. 11 needles cast on 50 (54, 58) sts. and work 5 rows in st.st.
6th row: k., inc. 1 st. at both ends of row (hemline).
Cont. with No. 11 needles and B., k. 1 row, p. 1 row, k. 1 row. Change to W. and p. 1 row. With B., k. 1 row, p. 1 row.
7th row: * k. 1 W., k.3 B.; rep. from * to end.
8th row: * p.1 W., p.1 B.; rep. from * to end.
9th row: k. in W.
10th row: p. in B.
Change to No. 9 needles and P. and, starting with a k. row, cont. in st.st. to complete 2 in. (or length required) from hemline, ending after a p. row.

Top of Sleeve
Follow instructions for shaping armholes for Front, cont. to dec. until 6 sts. rem. (all sizes). Leave sts. on a spare needle.

TO COMPLETE
Sew raglan seams, leaving seam open between Back and left sleeve.

Polo Neck
With right side facing and No. 11 needles, start at top of left sleeve and pick up all sts. from spare needles round neck, and also 8 sts. from each side of neck: 70 (74, 78) sts.
With P., and working in k.1, p.1 rib, work 1 in. on No. 11 needles and 2 in. on No. 9 needles. Cast off.

To Make Up.
Press well, blocking hems. Sew seam between Back and Left Sleeve, joining sides of polo neck. Sew side seams and sleeve seams. Turn up all hems and catch lightly in position. Press all seams.

Blue and cream cape set
illustrated in colour on pages 72 and 73

MATERIALS
For tunic: 10 (11, 12) balls (50 gr. each) Mahony's Blarney Bainin (USA Blarneyspun). **For cape:** 14 (15, 16) balls (50 gr. each) Mahony's Blarney Bainin (USA Blarneyspun). **For both:** one pair each Nos. 7, 9 and 10 knitting needles (USA sizes 7, 5 and 3). One cable needle. Three buttons ¾ in. in diameter. 1 yard facing ribbon, 1 in. wide.

MEASUREMENTS
To fit chest size 26 (28, 30) in.; length of tunic 23 (24½, 26) in.; length of cape 24½ (26, 27½) in.

TENSION
5 sts. and 6½ rows to 1 in. over rice st. with No. 7 needles.

ABBREVIATIONS
See page 46; k.f.b. (or p.f.b.), k. (or p.) into front and back of next st.; tw.r., twist right: slip next 2 sts. on to cable needle and leave at back of work, k.1, then k.2 from cable needle; tw.l., twist left: slip next st. on to cable needle and leave at front of work, k.2, then k.1 from cable needle.

TUNIC
BACK
With No. 10 needles cast on 85 (93, 101) sts.
1st rib row: k.2, * p.1, k.1; rep. from * to last st., k.1.
2nd rib row: k.1, * p.1, k.1; rep. from * to end. Rep. these 2 rows 3 times.
Inc. row (right side): k.f.b., rib 12 (14, 16), * k.1, (k.f.b., k.1) twice, p.f.b., (k.f.b., k.2) 4 times, k.f.b., p.f.b., (k.1, k.f.b.) twice, k.1 *, rib 9 (13, 17); rep. from * to *, rib 12 (14, 16), k.f.b.: 109 (117, 125) sts. Change to No. 7 needles.
Foundation row: k.14 (16, 18), * p.7, k.2, p.18, k.2, p.7 *, k.9 (13, 17); rep. from * to *, k.14 (16, 18). Now work in patt.
1st patt. row: (k.1 t.b.l., p.1) 7 (8, 9) times, * k.7, p.2, (tw.r., tw.l.) 3 times, p.2, k.7 *, p.1, (k.1 t.b.l., p.1) 4 (6, 8) times; rep. from * to *, (p.1, k.1 t.b.l.) 7 (8, 9) times.
2nd patt. row: as foundation row.
These 2 rows form rice st. patt. over 14 (16, 18) sts. at each side and 9 (13, 17) sts. in centre. Cont. working in rice st. over these sts.
3rd patt. row: rice st. 14 (16, 18), * tw.r., k.1, tw.l., p.2, (tw.l., tw.r.,) 3 times, p.2, tw.r., k.1, tw.l. *, rice st. 9 (13, 17); rep. from * to *, rice st. 14 (16, 18).
4th patt. row: as foundation row.
These 4 rows form patt. over rem. sts. Cont. in patt. Work 4 more rows straight then dec. 1 st. at each end of next row and every foll. 8th row until 97 (103, 109) sts. remain, then dec. 1 st. at each end of every foll. 12th row until 91 (97, 103) sts. remain: 5 (6, 7) sts. in rice st. at each side.
Cont. straight until work measures 16½ (17½, 18½) in.

Shape Armholes
Cast off 4 sts. at beg. of next 2 rows, 2 sts. at beg. of next 4 rows and 1 st. at beg. of next 10 (12, 14) rows: 65 (69, 73) sts.
Cont. straight in patt. with 1 st. at each end in garter st. until work measures 21½ (23, 24½) in., ending with a wrong-side row.

Shape Neck and Shoulders
1st row: patt. 29 (30, 31) and leave these sts. on a st. holder for right back, cast off 7 (9, 11) sts., patt. to end.
Cont. on the last set of 29 (30, 31) sts. for left back and work 1 row straight.
** Cast off 2 (3, 4) sts. at beg. of next row, 2 sts. at same edge on next 3 alt. rows and 1 st. at same edge on next alt. row.
Keeping neck edge straight cast off 9 sts. for shoulder shaping at beg. of next row, work 1 row, then cast off rem. 11 sts. **
With wrong side facing rejoin yarn to inner edge of right back sts. Complete to match left back from ** to **

FRONT
Work as Back until the first 10 rows of armhole shaping have been worked: 71 (77, 83) sts.

Shape Neck
1st row: cast off 1, patt. until there are 28 (31, 34) sts. on right-hand needle, leave these sts. on a st. holder for left front, cast off 13, patt. to end.
Cont. on the last set of 29 (32, 35) sts. for right front.
2nd row: cast off 1, patt. back to neck edge.
*** Cast off 2 sts. at beg. of next row and 1 st. at armhole edge on foll. row. Rep. last 2 rows 1 (2, 3) times. Cast off 2 sts. at beg. of foll. row, then cont. in patt. on rem. 20 sts. working 1 st. at each end in garter st. until work measures same as Back to beg. of shoulder shaping, ending at side edge.
Cast off 9 sts. at beg. of next row, work 1 row, then cast off rem. 11 sts. ***
With wrong side facing rejoin yarn to inner edge of left front sts. Complete as for right front from *** to ***

ARMHOLE BORDERS (make 2 alike)
With No. 9 needles cast on 89 (95, 101) sts. and work 4 rows in rib as for welt. Change to No. 10 needles and work 4 more rows. Cast off ribwise.

NECK BORDERS
Front Border
With No. 9 needles cast on 81 (87, 93) sts. and work as for armhole border.

Back Border
With No. 9 needles cast on 51 (53, 55) sts. and work as for armhole border.

TO COMPLETE
Do not press. Join shoulder and side seams using back st. Press seams on wrong side with warm iron and damp cloth. Join ends of armhole borders. With right sides tog. and join level with side seam, back st. cast-on edge of armhole borders to armholes stretching them to fit. Join front and back neck borders at ends. Placing seams at shoulders sew on as for armhole borders. Press border seams with point of iron so as not to flatten rib.

CAPE
BACK
With No. 9 needles cast on 103 (111, 119) sts. Work 8 rows in rib as for Tunic Back but reverse rib by beg. with a 2nd row and ending with a first row.
Inc. row (right side): rib 26 (30, 34), work from * to * of same row of Tunic Back, p.f.b., work from * to * again, rib 26 (30, 34): 126 (134, 142) sts. Change to No. 7 needles.
Foundation row: k.26 (30, 34), * p.7, k.2, p.18, k.2, p.7 *, k.2; rep. from * to *, k.26 (30, 34). Now work in patt.
1st patt. row: (k.1 t.b.l., p.1) 13 (15, 17) times, work from * to * of first patt. row of Tunic Back, p.2, work from * to * again, (p.1, k.1 t.b.l.) 13 (15, 17) times.
Cont. in patt. as now set working the 2 patt. panels with 26 (30, 34) sts. in rice st. at each side until the 6th (7th, 8th) patt. is completed. Dec. 1 st. at each end of next row, then work 11 rows straight. Rep. last 12 rows twice. Dec. 1 st. at each end of next row and every foll. 8th until 112 (120, 128) sts. remain. Work 7 rows after last dec. row: 23rd (24th, 25th) patt. completed. Now dec. 1 st. at each end of next row and every first patt. row until 100 (106, 112) sts. remain. Work 3 rows straight. Now dec. 1 st. at each end of next row and every right-side row until 86 (90, 94) sts. remain. Work 1 row straight.

Shape Shoulders
Cast off 2 sts. at beg. of next 12 rows, 3 sts. at beg. of next 4 rows, 4 (5, 6) sts. at beg. of next 2 rows and 7 sts. at beg. of next 2 rows. Cast off 28 (30, 32) sts.

RIGHT FRONT
With No. 9 needles cast on 60 (64, 68) sts.
1st rib row: k.2, * p.1, k.1; rep. from * to end. Rep. this row 7 times.
Inc. row (right side): rib 8 and slip these sts. on to a safety pin for border, p.f.b., work from * to * of the inc. row of Tunic Back, rib 26 (30, 34): 64 (68, 72) sts. Change to No 7 needles.
Foundation row: k.26 (30, 34), work from * to * of same row of Back, k.2.
1st patt. row: p.2, work from * to * of first patt. of Tunic Back, (p.1, k.1 t.b.l.) 13 (15, 17) times. Cont. in

continued on page 73

Junior-style cape sets: blue cape and its teaming cream dress are both worked in traditional Aran stitches (see page 70). Little Red Riding Hood outfit has a roll-collared, cable-patterned cape, warm trousers and a smart peaked cap (see page 74).

patt. as now set until the 6th (7th, 8th) patt. has been completed. Dec. 1 st. at end of next row, then work 11 rows straight. Dec. 1 st. at end of next row, work 7 rows straight.

Divide for Slit
1st row of next patt: p.2, patt. 36, k.1; turn.
Cont. on these 39 sts. for front section working in patt. with the st. next to opening in garter st. until the first row of the 23rd (24th, 25th) patt. has been worked, thus ending at opening edge. Break yarn.
With right side facing rejoin yarn to rem. 23 (27, 31) sts. at opening, rice st. to end. Work 3 rows straight. Dec. 1 st. at side edge on next row then work 11 rows straight. Dec. 1 st. at side edge on next row and every foll. 8th row until 18 (22, 26) sts. remain. Work 4 rows straight, thus having worked same number of rows as on front section, and ending at side edge.

2nd row of patt.: k.18 (22, 26), patt. across 39 sts. of main part pulling yarn tightly across join.
Work 2 rows straight, thus completing 23rd (24th, 25th) patt.
** Cont. across all sts., dec. 1 st. at side edge of next row and every first patt. row until 51 (54, 57) sts. remain. Work 3 rows straight. Dec. 1 st. at side edge on next row and every right-side row until 44 (46, 48) sts. remain. **
Work 2 rows straight, thus ending at side edge.

Shape Shoulder and Neck
Cast off 2 sts. at beg. of next row and next 3 alt. rows. Now cast off 5 (6, 7) sts. for neck shaping at beg. of next row. Cast off 2 sts. at beg. of next 4 rows. Now cast off 3 sts. for shoulder shaping at beg. of next row and 2 sts. at neck edge on foll. row. Rep. last 2 rows once. Cast off 4 (5, 6) sts. at beg. of next row and 2 sts. at neck edge on foll. row. Cast off rem. 7 sts.

LEFT FRONT
With No. 9 needles cast on 60 (64, 68) sts.
1st rib row: * k.1, p.1; rep. from * to last 2 sts., k.2. Rep. this row 7 times.
Inc. row: rib 26 (30, 34), work from * to * of the inc. row of Tunic Back, p.f.b.; turn and slip rem. 8 sts. on to a safety pin for front border.
Change to No. 7 needles.
Foundation row: k.2, work from * to * of same row of

Back, k.26 (30, 34).
1st patt. row: (k.1 t.b.l., p.1) 13 (15, 17) times, work from * to * of first patt. row, p.2.
Cont. in patt. as now set until the 6th (7th, 8th) patt. is completed. Dec. 1 st. at beg. of next row, then work 11 rows straight. Dec. 1 st. at beg. of next row, then work 7 rows.

Divide for Slit
1st row: rice st. 23 (27, 31); turn. Cont. on these sts. Work 3 rows straight, then dec. 1 st. at beg. of next row, work 11 rows straight. Dec. 1 st. at beg. of next row and every foll. 8th row until 18 (22, 26) sts. remain. Work 4 rows straight, thus ending at opening edge. Break yarn. With right side facing rejoin yarn to 39 sts. of front side of opening.
Next row: k.1, patt. 36, p.2.
Cont. in patt. with the st. next to opening in garter st. until the first row of the 23rd (24th, 25th) patt. has been worked.
2nd row: k.2, patt. 36, k.1, then k.18 (22, 26) sts. of side section.
Working shapings at opposite edge cont. as for Right Front from ** to **. Work 1 row straight thus ending at side edge. Work shoulder and neck shaping as for Right Front.

TO COMPLETE
Borders
Slip sts. of Left Front border on to a No. 9 needle with point at inner edge, cast on 1, k. this st. and next st., (p.1., k.1) 3 times, k.1.
Beg. with a 2nd rib row of Tunic Back cont. in rib on these 9 sts. until strip measures 22 (23½, 25) in., ending with a 2nd rib row.
Break yarn and leave sts. on a safety pin.
Slip sts. of Right Front border on to a No. 9 needle with point at inner edge, join yarn, cast on 1, k. this st., (p.1, k. 1) 4 times. Cont. in rib beg. with a first rib row of Tunic Back until strip measures 16½ (18, 19½) in. from beg., ending with a 2nd rib row.
Next (buttonhole) row: rib 3, cast off 3, rib to end. On next row cast on 3 sts. over buttonhole.
Work 2nd buttonhole when work measures 19½ (21, 22½) in. Cont. until strip measures same as Left Front border, ending with a 2nd row. Do not break yarn. Back st. borders to front edges stretching them slightly to fit as you work.

Neckband
First back st. side and shoulder seams, leaving neck edges open. Return to sts. of Right Front border, rib 9, then on to same needle pick up and k.19 (20, 21) sts. round front neck, 23 (25, 27) sts. across back neck and 19 (20, 21) sts. round Left Front neck, then rib sts. of Left Front border.
Work 1 row in rib across all sts.
3rd row: rib 7, k.2 tog. t.b.l., rib to last 9 sts., k.2 tog., rib 7.
4th row: rib 7, p.2, rib to last 9 sts., p.2, rib 7.
5th and 6th rows: as 3rd and 4th rows but making buttonhole in same way as before.
Rep. 3rd and 4th rows once, then 3rd row again. Cast off ribwise.

To Make Up
Press shoulder and side seams and border seams lightly on wrong side with warm iron and damp cloth; use point of iron along borders so as not to flatten rib. Lightly press ribbing at lower edge so that it does not pull in. Face both sides of front slits with ribbon. Sew buttons on to Left Front to match buttonholes.
Press again lightly.

Red cape set
illustrated in colour on pages 72 and 73

MATERIALS
14 (16, 17, 18) balls (50 gr. each) Wendy Kinvara. One pair each Nos. 9 and 7 knitting needles (USA sizes 5 and 7). One cable needle. ¾ yard elastic, 1 in. wide. Small piece cardboard.

MEASUREMENTS
To fit chest size 26 (28, 30, 32) in.; length 20 (22, 24, 26) in.; trousers inside leg measurement 16 (17, 19, 21) in.; length at side 23 (25, 28, 30) in.

TENSION
4½ sts. and 6 rows to 1 in. with No. 7 needles.

ABBREVIATIONS
See page 46; c.6, cable 6: slip next 3 sts. on to cable needle and leave at back of work, k. next 3 sts. then k. the sts. from the cable needle.

CAPE
BACK
With No. 9 needles cast on 46 (50, 56, 62) sts.
Work 8 rows in k.1, p.1 rib.
Change to No. 7 needles and work in st.st.
Continue straight until work measures 19 (21, 23, 25) in.

Shape Shoulders
Cast off 7 (7, 8, 10) sts. at beg. of next 4 rows. Slip rem. sts. on to a st. holder.

FRONT
With No. 9 needles cast on 57 (57, 66, 75) sts.
Work 8 rows in k.1, p.1 rib.
Change to No. 7 needles and cont. in patt.
1st row: p.3, * k.6, p.3; rep. from * to end.
2nd row: k.3, * p.6, k.3; rep. from * to end.
3rd row: p.3, * c.6, p.3; rep. from * to end.
4th row: as 2nd row.
5th to 8th rows: rep. first and 2nd rows twice. These 8 rows form patt. Cont. straight in patt. until work measures 19 (21, 23, 25) in., ending with a

right-side row.
Next row: (p.1, p.2 tog.) 5 (4, 4, 6) times, patt. to last 15 (12, 12, 18) sts., (p.2 tog., p.1) 5 (4, 4, 6) times.

Shape Shoulder
Next 3 rows: patt. 14 (14, 16, 20) sts.; turn; patt. 7 (7, 8, 10) sts.; turn; patt. 7 (7, 8, 10) sts.; turn.
Cast off these 14 (14, 16, 20) sts.
Leave centre 19 (21, 26, 23) sts. on st. holder, then work on rem. sts. to match first shoulder.

SIDE PANELS (make 2 alike)
With No. 9 needles cast on 56 (64, 72, 76) sts.
Work 8 rows in k.1, p.1 rib.
Change to No. 7 needles and cont. in st.st. Dec. 1 st. at each end of next and every foll. 6th row until 20 (22, 24, 26) sts. remain. Cont. straight until work measures 19 (21, 23, 25) in. Mark this row with a coloured thread.
Cont. straight until Side Panel from marked row matches cast-off sts. of Back shoulders. Slip these 20 (22, 24, 26) sts. on to a st. holder.

TO COMPLETE
Armflaps
With No. 9 needles pick up and k. 40 sts. along front side edges of one Panel, beg. approx. 6 in. from ribbing. Work in k.1, p.1 rib for 10 rows. Cast off in rib. Work other armflap in same way.

Neckband
With No. 9 needles, k. across sts. on st. holder at back neck, k.2 tog. across one Side Panel sts., pick up and k. 3 sts. down side of front neck, k. across centre sts., pick up and k.3 sts. up other side of front neck, k.2 tog. across 2nd Side Panel. Work 34 (34, 36, 36) rows in k.1, p.1 rib. Cast off in rib.

To Make Up
Press lightly on wrong side. Join side seams, leaving armflaps open. Sew sides of armflaps down on right side.

TROUSERS
LEFT LEG
With No. 9 needles cast on 46 (50, 56, 62) sts. Work in k.1, p.1 rib.
Change to No. 7 needles and cont. in patt.
1st row: k.17 (19, 22, 25), p.3, k.6, p.3, k. to end.
2nd row: p.17 (19, 22, 25), k.3, p.6, k.3, p. to end.
3rd row: k.17 (19, 22, 25), p.3, c.6, p.3, k. to end.
4th row: as 2nd row.
5th to 8th rows: rep. first and 2nd rows twice.
Cont. to work this 8-row patt.
Cont. straight until work measures 8 (8, 9, 9) in. Keeping patt. correct, inc. 1 st. at each end of next and every foll. 6th row until there are 56 (62, 68, 74) sts.
Cont. straight on these sts. until work measures 16 (17, 19, 21) in. (or length required to crutch). Inc. 1 st. at each end of every alt. row until there are 64 (70, 76, 80) sts.
Work 10 rows straight.
Dec. 1 st. at each end of next and every foll. 4th row until 50 (56, 62, 68) sts. remain.
Cont. straight until work measures 22 (24, 27, 29) in. (or length required to waist) ending with a wrong-side row.

Shape Back
Next 6 rows: patt. 32 sts.; turn; patt. back; turn; patt. 24 sts.; turn; patt. back; turn; patt. 16 sts.; turn; patt. back.

Waistband
With No. 9 needles work across all sts. in k.1, p.1 rib for 1 in. Cast off in rib.

RIGHT LEG
Work as Left Leg, but end with a right-side row before shaping back.

TO COMPLETE
Press lightly on wrong side. Join inside leg seams, then join back and front seams. Cut elastic to waist measurement and join ends. Place inside waist ribbing and work herringbone st. over it.

CAP
Main Piece
With No. 9 needles cast on 84 (92, 92, 92) sts.
Work 18 rows in k.1, p.1 rib.
Next (hem) row: k.1 st. tog. with 1 cast-on st. all along row.
Change to No. 7 needles and cont. in st.st., beg. with a p. row. Cont. straight until work measures 2½ (3, 3, 3) in., ending with a p. row.
Next row: k.2 (1, 1, 1), * k.2 tog., k.8; rep. from * to last 2 (1, 1, 1) sts., k.2 (1, 1, 1).
Work 3 rows straight.
Next row: k.2 (1, 1, 1), * k.2 tog., k.7; rep. from * to last 2 (1, 1, 1) sts., k.2 (1, 1, 1).
Work 3 rows straight.
Cont. in this way, working 1 st. fewer between decs. on each dec. row until 36 (38, 38, 38) sts. remain. Draw yarn through these sts., pull up tightly and fasten.

Peak
With No. 9 needles pick up the centre 36 (40, 40, 40) sts. on outer edge. Work 2 rows in st.st.
Next row: k.2 tog., k. to last 2 sts., k.2 tog.
Work 1 row.
Cont. to dec. at each end of every alt. row until 24 (28, 28, 28) sts. remain.
Work 1 row. Inc. 1 st. at each end of next and every foll. alt. row until there are 36 (40, 40, 40) sts. Work 1 row. Cast off.

TO COMPLETE
Press lightly on wrong side. St. back seam. Cut cardboard to fit peak, fold peak, insert cardboard and st. peak. Make pompon and stitch in place in centre of cap.

Big and little sister tunics
illustrated in colour on page 76

MATERIALS
3 (4, 4, 5) balls (25 gr. each) Mahony's Blarney Berella Baby yarn in white, 2 (2, 3, 3) balls in green. One pair each Nos. 10 and 11 knitting needles (USA sizes 3 and 2).

MEASUREMENTS
To fit chest size 20 (22, 24, 26) in.; length of tunic 17 (19, 21, 23) in.

TENSION
7 sts. and 14 rows to 1 in. over patt. on No. 10 needles.

ABBREVIATIONS
See page 46; W., white; G., green.

continued on page 78

Two-colour tunics for big and little sisters (see page 75)

Matching lace-up sweaters for all the family (see page 78)

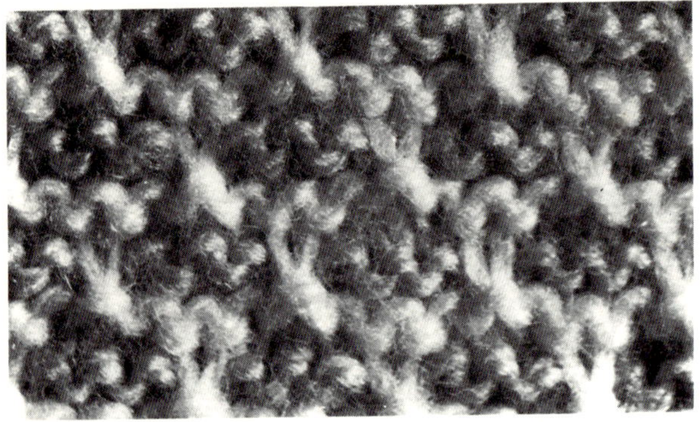

BACK

With No. 11 needles and W. cast on 91 (99, 111, 123) sts. and work in rib.

1st row (right side): k.2, * p.1, k.1; rep. from * to last st., k.1.

2nd row: k.1, * p.1, k.1; rep. from * to end.

Rep. these 2 rows 4 times more, then first row again. Change to No. 10 needles and k.1 row. Join on G. and work in patt. as follows.

1st row: with G. k.3, * sl.1 purlwise keeping y.b., k.3; rep. from * to end.

2nd row: with G. k.3, * y.fwd., sl.1 purlwise, y.b., k.3; rep. from * to end.

3rd and 4th rows: k. in W.

5th row: with G. k.1, * sl.1 purlwise keeping y.b., k.3; rep. from * to last 2 sts., sl.1 purlwise, k.1.

6th row: with G. k.1, * y.fwd., sl.1 purlwise, y.b., k.3; rep. from * to last 2 sts., y.fwd., sl.1 purlwise, y.b., k.1.

7th and 8th rows: k. in W.

These 8 rows form one patt. Continue until 2nd patt. is completed, then dec. 1 st. at both ends of next row and every foll. 16th row until 81 (89, 97, 107) sts. remain, then dec. 1 st. at both ends of every foll. 20th row until 75 (83, 91, 99) sts. remain, taking care to keep patt. correct. Continue without shaping until work measures 12 (13½, 15½, 17) in. from beg., ending with a 2nd or 6th patt. row. **

Armhole Shaping

Cast off 4 (5, 4, 5) sts. at beg. of next 2 rows and 2 sts. at beg. of next 2 (2, 6, 6) rows. Now dec. 1 st. at both ends of next 2 alternate rows after which dec. 1 st. at both ends of every following 4th row 2 (3, 2, 3) times: 55 (59, 63, 67) sts.

Continue without shaping until work measures 16 (18, 20, 22) in. from beg., ending with a 2nd or 6th patt. row.

Neck and Shoulder Shaping

Next row: with W. k.23 (25, 26, 28) and leave these sts. on a spare needle for right back, continue along row, cast off 9 (9, 11, 11) sts., k. to end.

Continue on the 23 (25, 26, 28) sts. now remaining on needle for left back and work 1 row straight. *** Cast off 2 sts. at beg. of next row and next 2 (2, 3, 3) alternate rows and 1 st. at same edge on next 4 (4, 3, 3) alternate rows. You have thus ended at side edge with 13 (15, 15, 17) sts. remaining. Keeping neck edge straight cast off for shoulder 6 (8, 8, 10) sts. at beg. of next row, work 1 row, then cast off remaining 7 sts. ***

With wrong side facing rejoin yarn to inner edge of right back sts. Complete to match left back from *** to ***

FRONT

Work as for Back to ** making sure there are the same number of patts.

Armhole and Neck Shaping

Cast off 4 (5, 4, 5) sts. at beg. of next 2 rows and 2 sts. at beg. of next 2 (2, 6, 6) rows: 63 (69, 71, 77) sts. remain and you have ended with a 2nd or 6th patt. row.

Next row: with W. k.28 (30, 31, 33) and leave these sts. on a spare needle for left front, continue along row, cast off 7 (9, 9, 11), k. to end.

Continue on the 28 (30, 31, 33) sts. now remaining on needle for right front and work 1 row straight.

**** Cast off 2 sts. at beg. of next row, then dec. 1 st. at armhole edge on following row.

Rep. last 2 rows once. Dec. 1 st. at neck edge on next row, work 1 row straight, dec. at neck edge on next row, then dec. at armhole edge on following row. Rep. last 4 rows once.

For size 20 only: keep armhole edge straight but dec. 1 st. at neck edge on every following 4th row 3 times.

For size 22 only: work 3 rows straight then dec. at both ends of next row, then work 3 rows straight and dec. at neck edge on following row.

For size 24 only: dec. 1 st. at neck edge on every following 4th row 4 times.

For size 26 only: dec. 1 st. at both ends of following 4th row, then dec. at neck edge on every 4th row twice more.

For all sizes: continue on remaining 13 (15, 15, 17) sts. until work measures 17 (19, 21, 23) in. from beg., ending at side.

Shoulder Shaping

Cast off 6 (8, 8, 10) sts. at beg. of next row, work 1 row, then cast off remaining 7 sts. **** With wrong side facing rejoin yarn to inner edge of left front sts. Complete as given for right front from **** to ****

ARMHOLE BORDERS (make 2 alike)

With No. 11 needles and W. cast on 107 (115, 119, 127) sts. and work 11 rows in rib as on welt. Cast off loosely ribwise.

NECK BORDERS

For front neck work one piece as given for armhole border of same size. For back neck cast on 47 (47, 53, 53) sts. using No. 11 needles and W. Work as for other borders.

TO COMPLETE

Press patt. sections very lightly on wrong side with cool iron; do not use a damp cloth. Backstitch shoulder and side seams carefully matching patt. along sides. Press seams. Join ends of armhole borders. With right side of border to wrong side of tunic and seam level with side seam, sew cast-on edge of borders to armhole edges with a flat join. Fold border over on to right side so that cast-off edge just covers previous seam. Hold in place by taking a small st. into each p. rib below cast-off edge. Join ends of front neck border to back neck border. Placing seams level with shoulder seams sew on as for armhole borders.

FAMILY

Lace-up sweater — in 5 sizes
illustrated in colour on page 77

MATERIALS. 5 (5, 6, 7, 7) balls Wendy Tricel/Nylon Crepe double knitting in main shade and 3 (3, 3, 4, 5) balls in each of 2 contrasting shades (or any Tricel/Nylon double knitting yarn to give tension indicated below). One pair each No. 9 and No. 11 knitting needles (USA: sizes 5 and 2). One crochet hook International Standard Size 5.00.

MEASUREMENTS. To fit chest size 28/29 (31/32, 34/35, 37/38, 40/41) in.; length 19 (20½, 22, 23, 24) in.; length of sleeve seam 2½ (4, 4, 4, 5½) in.

TENSION. 6½ sts. to 1 in. and 1 patt. to 1½ in.

ABBREVIATIONS. See page 46; M., main shade; A, first contrasting shade; B., 2nd contrasting shade.

PATT.
1st to 4th rows: with M., work in st.st. beg. with a k. row.
5th to 8th rows: with A., work in st.st., beg. with a k. row.
9th row: with B., k. winding yarn 3 times round needle for each st. **10th row:** with B., p., letting extra 2 loops drop.

BACK
With No. 11 needles and M. cast on 92 (102, 112, 122, 132) sts. and work 20 rows in k.1, p.1 rib.
Change to No. 9 needles and patt. as given above. Work 7 (8, 9, 10, 11) patts. (of 10 rows each) straight.

Shape Raglan. Cont. in patt., cast off 4 sts. at beg. of next 2 rows. K.2 tog. at each end of next row. Work 3 rows straight. K.2 tog. at each end of every right-side row and at each end of every 10th patt. row until 34 (40, 46, 52, 58) sts. remain. K.2 tog. at each end of first 8 patt. rows and k.3 tog. at each end of every 9th and 10th patt. row until 28 (30, 32, 34, 36) sts. remain. Leave sts. on st. holder.

FRONT
Work as Back until 6 (7, 8, 9, 10) patts. have been completed.

Divide for Front Opening. Next 2 rows: patt. 46 (51, 56, 61, 66) sts.; turn and work back. Working on these sts. only, complete this patt.

Shape Raglan. Next 2 rows: cast off 4 sts., patt. to neck edge; turn and work back. K.2 tog. at beg. of next row. Work 3 rows in patt. K.2 tog. at beg. of every right-side row and at end of every 10th patt. row until 25 (29, 33, 37, 41) sts. remain, ending at neck edge.
Next row: patt. 9 (10, 11, 12, 13) sts. and place on st. holder, patt. to end of row. Now dec. at armhole edge as before and at neck edge on every right-side row, until 6 (7, 9, 10, 11) sts. remain. Now dec. at armhole edge only on every right-side row and on every 10th patt. row until all sts. are worked off. Rejoin yarn to other half of front opening and work to match first, reversing shapings.

SLEEVES (make 2 alike)
With No. 11 needles and M., cast on 64 (70, 76, 82, 88) sts. and work 10 rows in k.1, p.1 rib. Change to No. 9 needles and work 1 (2, 2, 2, 3) patts.

Shape Raglan. Cont. in patt. cast off 4 sts. at beg. of next 2 rows. K.2 tog. at each end of every right-side row and every 10th patt. row until 6 sts. remain. Work 2 more rows if necessary to match Back. Place sts. on safety pin.

TO COMPLETE
Front Opening. With No. 11 needles and M. and right-side facing, pick up and k. 25 (33, 38, 43, 48) sts. down left side of front opening from neck to base and 25 (33, 38, 43, 48) sts. up right side of opening: 50 (66, 76, 86, 96) sts. Beg. with a p. row, work 3 rows in st.st. P. 1 row. Beg. with a p. row, work 4 rows in st.st. Cast off loosely. Fold half of border to wrong side and hem.

Collar. Carefully join raglan seams. With right side facing, No. 11 needles and M., beg. at right front and pick up and k. 3 sts. from top of front opening border, k. 9 (10, 11, 12, 13) sts. from st. holder, pick up and k. 14 (16, 18, 20, 22) sts.

round neck to shoulder, k. 6 sts. from shoulder safety pin, k. 28 (30, 32, 34, 36) sts. from neck st. holder, k. 6 sts. from other shoulder safety pin, pick up and k. 14 (16, 18, 20, 22) round neck to front st. holder, k. 9 (10, 11, 12, 13) sts. from holder, pick up and k. 3 sts. from front opening border: 92 (100, 108, 116, 124) sts.
Work 7 rows in k.1, p 1 rib. Cast off loosely in rib.

To Make Up. Join side and sleeve seams. With all 3 colours tog. and crochet hook, make a length of ch. to lace up front opening and tie at neck.

WOMEN

Jumper and tank top
illustrated in colour on page 81

MATERIALS
For jumper: 6 (6, 7, 7, 8, 8) balls (20 gr. each) Twilleys Mohair. One pair each Nos. 10 and 11 knitting needles (USA sizes 3 and 2). One crochet hook International Standard Size 3.00. Shirring elastic. 3 small buttons.
For tank top: 3 (3, 4, 4, 5, 5) balls (20 gr. each) Twilleys Mohair in each of two toning shades. One pair each No. 8 and No. 9 knitting needles (USA sizes 6 and 5).

MEASUREMENTS
To fit bust size 32 (34, 36, 38, 40, 42) in.; length of jumper 19 (19½, 20, 20½, 21, 21½) in.; length of jumper sleeve seam 19 in.; length of tank top 17½ (18, 18½, 19, 19½, 20) in.; length of tank top sleeve seam 6 in.

TENSION
Jumper: 5 sts. and 9 rows to 1 in. over st.st. with No. 10 needles. **Tank top:** 6 sts. and 8 rows to 1 in. over unstretched rib with No. 8 needles.

ABBREVIATIONS
See page 46.

JUMPER FRONT
With No. 11 needles and using yarn double cast on 80 (86, 90, 96, 100, 106) sts. Break off 1 strand and cont. with single yarn.
Work 4 in. in k.1, p.1 rib. Change to No. 10 needles. Cont. in st.st. Work straight until front measures 12 (12½, 12½, 13, 13, 13½) in. from beg.

Shape Armholes
Cast off 3 (4, 4, 5, 5, 6) sts. at beg. of next 2 rows then dec. 1 st. at each end of next 6 rows: 62 (66, 70, 74, 78, 82) sts. Cont. straight until work measures 17½ (18, 18½, 19, 19½, 20) in. from beg., ending with a p. row.

Shape Neck
Next row: k.22 (24, 26, 28, 30, 32), k.2 tog.; turn. Work on these sts. only. Dec. 1 st. at neck edge on next 7 rows: 16 (18, 20, 22, 24, 26) sts. Work 6 rows straight.

Shape Shoulder
Using yarn double cast off 8 (9, 10, 11, 12, 13) sts. very loosely at beg. of next and foll. alt. row.
Place centre 14 sts. on a st. holder. Complete other side of neck to match first, reversing shapings.

continued on page 82

Striped halter top

MATERIALS
Of Hayfield Beaulon 4-ply — 1 oz. each in each of three contrasting shades. One pair each Nos. 10 and 12 knitting needles (USA sizes 3 and 1). One crochet hook International Standard Size 2.50.

MEASUREMENTS
To fit bust size 30 (32, 34, 36) in.

TENSION
7 sts. and 9 rows to 1 in. over st.st. on No. 10 needles.

ABBREVIATIONS
See page 46; A, first colour; B, second colour; C, third colour.

THE COLOUR PATTERN
Work in st.st. in the following colour sequence: 2 rows A, 10 rows B, 2 rows A, 10 rows C.
When working in rib, work in colour sequence as above, but always k. the first row of colour change.

FRONT
With No. 12 needles, and A, cast on 80 (88, 94, 100) sts. and work in k.1, p.1 rib for 4 rows.

Change to No. 10 needles and st. st. and work in colour pattern. Inc. 1 st. at each end of first and every following 6th row until you have 104 (112, 118, 124) sts. Work straight until 3 complete patts. have been worked.

Shape Top
Keeping colour patt. correct, k.2 tog. at beg. of next row, k. across 43 (45, 47, 48) sts., cast off centre 14 (18, 20, 24) sts. and work to last 2 sts., k.2 tog.
Work on this set of sts. only. Cont. in patt., dec. 1 st. at neck edge of next 10 rows, and at the same time dec. 1 st. at side edge on every alt. row. Cont. with side decs., keeping neck edge straight, until 10 sts. remain.
Work straight on these sts. for 5 in., or length required (longer if a lower neck is required; shorter if a higher neck is required).
Cast off.
Rejoin yarn to sts. at other side and work to match first side, reversing shapings.

BACK
With No. 12 needles and A, cast on 76 (84, 92, 96) sts. and work in k.1, p.1 rib for 4 rows. Change to No. 10 needles and cont. in rib., beg. colour patt.
Inc. 1 st. at side edges of next and every 6th row for 12 incs. in all on each side.
When 12 rows of patt. have been worked, cast off centre 12 (20, 28, 32) sts. and on the first set of sts. dec. 1 st. at centre edge on next 30 rows, then on every alt. row until all sts. have been dec.
(Note. Side edge should measure as side of front to decreasings.)
Fasten off.
Rejoin yarn to rem. sts. and finish to match first side.

TO COMPLETE
Press. Join side and back neck seams. With crochet hook and A, work 2 rows of d.c. round neck and back edges. Fasten off. Press.

Pretty for a teenager—full-sleeved jumper with matching tank top (see page 79)

BACK

Work as Front until Back measures 16 (16½, 17, 17½, 18, 18½) in. from beg. ending with a p. row.

Divide for Opening
Next row: k.31 (33, 35, 37, 39, 41); turn.
Work straight on these sts. only until work measures 19 (19½, 20, 20½, 21, 21½) in. from beg., ending at armhole edge.

Shape Shoulder
Using yarn double cast off 8 (9, 10, 11, 12, 13) sts. very loosely at beg. of next and foll. alt. row. Work 1 row. Leave rem. 15 sts. on st. holder. Complete other side of opening to match first, reversing shapings.

SLEEVES (make 2 alike)
With No. 11 needles and using yarn double cast on 40 (40, 44, 44, 48, 48) sts. Break off 1 strand and cont. with single yarn. Work 1½ in. in k.1, p.1 rib.
Next row: k. twice into each st. to end.
Next row: * p. twice into next st., p.1; rep. from * to end: 120 (120, 132, 132, 144, 144) sts.
Change to No. 10 needles. Cont. in st.st., beg. with a k. row. Work straight until Sleeve measures 13 in. from beg., ending with a p. row.
Next row: * k.2 tog.; rep. from * to end: 60 (60, 66, 66, 72, 72) sts.
Now work in k.1, p.1 rib until work measures 19 in. from beg.

Shape Top
Cont. in rib, cast off 4 sts. at beg. of next 2 rows then dec. 1 st. at each end of every alt. row until 20 (20, 20, 20, 20, 20) sts. remain. Dec. 1 st. at each end of next 6 rows.
Cast off.

TO COMPLETE
Collar
Join shoulders. With No. 11 needles and using yarn double k. sts. from left side of back neck, pick up and k. 18 sts. down left side of front neck, k. sts. from st. holder, pick up and k. 18 sts. up right side of front neck then k. sts. from right side of back neck: 80 sts. Break off 1 strand and cont. with single yarn.
Work 7 rows in k.1, p.1 rib.
Next row: rib 40; turn.
Work on these sts. only for first half of collar.
Next row: rib 2, * work k.1, p.1 and k.1 all into next st., rib 3; rep. from * ending last rep. rib 1: 60 sts.
Work 4 in. in k.1, p.1 rib on these sts. Dec. 1 st. at each end of next 6 rows.
Cast off loosely ribwise.
Rejoin yarn to rem. 40 sts. and complete 2nd half of collar to match first, reversing shapings.

To Make Up
Press lightly, omitting ribbing. Join side and sleeve seams. Set in Sleeves. With crochet hook and using yarn double work 2 rows of d.c. around collar edges and back opening edges, working loosely around collar and making 3 evenly-spaced buttonhole loops on right side of back opening on 2nd row by working 3 ch., miss 3 d.c. for each. Press collar and press all seams. Sew buttons on to left side of back opening. Thread shirring elastic through wrong side of wrist ribbing.

TANK TOP
Note. Use one strand of each shade together throughout.

BACK AND FRONT (make 2 pieces alike)
With No. 9 needles cast on 81 (87, 93, 99, 105, 111) sts. Work 5 in. in k.1, p.1 rib, beg. 2nd and alt. rows p.1. Change to No. 8 needles and cont. in rib. Work straight until work measures 10 (10½, 10½, 11, 11, 11½) in. from beg.

Shape Armholes
Still working in rib, cast off 2 sts. at beg. of next 2 rows then dec. 1 st. at each end of next 6 rows: 65 (71, 77, 83, 89, 95) sts. Cont. straight in rib until work measures 13½ (14, 14½, 15, 15½, 16) in. from beg., ending with a 2nd row.

Shape Neck
Next row: rib 13 (15, 17, 19, 21, 23), cast off 39 (41, 43, 45, 47, 49) loosely ribwise, rib to end.
Work on last set of sts. only.
Next row: rib to last 2 sts., k.2.
Next row: k.2, rib to end.
Rep. last 2 rows for 4 in., ending at armhole edge.

Shape Shoulder
Cast off 7 sts. loosely at beg. of next row. Work 1 row.
Cast off rem. sts. loosely.
Rejoin yarn to inner edge of rem. sts.
Next row: k.2, rib to end.
Next row: rib to last 2 sts., k.2.
Working in this way, complete to match first side of neck.

SLEEVES (make 2 alike)
With No. 9 needles cast on 73 (73, 79, 79, 85, 85) sts. Work 2 in. in k.1, p.1 rib, beg. 2nd and alt. rows p.1. Change to No. 8 needles and work 4 in. more in rib.

Shape Top
Cont. in rib, cast off 2 sts. at beg. of next 2 rows then dec. 1 st. at each end of every alt. row until 43 (43, 45, 45, 47, 47) sts. remain. Dec. 1 st. at each end of next 10 rows. Cast off.

TO COMPLETE
Do not press. Join shoulder, side and sleeve seams. Set in sleeves. Press seams lightly.

Ladybird jacket
illustrated on page 84

MATERIALS
9 (10, 11) oz. Robin Vogue Double Knitting in main shade (grey), 1 ball each in red and black, plus an oddment of yellow. One pair each Nos. 8 and 10 knitting needles (USA sizes 6 and 3). One crochet hook International Standard Size 3.00.

MEASUREMENTS
To fit bust size 32 (34, 36) in.; length 19 (19½, 20) in.; sleeve seam 3½ in.

TENSION
6 sts. and 8 rows to 1 in. over st.st. on No. 8 needles.

ABBREVIATIONS
See page 46; M., main shade; R., red; B., black; Y., yellow.

BACK

With No. 10 needles and M. cast on 89 (95, 101) sts.
and work 26 rows in k.1, p.1 rib.
Change to No. 8 needles and work in st.st., inc. 1 st. at
each end of the 9th and every following 10th row to
99 (105, 111) sts. Continue without further shaping
until work measures 12½ in. from beg. ending with a
wrong-side row.

Shape Armholes

Cast off 2 (3, 4) sts. at beg. of each of next 2 rows.
Dec. 1 st. at each end of next 5 rows, then the next
5 alternate rows: 75 (79, 83) sts.
Continue without further shaping until work measures
19 (19½, 20) in. from beg. ending with a wrong-side row.

Shape Shoulders

Cast off 8 (9, 9) sts. at beg. of next 4 rows, then 9 (8, 9)
sts. at beg. of next 2 rows. Cast off.

LEFT FRONT

With No. 10 needles and M. cast on 46 (48, 52) sts. and
work 26 rows in k.1, p.1 rib.
1st and 3rd sizes only: dec. 1 st. at end of last row.
All sizes. Change to No. 8 needles and st.st. inc. 1 st.
at beg. of 9th and every following 10th row to 50 (53, 56)
sts. Continue without further shaping until work
measures same as back to armhole shaping, ending with
a wrong-side row.

Shape Armhole and Commence Motif

*Note. 18-in. lengths of B. yarn can be used for each
spot and 2 separate balls of M. for each side of Motif
to avoid carrying all yarns right across back of work.*

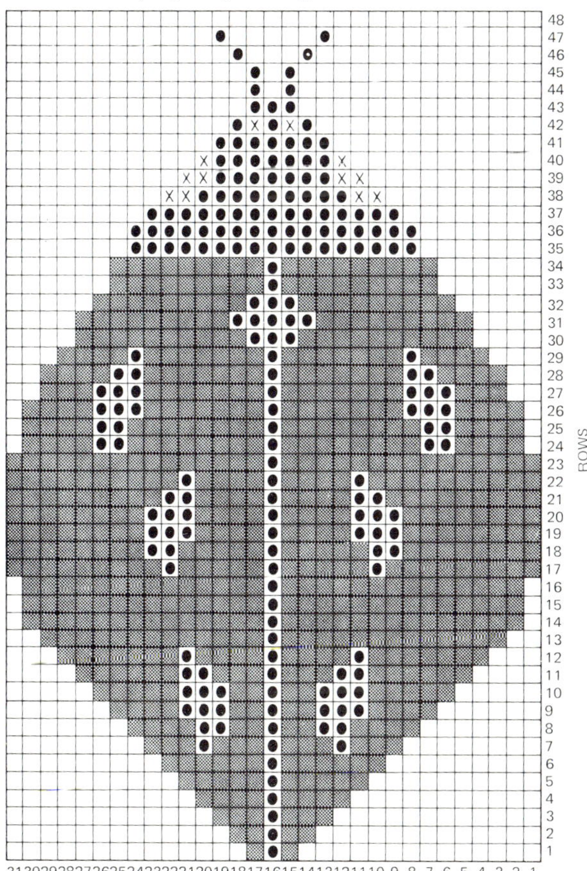

RED
BLACK
YELLOW
MAIN

1 SQUARE = 1 STITCH

1st row: cast off 2 (3, 4) sts., k.27 (28, 29) M., 1 R.,
1 M., 1 R., 18 (19, 20) M.
2nd row: p.17 (18, 19) M., 2 R., 1 B., 2 R., 26 (27,
28) M.
Keeping the Motif correct beg. on 3rd row of chart but
at the same time dec. 1 st. at armhole edge on next
5 rows, then the 5 following alternate rows: 38 (40, 42)
sts. Continue without further shaping until the 35th
row from chart has been worked.

Shape Neck

1st row: cast off 2 sts., patt. to end.
Dec. 1 st. at neck edge on every row until 25 (26, 27) sts.
remain, ending on wrong side. Continue until work
measures same as Back to shoulder shaping, ending on
wrong side.

Shape Shoulder

Cast off 8 (9, 9) sts. at beg. of next and following
alternate row. Patt. one row then cast off.

RIGHT FRONT

Work to correspond with Left Front making inc. at end
of row unstead of beg. until work measures same as
Left Front to armhole shaping, ending on wrong side.
Next row: k.18 (19, 20) M., 1 R., 1 M., 1 R., 29 (31,
33) M.

Shape Armhole

Next row: cast off 2 (3, 4) sts., p.26 (27, 28) M., 2 R.,
1 B., 2 R., 17 (18, 19) M.
Complete to correspond with Left Front reversing all
shapings.

SLEEVES (make 2 alike)

With No. 10 needles and M. cast on 58 (60, 62) sts.
and work 8 rows in k.1, p.1 rib.
Change to No. 8 needles and work in st.st. until work
measures 3½ in. from beg., ending on wrong side.

Shape Top

1st row: k.27, cast off 4 (6, 8) sts., k. to end. Dec. 1 st.
at inside edge on each of the next 5 rows, then on every
alternate row to 8 sts. Leave these sts. on a spare needle.
With wrong side facing rejoin yarn to sts. left for other
side, patt. to end. Dec. 1 st. at inside edge on each of the
next 5 rows then every alternate row to 8 sts.
Next row: p.8, cast on 6 (8, 10) sts. taking care not to
twist work, p. across 8 sts. left on needle.
Next row: k.2 tog., k. to last 2 sts., k.2 tog. Patt. one
row. Cast off 3 sts. at beg. of next 4 rows. Cast off.

TO COMPLETE

Press each piece carefully using a warm iron over a
damp cloth.
Join shoulder and side seams. Set in sleeves placing
centre of cast-on sts. at sleeve top to shoulder seam.

Sleeve Vent Edging

With crochet hook and M., and with right side facing
beg. at lower edge and work one row d.c. evenly around
vent.
Next row: 1 d.c. in each of first 3 d.c., 1 ch., miss
1 d.c.: a lace hole made. Continue in d.c. making 4 more
lace holes at 1¼-in. intervals to sleeve top, miss 1 d.c. at
each corner of vent then work down other side to
correspond. Work one more row d.c. all round working
1 d.c. in ch. spaces of previous row.

continued on page 84

Front Borders

With crochet hook and M. work one row d.c. evenly all round front edges, work up front edge making 11 lace holes as given for sleeves evenly spaced, the first lace hole to be 3 sts. up from lower edge and the last 3 sts. from neck edge. Break off yarn, rejoin at neck edge of other side and work to correspond with first side. Fasten off.
With right side facing and R., beg. at lower edge and work 1 d.c. in first st., 1 tr. in next st. Continue in this manner all round front and neck edge. Break off R.
With right side facing and B., work 1 tr. in each d.c., 1 d.c. in each tr., all round. Break off B.

To Make Up

Press all seams and borders carefully. Using yarn double and B. make 2 crochet chains each 26 in. long. Thread one cord through holes in each sleeve to fasten at lower edge of sleeve. Make another chain 52 in. long and thread through holes up front of jacket.

Peasant-style suit, in simple stocking stitch, has a lace-up front fastening (see page 86)

Peasant-style suit
illustrated in colour on page 85

MATERIALS
20 (21, 22) balls (20 gr. each) Wendy Tricel Nylon Crêpe Double Knit for skirt, 12 (13, 13) balls for waistcoat. One pair each Nos. 9 and 11 knitting needles (USA sizes 5 and 2). A medium crochet hook. A 7-in. zip fastener. A waist length of elastic.

MEASUREMENTS
To fit bust size 34 (36, 38) in.; hip size 36 (38, 40) in.; length of waistcoat 21 (21½, 22) in.; length of skirt 30 in.

TENSION
6½ sts. to 1 in. over st.st. on No. 9 needles.

ABBREVIATIONS
See page 46; inc. 1, increase one st., by picking up loop between sts. and k. into back of it.

SKIRT
BACK AND FRONT (make 2 pieces alike)
With No. 11 needles cast on 85 (91, 97) sts.
1st row: k.1, * p.1, k.1; rep. from * to end.
2nd row: p.1, * k.1, p.1; rep. from * to end.
Rep. these 2 rows for 1¼ in., ending with 2nd row.
Change to No. 9 needles and beg. with a k. row work 4 rows in st.st.
Next row: k.2, inc. 1, k.25 (27, 29), inc. 1, k.2, inc. 1, k.27 (29, 31), inc. 1, k.2, inc. 1, k.25 (27, 29), inc. 1, k.2. Work 7 rows in st.st.
Next row: k.2, inc. 1, k.27 (29, 31), inc. 1, k.2, inc. 1, k.29 (31, 33), inc. 1, k.2, inc. 1, k.27 (29, 31), inc. 1, k.2.
Cont. to inc. in this way on every 8th row until there are 127 (133, 139) sts., then omitting inc. at each end of row, cont. to inc. at each side of the 2 dart sts. on every 20th row until work measures 29½ in. from beg., or ½ in. less than final length required, ending with a p. row.
Change to No. 11 needles and work 2 rows in rib as at beg.
Cast off loosely in rib.

WAISTCOAT
BACK
With No. 11 needles cast on 135 (145, 153) sts. and work 2 rows in rib as on Skirt, inc. 1 st. at end of 2nd row on first and 3rd sizes only: 136 (145, 154) sts.
Change to No. 9 needles and beg. with a k. row cont. in st.st. until work measures 5 in. from beg., ending with a p. row.
Next row: k.1, * k.2 tog., k.1; rep. from * to end: 91 (97, 103) sts.
Cont. in st.st. for 5 rows.
Next row: k.2, * inc. 1, k.29 (31, 33); rep. from * twice more, inc. 1, k.2.
Work 7 rows.
Next row: k.2, inc. 1, k.30 (32, 34), inc. 1, k.31 (33, 35), inc. 1, k.30 (32, 34), inc. 1, k.2. Cont. to inc. in this way on every 8th row until there are 119 (125, 131) sts., then cont. straight until work measures 14 in. from beg. ending with a p. row.

Shape Armholes
Cast off 6 sts. at beg. of next 2 rows, then 2 sts. at beg. of next 4 rows.
Next row: k.1, sl.1, k.1, p.s.s.o., k. to last 3 sts., k.2 tog., k.1.
Next row: p. to end.
Rep. the last 2 rows 6 (7, 8) times more: 85 (89, 93) sts.
Cont. straight until armhole measures 7 (7½, 8) in., ending with a p. row.

Shape Shoulders
Cast off 6 sts. at beg. of next 6 rows, then 6 (7, 8) sts. at beg. of next 2 rows.
Change to No. 11 needles and work 2 rows in rib as at beg.
Cast off in rib.

LEFT FRONT
With No. 11 needles cast on 63 (67, 73) sts. and work 2 rows in rib as on Back, inc. 1 st. at end of 2nd row on first and 2nd sizes: 64 (68, 73) sts.
Change to No. 9 needles and cont. in st.st. until work measures 5 in. from beg., ending with a p. row.
Next row: k.1 (2, 1), * k.2 tog., k.1; rep. from * to end: 43 (46, 49) sts.
Cont. in st.st. for 5 rows.
Next row: k.2, inc. 1, k.29 (31, 33), inc. 1, k. to end.
Work 7 rows.
Next row: k.2, inc. 1, k.30 (32, 34), inc. 1, k. to end.
Cont. to inc. in this way on every 8th row until there are 57 (60, 63) sts., then cont. straight until work measures 12 rows less than Back to armholes, ending with a p. row.

Shape Front Edge
Next row: k. to last 3 sts., k.2 tog., k.1.
Work 3 rows straight.
Rep. the last 4 rows twice more.

Shape Armhole
Next row: cast off 6, k. to last 3 sts., k.2 tog., k.1.
Cont. to shape armhole to match Back, at the same time cont. to dec. at front edge on every 4th row until 25 (26, 27) sts. rem. Cont. straight, if necessary, until armhole measures the same as on Back, ending with a p. row.

Shape Shoulder
Cast off 6 sts. at beg. of next and foll. 2 alt. rows. P. 1 row, then cast off rem. 7 (8, 9) sts.

RIGHT FRONT
Work to match Left Front, reversing all shaping.

LEFT FRONT BORDER
With No. 11 needles and right side facing pick up and k. 131 (135, 139) sts. along front edge. Work 1 row rib as at beg.
Next row: rib 54 (58, 62) sts., m.1, work 2 tog., (rib 13, m.1, work 2 tog.) 3 times, rib to end.
Cast off in rib.

RIGHT FRONT BORDER
Work to match Left Front Border but ribbing 30 sts. at beg. of row of holes instead of 54 (58, 62) sts.

ARMHOLE BORDERS (make both alike)
Join shoulder seams.
With No. 11 needles and right side facing, pick up and k. 95 (101, 107) sts. along armhole edge. Work 2 rows in rib.
Cast off in rib.

TO COMPLETE
Press work very lightly with a cool iron over a slightly damp cloth.
Join side seams of skirt, leaving one side open for zip. Sew in zip. Sew elastic behind waist with herringbone sts.
Join side seams of waistcoat. Press all seams well. Make a crochet chain 60 in. long and thread through holes of Waistcoat to form lace-up fastening.

Brown and white coat
illustrated in colour on page 88

MATERIALS
27 (29, 31) oz. Wendy Double Knit Nylonised in main colour, 3 (4, 4) in a contrasting colour. One pair each Nos. 9 and 11 knitting needles (USA sizes 5 and 2). 1 (1¼, 1¼) yards petersham ribbon, 2 in. wide. One large button. Two press fasteners.

MEASUREMENTS
To fit bust size 34 (36, 38) in.; length from top of shoulder 42 (42½, 43) in.; sleeve seam 17½ (18, 18) in.

TENSION
6 sts. and 7 rows to 1 in.

ABBREVIATIONS
See page 46; M., main shade; C., contrasting shade.

BACK
With No. 9 needles and M., cast on 140 (146, 152) sts. Work in st.st. Dec. 1 st. at each end of every 8th row 14 times, then every 6th row 5 times and then every 4th row 6 times. Now inc. 1 st. at each end of every 8th row 5 times: 100 (106, 112) sts. When work measures 32 (32, 32½) in. from beg. shape armholes as follows. Cast off 6 sts. at beg. of next 2 rows, then dec. 1 st. at each end of every row until 76 (80, 84) sts. remain. When armholes measure 7 (7½, 7½) in., shape shoulders and neck as follows:
Next row: cast off 5, work 24 (25, 26) including st. on needle, place rem. sts. on a st. holder. Cast off at neck edge 3 sts. 3 times and continue to cast off at armhole edge 5 sts. twice more and 5 (6, 7) sts. once. Go back to sts. left on st. holder and join yarn at centre edge. Cast off the first 18 (20, 22) sts. then work on rem. sts. to correspond with other side of neck. With No. 11 needles and C., pick up and k. 138 (144, 150) sts. along cast-on edge. Work in garter st. for 11 rows. Change to M. Work in garter st. for 11 rows. Cast off on wrong side.

LEFT FRONT
With No. 9 needles and M., cast on 74 (77, 80) sts. Work in st.st. Work 7 rows. Dec. 1 st. at end of next row. Rep. this dec. at this edge every 8th row 13 times more, then every 6th row 5 times and then every 4th row 6 times. Now inc. 1 st. at this edge every 8th row 5 times. At the same time when work measures 27 in. from beg., finishing at centre edge, shape neck as follows.
Dec. 1 st. at beg. of next row. Rep. this dec. at this edge every 4th row 21 (22, 23) times more. At the same time when work measures 32 (32, 32½) in. from beg., finishing at outside edge, shape armhole as follows. Cast off 6 sts. at beg. of next row then dec. 1 st. at this edge on every row 6 (7, 8) times. When armhole measures 7 (7½, 7½) in., shape shoulder as follows. Cast off at armhole edge 5 sts. 3 times and 5 (6, 7) sts. once.
With No. 11 needles and C., pick up and k. 73 (76, 79) sts. along cast-on edge. Work in garter st. Work 11 rows C., 11 rows M., inc. 1 st. at centre edge on every alternate row. Cast off.

RIGHT FRONT
Work as for Left Front, reversing shapings.

SLEEVES (make 2 alike)
With No. 9 needles and M., cast on 48 (52, 52) sts. Work in st.st. Inc. 1 st. at each end of every 6th row until there are 76 (80, 80) sts. When sleeve measures 15½ (16, 16) in. from beg., shape top of sleeve as follows.

Cast off 6 sts. at beg. of next 2 rows, dec. 1 st. at beg. only of foll. 16 (20, 20) rows, then dec. 1 st. at each end of every row until 20 sts. remain. Cast off. With No. 11 needles and C., pick up and k.46 (50, 50) sts. along cast-on edge then work border as for lower edge of Back.

BELT
With No. 9 needles and M., cast on 28 sts. Work in st.st. Work straight for 30 (32, 34) in., finishing with a p. row.

Next row: k.14; turn.
Work 6 rows on these sts. Break yarn. Rejoin yarn at centre and work 7 rows on rem. sts. Work 3 rows across all sts. Shape point as follows.
Next row: k.7; turn.
Dec. 1 st. at beg. of next row. Rep. this dec. at this edge on every alternate row twice more.
Cast off rem. sts. Rejoin yarn, k. across next 14 sts. Work on these sts., dec. 1 st. at each end of next row. Rep. this dec. on every alternate row twice more. Cast off. K. across rem. 7 sts. Dec. 1 st. at inside edge on every alternate row 3 times. Cast off.

TO COMPLETE
Press all pieces under a damp cloth. Back st. side, shoulder and sleeve seams, oversewing garter st. borders. Set in Sleeves.

Front Borders
Beg. at bottom of Right Front, with No. 11 needles and C., pick up and k. 163 (163, 163) sts. along straight edge of Right Front, 73 (77, 81) sts. along shaped edge of neck and 21 (22, 23) sts. to centre back of neck. Work in garter st. Work 11 rows C., 11 rows M., inc. 1 st. at bottom of coat on every alternate row. Cast off. In a similar way, work border for Left Front. Join borders tog. at centre back of neck. Place the petersham on to the wrong side of belt and join side edges of belt tog. in the centre of the petersham. Cut a space in the petersham to correspond with buttonhole and shape point. Work round buttonhole. Press seams, front borders and belt. Sew 2 press studs to borders of coat at waist. Sew button to belt.

Knickerbocker suit
illustrated on page 89

MATERIALS
35 (37, 39) oz. Lee Target Motoravia Double Knitting. One pair each Nos. 9, 10 and 11 knitting needles (USA sizes 5, 3 and 2). A 9-in. zip fastener. 1¼ yd. of elastic, 1 in. wide.

MEASUREMENTS
To fit bust size 32 (34, 36) in.; hip size 34 (36, 38) in.; length of jersey 27½ (28, 28½) in.; sleeve seam 17 in.; inside leg seam of knickerbockers including band 22 in.

TENSION
13 sts. to 2 in. over st.st. with No. 10 needles; 13 sts. over rib with No. 9 needles.

ABBREVIATIONS
See page 46; inc., increase (by working into the back and front of the same st.); dec., decrease (by working 2 sts. tog.).

JERSEY BACK
With No. 11 needles cast on 116 (122, 128) sts. and work in rib as follows:

continued on page 90

Elegant brown and white coat has wrap-over
fastening and matching belt (see page 87)

Knickerbocker suit (see page 87)

1st row: k.3, * p.2, k.4; rep. from * ending last repeat with k.3.
2nd row: p.3 * k.2, p.4; rep. from * ending last repeat with p.3.
Repeat these 2 rows twice. Change to No. 10 needles and work in st.st. for 16 rows, then dec. 1 st. at each end of the next row and 2 following 20th rows. On 110 (116, 122) sts. work in st.st. for 9 rows. Change to No. 9 needles and work 90 rows in rib as given at beg. of Back.

To Shape Armholes
Cast off 6 sts. at the beg. of each of the next 2 rows, then dec. 1 st. at the beg. of the next 10 (12, 14) rows. Rib 4 rows. **
Change to No. 10 needles and work in st.st. for 38 rows.

To Slope Shoulders
Cast off 7 sts. at the beg. of each of the next 6 rows: 7 (8, 9) sts. on the following 2 rows. Leave the remaining 32 (34, 36) sts. on a spare needle for collar.

FRONT
Work as given for Back until ** is reached. Change to No. 10 needles and work in st.st. for 25 rows. Now divide the sts. for neck.
Next row: p.32 (34, 36) and leave for right front shoulder, p.24 and leave for collar, p. to end and work on these last 32 (34, 36) sts.

Left Front Shoulder
Dec. 1 st. at neck edge of the next row and 4 following alternate rows. Work 3 rows.

To Slope Shoulder
Cast off 7 sts. at the beg. of next row and 2 following alternate rows. Work 1 row then cast off the 7 (8, 9) remaining sts. With right side of work facing, rejoin yarn to the 32 (34, 36) sts. and k. to end of row.

Right Front Shoulder
Work as for left front shoulder.

SLEEVES (make 2 alike)
With No. 11 needles cast on 62 sts. and work 12 rows in rib as on Back. Change to No. 9 needles and work 2 rows more. Continue in rib and inc. 1 st. at each end of the next row and every following 6th row until the 17th (18th, 19th) inc. row has been worked: 96 (98, 100) sts.
Continue until sleeve measures 17 in. or length required.

To Shape Top
Cast off 6 sts. at the beg. of each of the next 2 rows, then dec. 1 st. at the beg. of the next 22 (24, 26) rows. Cast off 4 sts. at the beg. of the next 6 rows, 3 sts. on next 6 rows. Cast off remaining 20 sts.

TO COMPLETE
Join right shoulder seam.

Polo Collar
With right side of work facing and No. 11 needles, pick up and k.21 (20, 22) sts. down left neck edge, k. across the 24 sts. at centre front, pick up and k.21 (20, 22) sts. from right neck edge, k. across the 32 (34, 36) sts. of back: 98 (98, 104) sts. Beg. with first rib row, work 2 in. in rib as on back. Change to No. 10 needles and work 2 in. more. Change to No. 9 needles and work a further 1 in.
Cast off in rib.

To Make Up
Press lightly on the wrong side with a hot iron over a damp cloth. Join left shoulder seam and polo collar. Set in sleeves. Join sleeve and side seams. Press seams.

KNICKERBOCKERS LEFT FRONT LEG
With No. 11 needles cast on 49 (52, 55) sts. Work in st.st. for 8 rows. P.1 row on right side to mark hemline. Change to No. 10 needles and work in st.st. for 7 (7, 9) rows (when working right front leg work 8 (8, 10) rows here of st.st.).
Inc. 1 st. at end (side seam) of the next row and 5 following 6th rows, then on the 4 following 8th rows: 59 (62, 65) sts.
Work in st.st. for 1 (3, 5) rows.
Inc. 1 st. at beg. (centre front edge) of the next row and at the same edge on the 11 following rows. Place a marker at each end of row: 71 (74, 77) sts.
Work in st.st. for 4 rows.
Dec. 1 st. at centre front edge on the next row and 3 following 6th rows. Work in st.st. for 5 rows.
** Dec. 1 st. at each end of the next row and 2 following 8th rows. Work in st.st. for 9 rows. Inc. 1 st. at each end of the next row and 4 following 22nd rows. Work in st.st. for 15 rows. (Adjust length here if necessary.)
Dec. row: k. or p.2, * dec. 1, k. or p.1; rep. from * to end: 48 (50, 52) sts.
Work in st.st. for 3 rows, then cast off.

RIGHT FRONT LEG
Work as given for Left Front Leg, working the extra row where indicated.

RIGHT BACK LEG
With No. 11 needles cast on 43 (46, 49) sts. and work in st.st. for 8 rows.
P. 1 row on the right side to mark the hemline. Change to No. 10 needles and work in st.st. for 7 (7, 9) rows (8 (8, 10) rows here for left back leg).
Inc. 1 st. at each end of the next row and 4 following 6th rows. Work in st.st. for 5 rows, then inc. 1 st. at the beg. (centre back) of the next row and 4 following 8th rows. Work in st.st. for 1 (3, 5) rows. Inc. 1 st. at centre back edge of next row and 3 following alternate rows. Work one row then cast on 12 sts. at the beg. of following row. Place marker at each end of last row. Work one row in st.st.
Dec. 1 st. at centre back edge of the next row and 6 following 4th rows. Work in st.st. for 3 rows.
Now work from ** to end as give for Left Front Leg.

LEFT BACK LEG
Work as given for Right Back Leg, working the extra row where indicated.

LEG BANDS (make 2 alike)
With No. 10 needles cast on 92 sts. and work in st.st. for 10 rows. P. 1 row on right side to mark the hemline. Work in st.st. for 9 rows, then cast off.

TO COMPLETE
Press as given for the jersey. Join front and back seams as far as markers, then join leg seams, leaving 8 in. free below hemline in left side seam. Fold top over at marked hemline and sew cast-on edge in position. Thread a waist length of elastic through hem and secure ends. Sew in zip fastener. Sew cast-on edge of band to dec. row on leg, easing in any fullness. Fold band in half and sew cast-off edge in position. Thread through elastic and secure ends to fit. Sew up opening. Press all seams.

Yellow skirt

illustrated in colour on page 92

MATERIALS

20 (21, 22) oz. Hayfield Gaylon Double Knitting in gold, 6 balls in navy and 3 balls in red. One pair each Nos. 9 and 10 knitting needles (USA sizes 5 and 3). $\frac{3}{4}$ yd. boned petersham ribbon, $1\frac{1}{2}$ in. wide. An 8-in. gold zip fastener. Two large hooks and eyes.

MEASUREMENTS

To fit hip size 36 (38, 40) in.; length 41 in.

TENSION

6 sts. and 8 rows to 1 in. over st.st. with No. 9 needles.

ABBREVIATIONS

See page 46; G., gold; N., navy; R., red.

FRONT AND BACK (make 2 pieces alike)

With No. 10 needles and N. cast on 186 sts. and work 1 in. in st.st., beg. and ending with a k. row.
K. 1 row for hemline.

Now beg. with a k. row, work 1 in. more.
Change to No. 9 needles and border patt. as given in chart below. Beg. each row with a k. st. worked in same colour as first st. of patt. and ending each row with a k. st. worked in same colour as last st. of patt., work 4 reps. of the 46-st. chart patt. between, in st.st. Read chart from right to left for k. rows and from left to right for p. rows. Weave yarn not in use at back of work.
When the 44 patt. rows have been completed work 4 rows in N. in st.st. Cont. in N. and st.st.
1st dec. row: * k.6, k.2 tog. t.b.l., k.46, k.2 tog., k.6; rep. from * twice: 180 sts.
Work 3 more rows in N. then change to G. and work 18 (22, 26) rows straight.
2nd dec. row: * k.6, k.2 tog. t.b.l., k.44, k.2 tog., k.6; rep. from * twice: 174 sts.
Work 17 (21, 25) rows straight.
3rd dec. row: * k.6, k.2 tog. t.b.l., k.42, k.2 tog., k.6; rep. from * twice: 168 sts.
Work 17 (17, 21) rows straight.

continued on page 93

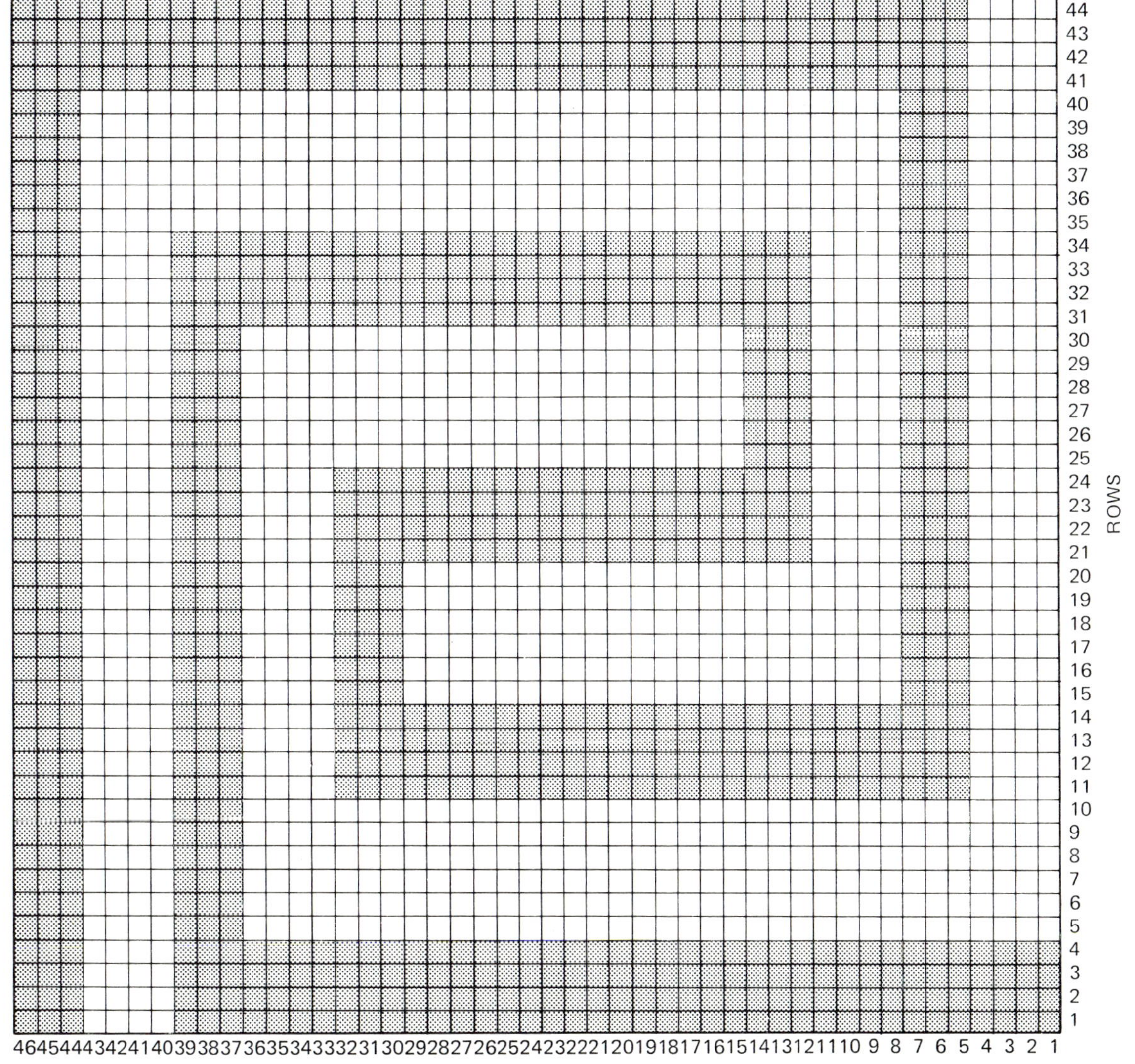

Below and left: yellow skirt, with close-up of red and navy border pattern (see page 91).
Opposite: tartan skirt, with close-up of the colour pattern (see page 94).

4th dec. row: * k.6, k.2 tog. t.b.l., k.40, k.2 tog., k.6;
rep. from * twice: 162 sts.
Work 15 rows straight.
5th dec. row: * k.6, k.2 tog. t.b.l., k.38, k.2 tog., k.6;
rep. from * twice: 156 sts.
Work 15 rows straight.
6th dec. row: * k.6, k.2 tog. t.b.l., k.36, k.2 tog., k.6;
rep. from * twice: 150 sts.
Work 15 (13, 15) rows straight.
7th dec. row: * k.6, k.2 tog. t.b.l., k.34, k.2 tog., k.6;
rep. from * twice: 144 sts.
Work 15 (13, 13) rows straight.
8th dec. row: * k.6, k.2 tog. t.b.l., k.32, k.2 tog., k.6;
rep. from * twice: 138 sts.
Work 15 (13, 13) rows straight.
9th dec. row: * k.6, k.2 tog. t.b.l., k.30, k.2 tog., k.6;
rep. from * twice: 132 sts.
Work 11 (13, 13) rows straight.
10th dec. row: * k.6, k.2 tog. t.b.l., k.28, k.2 tog., k.6;
rep. from * twice: 126 sts.

Work 11 (13, 13) rows straight.
11th dec. row: * k.6, k.2 tog. t.b.l., k.26, k.2 tog., k.6;
rep. from * twice: 120 sts.
Work 11 (13, 13) rows straight.
12th dec. row: * k.6, k.2 tog. t.b.l., k.24, k.2 tog., k.6;
rep. from * twice: 114 sts.
Work 11 (11, 13) rows straight.
13th dec. row: * k.6, k.2 tog. t.b.l., k.22, k.2 tog., k.6;
rep. from * twice: 108 sts.
Work 11 rows straight.
14th dec. row: * k.6, k.2 tog. t.b.l., k.20, k.2 tog., k.6;
rep. from * twice: 102 sts.
Work 11 rows straight.
15th dec. row: * k.6, k.2 tog. t.b.l., k.18, k.2 tog., k.6;
rep. from * twice: 96 sts.
Work 11 (11, 7) rows straight.
16th dec. row: * k.6, k.2 tog. t.b.l., k.16, k.2 tog., k.6;
rep. from * twice: 90 sts.
Work 11 (7, 3) rows straight.
For size 40 hip only. Cast off.
For sizes 36 and 38 hip only. 17th dec. row: * k.6,
k.2 tog. t.b.l., k.14, k.2 tog., k.6; rep. from * twice:
84 sts.
Work 7 (3) rows straight.
For size 38 hip only. Cast off.
For size 36 hip only. 18th dec. row: * k.6, k.2 tog.
t.b.l., k.12, k.2 tog., k.6; rep. from * twice: 78 sts.
Work 3 rows. Cast off.

TO COMPLETE
Press well under damp cloth. Join side seams leaving
left seam open for 8 in. from top. Insert zip in opening.
Attach petersham ribbon to inside of top of Skirt with
herringbone casing. Close with 2 large hooks and eyes.
Turn up hem and slip st. in place.

Tartan skirt
illustrated in colour on page 93

MATERIALS
21 (23, 25) oz. Hayfield Gaylon Double Knitting in
green, 8 (9, 9) oz. in red, 4 oz. in each of yellow and
white and 3 oz. in blue. One pair each Nos. 10 and 11
knitting needles (USA sizes 3 and 2). One medium-sized
crochet hook. Waist length elastic, 1 in. wide. Two large
hooks and eyes. An 8-in. green zip fastener.

MEASUREMENTS
To fit hip size 36 (38, 40) in.; length 40-41 in.

TENSION
6 sts. and 8 rows to 1 in. over st.st. with No. 10 needles.

ABBREVIATIONS
See page 46; G., green; R., red; Y., yellow; W., white;
B., blue.

BACK AND FRONT (make 2 pieces alike)
With No. 11 needles and G., cast on 188 sts. and work
1 in. in st.st. K. 1 row for hemline.
Now begin patt. as follows, joining in R. and changing
to No. 10 needles after 1 in. has been worked.
1st row: k.1G., (k.6G., p.1G., k.5G., p.1G., k.1G., k.3R.,
k.1G., p.1G., k.9G., p.1G., k.2G.) 6 times, k.1G.
2nd row: p.1G., (p.2G., k.1G., p.9G., k.1G., p.1G.,
p.3R., p.1G., k.1G., p.5G., k.1G., p.6G.) 6 times, p.1G.
3rd to 6th rows: work first and 2nd rows twice.
7th row: as first row but use B. only.
8th row: as 2nd row.
9th to 18th rows: work first and 2nd rows 5 times.

19th row: as first row but use W. only.
20th row: as 2nd row.
21st row: with R. only, k.
22nd row: with R. only, p.
23rd and 24th rows: as 21st and 22nd rows.
25th row: as first row.
26th row: as 2nd row but use W. only.
27th to 38th rows: work first and 2nd rows 6 times.
39th row: as first row but use Y. only.
40th row: as 2nd row but use Y. only.
41st to 46th rows: work first and 2nd rows 3 times.
These 46 rows form patt. Continue in patt. throughout.
When 54 rows of patt. have been worked begin dec.
rows, being careful to keep continuity of patt. correct.
1st dec. row: k.1, k.2 tog., (patt. 58, k.2 tog. t.b.l., k.2
tog.) twice, patt. 58, k.2 tog. t.b.l., k.1: 182 sts.
Work 31 (33, 35) rows.
2nd dec. row: k.1, k.2 tog., (patt. 56, k.2 tog. t.b.l.,
k.2 tog.) twice, patt. 56, k.2 tog. t.b.l., k.1: 176 sts.
Work 27 (29, 31) rows.
3rd dec. row: k.1, k.2 tog., (patt. 54, k.2 tog. t.b.l., k.2
tog.) twice, patt. 54, k.2 tog. t.b.l., k.1: 170 sts.
Work 23 (25, 27) rows.
4th dec. row: k.1, k.2 tog., (patt. 52, k.2 tog. t.b.l.,
k.2 tog.) twice, patt. 52, k.2 tog. t.b.l., k.1: 164 sts.
Work 19 (21, 21) rows.
5th dec. row: k.1, k.2 tog., (patt. 50, k.2 tog. t.b.l., k.2
tog.) twice, patt. 50, k.2 tog. t.b.l., k.1: 158 sts.
Work 15 (15, 17) rows.
6th dec. row: k.1, k.2 tog., (patt. 48, k.2 tog. t.b.l., k.2
tog.) twice, patt. 48, k.2 tog. t.b.l., k.1: 152 sts.
Work 15 (15, 17) sts.
7th dec. row: k.1, k.2 tog., (patt. 46, k.2 tog. t.b.l., k.2
tog.) twice, patt. 46, k.2 tog. t.b.l., k.1: 146 sts.
Work 15 (15, 15) rows.
8th dec. row: k.1, k.2 tog., (patt. 44, k.2 tog. t.b.l., k.2
tog.) twice, patt. 44, k.2 tog. t.b.l., k.1: 140 sts.
Work 15 (15, 15) rows.
9th dec. row: k.1, k.2 tog., (patt. 42, k.2 tog. t.b.l., k.2
tog.) twice, patt. 42, k.2 tog. t.b.l., k.1: 134 sts.
Work 15 (13, 15) rows.
10th dec. row: k.1, k.2 tog., (patt. 40, k.2 tog. t.b.l., k.2
tog.) twice, patt. 40, k.2 tog. t.b.l., k.1: 128 sts.
Work 9 (11, 11) rows.
11th dec. row: k.1, k.2 tog., (patt. 38, k.2 tog. t.b.l., k.2
tog.) twice, patt. 38, k.2 tog. t.b.l., k.1: 122 sts.
Work 7 (7, 11) rows.   8 8 8
12th dec. row: k.1, k.2 tog., (patt. 36, k.2 tog. t.b.l., k.2
tog.) twice, patt. 36, k.2 tog. t.b.l., k.1: 116 sts.
Work 7 (7, 7) rows.
13th dec. row: k.1, k.2 tog., (patt. 34, k.2 tog. t.b.l.,
k.2 tog.) twice, patt. 34, k.2 tog. t.b.l., k.1: 110 sts.
Work 7 (7, 7) rows.
14th dec. row: k.1, k.2 tog., (patt. 32, k.2 tog. t.b.l., k.2
tog.) twice, patt. 32, k.2 tog. t.b.l., k.1: 104 sts.
Work 7 (7, 3) rows.
15th dec. row: k.1, k.2 tog., (patt. 30, k.2 tog. t.b.l., k.2
tog.) twice, patt. 30, k.2 tog. t.b.l., k.1: 98 sts.
Work 7 (7, 3) rows.
16th dec. row: k.1, k.2 tog., (patt. 28, k.2 tog. t.b.l., k.2
tog.) twice, patt. 28, k.2 tog. t.b.l., k.1: 92 sts.
For size 36 only: work 7 rows.
For size 38 only: work 3 rows.
For size 40 only: cast off.
17th dec. row: k.1, k.2 tog., (patt. 26, k.2 tog. t.b.l., k.2
tog.) twice, patt. 26, k.2 tog. t.b.l., k.1.
Work 3 rows.
For size 38 only: cast off.
For size 36 only: 18th dec. row: k.1, k.2 tog., (patt.
24, k.2 tog. t.b.l., k.2 tog.) twice, patt. 24, k.2 tog. t.b.l.,
k.1.
Work 3 rows.
Cast off.

TO COMPLETE
Press both pieces well with warm iron over damp cloth.

Tartan Pattern
With crochet hook, work a line of ch. in B. right up first p. line of patt. on Back. Work a line of ch. in W. up 2nd p. line of patt. Work another line of ch. in W. up 3rd p. line of patt.
Work 2 rows of ch. in Y. up 4th p. line of patt. Rep. these ch. lines across Back and then Front. When p. sts. stop because of skirt shapings, then stop the line of ch. being worked—i.e. the only ch. lines which will go all the way up to the waist are 3 B. lines and 3 double Y. lines.
Join side seams of Skirt, leaving left one open at waist edge for 8 in. Insert zip in opening. Attach elastic to inside top of Skirt with herringbone casing. Fasten ends with 2 large hooks and eyes. Turn up hem and slip st. in place on wrong side of work. Press again, paying special attention to lines of crochet and also to seams.

Party tunic
illustrated in colour on page 96

MATERIALS
16 (17, 18, 19) oz. Twilleys Goldfingering.
One pair each Nos. 9 and 11 knitting needles (USA sizes 5 and 2).

MEASUREMENTS
To fit bust size 32 (34, 36, 38) in.; length 27 (27, 28, 28) in.; sleeve seam 18½ in.

TENSION
6 sts. and 9 rows to 1 in. over main patt.

ABBREVIATIONS
See page 46; m.1, make 1 st. by picking up loop before next st. and k. into back of it.

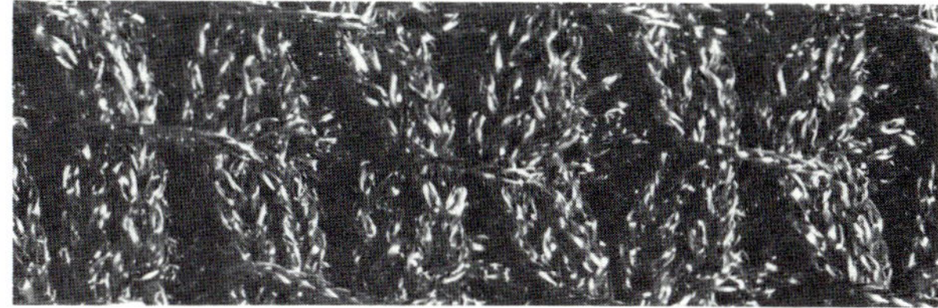

BACK
With No. 9 needles cast on 117 (125, 133, 141) sts. and k. 4 rows. Work in patt. as follows:
1st row (right side): k.1, * p.1, y.b., y.o.n., k.2 tog., k.1; rep. from * to end.
2nd row: k.1, * p.2, k.2; rep. from * to end.
These 2 rows form main patt. Continue in patt. until work measures 8½ (8½, 9, 9) in. from beg., ending with a 2nd row and inc. 1 st. at end of last row: 118 (126, 134, 142) sts.
Now work smock patt. thus:
1st row: p.2, * k.2, p.2; rep. from * to end.
2nd row: k.2, * p.2, k.2; rep. from * to end.
3rd row: p.2, * k.2, m.1 (see Abbreviations), p.2, k.2, insert point of left-hand needle into 7th st. from point of right-hand needle and lift this st. over last 6 sts. and off needle, p.2 *; rep. from * to * to last 4 sts., k.2, p.2. Rep. 2nd row then first and 2nd rows again.
7th row: p.2, k.2, p.2, now rep. from * to * of 3rd row to end.
8th row: as 2nd row.
These 8 rows form smock patt. Continue in smock patt. until work measures 12 (12, 12½, 12½) in. from beg., ending with a 4th or 8th patt. row and dec. 1 st. at end of last row: 117 (125, 133, 141) sts. Now work in main

patt., beg. with a first patt. row, until work measures 19½ (19½, 20, 20) in. from beg.

Armhole Shaping
Keeping main patt. correct, cast off 4 sts. at beg. of next 2 rows then dec. 1 st. each end of next 12 rows: 85 (93, 101, 109) sts.
Continue in main patt. until work measures 27 (27, 28, 28) in. from beg.

Shoulder Shaping
Cast off 6 (7, 8, 9) sts. loosely at beg. of next 8 rows. Cast off remaining 37 sts. loosely.

FRONT
Work as for Back until work measures 22 (22, 23, 23) in. from beg.

Front dividing row: patt. 41 (45, 49, 53) sts.: turn. Leave remaining sts. on st. holder or spare needle. Work in main patt. on these sts. until work measures 25 (25, 26, 26) in. from beg., ending at inner edge.

Neck Shaping
Cast off 9 sts. loosely at beg. of next row then dec. 1 st. at neck edge on next 8 rows: 24 (28, 32, 36) sts. Continue straight until work measures 27 (27, 28, 28) in. from beg., ending at armhole edge.

Shoulder Shaping
Cast off 6 (7, 8, 9) sts. loosely at beg. of next and following 3 alternate rows. Return to remaining sts., place centre 3 sts. on a safety pin or st. holder, rejoin yarn and patt. across remaining 41 (45, 49, 53) sts. Complete to match other side of front.
Place 3 sts. from safety pin on to a No. 11 needle. With right side facing k. into front then into back of each st.: 6 sts.
Next row: inc. in first st., p.1, k.1; turn.
Work on these sts. only for right front band.
Work in p.1, k.1 rib for 3 in. Cast off.
Rejoin yarn to wrong side of remaining 3 sts., k.1, p.1, inc. in last st. Work 3 in. in k.1, p.1 rib for left front band. Cast off.

SLEEVES (make 2 alike)
With No. 11 needles cast on 52 (52, 58, 58) sts. Work 2 in. in k.1, p.1 rib.
Next row: k.1 (1, 2, 2), * inc. in next st.; rep. from * to end: 103 (103, 114, 114) sts.
Next row: p.3 (3, 6, 6), * inc. in next st., p.1; rep. from * to end: 153 (153, 169, 169) sts.
Change to No. 9 needles and work in main patt. as for Back, beg. with a first patt. row, until work measures 11 in. from beg., ending with a 2nd patt. row.
Next row: k.1, * k.2 tog.; rep. from * to end: 77 (77, 85, 85) sts.
K. 7 rows. Now continue in main patt., beg. with a first patt. row, until work measures 18½ in. from beg.
To shape top continue in main patt., casting off 4 sts. at beg. of next 2 rows then dec. 1 st. each end of every alternate row until 33 (33, 37, 37) sts. remain. Dec. 1 st. each end of next 10 rows. Cast off.

NECKBAND AND TIE
With No. 11 needles cast on 5 sts. Work 60 in. in k.1, p.1 rib, beg. 2nd row p.1. Cast off.

TO COMPLETE
Press lightly, omitting rib and smocking. Join shoulder, side and sleeve seams. Set in sleeves.
Sew on front bands. Sew on neckband and tie, leaving 20 in. approx. free at each end to tie. Press seams.

Silver and gold evening bag
illustrated left

MATERIALS
Of Twilleys Double Gold—one ball each (50 gr. each) in gold and silver. One pair No. 9 knitting needles (USA size 5). An 8-in. evening bag frame. ½ yd. lining material, 36 in. wide.

MEASUREMENTS
Finished bag measures 8 in. by 8 in.

TENSION
5 sts. and 10 rows to 1 in.

ABBREVIATIONS
See page 46.

TO MAKE TRIANGLE MOTIF (make 4 in silver, 4 in gold)
Cast on 40 sts.

1st row: k.
2nd row: cast off 1 st., k. to last 2 sts., k.2 tog. Cont. to dec. 1 st. at both ends of every alt. row until there are 2 sts. Cast off.

TO COMPLETE

Place 4 triangles to form a square, alternating the colours. Sew tog. on the wrong side. Stitch other 4 triangles tog. in a similar way. Place the 2 squares tog., right sides facing. Sew the bottom edges tog., then open bag out flat, and use as a pattern to cut out lining material. Add $\frac{1}{2}$ in. to all edges on lining for seam allowances. Sew up the side seams on the bag and the lining, leaving 2 in. of the seam unstitched at the top. Sew bag to the frame along the open edges and along the top. Place lining inside bag, wrong sides together, and trim remaining open edges to $\frac{1}{4}$ in., turn in and stitch lining neatly in place to inside of knitted fabric.

Opposite: *party tunic (see page 95).*
Below and right: *gold dress (see page 98).*

Gold dress
also illustrated in colour on page 97

MATERIALS
16 (17, 18) balls (50 gr. each) Lister Bel-Air Starspun 4-ply.
One pair each Nos. 12 and 13 knitting needles (USA sizes 1 and 0).

MEASUREMENTS
To fit bust size 34 (36, 38) in.; length 34½ (34¾, 35) in.; sleeve seam 18 in.

TENSION
8 sts. and 11 rows to 1 in. over st.st. with No. 12 needles.

ABBREVIATIONS
See page 46; m.b., make bobble: into next st. work k.1, y.f., k.1; turn; p. these 3 sts., turn; k.3; turn; p.3; turn; now slip 2nd st. of bobble over first st. and off needle then k. tog. t.b.l. rem. 2 sts.

BACK AND FRONT (make 2 pieces alike)
With No. 13 needles cast on 166 (174, 182) sts.
1st row: k.2, * p.1, k.1; rep. from * to end.
Rep. this row once. Now, beg. with a k. row, work in st.st. for 15 rows. K. next row to make a ridge on right side for hemline.
Change to No. 12 needles and, beg. with another k. row, cont. in st.st. Cont. straight until work measures 2½ in. from hemline.
Dec. 1 st. at each end of next row and every foll. 12th row until 138 (146, 154) sts. remain, then cont. straight until work measures 18 in. from hemline. Place marker loops of contrast yarn at each end of last row to indicate waistline. Cont. in st.st., inc. 1 st. at each end of row when work measures 20 in., 22 in. and 24 in. from hemline. Cont. on these 144 (152, 160) sts. until work measures 27 in. from hemline.

Shape Armholes
Cast off 5 sts. at beg. of next 4 rows and 5 (6, 7) sts. at beg. of next 4 rows.
Cont. straight on rem. 104 (108, 112) sts. until work measures 33 (33¼, 33½) in. from hemline, ending with a p. row.

Shape Neck and Shoulders
1st row: k.44 (46, 48) and leave these sts. on a st. holder, cast off 16, k. to end.
Cont. on last 44 (46, 48) sts. and work 1 row straight.
** Cast off 4 sts. at beg. of next row and 3 sts. at same (neck) edge on next 7 alt. rows. Cast off 8 sts. at armhole edge at beg. of next row and 3 sts. at neck edge on foll. row. Cast off rem. 8 (10, 12) sts. **
With wrong side facing rejoin yarn to inside edge of sts. on st. holder. Complete to match first side from ** to **.

SLEEVES (make 2 alike)
With No. 13 needles cast on 63 (67, 71) sts. Beg. with a k. row work 5 rows in st.st. K. next row to make hemline ridge.
Change to No. 12 needles and patt.
1st row: k.4, * m.b., k.3; rep. from * to last 3 sts., m.b., k.2.
2nd row: p., but pull the st. above each bobble fairly tightly to prevent bobble slipping through.
3rd row: k.2, * m.b., k.3; rep. from * to last st., k.1.
4th row: as 2nd row.
Now work in st.st., working next (5th) row straight, inc. 1 st. at each end of 6th row, then working 5 rows straight. Rep. last 6 rows twice more, then inc. 1 st. at each end of next row.

These 24 rows form 1 patt: 4 sts. inc. at each side.
Cont. to rep. these 24 rows until there are 111 (115, 119) sts. and 6th patt. is completed. Cont. in patt. without any incs. until work measures 18 in. from hemline. Place marker loops at each end to indicate end of sleeve seam.
Cont. in patt., work 28 (31, 34) rows straight.
Keeping patt. correct cast off 6 sts. at beg. of next 16 rows. Cast off 15 (19, 23) sts.

NECKBANDS (make 2 alike)
With No. 12 needles cast on 87 sts. Beg. with a k. row work 2 rows in st.st. Now work the first patt. row of Sleeves.
Change to No. 13 needles and work 2nd, 3rd and 4th patt. rows of Sleeves. Now p. the next row to make a ridge on right side. P. 1 more row, dec. 1 st. at end of row. Now work the rib row given at beg. of Back 5 times. Cast off ribwise.

BELT
With No. 13 needles cast on 8 sts. and rep. the rib row given at beg. of Back until strip measures 54 (56, 58) in. Cast off.

TO COMPLETE
Press st.st. sections on wrong side with cool iron. Join shoulder seams, using back st. for these and all seams. Press seams.
Sew cast-off edges of Sleeves to sides of armholes and straight rows of Sleeves above markers to armhole casting-off. Remove markers. Press seams.
Join side seams matching shapings and waistline markers, ending seam just below hemline ridge. Remove markers. Press seams.
Turn up hem to wrong side along the ridge and slip st. cast-on edge in place. At side seams catch the sides of hems in place next to the seams but do not sew them over seams.
Join sleeve seams matching patt. Turn up hems on Sleeves and slip st. in place.
Join ends of neckbands. With right sides together sew cast-on edge to neck edge. Press seam carefully using point of iron. Fold the last 6 rows inside and slip st. over first seam.

Evening suit
illustrated in colour on page 100

MATERIALS. For waistcoat: 6 (7, 7, 8) oz. Twilley's
Cortina Super Crochet Wool and 7 (7, 8, 9) oz. Twilley's
Goldfingering. One pair each No. 10 and No. 12 Knitting
needles (USA: sizes 3 and 1). **For skirt:** 8 (9, 10, 11) oz.
Twilley's Cortina Super Crochet and 8 (9, 10, 11) oz. Twilley's
Goldfingering. One pair each No. 10 and No. 12 knitting
needles (USA: sizes 3 and 1). ¾ yard elastic 1 in. wide.

MEASUREMENTS. to fit bust size 32 (34, 36, 38) in. and
hip size 34 (36, 38, 40) in.; length of Waistcoat 27 (27, 28,
28) in.; length of Skirt 30 in. (adjustable).

TENSION. 8 sts. and 11 rows to 1 in. with Goldfingering;
7 sts. and 10 rows to 1 in. with Cortina.

ABBREVIATIONS. See page 46; G., Goldfingering; C.,
Cortina.

WAISTCOAT BACK
With No. 12 needles and G. cast on 136 (144, 152, 160) sts.
Work 6 rows st.st., beg. with a p. row. K. 1 row for hemline.
Now work in patt.
** With No. 12 needles and G. work 6 rows in st.st. beg. with
a k. row.
With C. k. 1 row.
Change to No. 10 needles. With C. work 7 rows in reversed
st.st., beg. with a k. row.
Change to No. 12 needles. With G. work 6 rows in st.st., beg.
with a k. row.
With C. k. 1 row.
Change to No. 10 needles. With C. work 3 rows in reversed
st.st. beg. with a k. row. **
These 24 rows from ** to ** form patt. Cont. straight in patt.
until work measures 19 (19, 19½, 19½) in. from hemline.

Shape Armholes. Keeping patt. correct, cast off 10 (11, 12,
13) sts. at beg. of next 2 rows then dec. 1 st. at each end of
next 10 rows: 96 (102, 108, 114) sts. Cont. straight in patt.
until work measures 27 (27, 28, 28) in. from hemline.

Shape Shoulders. Cast off 8 (9, 10, 11) sts. at beg. of next
6 rows. Cast off.

RIGHT FRONT
With No. 12 needles and G. cast on 60 (64, 68, 72) sts. Work
as Back until Front measures 19 (19, 19½, 19½) in. from
hemline, ending with a right-side row.

Shape Armhole. Cast off 10 (11, 12, 13) sts. at beg. of next
row then dec. 1 st. at armhole edge on next 10 rows: 40 (43,
46, 49) sts. Cont. straight in patt. until work measures 25 (25,
26, 26) in. from hemline, ending with a wrong-side row.

Shape Neck. Cast off 8 sts. at beg. of next row then dec. 1 st.
at neck edge on next 8 rows: 24 (27, 30, 33) sts. Cont.
straight until work measures 27 (27, 28, 28) in. from hemline
ending at armhole edge.

Shape Shoulder. Cast off 8 (9, 10, 11) sts. at beg. of next
and foll. 2 alt. rows.

LEFT FRONT
Work as Right Front reversing all shapings.

TO COMPLETE
Press lightly. Join shoulder and side seams. Fold hem at lower
edge to wrong side and sew down. Press seams.

SKIRT
BACK AND FRONT (make 2 pieces alike)
With No. 12 needles and G. cast on 104 (112, 120, 128) sts.
Work 24 rows in patt. as for Waistcoat Back.
Next row: with No. 12 needles and G. k.8, * k. twice into
next st., k.7; rep. from * to end.
Work 47 rows straight in patt.
Next row: with No. 12 needles and G. k.8, * k. twice into
next st., k.8; rep. from * to end.
Work 47 rows in patt.
Next row: with No. 12 needles and G. k.8, * k. twice into
next st., k.9; rep. from * to end. Inc. in this way on first patt.
row of every alt. patt. until the 6th inc. row has been completed:
176 (190, 204, 218) sts.
Cont. straight in patt. until work measures 30 in. from beg.,
ending with 6 rows in G. (adjust length here if required).
With No. 12 needles and G. p. 1 row for hemline, then work
6 rows in st.st., beg. with a p. row. Cast off loosely purlwise.

TO COMPLETE
Press lightly. Join side seams. Fold hem at lower edge to
wrong side and sew down. Cut elastic to fit waist and join.
Place inside waist and work herringbone st. over it to hold it
in position. Press seams.

MEN
Sleeveless slip-on
illustrated in colour on page 101
MATERIALS
11 (12, 13) balls (25 gr. each) Patons Limelight Crêpe
4-ply. One pair each Nos. 13, 12 and 11 knitting
needles (USA sizes 0, 1 and 2). Seven medium-sized
buttons. Two small buttons. Two press studs.

MEASUREMENTS
To fit chest size 38 (40, 42) in.; length 25 (25¼, 25½) in.

TENSION
7½ sts. and 9½ rows to 1 in. over st.st. with No. 11 needles.

ABBREVIATIONS
See page 46; k. (or p.) 1 b., k. (or p.) into back of st.; m. 1,
make 1: pick up loop between st. just worked and foll. st.
and k. it t.b.l.

FEATHER PATT. (23 sts.)
1st row: p.2, k.1 b., k.17, k.1 b., p.2.
2nd row: p.2, p.1 b., p.17, p.1 b., p.2.
3rd row: p.2, k.1 b., (k.2 tog.) 3 times, (m.1, k.1),
5 times, m.1, (k.2 tog. t.b.l.) 3 times, k.1 b., p.2.
4th row: p.2, p.1 b., p.17, p.1 b., p.2.

continued on page 102

Elegant evening suit in plain and glitter yarns (see page 99)

Sleeveless slip-on (see page 99)

POCKETS (make 2 alike)

With No. 12 needles cast on 37 (39, 41) sts. Work in st.st. for 5 in. Leave sts. on a st. holder.

FRONT

With No. 13 needles cast on 151 (159, 167) sts. K. 8 rows. Change to No. 11 needles and work in st.st. until front measures 6½ in. from cast-on edge, ending with a p. row.

Place Pockets

Next row: k.18 (19, 20), k. next 37 (39, 41) sts. on to st. holder, k.41 (43, 45), k. next 37 (39, 41) sts. on to st. holder, k.18 (19, 20).

Next row: p.18 (19, 20), slip 37 (39, 41) sts. of one pocket to left-hand needle, p.37 (39, 41), p.17 (18, 19), cast off 7, p.17 (18, 19) including st. used in casting off, slip 37 (39, 41) sts. from 2nd pocket on to left-hand needle, p. to end.

Work on first group of 72 (76, 80) sts. only.

1st row: k.25 (27, 29), work first row of feather patt. over next 23 sts., k.24 (26, 28).

2nd row: k.1, p.23 (25, 27), work 2nd row of feather patt., p.25 (27, 29).

3rd and 4th rows: keeping feather patt. correct as 3rd and 4th rows work rem. as first and 2nd rows.

These 4 rows form patt.

Cont. straight in patt. until work measures 16 in. from beg., ending with a wrong-side row.

Shape Armhole

Cast off 7 (8, 9) sts. at beg. of next row, 3 sts. at beg. of foll. alt. row, then 2 sts. at beg. of foll. alt. row. Now dec. 1 st. at armhole edge on every alt. row until 55 (58, 61) sts. remain. Cont. on these sts. until armhole measures 5 (5¼, 5½) in. ending at inside edge.

Shape Neck

Cast off 9 (10, 11) sts. at beg. of next row, then dec. 1 st. at neck edge on every alt. row until 39 (41, 43) sts. remain.

Cont. on these sts. until armhole measures 8 (8¼, 8½) in. ending at armhole edge.

Change to No. 13 needles.

Shape Shoulder

1st row: cast off 13 (13, 14), patt. to end.
2nd and 4th rows: patt. to end.
3rd row: cast off 13 (14, 14), patt. to end.
Cast off rem. sts.

Pocket Top

Slip the 37 (39, 41) sts. from st. holder on to No. 13 needle with right side facing. K. 4 rows.

Next row: k.18 (19, 20), y.f., k.2 tog., k.17 (18, 19). K. 3 rows. Cast off.

Slip the 2nd set of 72 (76, 80) sts. on to No. 11 needle with point at inside edge.

1st row: k.24 (26, 28), work first row of feather patt. over next 23 sts., k.25 (27, 29).

2nd row: p.25 (27, 29), work 2nd row of feather patt., p.23 (25, 27), k.1.

3rd and 4th rows: keeping feather patt. correct as 3rd and 4th rows work rem. as first and 2nd rows.

Complete to match first half reversing all shapings.

LEFT FRONT BAND

With No. 13 needles cast on 10 sts. K.14 (16, 18) rows.
1st row: k.4, cast off 2, k. to end.
2nd row: k.4, cast on 2, k.4.
3rd to 24th rows: k.
Rep first to 24th rows 4 times more, then work first to 20th rows again.
Leave sts. on st. holder.

RIGHT FRONT BAND

With No. 13 needles cast on 10 sts. K. 154 (156, 158) rows. Leave sts. on st. holder.

BACK

With No. 13 needles cast on 151 (159, 167) sts. K. 8 rows. Change to No. 11 needles and work in st.st. until Back matches Front to beg. of armholes.

Shape Armholes

Cast off 7 (8, 9) sts. at beg. of next 2 rows, 3 sts. at beg. of next 2 rows, 2 sts. at beg. of next 2 rows. Then dec. 1 st. at each end of every alt. row until 117 (123, 129) sts. remain. Cont. on these sts. until work matches Front to beg. of shoulders.
Change to No. 13 needles.

Shape Shoulders

1st and 2nd rows: cast off 13 (13, 14), patt. to end.
3rd and 4th rows: cast off 13 (14, 14), patt. to end.
5th and 6th rows: cast off 13 (14, 15), patt. to end.
Cast off.

TO COMPLETE
Armbands

Join shoulders. With No. 13 needles pick up and k. 173 (179, 185) sts. round one armhole. Work 12 rows in k.1, p.1 rib. Cast off.
Work round other armhole in same way.

Neckband

Slip 10 sts. from top of Right Front Band on to No. 13 needle with point at outside edge, rejoin yarn and k. 10 sts. of band, then with same needle pick up and k. 109 (115, 121) sts. round neck, then slip sts. from top of Left Front Band on to left-hand needle with point to end of last row and k.10 sts. of band.

1st row: k.10, * p.1, k.1; rep. from * to last 11 sts., p.1, k.10.

2nd row: k.11, * p.1, k.1; rep. from * to last 10 sts., k.10.

3rd and 4th rows: as first and 2nd rows.

5th row: k.4, cast off 2, k.4, p.1, rib to last 11 sts., p.1, k.10.

6th row: k.11, * p.1, k.1; rep. from * to last 4 sts. before buttonhole, k.4, cast on 2, k.4.

7th to 11th rows: rep. first and 2nd rows twice, then first row again.
Cast off in rib.

To Make Up

Omitting ribbing block and press on wrong side using warm iron and dry cloth. St. pockets down on wrong side and pocket tops on right side. St. front bands in position; now st. ends of Left Front Band over Right Front Band, then st. to 7 cast-off sts. at centre Front. Join side seams and ends of armbands.
Sew medium-sized buttons on Right Front Band to match buttonholes. Sew 2 press studs at top of bands. Sew small buttons to match buttonholes on top of pockets. Lightly press seams.

Man's Aran sweater

illustrated in colour on page 104

MATERIALS. 18 (19, 21, 22) 50-gram balls of Mahony's Blarney Bainin (USA: Blarneyspun) wool. One pair each Nos. 7, 9 and 10 knitting needles (USA: sizes 7, 5 and 3). A cable needle.

MEASUREMENTS. To fit chest size 36/38 (39/41, 42/44, 45/47) in.; sleeve seam 19 (19½, 20, 20) in.; centre back length 26 (27, 28, 29) in.

TENSION. One patt. of 12 sts. over small size patt. measures 2 in.; 7½ rows to 1 in. over patt.

ABBREVIATIONS. See page 46; C.4 B. (or C.4 F.), cable 4 back (or front) thus — slip next 2 sts. on to cable needle, leave at back (or front) of work, k.2, then k.2 from cable needle; k.f.b. (or p.f.b.), knit (or purl) into front and back of next st.

BACK
With No. 10 needles cast on 93 (101, 109, 117) sts.
Work in rib.
1st row (right side): k.2, * p.1, k.1; rep. from * to last st., k.1.
2nd row: k.1, * p.1, k.1; rep. from * to end.
Rep. these 2 rows 6 times more, then the first row again.
Inc. row (wrong side): k.3, * p.3, p.f.b., p.3, k.1 (1, 2, 2), k.f.b., k.1 (2, 2, 3); rep. from * to last 10 sts., p.3, p.f.b., p.3, k.3: 110 (118, 126, 134) sts.
Change to No. 7 needles and patt.
1st row: k.2, * p.1, k.8, p.1, k.2 (3, 4, 5); rep. from * to last 12 sts., p.1, k.8, p.1, k.2.
2nd row: k.3, * p.8, k.4 (5, 6, 7); rep. from * to last 11 sts., p.8, k.3.
Rep. these 2 rows once.
5th row: k.2, * p.1, C.4 B., C.4 F., p.1, k.2 (3, 4, 5); rep. from * to last 12 sts., p.1, C.4 B., C.4 F., p.1, k.2.
6th row: as 2nd.
Rep. first and 2nd rows once.
9th row: as 5th.
10th row: as 2nd.
Rep. first and 2nd rows twice.
15th row: k.2, * p.1, C.4 F., C.4 B., p.1, k.2 (3, 4, 5); rep. from * to last 12 sts., p.1, C.4 F., C.4 B., p.1, k.2.
16th row: as 2nd.
Rep. first and 2nd rows once.
19th row: as 15th.
20th row: as 2nd.
These 20 rows form one patt. Continue in patt. but inc. 1 st. at both ends of row when work measures 7 in. and 11 in. from beg., keeping extra sts. at sides in g.st. Continue on these 114 (122, 130, 138) sts. without shaping until work measures 17½ (18, 18½, 19) in. from beg.

Armhole Shaping. Cast off 4 (5, 6, 7) sts. at beg. of next 4 rows and 4 sts. at beg. of next 2 rows: 90 (94, 98, 102) sts. remain. Continue in patt. with 4 (3, 2, 1) sts. in g.st. at each end of row, until work measures 25 (26, 27, 28) in. from beg., ending with a wrong-side row.

Shoulder and Neck Shaping. 1st row: cast off 5 (6, 7, 8), patt. until there are 33 sts. on right-hand needle, leave these sts. on a spare needle for right back, continue along row, cast off 14 (16, 18, 20) sts., then patt. to end. Continue on the 38 (39, 40, 41) sts. now remaining on needle for left back.
2nd row: cast off 5 (6, 7, 8), patt. back to neck edge.
** **3rd row:** cast off 4, patt. to end.

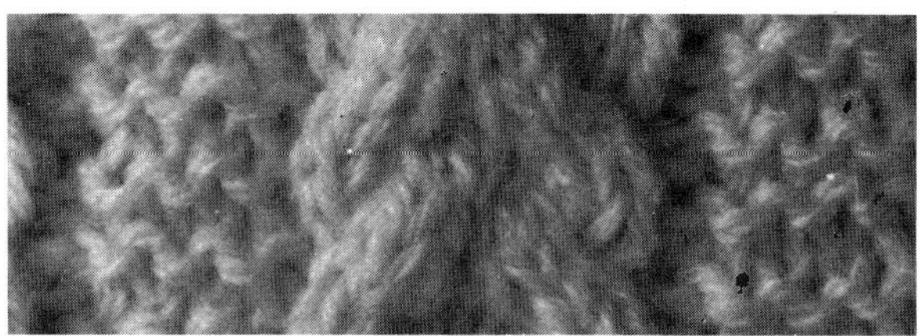

4th row: cast off 7, patt. back to neck edge. Rep. last 2 rows once, then 3rd row again. Cast off remaining 7 sts. **
With wrong side facing, rejoin wool to inner edge of right back sts. Complete as given for left back from ** to **.

FRONT
Work as given for back until you have worked 10 rows less than on back to start of neck shaping, thus ending with a wrong-side row.
Neck and Shoulder Shaping. 1st row: patt. 40 (41, 42, 43) and leave these sts. on a spare needle for left front, continue along row, cast off 10 (12, 14, 16) sts., then patt. to end. Continue on the 40 (41, 42, 43) sts. now remaining on needle for right front and work 1 row straight. *** Cast off 3 sts. at beg. of next row, then dec. 1 st. at same edge on next 8 rows. Now cast off for shoulders 5 (6, 7, 8) sts. at beg. of next row, then dec. 1 st. at neck edge on following row. Cast off 7 sts. at beg. of next row and dec. 1 st. at neck edge on following row. Rep. last 2 rows once. Cast off remaining 7 sts. *** With wrong side facing, rejoin wool to inner edge of left front sts. Complete as for right front from *** to ***.

SLEEVES (make 2 alike)
With No. 10 needles cast on 53 (57, 61, 65) sts. and work first 16 rows exactly as for back; when the inc. row has been worked you will have 62 (66, 70, 74) sts.
Change to No. 7 needles and work in patt. as given for back but when first patt. is completed, inc. 1 st. at both ends of first, 7th and 14th rows of every patt. until there are 88 (94, 100, 106) sts. taking extra sts. into patt. When all incs. are completed you will have 3 sts. in g.st. at each end. Continue without shaping until work measures 19 (19½, 20, 20) in. from beg. Place marker loops of contrast wool at each end of last row, then work 16 (19, 21, 24) rows straight.

To Shape Top. Cast off 4 sts. at beg. of next 4 rows and 4 (5, 6, 7) sts. at beg. of next 2 rows. Rep. last 6 rows once. Cast off 6 sts. at beg. of next 2 rows and 6 (7, 8, 9) sts. at beg. of next 2 rows: 16 sts. remain for all sizes. Continue on these sts. in patt. with the cable in centre and 3 sts. in g.st. at each edge until this strip is long enough to fit along front shoulder edge. Cast off.

NECKBAND
With No. 9 needles cast on 127 (131, 135, 139) sts. and work in rib as on welt for 4 rows. Change to No. 10 needles and work 8 rows. Change back to No. 9 needles and work 4 rows. Cast off ribwise.

TO COMPLETE
Do not press. First pin sleeves in place matching markers to beg. of armhole casting-off, pinning straight rows of sleeves above markers to armhole casting-off, shaped edges of sleeves to sides of armholes and sides of extension strip to shoulder edges. The cast-off edge of extension strips forms part of neckline. Remove markers and sew sleeves in place backstitching these and all seams. Press seams lightly on wrong side with warm iron and damp cloth taking care not to stretch patt. Join side and sleeve seams and press. Join ends of neckband. With right sides together and join level with left back shoulder seam, sew cast-on edge of neckband to neck edges, easing in neckline to fit band. Press seam using point of iron so as not to flatten rib. Fold band in half to inside and slip-st. cast-off edge to previous seam.

Aran knitwear is a winner with men who enjoy the outdoor life. Pattern for sweater (left) is on page 103.

CROCHET

Crochet is easy to learn, quick to do and instantly effective for all manner of exciting designs – not only in its traditional form for fine lace edgings and insertions, but for top-fashion outfits and accessories, clothes for babies and children, and for elegant household furnishings too.

The technique which is based on a single stitch is extremely simple, although sometimes learning to hold and control the crochet hook is not so easy for a beginner. Once this has been mastered however, you can go on to work the limitless fascinating pattern variations of the single basic stitch.

Part 1—General

BASIC EQUIPMENT

A crochet hook and a ball of yarn are all you need to begin to crochet, but you will find it useful also to have a tape measure for measuring your work as you go along (ideally, one marked with inches and centimetres), good-quality, rustless pins for pinning the finished work out to the correct size, plus an iron, ironing board and cloth for pressing the completed item, and a sewing needle for making it up.

Crochet hooks

Hooks are available in many sizes from very thin to quite thick. The thin ones are used with fine cotton yarn, the thick with heavy wools or synthetics. In the system of sizing called International Standard Sizing the higher the size number the thicker the hook (see chart below). Hooks are available in steel, aluminium, bone or plastic; steel hooks are generally used for work with fine cotton yarns, and aluminium, plastic or bone for work with other yarns.

Although a pattern normally recommends a particular size of hook, it is important not necessarily to use this hook size, but to use the one with which you can achieve the correct tension as quoted in the pattern (see page 115).

Throughout the patterns in this book, the International Standard Sizing of hooks has been used; if it is wished to convert these sizes into other size ranges, please refer to the chart below.

International Standard Size	Old UK Sizes		American Sizes	
	Wool	Cotton	Wool	Cotton
7.00	2	—	K	—
—	3	—	—	—
6.00	4	—	—	—
5.50	5	—	—	—
5.00	6	—	J	—
4.50	7	—	I	—
4.00	8	—	H	—
3.50	9	—	G	—
3.00	10	3/0	F	2/0
—	11	2/0	E	0
2.50	12	0	D	1
—	13	1	C	2
—	—	—	—	3
2.00	14	$1\frac{1}{2}$	B	4
—	—	2	A	5
1.75	15	$2\frac{1}{2}$	—	6
—	—	3	—	6
1.50	16	$3\frac{1}{2}$	—	7
—	—	4	—	8
1.25	—	$4\frac{1}{2}$	—	9
—	—	5	—	10
1.00	—	$5\frac{1}{2}$	—	11
—	—	6	—	12
0.75	—	$6\frac{1}{2}$	—	13
0.60	—	7	—	14
—	—	$7\frac{1}{2}$	—	—

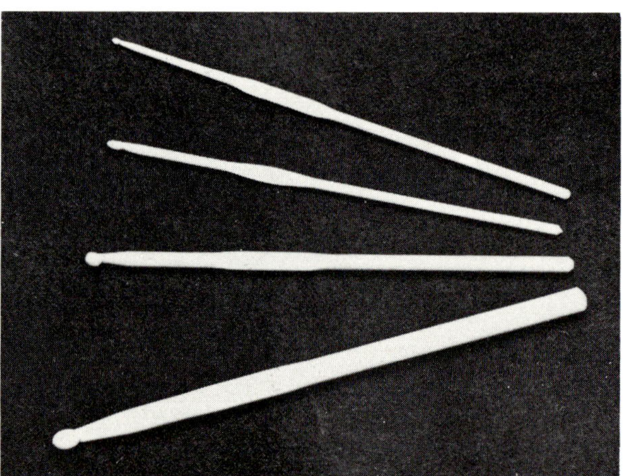

Yarns

Traditionally very fine thread – usually cotton – is used for crochet trimmings and laces, but now that so many other items can be successfully crocheted, wool and synthetic yarns and mixtures can all be used as well. In fact the extensive range of yarn types, thicknesses and colours available for knitting can be used with equal success for crochet work. The choice of yarn is, of course, dependent on the article being made, and the amount of wear it will have to withstand.

HOLDING YOUR HOOK AND YARN

There is no hard and fast rule about the correct way to hold your crochet hook, and manipulate the yarn – really the ideal position is the one in which you feel comfortable, and you can produce even, regular work smoothly and quickly. The following method however is the one generally recommended: pass the yarn round the little finger of the left hand, under the middle two fingers then over the first finger. The hook is held in the right hand; it rests between thumb and first finger rather like holding a pencil, with the second finger on the tip of the hook. Initially the loose end of the yarn is held tight between thumb and first finger of the left hand. When work begins, the work is held by the left hand between thumb and first finger. The left hand also controls the yarn from the main ball while the right hand moves the hook.

Left-handed workers will work in reverse, holding the hook in the left hand and controlling yarn with the right hand. The easiest way for left-handed workers to follow diagrams intended for right-handed workers is to place a pocket mirror at right angles to the diagrams, and to follow the mirror-reflected diagrams. There is available a simple but clever gadget called a crochet tension

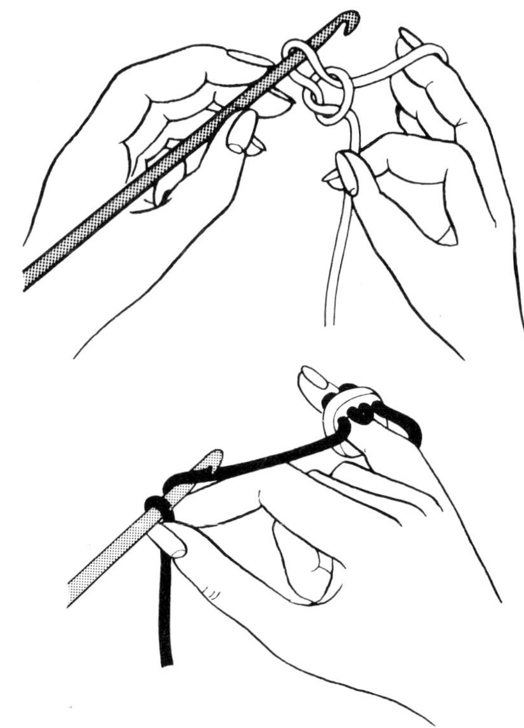

ring which is intended to help not only left-handed workers, but also arthritic and disabled people who are anxious to crochet but find difficulty in controlling the yarn. The tension ring is slipped over the little finger, and then the yarn is fed through the ring, so an even and regular tension is automatically maintained.

STITCHES
Chain

This is the foundation of all crochet work, and for this reason it is often called 'foundation chain', though this stitch is also used at other times in the course of a pattern.

When making foundation chain you must start with a slip loop. To make a slip loop, undo a short length of yarn from the ball. Hold yarn between

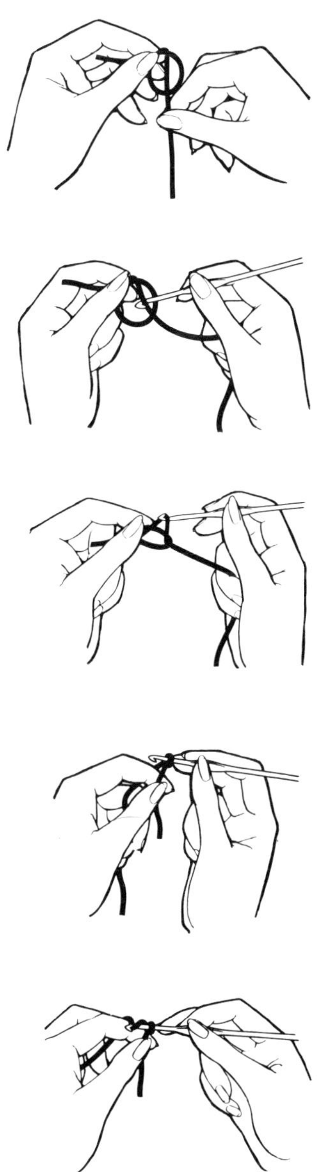

thumb and first finger of left hand and take yarn from ball in the right hand; cross main yarn from ball over short length to make a loop then hold this loop firmly in the left hand. Take crochet hook in right hand and insert it into loop and with it pull through the main yarn so a loop forms on the hook. Pull short length of yarn to tighten loop on hook.

Crochet stitches vary enormously—compare the looped bolero and hat **(above)** _with the more traditional coffee table-cloth_ **(opposite).**

You are now ready to work your commencing chain – chain used as part of a pattern are worked in a similar way. Holding the short end of the yarn and the bottom of the slip loop between your left thumb and first finger, and yarn and hook in correct positions, take the hook under the yarn on the left hand first finger and pull the yarn and the hook through the loop on the hook. You have now worked one chain.

The action of taking the hook under the yarn is called 'yarn over hook'. Continue making chain in this way until you have the number you want. Move your first finger and thumb of left hand up the chain as you work so you are always holding the chain just made.

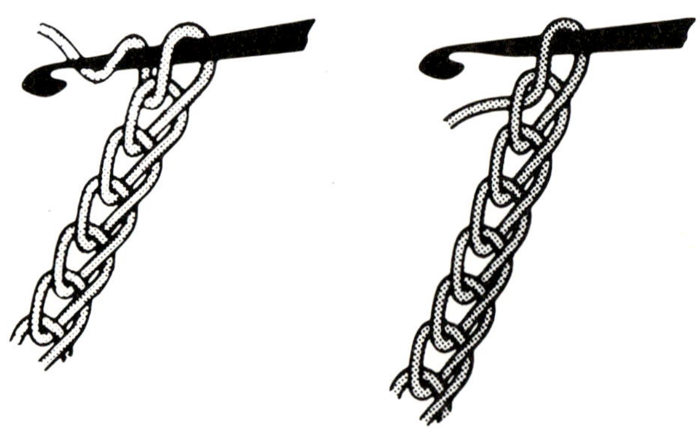

Slip stitch or single crochet

This stitch adds no height to the work, so can be
used to take yarn across the work to another
point, for joining or for making an edge firm. Work
from right to left across foundation chain. Insert
hook under top two loops of next chain (or stitch
when working into a row of stitches instead of the
foundation chain), yarn over hook and pull yarn
through the chain stitch and through the loop on
the hook. Insert hook into next stitch and repeat;
continue in this way along row.

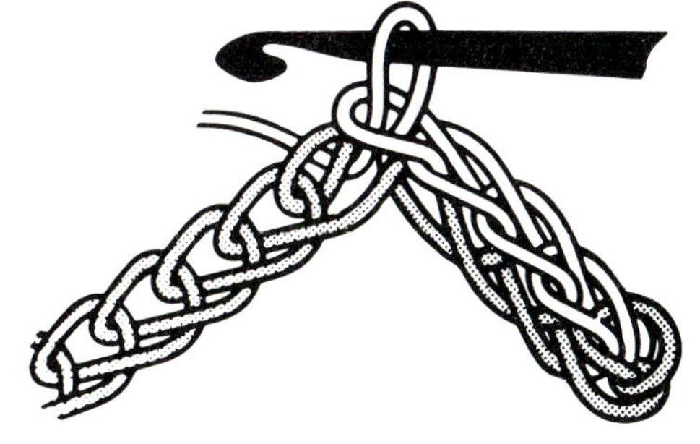

Double crochet

Insert hook into chain or stitch through top two loops, **yarn** over hook and draw through the stitch. This makes two loops on the hook. Take yarn over the hook again and draw through the two loops on the hook. Continue in this way along row.

Double crochet worked to give a dense, interlocked fabric.

Half treble

Take yarn over hook then insert hook into next stitch. Yarn over hook again and pull a loop through the stitch – three loops on the hook. Pass yarn over hook again and draw yarn through all three loops. Work along row in this way.

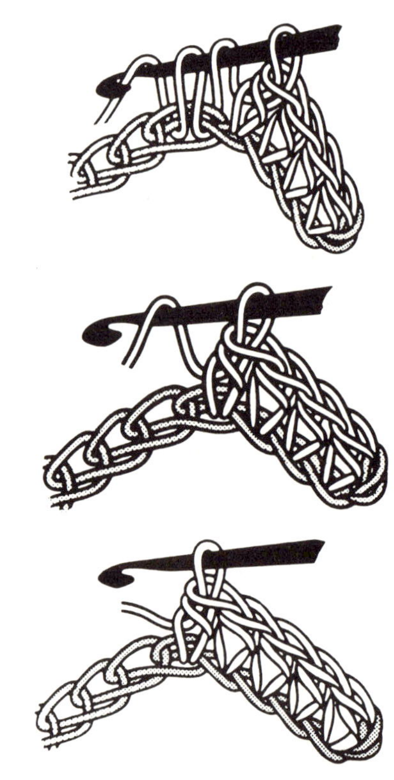

Treble

Pass yarn over hook then insert hook into next stitch. Yarn over hook and draw through stitch – three loops on hook. Yarn over hook again and draw through the first two loops on the hook. Yarn over hook once more and draw through remaining two loops on hook. Continue in this way along row.

work another cluster, and continue along row in this way. On the next row work the clusters into the chain spaces of previous row.

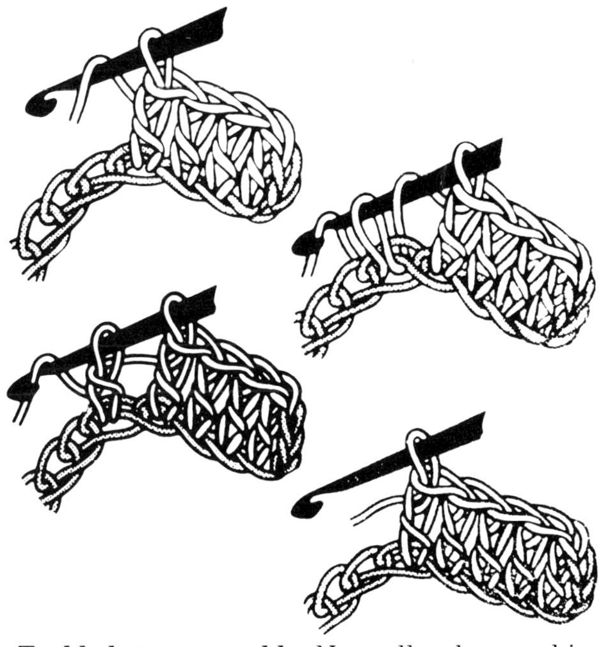

Example of a treble cluster pattern.

Treble between treble. Normally when working in a treble pattern, each consecutive row of stitches is worked into the top of the stitches of the previous row. To produce a denser fabric, the pattern can be varied by working each row of trebles into the spaces between the trebles worked in the previous row.

Shell patterns. This is another traditional stitch pattern which is a combination of double crochets and trebles. Working into foundation chain, miss two chain, work one double crochet into the next chain, miss two chain, work five trebles into the next chain, and continue in this way to end of row. On next row, work the double crochet stitches into the centre trebles of the shells, and work the shells into the double crochet stitches.

Example of treble between treble pattern.

Clusters or groups. This stitch variation is usually worked in trebles. If you are working into foundation chain, leaving last loop of each on hook, work three trebles into one chain (four loops on hook), yarn over hook and draw through all loops on hook, one chain, miss one chain,

Above: two shell pattern variations.

Crochet caters for the conventionally fashionable

—or the more exotic tastes.

Double treble
(also sometimes called a long treble)

Take yarn over hook twice, then insert hook into next stitch. Yarn over hook and draw a loop through the stitch – four loops on hook. Yarn over hook and draw through two loops, yarn over hook again and draw through a further two loops, yarn over hook once more and draw through last two loops. Continue in this way all along row.

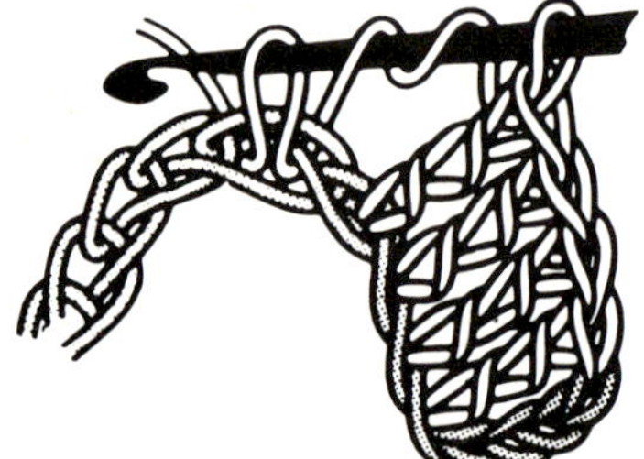

Triple treble

Yarn over hook three times, insert hook into next stitch, yarn over hook and draw through a loop – five loops on the hook. Yarn over hook and draw through two loops on the hook, yarn over hook and draw through two more loops on hook, yarn over hook and draw through two more loops, yarn over hook and draw through last two loops. Continue in this way along row.

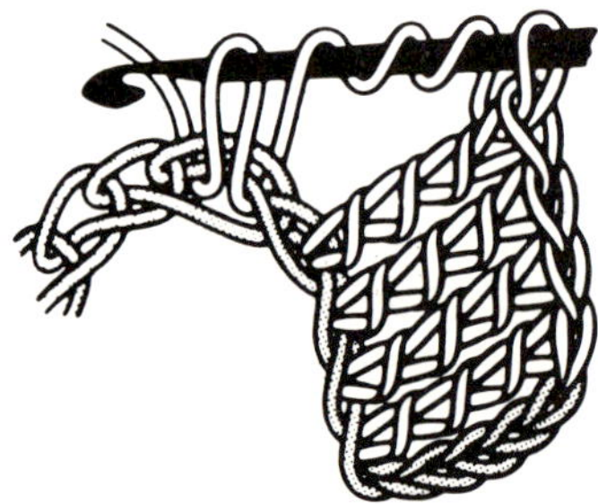

Quadruple treble

Yarn over hook four times, and complete as for triple treble until only one loop remains.

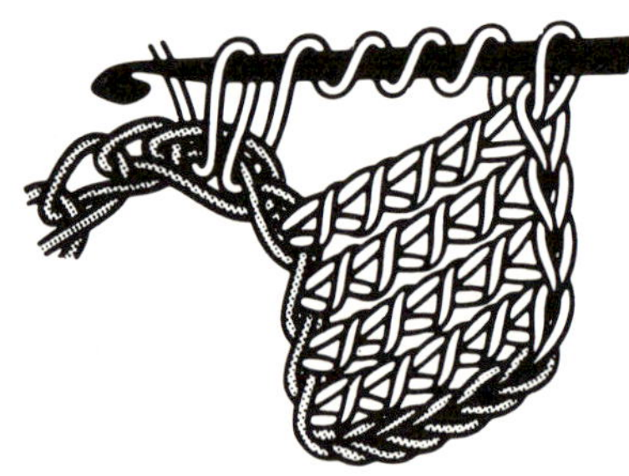

TURNING CHAIN

As crochet stitches are worked from the top down, when crocheting in rows a new row cannot start until the yarn has been taken up to the correct height to begin the new row. To do this, a number of chain stitches are worked and these chain count as the first stitch in the row. At the end of the following row, the last stitch is worked into the top of these 'turning chain' as they are called. The number of turning chain worked will depend on the depth of the stitch being used in the pattern. Most patterns will tell you how many chain to work, but as a general guide work two chain for a double crochet stitch or a half treble, three chain for a treble stitch, four chain for a double treble, and five chain for a triple treble.

INCREASING

The most usual method of increasing is to work two stitches into the same stitch of the previous row – or more if this is required. If extra stitches are required at the edge of the work, a length of chain can be made at the end of a row and these chain stitches worked into on the following row.

DECREASING

If several stitches are to be decreased at the edge of the work, this can be done in the following way: at the beginning of a row work slip stitches over the number of stitches you want decreased; at the end of a row stop working the required number of stitches before the end, turn and work next row. In some patterns, decreases can be made merely by missing a stitch, but a more successful method is to work two stitches together.

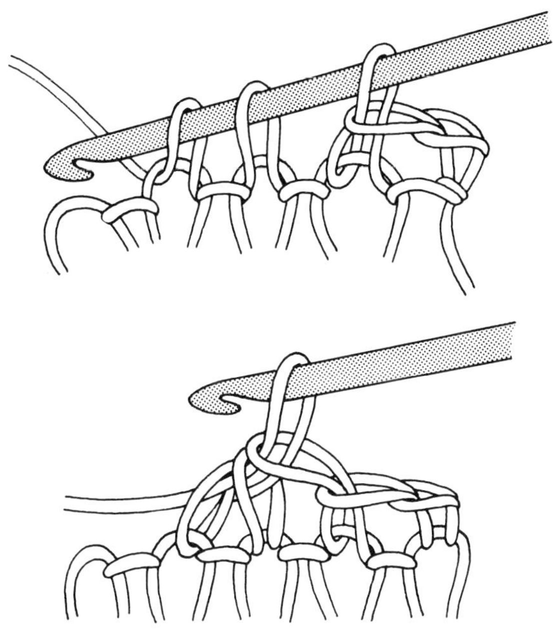

Work the first stitch in the usual way but leave the last loop of it on the hook (so there are two loops on hook); move on to next stitch and work this but leave the last loop on the hook. Take yarn over hook and draw through the last three loops on the hook.

FASTENING OFF

When your piece of work is complete – or if you are changing the colour of your yarn, or for some other reason want to fasten off – cut the yarn a few inches from the work. Pull this end through the last loop on the hook and draw tightly. Darn this loose end in later.

TENSION

The tension is the number of stitches and rows which measure one square inch for a particular pattern. In order to make an item of the correct finished size, you must work to the tension measurement given – e.g. if a pattern gives a tension of 6 rows and 8 stitches to the square inch, then you must make sure that your work achieves exactly this measurement, being neither slacker nor tighter. Before starting work on any pattern, check your tension by working a 3 or 4-in. square in the stitch pattern, yarn and hook size given in the pattern. Press the square then mark off on it with pins a 2-in. square. Count the number of stitches and rows contained in this square and compare them with the tension measurement given in the pattern. If they are more than those given, work another square with a hook a size larger; if they are fewer try again with a hook a size smaller. Continue to make tension checks until you achieve exactly the right measurement. Do not ever start work on a pattern until you have found the right hook to give you the correct tension measurement.

JOINING YARN

When your ball of yarn is running out, take the new ball and lay the end of it on top of your work. Crochet over this with the last of the old ball for a few stitches, then lay the end of the old ball over the top of the work and crochet over it with the new ball.

EDGINGS

A crochet edging worked round neck, sleeve and hem edges of a completed garment will give a decorative and neat finish not only to a crocheted garment but a knitted one as well. Simply work round the edge picking up stitches evenly through the loops of the last row of knitting or crochet worked on the garment (usually double crochet is used for this foundation row), then work in any crochet pattern as wished. Two or three rows of double crochet give a neat, plain border. For a more decorative border try a picot edging, as follows:

Work a foundation row of double crochet all round edge.

Next row or round: slip stitch to the required position for picot, then make four chain, and work a slip stitch into the fourth chain from the hook: a picot made. Slip stitch across stitches of previous row to required position for next picot, then repeat the picot.

A scalloped edging can be produced by working shell pattern round the edge. Work a foundation row of double crochet, as for picot edging. On the next row, work one slip stitch, then miss two stitches and work five treble all into the next stitch, miss two stitches, work a slip stitch into the next stitch. Continue in this way all round edge.

Crab stitch

This is double crochet worked from left to right. It makes a good edging, particularly for a jacket or similar item.

Keeping in trim—pom-pons are added to tot's dress **(above)** *while flower motifs give the finishing touch to the tank top* **(opposite).** See Motif Crochet *on page 118.*

BUTTONHOLES

It is usual for buttonholes to be worked in a double crochet edging. Sometimes however a buttonhole will occur in the main body of a design, and in this case instructions are usually given in full within the pattern.

The principle of working buttonholes in crochet is fairly simple: work in pattern to the point where the buttonhole is required, then work a number of chain, and do not work into this same number of stitches on the previous row – i.e. if you work five chain, then miss five stitches, and resume pattern in the sixth stitch. Continue working into stitches of previous row in pattern until the next button-hole position is reached; work the same number of chain as before, and miss the equivalent number of stitches. Continue in this way. On the subsequent row work in pattern across all stitches, including the chain stitches worked for the buttonholes. A short opening is thus formed in the work. The number of chain stitches worked will depend on the size of buttons being used.

WORKING WITH MORE THAN ONE COLOUR

Colour work in crochet is considerably easier than it is in knitting chiefly because the nature of crochet, where you work with only one stitch on the hook at a time, allows new colours to be easily joined in at the beginning of rows or rounds. If you are working in a simple regular stripe pattern (equal number of rows of each colour) then just carry the two colours of yarn up the sides of the work without breaking off the yarn. Loosely wind the two colours round each other when changing colours.

However if you are working in an irregular colour pattern where only occasional rows of a contrast colour are used then it is probably easier just to join in the contrast colour where required and break it off again at the end of the row. The loose ends can be darned into the seams afterwards when the garment is made up.

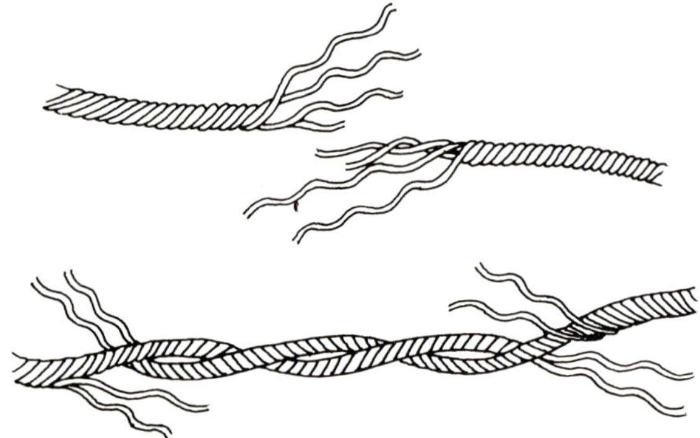

The same principle can be used when working in rounds. To work a multi-coloured square motif for instance, a different coloured yarn can be used for each round. If you wish to change colours in mid-round then splicing is the best joining method to use: to do this, untwist a few inches of yarn from the two ends, cut away half the strands from each and overlaying the remaining strands in opposite directions, twist them together until they hold – the twisted yarn should thus be equivalent to the original thickness. Any loose ends can be trimmed away on the wrong side of work afterwards.

MOTIF CROCHET

The nature of the crochet technique in which it is easy to begin at a centre point and work round and round this central point, increasing stitches with each successive round, makes it particularly suitable for motif work. All sorts of motifs in plain or multiple colours can be quickly and easily worked, including not only plain squares but circles, stars and flower shapes as well. Also as only oddments of yarn are needed for each motif this is a good way to use up left-over yarns, and as motifs are easily portable this is an ideal form of crochet to take with you to do on a train or car journey. Save the assembling of multiple motifs into garments, blankets, pram covers, handbags, shawls, cushions covers or whatever you wish until later when you are home by your own fireside.

If you find a motif pattern which you particularly like, then it can be varied by working it in entirely different yarns and hook sizes – worked in fine cotton on a fine hook, for instance, will produce a small delicate lacy motif, suitable for a table runner, or edging for a party dress. The same motif worked in a chunky wool with a thick hook, will be totally different in size, texture and character – use it for a winter scarf or pullover, a cot blanket, or a handbag.

Several motif patterns are given in the stitch pattern dictionary, starting on page 123—experiment with one or two of these, trying out different yarns and hook sizes to see the variety of effects which can be produced.

Joining motifs

Motifs may be either sewn together or crocheted together to form the finished design required.

To sew them together, place motifs together right sides facing, and using a large blunt-ended darning needle and thread to match the yarn used for the crochet (ideally use the same yarn, or a strand of it – if it is too thick to thread on to the darning needle, use a sewing thread in a colour as close as possible to the yarn colour), work overcasting stitches fairly loosely along the two edges.

To crochet motifs together, place motifs together right sides facing, and then insert hook into the loop at the edge of one motif and then into the corresponding loop on the other motif. Make a slip stitch with both stitches at once. Continue in this way along the edge.

FILET CROCHET

This is a traditional form of lace-work crochet in which designs are formed from a series of solid squares, produced by working blocks of trebles, and open areas, made by working individual trebles and chains. The resulting fabric is similar to net, and is suitable for all sorts of household furnishings, including tablecloths and curtains. Patterns are often given in the form of charts, one square on the chart representing one stitch in your work – the open or blank squares usually represent the spaces, the solid or black squares are the blocks.

To work the spaces in filet crochet

Work two chain, miss two stitches, one treble into next stitch.

Blocks and spaces

Work one treble into each of next four stitches, two chain, miss two stitches, one treble into next stitch, one treble into each of next three stitches.

Bars and lacet

A bar consists of five chain, miss five stitches or a lacet, one treble into next stitch. A lacet consists of three chain, miss two stitches, one double crochet into next stitch, three chain, miss two stitches, one treble into next stitch.

MAKING UP YOUR GARMENTS

When you have finished crocheting the individual parts of a garment or household design, they then have to be sewn together to make the complete item. First the individual pieces should be pressed: if specific instructions are given in the pattern, follow these as different yarns require different treatments. Wool is usually pressed with a warm iron over a damp cloth; synthetics with a cool iron over a dry cloth. Before pressing, pin out each piece of work to its correct measurements, with the wrong side up, then press in the appropriate way. Sew in any loose ends of yarn, and join seams using a large-eyed needle threaded with the same yarn as used for the crochet (or a strand of it). Use a backstitch seam to join side, sleeve and shoulder seams, an overcasting stitch to join edgings or trimmings to the main work.

AFTER-CARE

Never allow a crocheted garment to get too dirty. Careful washing does not damage any fabric but when a garment is very soiled, normal use of washing agents will not remove all the dirt without rubbing and it is this rubbing which causes damage to the fibres.
Make sure the washing agent, whether it is soap, soap flakes, soap powder or a detergent, is thoroughly dissolved in hot water, and then add cold water to reduce the temperature before placing the garment in the solution. Always make sure that enough washing water is prepared to cover the garment completely. Never boil a crocheted garment. The water temperature should be about 40 deg. C (104 deg. F.), just hot enough for your hand. Do not use any form of bleach.
Allow the washing agent to remove the dirt. Do not rub the fabric. Gently ease the fabric in the washing water, but do not lift the garment in and out of the water as this causes stretching. All fabrics are more easily harmed or distorted when wet than in a dry state.
Take the garment from the washing water and gently squeeze to remove as much of the water as possible. Rinse the garment in at least three changes of warm water. The third rinsing water should be quite clear after rinsing the garment in it. If it is not, it means that there is still some soap or detergent in the garment and another rinse is needed until the water is absolutely clear. Gently squeeze the garment on removing it from the final rinse and roll it in a clean dry white towel without twisting. This will absorb most of the excess moisture. Spread the garment out flat on a clean towel and ease it into the correct shape and size. Allow it to dry slowly in the shade or in an airing cupboard.
Items worked in fine crochet cotton should be carefully pinned out to shape when half-dry – place a piece of paper, either plain white or squared, on top of a clean, flat board. Following the correct measurements as given in the pattern, draw the shape of the finished article on to the paper. Using rustless pins, pin the crochet out to the pencilled shape, taking care not to strain the crochet. Pin out the general shape first, then finish by pinning each picot, loop or space into position.
If a slight stiffening is required, use a solution of starch (one dessertspoon to one pint of hot water), and dab lightly over the article. Raise the crochet up off the paper to prevent it sticking as it dries. When completely dry, remove the pins and press the article lightly with a hot iron.

TUNISIAN CROCHET

This technique – also known as tricot crochet, and sometimes as crochet-knitting – is in a way a combination of knitting and crochet. It is worked on a special Tunisian crochet hook which looks like a knitting needle with a knob at one end, but the other end instead of being pointed like a normal knitting needle is hooked like a crochet hook.

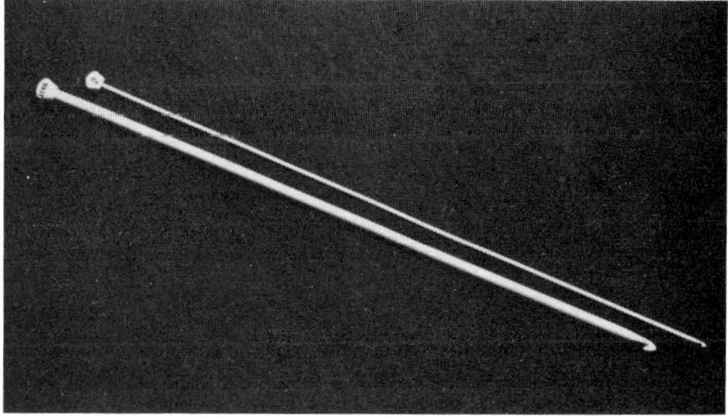

The principle of the technique is simple: all patterns including the basic plain Tunisian stitch are worked in two-row sequences – in the first row all the stitches across work are picked up and kept on the hook; in the second row the stitches are worked off one by one until you have at the end of the row only one stitch on the hook.

The fabric thus produced is firm and strong: it is in fact sometimes difficult to tell whether a fabric has been made by Tunisian crochet or by knitting, especially as many of the Tunisian stitch variations are worked to resemble knitting patterns – there is a stocking stitch variation, for example, which looks almost identical to knitting stocking stitch.

To work plain Tunisian stitch, work a chain to length required. Insert the hook into the second chain from the hook, and draw yarn through to form a loop on the hook; leave this loop on the hook and repeat the process into the next chain. Continue in this way all along the chain, so at the end of it you have a row of loops on the hook.

Do not turn the work as you would normally do for conventional crochet.

Next row: take the yarn round hook and draw through the first stitch, take the yarn round the hook and draw it through the next two stitches, continue taking yarn round hook and drawing it through two stitches to the end of the row.

In the following row loops are taken back on to the hook by inserting the hook into each vertical stitch in turn and drawing through a loop. In the next row the stitches are worked off one by one as before. Continue in this way.

HAIRPIN CROCHET

This is a form of crochet worked with a normal crochet hook but the stitches are 'mounted' on a large steel hairpin or two-pronged fork. The hairpin acts as a frame for the work. Usually hairpin crochet is worked in fine cotton yarns, and it is possible to make pretty lace edgings and fringings. Strips can be joined together to give broader bands of lace fabric.

Crocheted waistcoats are great favourites—thigh-length **(opposite)** *or midi- or maxi-length* **(above).**

Begin as usual with a very loose chain stitch, then withdraw the crochet hook from the loop and insert the left prong of the fork upwards from below and take hold of it with the thumb and middle finger of the left hand. Now take the yarn in front of and round the right prong of the fork. Place the hook into the loop, lift up the yarn, take it through the stitch and fix it in place with a double crochet. Then take the yarn behind and over the left prong of the fork. Turn the fork, place the hook into the loop on the left prong and work another double crochet. Continue in this way. As the prong becomes covered with loops slip off the lower ones, to leave room for new loops as work progresses.

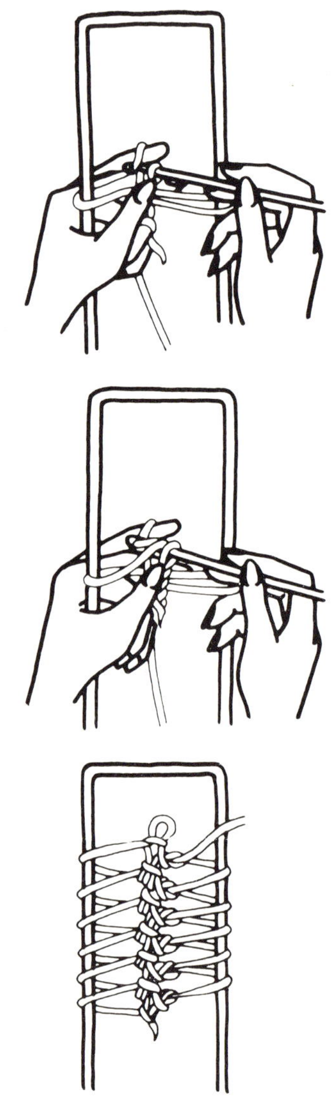

To join strips together, lay them side by side then, using a crochet hook, take two loops along the edge of the first strip and work a chain; take up two loops along the edge of the second strip and work a chain. Continue in this way.

ABBREVIATIONS

The following are the abbreviations normally used in crochet patterns.

alt.	alternate
beg.	beginning
blk(s).	block(s)
ch.	chain
cl.	cluster
cont.	continue
d.c.	double crochet
dec.	decrease(d)(ing)
d.tr.	double treble
foll.	following
gr(s).	group(s)
h.tr.	half treble
in.	inch(es)
inc.	increase(d)(ing)

p.   picot
patt.   pattern
qd.tr.   quadruple treble
rep.   repeat
sh.   shell
sp(s).   space(s)
sl.st.   slip stitch
st(s).   stitch(es)
tog.   together
tr.   treble
tr.tr.   triple treble
y.o.h. yarn over hook

Pattern sizes. If a pattern gives a range of different sizes then normally instructions are given in size order, with the different instructions relating to larger sizes in brackets. Where only one set of figures occurs this refers to all sizes.

IMPORTANT NOTE

Stitch terminology in crochet varies not only from country to country, but also from region to region. For instance, a double crochet in some areas is called a single crochet in others. In all the patterns and instructions in this book, stitch terms used refer to the specific directions given in Part 1—e.g. wherever the instruction 'double crochet' occurs in a pattern, then work double crochet as described on page 110.

Part 2—Dictionary of Stitch Patterns

Afghan square
illustrated in colour on page 124

This is the traditional multicoloured square which can be used to make all manner of household furnishings, including bedspreads, as well as fashion garments. Squares may all be made in single colours, or in two colours only, alternating the colours on rounds, or in multiple colours, having a different colour for every round. If multiple colours are used it is a good idea to finish each square with the same colour, and then to use this colour as the joining yarn – this creates the effect of a basic background colour, on which are superimposed all the other contrasting colours.
Our sample is worked in three colours: white, pink and blue.

With white, make 6 ch. Join into a ring with sl. st.
1st round: 2 ch., 2 tr., 3 ch., * 3 tr., 3 ch. into ring; rep. from * twice, sl.st. to first 2 ch. Join in pink.
2nd round: sl.st. to first sp., (2 ch., 3 tr., 3 ch., 3 tr.) into first 3 ch.sp., * (1 ch., 3 tr., 3 ch., 3 tr.) into next 3 ch.sp.; rep. from * twice, join with sl.st.
Join in blue.
3rd round: sl.st. to first sp., (2 ch., 2 tr., 3 ch., 3 tr.) into first 3 ch.sp., * 1 ch., 3 tr. into 1 ch.sp., (1 ch., 3 tr., 3 ch., 3 tr.) into each corner; rep. from * ending 1 ch., sl.st. to join. Join in white.
4th round: sl.st. to first sp., (2 ch., 2 tr., 3 ch., 3 tr.) into first 3 ch.sp., * 1 ch., 3 tr. into each 1 ch.sp., (1 ch., 3 tr., 3 ch., 3 tr.) into each corner; rep. from * ending 1 ch., sl.st. to join. Fasten off.

Arches

A regular openwork pattern in a firm, close fabric with a scalloped edge.

Work a ch. in a multiple of 6, plus 1 (e.g. 37).
1st row: 1 d.c. into 2nd ch. from hook, 1 d.c. into next st., * 3 ch., miss 3 sts., d.c. into each of the next 3 sts.; rep. from * ending 3 ch., miss 3 sts., 2 d.c. into each of next 2 sts., 1 ch., turn.
2nd row: 1 d.c. into first st., * 5 tr. into 3 ch.sp., miss 1 d.c., 1 d.c. into next st.; rep. from * ending 1 d.c. into centre of 3 d.c., 1 ch., turn.
3rd row: * 3 ch., 1 d.c. into each of 3 centre tr. of group; rep. from * ending 2 ch., 1 d.c. into last st., 3 ch., turn.
4th row: 2 tr. into 2 ch.sp., * 1 d.c. into centre of 3 d.c. of previous row, 5 tr., into 3 ch.sp.; rep. from * ending 1 d.c. into centre of 3 d.c., 3 tr. in last sp., 1 ch., turn.
5th row: as first row, beginning with 2 d.c.
Rep. 2nd-5th rows until work is length required.

Balancing trebles

Alternating sets of treble groups give a firm yet lacy fabric.

Work a ch. in a multiple of 4, plus 3 (e.g. 27).
1st row: (2 tr., 1 ch., 1 tr.) into 4th ch. from hook, * miss 3 ch., (3 tr., 1 ch., 1 tr.) into next st.; rep. from * ending miss 2 sts., 1 tr. in last st., 3 ch., turn.
2nd row: (2 tr., 1 ch., 1 tr.) into 1 ch.sp., * (3 tr., 1 ch., 1 tr.) into next 1 ch.sp.; rep. from * ending 1 tr. into turning ch., 3 ch., turn.
Rep. 2nd row until work is length required.

Clusters

Groups of stitches set above each other in even rows.

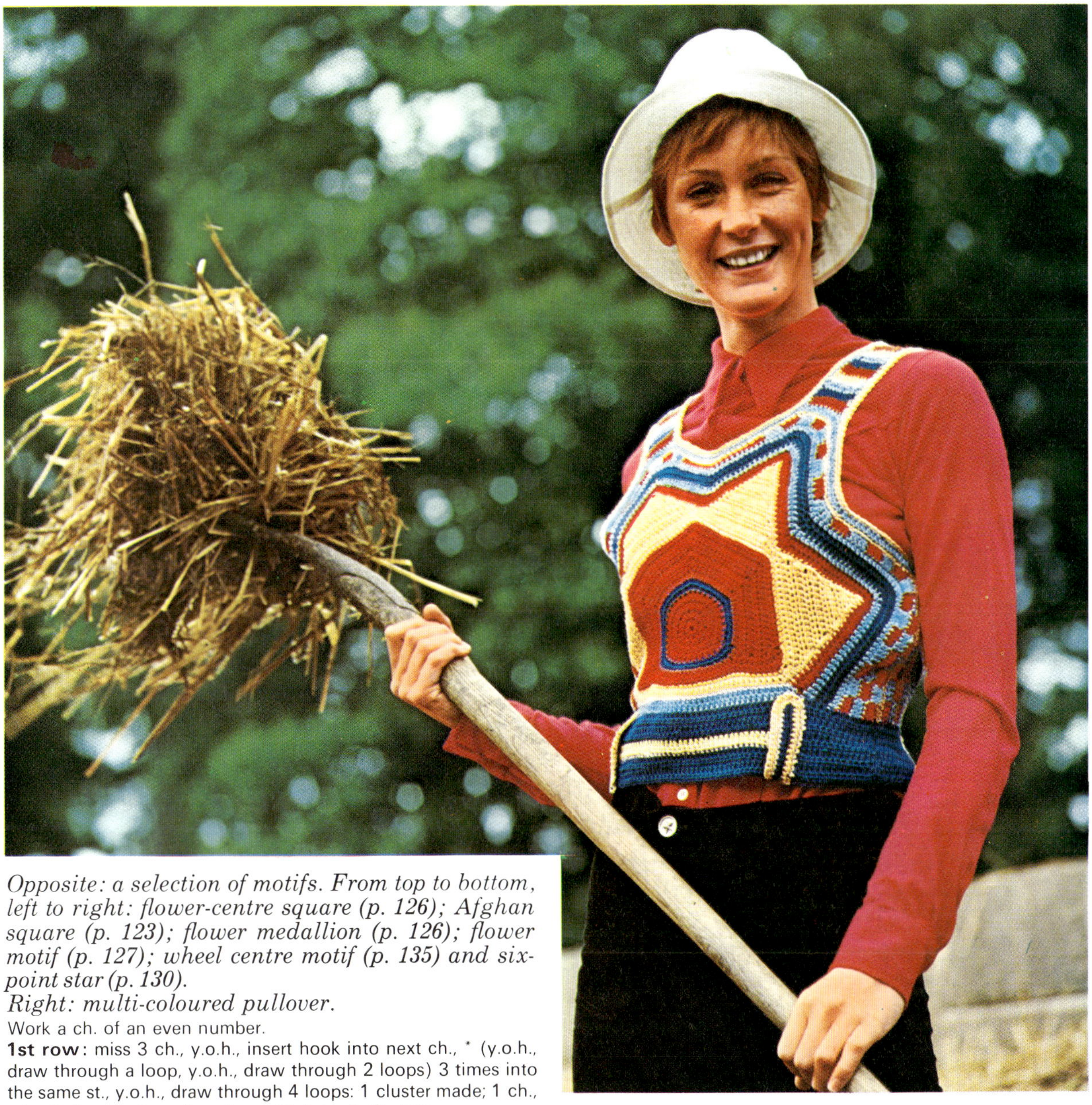

Opposite: a selection of motifs. From top to bottom, left to right: flower-centre square (p. 126); Afghan square (p. 123); flower medallion (p. 126); flower motif (p. 127); wheel centre motif (p. 135) and six-point star (p. 130).
Right: multi-coloured pullover.

Work a ch. of an even number.
1st row: miss 3 ch., y.o.h., insert hook into next ch., * (y.o.h., draw through a loop, y.o.h., draw through 2 loops) 3 times into the same st., y.o.h., draw through 4 loops: 1 cluster made; 1 ch., miss 1 ch.; rep. from * ending with 1 tr., 1 ch., turn.
2nd row: work 1 d.c. on each cluster and 1 d.c. on each single ch. to end, 3 ch., turn.
3rd row: * miss 1 ch., work cluster into next st., 1 ch.; rep. from * ending 1 tr., 1 ch., turn.
Rep. 2nd and 3rd rows until work is length required.

Clusters and spaces

This stitch pattern combines clusters and openwork. The fabric produced is firm enough for a sports sweater, yet open and light enough for an evening dress.

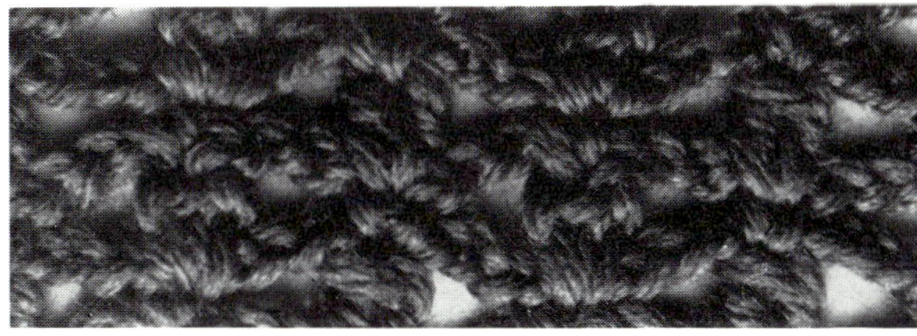

Work a ch. in a multiple of 6, plus 1 (e.g. 37).
1st row: work 1 d.c. in 2nd ch. from hook and then 1 d.c. in each ch. to end, 6 ch., turn.
2nd row: miss first 2 d.c., 1 d.c. in next d.c., * 3 ch., miss 2 d.c., (y.o.h., draw up loop, y.o.h. and draw through 2 loops) twice in next st., y.o.h. and draw through 3 loops: 1 cluster made; 3 ch., miss 2 d.c., 1 d.c. in next d.c.; rep. from * to last 3 sts., 3 ch., 1 tr. in last d.c., 1 ch., turn.
3rd row: 1 d.c. in first tr., * 3 ch., make cluster in next d.c., 3 ch., 1 d.c. in top of next cluster; rep. from * ending 1 d.c. in 3rd ch. of turning 6 ch., 6 ch., turn.
4th row: 1 d.c. in top of first cluster, * 3 ch., make cluster in next d.c., 3 ch., 1 d.c. in top of next cluster; rep. from * ending 3 ch., 1 tr. in next d.c., 1 ch., turn.
Rep. 3rd and 4th rows until work is length required.

Double shell

An interesting use of shells to give an alternating, balanced effect.

Work a ch. in a multiple of 7, plus 5 (e.g. 26).
1st row: 1 d.c. into 2nd st., miss 2 sts., 3 tr. into next st., * 3 ch., miss 3 sts., 1 d.c. into next st., miss 2 sts., 3 tr. into next st.; rep. from * to end, 1 ch., turn.
2nd row: 1 d.c. into first tr., 3 tr. into next d.c., * 3 ch., 1 d.c. into 3 ch.sp., 3 tr. into next d.c.; rep. from * to end, 1 ch., turn.
Rep. 2nd row until work is length required.

Fancy squares

A spectacular stitch pattern which is nevertheless simple to work, giving open squares in a regular sequence.

Work a ch. in a multiple of 9, plus 2 (e.g. 38).
1st row: work 1 tr. in 3rd ch. from hook and 1 tr. in each ch. to end, 4 ch., turn.
2nd row: miss first tr., 1 d.tr. in next tr., * 4 ch., miss 1 tr., 1 tr. in each of next 3 tr., 4 ch., miss 1 tr., 1 d.tr. in each of next 4 tr.; rep. from * ending 4 ch., miss next tr., 1 d.tr. in next tr., 1 d.tr. in top of turning ch., 1 ch., turn.
3rd row: 1 d.c. in each of first 2 d.tr., * 4 ch., 1 tr. in each of next 3 tr., 4 ch., 1 d.c. in each of next 4 d.tr.; rep. from * ending 4 ch., 1 d.c. in last d.tr., 1 d.c. in top of turning ch., 1 ch., turn.
4th row: 1 d.c. in each of first 2 d.c., * 4 ch., 1 tr. in each of next 3 tr., 4 ch., 1 d.c. in each of next 4 d.c.; rep. from * ending 4 ch., 1 d.c. in each of last 2 d.c., 1 ch., turn.
5th row: rep. 4th row, 4 ch., turn.
6th row: 1 d.tr. in 2nd d.c., * 1 d.c., 1 tr. in each of next 3 tr., (1 ch., 1 d.tr.) in next d.c. 4 times; rep. from * ending (1 ch., 1 d.tr. in next d.c.) twice, 3 ch., turn.
7th row: 1 tr. in next d.tr., * 1 tr. in next 1 ch.sp., 1 tr. in each of next 3 tr., (1 tr. in next 1 ch.sp., 1 tr. in next d.tr.) 4 times; rep. from * ending 1 tr. in each of next 3 tr., 1 tr. in next 1 ch.sp., 1 tr. in next d.tr., 1 tr. in top of turning ch., 4 ch., turn.
8th row: 1 d.tr. in 2nd tr., * 4 ch., miss next tr., 1 tr. in each of next 3 tr., 4 ch., (miss next tr., 1 d.tr. in next tr.) 4 times; rep. from * ending 4 ch., 1 d.tr. in last tr., 1 d.tr. in top of turning ch., 1 ch., turn.
Rep. 3rd-8th rows until work is length required.

Flower-centre square
illustrated in colour on page 124

A multicoloured square with a central, raised flower. Particularly attractive for cushion covers, bedspreads and so forth. Our square is worked in four colours: yellow, dark green, white and purple.

With yellow, make 5 ch., and sl.st. to form a ring.
1st round: (1 d.c., 1 tr., 1 d.c.) in each of 4 ch.
2nd round: * 2 ch., from wrong side sl.st. to base of 2nd d.c. of next st.; rep. from * 3 times.
3rd round: * 4 tr. and 1 sl.st. under next 2 ch.; rep. from * 3 times, draw dark green yarn through loop on hook, and fasten off yellow.
4th round: * 3 ch., sl.st. in base of next sl.st. of previous round; rep. from * 3 times.
5th round: * 8 tr. and 1 sl.st. under next ch.; rep. from * 3 times.
6th round: as 4th round.
7th round: * 10 tr. and 1 sl.st. under next ch.; rep. from * 3 times, draw white yarn through loop on hook, and fasten off dark green.
8th round: 3 tr. in sl.st. just made, * 2 ch., 3 tr. in 5th tr. of next petal, 1 ch., 3 tr. in same tr., 2 ch., 3 tr. in sp. before next petal; rep. from * ending 2 ch., sl.st. in top of first tr. Fasten off white yarn.
9th round: attach purple yarn in any corner ch. (between two 3 tr. groups). Work 3 ch. and in same sp. work (2 tr., 1 ch., 3 tr.), 2 ch., * (3 tr. in next sp., 2 ch.) twice, in next sp. work (3 tr., 1 ch., 3 tr.), 2 ch.; rep. from * all round, join with sl.st. to top of first tr. and fasten off.

Flower medallion
also illustrated in colour on page 124

A light and lacy motif with eight petal points.

Work 6 ch., and join into a ring with sl.st.
1st round: 7 ch., (1 d.tr. into ring, 3 ch.) 7 times, sl.st. into 4th of 7 ch.
2nd round: 3 ch., * miss 3 ch., (1 tr., 6 ch., 1 tr.) into top of d.tr.; rep. from * ending last rep. miss 3 ch., 1 tr. into first d.tr., 6 ch., sl.st. into top of 3 ch.
3rd round: * (3 tr., 5 ch., 3 tr.) into next ch.sp., 1 sl.st. into 2nd tr.; rep. from * to end. Fasten off.

Flower motif
illustrated in colour on page 124

A regular, eight-petalled flowerhead shape which can be used as a trimming or, joined together, to form an attractive fabric.

Work 6 ch. and join into ring with sl.st.
1st round: 2 ch., work 23 tr. into ring, join into ring with sl.st. to 2 ch. at beg. of round.
2nd round: 4 ch., 1 tr. into same st. as sl.st., 1 ch., * miss 2 sts., (1 tr., 2 ch., 1 tr.) into next st., 1 ch.; rep. from * 6 times, sl.st. to 2 ch. at beg. of round.
3rd round: 2 ch., (1 tr., 2 ch., 2 tr.) into first 2 ch.sp., 1 d.c. into 1 ch.sp., (2 tr., 2 ch., 2 tr.) into next 2 ch.sp.; rep. from * 6 times, 1 d.c. into last 1 ch.sp., sl.st. to 2nd ch. of first 2 ch.
4th round: * (3 tr., 1 ch., 3 tr.) into 2 ch.sp., 1 d.c. on d.c. of previous round; rep. from * 7 times, sl.st. to join. Fasten off.

Lace and bars
A combination of close work and lacy sections alternating in vertical panels.

Work a ch. in a multiple of 13, plus 1 (e.g. 27).
1st row: 1 tr. into 3rd ch. from hook, 1 tr. into each st., 3 ch., turn.
2nd row: 1 tr. into first 3 sts., * 3 ch., miss 3 tr., 1 d.c. into next st., 3 ch., miss 3 tr., 6 tr. on 6 tr.; rep. from * ending with 3 ch., 1 d.c., 3 ch., 3 tr., 1 tr. into turning ch., 3 ch., turn.
3rd row: 1 tr. into each of next 3 sts., * 1 ch., 1 d.c. into 3 ch.sp., 3 ch., 1 d.c. into next 3 ch.sp., 1 ch., 6 tr. on 6 tr.; rep. from * ending with 4 tr. as 2nd row, 3 ch., turn.
4th row: 3 tr. on 3 tr., * 7 tr. into 3 ch.sp., 6 tr. on 6 tr.; rep. from * ending with 4 tr., 3 ch., turn.
Rep. 2nd–4th rows until work is length required.

Lace and picot
An ideal stitch pattern for babywear and delicate evening tops.

Work a ch. in a multiple of 7, plus 2 (e.g. 23).
1st row: 2 ch., * 1 h.tr. into each of next 2 sts., 3 ch., miss 2 sts., 1 d.c. into next st., 3 ch., miss 2 sts.; rep. from * ending with 1 h.tr. into each of last 2 sts., 2 ch., turn.
2nd row: 1 h.tr. on 2nd h.tr., * 3 ch., (1 d.c., 3 ch., 1 d.c.) on d.c., 3 ch., 2 h.tr. on 2 h.tr.; rep. from * to end, 1 ch., turn.
3rd row: 1 d.c. on 2nd h.tr., * 1 d.c. into 3 ch.sp., 5 ch., 1 d.c. into next 3 ch.sp., 1 d.c. into each of next 2 h.tr.; rep. from * to end, 1 ch., turn.
4th row: 1 d.c. on 2nd d.c., * 7 d.c. into ch. arch, 2 d.c. on 2 d.c.; rep. from * to end, 2 ch., turn.
5th row: 1 h.tr. on 2nd d.c., * 3 ch., miss 3 d.c., 1 d.c. into centre d.c. of arch, 3 ch., miss 2 d.c., 2 h.tr. on 2 d.c.; rep. from * to end, 2 ch., turn. **6th row:** as 2nd row.
Rep. 2nd–6th rows until work is length required.

Lattice and loops
Vertical bars of clusters set in lattice panels.

Work a ch. in a multiple of 8.
1st row: 1 d.c. in 8th ch. from hook, * 4 ch., miss 3 ch., 1 d.c. in next ch.; rep. from * to end, 4 ch., turn.
2nd row: (y.o.h., draw loop under first 4 ch. loop, y.o.h. and draw through 2 loops) 4 times, y.o.h. and draw through 4 loops, y.o.h. and draw through 2 loops: a cluster made; * 4 ch., 1 d.c. under next loop, 4 ch., work cluster under next loop; rep. from * ending with a cluster under turning ch., d.tr. in 5th ch. of turning ch., 4 ch., turn.
3rd row: * 1 d.c. under next 4 ch. loop, 4 ch.; rep. from * ending 4 ch., 1 d.c. under turning ch., 4 ch., turn.
4th row: * work cluster under next loop, 4 ch., 1 d.c. under next loop, 4 ch.; rep. from * ending with a cluster under turning ch., 1 d.tr. in top of d.tr. of last cluster row, 4 ch., turn.
Rep. 3rd and 4th rows until work is length required.

Lattice squares
A firm, openwork stitch pattern which is ideal for tailored garments.

Work a ch. in a multiple of 4.
1st row: 1 tr. in 4th ch. from hook, * 2 ch., miss 2 ch., 1 tr. in each of next 2 ch.; rep. from * to end, 1 ch., turn.
2nd row: 1 d.c. in each of first 2 tr., * 1 d.c. in each ch. of 2 ch., 1 d.c. in each of next 2 tr.; rep. from * ending 1 d.c. in last tr., 1 d.c. in top of turning ch., 2 ch., turn.
3rd row: miss first ch., 1 tr. in next d.c., * 2 ch., miss 2 d.c., 1 tr. in each of next 2 d.c.; rep. from * to end, 1 ch., turn.
Rep. 2nd and 3rd rows until work is length required.

Open shells
Groups of shells spaced to give a lacy texture.

Work a ch. in a multiple of 5, plus 4 (e.g. 34).
1st row: 1 d.c. in 2nd ch. from hook and in each ch. to end, 3 ch., turn.
2nd row: miss first d.c., 1 tr. in next d.c., * 5 ch., miss 4 d.c., (2 tr., 1 ch., 2 tr.) in next d.c. (shell): a shell made; rep. from * ending 5 ch., 1 tr. in last tr., 3 ch., turn.
3rd row: miss first tr., 1 tr. in next tr., * 5 ch., make shell under 1 ch.sp. of next shell; rep. from * ending 5 ch., 1 tr. in last tr., 1 tr. in top of turning ch., 3 ch., turn.
4th row: miss first tr., 1 tr. in next tr., * 2 ch., 1 d.c. in centre ch. of 5 ch. of 2nd row, working over the 5 ch. of 3rd row, 2 ch., make a shell in centre of next shell; rep. from * ending 1 tr. in last tr., 1 tr. in top of turning ch., 3 ch., turn.
5th row: miss first tr., 1 tr. in next tr., * 5 ch., make shell in next shell; rep. from * ending 1 tr. in last tr., 1 tr. in top of turning ch., 3 ch., turn.
Rep. 3rd–5th rows until work is length required.

Pique stitch

This pattern is excellent for skirts, jackets, coats or any garment which needs a firm, stable texture.

Work a ch. to any length.
1st row: work 1 d.c. into each ch., beg. with 2nd ch. from hook.
2nd row: 2 ch., * draw loop through each of next 2 ch., y.o.h. draw through 2 loops, y.o.h. and draw through last 2 loops, 1 ch.; rep. from * to end, 1 ch., turn.
3rd row: work 1 d.c. on each group and 1 d.c. on each ch. between groups all along, 1 ch., turn.
4th row: as first row, working first 2 loops on 2nd and 3rd d.c. of previous row, 1 ch., turn.
Rep. 3rd and 4th rows until work is length required.

A simple round motif forms the basis for this elegant cheval set (see page 130).

Popcorn stitch

In this pattern raised bobbles stand out from a flat fabric thus giving a three-dimensional effect.

Work a ch. in a multiple of 4.
1st row: beg. with 2nd ch. from hook, 1 d.c. in each ch. to end, 1 ch., turn.
2nd row: * 1 d.c. in each of first 3 d.c., 3 tr. in next d.c., take hook out of st. and insert it in first of the 3 tr., pick up loop and pull through tr.: a popcorn st. made; 1 ch. to tighten st.; rep. from * to last 3 d.c., 1 d.c. in each of last 3 d.c., 1 ch., turn.
3rd row: * 1 d.c. in each of first 3 d.c., 1 d.c. in popcorn st.; rep. from * to last 3 d.c., 1 d.c. in each of last 3 d.c., 1 ch., turn.

continued on page 130

Don't forget that crochet is as suitable for items like this blue/white and red bag as for clothes.

Top: *the same square motif worked in (from left to right) No. 40,
No. 20 and No. 10 cotton (see instructions on page 131).*
Bottom: *green square with diagonals and pale blue square with trebles (see page 131).*

4th row: 1 d.c. in first d.c., * popcorn st. in next d.c., 1 d.c. in each of next 3 d.c.; rep. from * to end, ending with 1 d.c. instead of 3 d.c., 1 ch., turn.
5th row: 1 d.c. in first d.c., * 1 d.c. in popcorn st., 1 d.c. in each of next 3 d.c.; rep. from * to last 2 sts., 1 d.c. in popcorn st., 1 d.c. in last d.c., 1 ch., turn.
Rep. last 4 rows until work is length required.

Round motif in fine crochet cotton
illustrated on page 128

Our sample is worked in No. 20 mercer-crochet cotton, with a steel crochet hook International Standard Size 1.25, and has four round motifs joined together with a central diamond filling motif. The motifs are joined as work progresses and the filling worked between the joined motifs.

Make 7 ch., and join with sl.st. to form a ring.
1st round: 16 d.c. into ring, 1 sl.st. into first d.c.
2nd round: 8 ch., * miss 1 d.c., 1 tr. into next d.c., 5 ch.; rep. from * ending with 1 sl.st. into 3rd of 8 ch.
3rd round: * into next loop work 3 d.c., 3 ch. and 3 d.c.; rep. from * ending with 1 sl.st. into first d.c.
4th round: 1 sl.st. into each of next 2 d.c., 1 sl.st. into next loop, 1 d.c. into same loop, * 7 ch., 1 d.c. into next loop; rep. from * ending with 7 ch., 1 sl.st. into first d.c.
5th round: 1 d.c. into same place as sl.st., * 9 d.tr. into centre ch. of next loop, 1 d.c. into next d.c.; rep. from * omitting 1 d.c. at end of last rep., 1 sl.st. into first d.c.
6th round: 1 sl.st. into each of next 3 d.tr., * 1 d.c. into each of next 3 d.tr., 7 ch., miss 7 sts.; rep. from * ending with 1 sl.st. into first d.c.
7th round: 1 sl.st. into next d.c., 8 ch., 1 tr. into same place as last sl.st., * 2 ch., into centre ch. of next loop work 1 tr., 5 ch. and 1 tr., 2 ch., miss next d.c., into next d.c. work 1 tr., 5 ch. and 1 tr.; rep. from * omitting 1 tr., 5 ch. and 1 tr. at end of last rep., 1 sl.st. into 3rd of 8 ch.
8th round: 1 sl.st. into each of next 3 ch., 8 ch., 1 tr. into same place as last sl.st., * 3 ch., miss next 2 ch.sp., into centre ch. of next loop work 1 tr., 7 ch. and 1 tr., 3 ch., miss next 2 ch.sp., into centre ch. of next loop work 1 tr., 5 ch. and 1 tr.; rep. from * omitting 1 tr., 5 ch. and 1 tr. at end of last rep., 1 sl.st. into 3rd of 8 ch. Fasten off.
This completes the basic circular motif.
To make second motif and join it on to the first as you work, complete as for first motif to the end of the 7th round.
8th round: 1 sl.st. into each of next 3 ch., 8 ch., 1 tr. into same place as last sl.st., * 3 ch., miss next 2 ch.sp., 1 tr. into centre ch. of next loop, 3 ch., 1 d.c. into corresponding loop on first motif, 3 ch., 1 tr. into same place as last tr. on second motif, * 3 ch., miss next 2 ch.sp., 1 tr. into centre ch. of next loop, 2 ch., 1 d.c. into corresponding loop on first motif, 2 ch., 1 tr. into same place as last tr. on second motif; rep. from * to * once more, complete as first motif.
Make a second row of two motifs below the first, joining motifs as second motif was joined to the first and leaving one 5 ch. loop free on each motif between joinings.

To work filling motif
Work as for first motif for one round.
2nd round: 3 ch., 1 tr. into same place as sl.st., 2 tr. into each d.c., 1 sl.st. into 3rd of 3 ch.
3rd round: 1 d.c. into same place as sl.st., 1 ch., 1 d.c. into any free 5 ch. loop between joinings, * 1 ch., 1 d.c. into same place as last d.c. on filling, miss 3 tr., 5 d.tr. into next tr., 2 ch., 1 d.c. into next joining between motifs, 2 ch., 5 d.tr. into same place as last d.tr. on filling, miss 3 tr., 1 d.c. into next tr., 1 ch., 1 d.c. into next free 5 ch. loop on next motif; rep. from * omitting 1 d.c., 1 ch. and 1 d.c. at end of last rep., 1 sl.st. into first d.c. Fasten off.

Scalloped edging

An attractive finish for the edge of a sweater, dress, blouse or even a tablecloth.

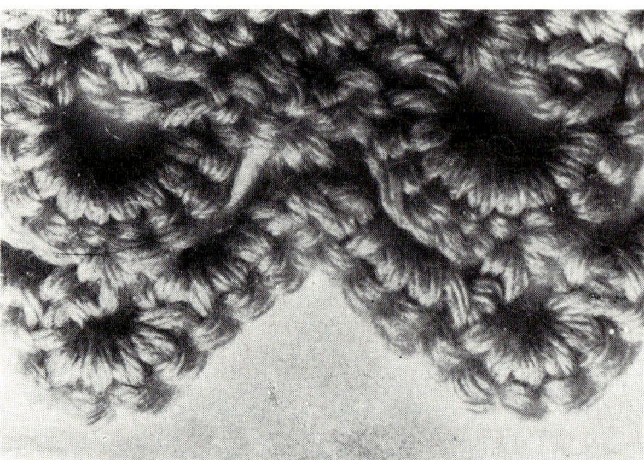

Work a ch. in a multiple of 8, plus 2 (e.g. 26).
1st row: 1 d.c. in 2nd ch., from hook and work 1 d.c. into each ch. to end, 1 ch., turn.
2nd row: working through front loops of sts., 1 d.c. in each of first 4 d.c., * (1 d.c., 7 ch., 1 d.c.) in next d.c., 1 d.c. in each of next 7 d.c.; rep. from * to last 5 d.c., (1 d.c., 8 ch., 1 d.c.) into next d.c., 1 d.c. in each of last 4 d.c., 3 ch., turn.
3rd row: working through back loops of sts., miss first d.c., 1 d.c. in next d.c., * miss 3 d.c., 9 d.c. under 7 ch.sp., miss next 3 d.c., 1 d.c. in next d.c., 1 tr. in next d.c., 1 d.c. in next d.c.; rep. from * ending miss next 3 d.c., 9 d.c. under 7 ch.sp., miss next 3 d.c., 1 d.c. in next d.c., 1 tr. in last d.c., 1 ch., turn.
4th row: 1 d.c. in first d.c., * 4 ch., (1 d.c., 5 ch., 1 d.c.) in centre d.c. of next 9 d.c., 1 d.c. in next d.c.; rep. from * working last d.c. in top of turning ch. instead of a tr., 1 ch., turn.
5th row: 1 d.c. in first d.c., * 3 d.c. under next 4 ch.sp., 5 d.c. under next 5 ch.sp., 3 d.c. under next 4 ch.sp., 1 d.c. in next d.c.; rep. from * to end. Fasten off.

Single shell

A delicate and pretty stitch pattern, but firm enough for most purposes.

Work a ch. in a multiple of 6, plus 3 (e.g. 27).
1st row: work 2 tr. in 3rd ch. from hook, * miss 2 ch., 1 d.c. in next ch., miss 2 ch., 5 tr. in next ch.: a shell made; rep. from * ending miss 2 ch., 3 tr. in last ch., 1 ch., turn.
2nd row: 1 d.c. in first tr., * 5 tr. in next d.c., 1 d.c. in centre tr. of shell; rep. from * ending 1 d.c. in top of turning ch., 2 ch., turn.
3rd row: 2 tr. in first d.c., * 1 d.c. in centre tr. of shell, shell in next d.c.; rep. from * ending 3 tr. in top of turning ch., 1 ch., turn.
Rep. 2nd and 3rd rows until work is length required.

Six-point star
illustrated in colour on page 124

An attractive motif which is easy to make and which can be used as a trimming.

Centre piece
Make 25 ch.
1st row: 1 d.c. in 2nd ch. from hook, 1 d.c. in each ch. to end:
24 sts.
**** 2nd row**: 1 ch., 1 d.c. in first st., miss next st., 1 d.c. in each
st. to last 2 sts., miss next st., 1 d.c. in last st.
3rd row: 1 ch., 1 d.c. in each st. to end. **
Rep. last 2 rows until 4 sts. remain ending with a 3rd row.
***** Next row**: 1 ch., 1 d.c. in first st., 1 d.c. in last st.
Next row: 1 ch., draw loop through first st., draw loop through
last st., yarn round hook and draw loop through 3 loops on hook.
Fasten off.

First side piece
Rejoin yarn in 9th st. of first ch. and work 1 d.c. in this st.,
1 d.c. in each of next 7 sts., turn: 8 sts.
Work as Centre Piece from ** to **.
Rep. last 2 rows once: 4 sts. Complete as for Centre Piece from
*** to end.

Second and third side pieces (make both alike)
Rejoin yarn to 8th row of one side of Centre Piece and work
1 d.c. into this row, 1 d.c. in each of next 7 rows, turn: 8 sts.
Work as for Centre Piece from ** to **. Rep. last 2 rows once:
4 sts. Complete as Centre Piece from *** to end.

Square motif in fine crochet cotton
illustrated in colour on page 129

This delicate lacy motif is ideal for making up into
a bedspread. Our sample is in No. 10 mercer-
crochet cotton, with a steel crochet hook International Standard Size 1.50. This produces a motif
of about $4\frac{1}{2}$ in. square. If the motif is worked in
No. 20 cotton (same hook size) you will get a $3\frac{3}{4}$ in.
square; and in No. 40 cotton, a 3-in. square. See
illustrations on page 129.

Make 20 ch. and join with a sl.st. to form a ring.
1st round: work 32 d.c. into ring, 1 sl.st. into first d.c.
2nd round: 1 d.c. into same place as sl.st., * 5 ch., miss 3 d.c.,
1 d.c. into next d.c.; rep. from * ending with 5 ch., 1 sl.st. into
first d.c.
3rd round: 1 sl.st. into first loop, into same loop work 3 d.c.,
3 ch. and 3 d.c., * 1 ch., into next loop work 3 d.c., 3 ch. and

3 d.c.; rep. from * ending with 1 ch., 1 sl.st. into first d.c.
4th row: 1 sl.st. into each of next 2 d.c., 1 sl.st. into next loop,
6 ch., leaving the last loop of each on hook, work 4 quadruple
tr. into same loop, yarn over and draw through all loops on hook:
a 4 quad. tr. cluster made; * 9 ch., a 3 tr. cluster into next 1 ch.sp.,
9 ch., a 5 quad. tr. cluster into next loop; rep. from * omitting
9 ch. and a 5 quad. tr. cluster at end of last repeat, 6 ch., 1 tr.
into first cluster.
5th row: 1 d.c. into last tr. made, * 7 ch., 1 d.c. into 3rd ch. of
next loop, 7 ch., 1 d.c. into 7th ch. of next loop; rep. from *
omitting 1 d.c. at end of last repeat, 1 sl.st. into first d.c.
6th row: 1 sl.st. into each of next 2 ch., 5 d.c. into same loop, *
13 tr. into next loop, 5 d.c. into next loop; rep. from * omitting
5 d.c. at end of last rep., 1 sl.st. into first d.c.
7th row: 1 sl.st. into next d.c., * 1 d.c. into next d.c., 1 tr. into
each of next 6 tr., into next tr. work 1 tr., 7 ch. and 1 tr., 1 tr.
into each of next 6 tr., miss 2 d.c., 1 d.c. into next d.c., 1 tr.
into each of next 13 tr., miss 2 d.c.; rep. from * ending with
1 sl.st. into first d.c.
8th round: 1 sl.st. into each of next 3 tr., 3 ch., * 1 tr. into each of
next 4 tr., into next loop work 4 tr., 7 ch. and 4 tr., 1 tr. into each
of next 5 tr., 7 ch., miss 5 sts., 1 d.c. into each of next 4 tr., into
next tr. work 1 d.c., 3 ch. and 1 d.c., 1 d.c. into each of next
4 tr., 7 ch., miss 5 sts., 1 tr. into next tr.; rep. from * omitting
1 tr. at end of last rep., 1 sl.st. into 3rd of 3 ch. Fasten off.

Square with diagonals
illustrated in colour on page 129

The central flower of this square motif has 'arms'
that radiate out towards the corners.

Make 8 ch., and join into a ring with sl.st.
1st round: 3 ch., * (y.o.h. and insert hook into ring, y.o.h. and
draw through a loop, y.o.h. and draw through 1 loop, y.o.h. and
draw through 2 loops) * twice, y.o.h. and draw through 3
loops, ** 5 ch., work from * to * 3 times, y.o.h. and draw through
4 loops, 2 ch., work from * to * 3 times, y.o.h. and draw through
4 loops; ** rep. from ** to ** twice, 5 ch., work from * to *
3 times, y.o.h. and draw through 4 loops, 2 ch., sl.st. to 3rd ch.
of first 3 ch.
2nd round: 2 sl.st. over 2 tr., 3 ch., work from * to * of first
round twice into 5 ch.sp., y.o.h., and draw through 3 loops, 2
ch., work from * to * 3 times into same ch.sp., y.o.h. and draw
through 4 loops, 2 ch., 3 tr. into 2 ch.sp., 2 ch.
Continue in this way working (1 cluster, 2 ch., 1 cluster) into
5 ch.sp. and (2 ch., 3 tr., 2 ch.) into 2 ch.sp. to end of round,
join with sl.st. into 3rd of 3 ch.
3rd round: 1 sl.st., 3 ch., * work (1 cluster, 2 ch., 1 cluster)
into corner ch., 2 ch., 2 tr. into 2 ch.sp., 3 tr. on 3 tr. of previous
round, 2 tr. into 2 ch.sp., 2 ch.; rep. from * to end, join with sl.st.
4th round: work as previous round, working tr. in tr. of previous
round with 2 tr. on either side in 2 ch.sp., join with sl.st.
5th round: as 4th round.
Subsequent rounds are worked in a similar way to enlarge the
square to size required.

Square with trebles
illustrated in colour on page 129

This is a close-textured square motif which can
be made into any size required.

Make 10 ch. and join into a ring with sl.st.
1st round: 10 ch., (4 d.tr., 7 ch.) 3 times into ring, 3 d.tr.,
sl.st. to 3rd st. of first 10 ch., sl.st. over 3 sts. and turn work.
2nd round: 10 d.c. along each side, join with sl.st.
3rd round: 10 ch., (2 d.tr. into first d.c., 1 d.tr. in each of next
8 d.c., 2 d.tr. into next d.c., 7 ch.) 3 times, 2 d.tr. into first d.c.
of next 10 d.c., 1 d.tr. into each of next 9 d.c., sl.st. to 3rd ch. of
first 10 ch., turn work.
4th round: as 2nd round, with 18 d.c. worked on each side
instead of 10.
5th round: 3 ch., 1 d.tr. into each st. and 6 into each corner.
Fasten off.

This sporting life—striped sweater in hard-wearing double-knitting yarn.

Soft and sentimental—Tricel top with mohair skirt.

Trebles and arches

An open, delicate stitch pattern.

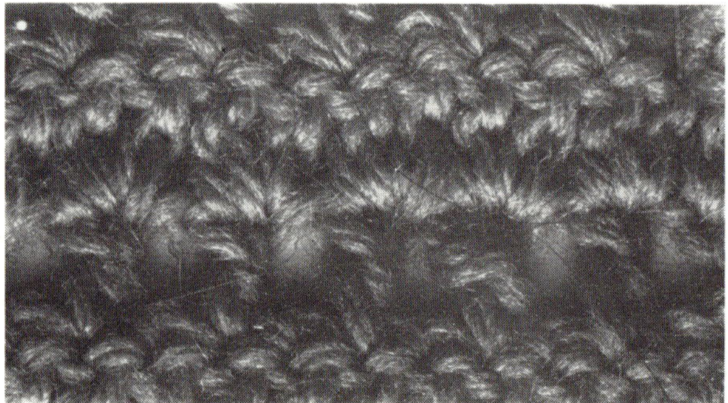

Work a ch. in a multiple of 10, plus 7 (e.g. 37).
1st row: 1 tr. in 4th ch. from hook, 1 tr. in each of next 3 ch., * 3 ch., miss 2 ch., 1 d.c. in next ch., 3 ch., miss 2 ch., 1 tr. in each of next 5 ch.; rep. from * to end, 2 ch., turn.
2nd row: miss first tr., 1 tr. in each of next 4 tr., * 4 ch., 1 tr. in each of next 5 tr.; rep. from * ending 1 tr. in each of last 4 tr., 1 tr. in top of turning ch., 6 ch., turn.
3rd row: 1 d.c. in centre tr. of 5-tr. group, * 3 ch., 5 tr. under 4 ch.sp., 3 ch., 1 d.c. in centre tr. of next 5 tr. group; rep. from * ending 3 ch., 1 tr. in top of turning ch., 6 ch., turn.
4th row: miss 1 d.c., * 1 tr. in each of next 5 tr., 5 ch.; rep. from * ending 4 ch., 1 tr. in 3rd ch. of turning ch., 3 ch., turn.
5th row: 4 tr. in first ch.sp., * 3 ch., 1 d.c. in centre tr. of 5 tr. group, 3 ch., 5 tr. under next 5 ch.sp.; rep. from * ending 4 tr. under turning ch., 1 tr. in 3rd ch. of turning ch., 3 ch., turn.
Rep. 2nd–5th rows until work is length required.

Trebles and spaces

A pleasing, tailored stitch pattern which is excellent for men's wear and also fashion jackets and coats.

Make a ch. of an even number.
1st row: 1 tr. in 6th ch. from hook, * 1 ch., miss 1 ch., 1 tr. in next ch.; rep. from * to end, 3 ch., turn.
2nd row: miss first tr., * 2 tr. in next tr.; rep. from * ending 2 tr. in last tr., miss next ch. of turning ch., 1 tr. in next ch., 3 ch., turn.
3rd row: miss first 2 tr., 1 tr. in next tr., * 1 ch., miss 1 tr., 1 tr. in next tr.; rep. from * ending 1 tr. in last tr., 1 ch., 1 tr. in 2nd ch. of turning ch., 3 ch., turn.
Rep. 2nd and 3rd rows until work is length required.

Triangle stitch

A classic stitch pattern which is regular and firm but has a look of lightness.

Work a ch. in a multiple of 3, plus 2 (e.g. 23).
1st row: 1 tr. in 5th ch. from hook, * miss 2 ch., (1 tr., 1 ch., 1 tr.) in next ch.; rep. from * to end, turn with 5 ch.
2nd row: 1 tr. in first ch.sp., * (1 tr., 2 ch., 1 tr.) in next ch.sp.; rep. from * ending (1 tr., 2 ch., 1 tr.) into loop of 5 ch., turn with 5 ch.
Repeat 2nd row until work is length required.

Two-colour drop stitch

Stripes in two colours – use more if you wish – with an interesting stepped effect.

With first colour, work a ch. in a multiple of 8, plus 4 (e.g. 36).
1st row: 1 d.c. in 4th ch. from hook, * 1 ch., miss next ch., 1 d.c. in next ch.; rep. from * to end, 2 ch., turn.
2nd row: * 1 d.c. in next 1 ch.sp., 1 ch.; rep. from * ending 1 d.c. under turning ch., draw second colour through loop, and drop first colour, 2 ch., turn.
Repeat 2nd row until work is length required, alternating colours after every two rows.

Two-colour octagon

An attractive eight-sided motif which could be used as a trimming.

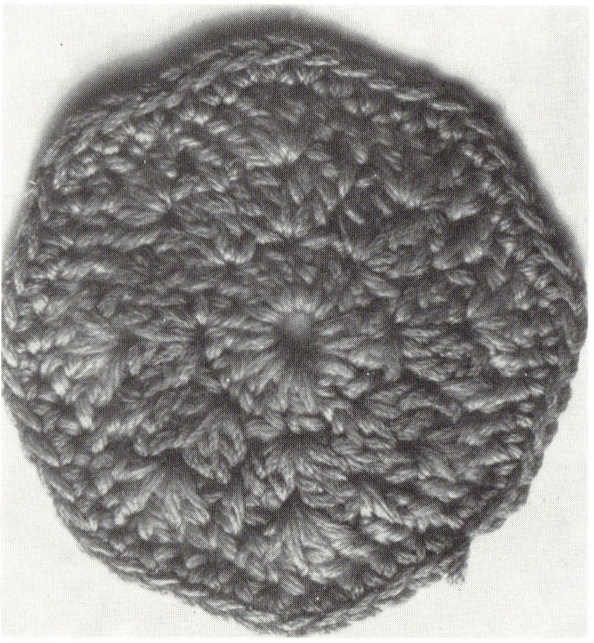

With first colour, work 6 ch., and join into a ring with sl.st.
1st round: 2 ch., work 15 tr. into ring, join with sl.st., joining in second colour.
2nd round: (2 ch., 1 tr., 1 ch., 2 tr.) into first st., miss 1 st., * (2 tr., 1 ch., 2 tr.) into next st., miss 1 st.; rep. from * 6 times, sl.st. to join, joining in first colour.
3rd round: (2 ch., 1 tr., 1 ch., 2 tr.) into first ch.sp., * 1 tr. between 4 tr. groups, (2 tr., 1 ch., 2 tr.) into next ch.sp.; rep. from * 7 times, 1 tr. between last 4 tr. group, sl.st. to join, joining in second colour.
4th round: work 1 d.c. into each tr. and ch.
Fasten off.

Wheel centre motif

illustrated in colour on page 124

Another version of the Afghan square, using three colours.

With first colour, make 8 ch., and join into a ring with sl.st.
1st round: 6 ch., * (1 tr., 3 ch.) 7 times into ring, sl.st. to join, joining in second colour.
2nd round: 2 ch., 3 tr., 2 ch. into first sp., * 4 tr., 2 ch. into next sp.; rep. from *, sl.st. to join, joining in third colour.
3rd round: 2 ch., 5 tr., 1 ch. into first sp., * 6 tr., 3 ch. into next sp., 6 tr., 1 ch. into next sp.; rep. from * 3 times, 6 tr., 3 ch. into next sp., sl.st. to join, joining in first colour.
4th round: 2 ch., 1 tr., 3 ch., 2 tr. into 3 ch.sp. at corner, * 3 ch., 1 d.c. between 3rd and 4th tr. of next group, 3 ch., 1 d.c. into 1 ch.sp., 3 ch., 1 d.c. between 3rd and 4th tr. of next group, 3 ch., (2 tr., 3 ch., 2 tr.) into 3 ch.sp. at corner; rep. from * 3 times, sl.st. to join. Fasten off.

Part 3—Patterns

CHILDREN

Gold pram cover

illustrated in colour on page 136

MATERIALS
19 oz. Emu Scotch double knitting in main shade, 11 oz. in first contrast shade and 8 oz. in second contrast shade. One crochet hook International Standard Size 5.50.

MEASUREMENTS
Length 64 in. approx.; width 43 in. approx.

TENSION
Three 3-tr. gr. measure 2 in.; 1 tr. is 1 in. deep.

ABBREVIATIONS
See page 122; M., main shade; A., first contrast shade; B., second contrast shade.

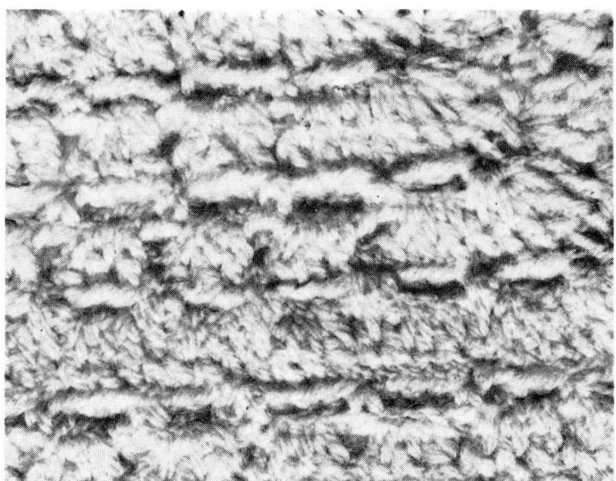

TO MAKE
With A., commence with 60 ch.
1st round: working through upper loops of ch., 1 d.c. into 2nd ch. from hook, 1 d.c. into each ch. to end, working along other side of ch. through upper loops, 1 d.c. into each ch. to end, sl.st. to first d.c.
2nd round: * 3 ch., miss 1 d.c., 1 d.c. into next d.c.; rep. from * 29 times, 3 ch., 1 d.c. across end of work, 3 ch., 1 d.c. into first d.c. on other side, ** miss 1 d.c., 3 ch., 1 d.c. into next d.c.; rep. from ** to end, 3 ch., 1 d.c. across end of work, 3 ch., sl.st. into ch.sp.
3rd round: 6 tr. into first 3-ch.sp., 3 tr. into each 3-ch.sp. to last sp. of first side, 6 tr. into next sp., 3 tr. into next sp., 6 tr. into next sp., 3 tr. into each ch.sp. to last sp. of 2nd side, 6 tr. into next sp., 3 tr. into next 3 ch. sp., sl.st. to first tr.
4th round: 3 ch., 1 d.c. into centre sp. of corner 6 tr., * 3 ch., 1 d.c. into sp. between next 3 tr.; rep. from * to corner 6 tr., 3 ch., 1 d.c. into centre sp. of corner 6 tr., 3 ch., 1 d.c. into sp. between next 3 tr., 3 ch., 1 d.c. into centre sp. of corner 6 tr., ** 3 ch., 1 d.c. into sp. between next 3 tr.; rep. from ** to corner, 3 ch., 1 d.c. into centre sp. of corner tr., 3 ch., 1 d.c. into sp. between next 3 tr., sl.st. to first ch.
5th round: work 6 tr. into each d.c. at centre of previous corner 6 tr. and 3 tr. into each 3-ch.sp. all round, sl.st. to first tr.
The 4th and 5th rounds form the patt.
Work 8 more rounds.
Change to B.
Note. When changing colour, on the 2nd round of the new colour (tr. round), work 1 tr. into sp. between each 3 tr. of previous tr. round (making a long st.) and between each of the 3 tr. of round being worked.
Work 6 rounds with B.
Change to A. and work 12 rounds.
Change to B. and work 6 rounds.
Change to M. and work 18 rounds, then 1 more 4th patt. round.

EDGING
With M. work 1 d.c., 3 tr. and 1 d.c. into each 3-ch.sp. and 6 tr. into each corner d.c., sl.st. to first d.c.
Fasten off.

TO COMPLETE
Press lightly.

Matinee coat and bonnet

illustrated in colour on page 136

MATERIALS
5 oz. Emu Baby Nylon 3 ply. One crochet hook International Standard Size 3.00. $\frac{3}{4}$ yd. narrow ribbon for jacket. $1\frac{1}{2}$ yd. ribbon, 1 in. wide, for bonnet.

MEASUREMENTS
To fit chest size 16–18 in. **Bonnet**: face edge measures 11 in.

TENSION
7 cl. to 2 in.

ABBREVIATIONS
See page 122.

COAT BACK
Make 98 ch., turn, * miss 1 st., 1 d.c. and 1 tr. into next st.; rep. from * ending 1 d.c. into last st., 1 ch.: 97 sts. and 48 cls. This row forms the patt. Cont. in patt. until 40 rows of patt. have been completed, always remembering to turn with 1 ch.

Shape Waist
Next row: 1 d.c. into first st., (miss 1 st., 1 d.c. on each of next 2 sts., miss 1 st., 1 d.c. on each of next 2 sts., miss 1 st., 1 d.c. on next st.) to end: 61 d.c.

Work 5 more rows in d.c. still turning each row with 1 ch.
Change back to main patt. and work 4 rows.

Shape Armholes
Next row : patt. to within 3 sts. of end of previous row, 1 d.c.
into next st., turn leaving 2 sts. unworked.
Rep. this row 5 times more: 49 sts.
Cut yarn and leave for yoke.

COAT RIGHT FRONT
Make 50 ch. and work exactly as for Back until the 40th row has
been worked, then dec. for waist as for Back: 31 d.c.
Work 5 rows of d.c. on d.c., then change back to patt. for 4 rows.

Shape Armhole
Next row : as first row of Back armhole shaping.
Next row : in patt.
Rep. the last 2 rows twice more, thus leaving 2 sts. unworked
at armhole edge 3 times: 25 sts. and 12 cls.
Cut yarn and leave for yoke.

COAT LEFT FRONT
Work exactly as for Right Front (as work is reversible).

COAT SLEEVES (make 2 alike)
Make 38 ch. and work in patt. as for Back until 30 rows are
completed, shaping sides by inc. on 5th row thus: 1 d.c. and
1 tr. into each of the first 3 sts., patt. to last 3 sts., 1 d.c. and 1 tr.
into each of the next 2 sts., 1 d.c. in last st.: 41 sts.
Work 5 rows straight. Rep. last 6 rows twice more, then 5th
row again. There are now 53 sts. and 26 cls.
Work 1 more row. (Cont. for more rows for longer sleeve.)

Shape Top
Work as for Back armhole shaping until 41 sts. and 20 cls. rem.
Cut yarn and leave for yoke.   *continued on page 138*

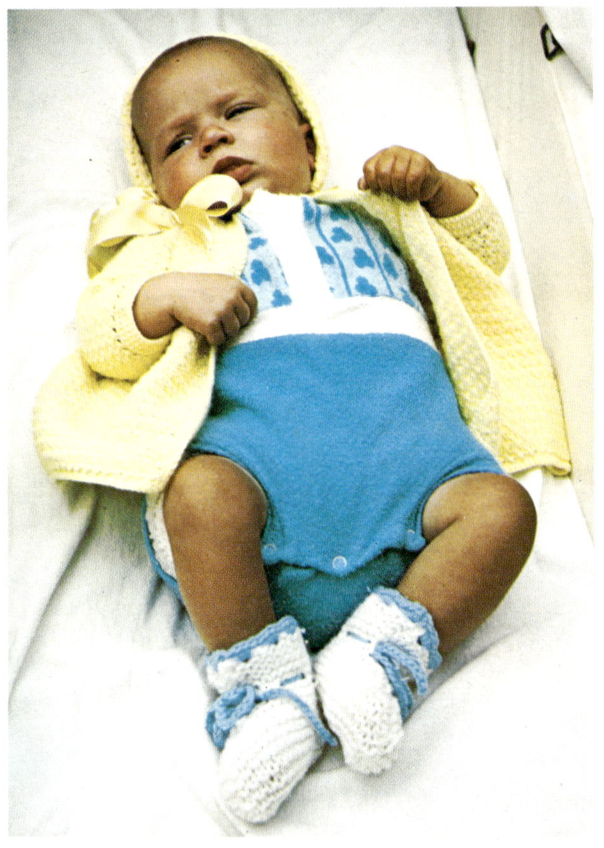

*Top: matinee coat and bonnet. Above: pram cover.
See page 135.*

Smockeasy dress (see page 138).

COAT YOKE

Arrange all pieces in order, 25 sts. of Right Front, 41 sts. of one Sleeve, 49 sts. of Back, 41 sts. of other Sleeve, and 25 sts. of Left Front. Across these, joining yarn work thus: 1 ch., 12 cls., hook through last st. of Front and first st. of Sleeve, yarn over hook and pull through 2 loops, yarn over hook and pull through last 2 loops (as for d.c.), 1 tr. into same st., miss 1 thus completing a cl., 1 cl. 19 times, hook through last d.c. of sleeve and first d.c. of back, yarn over hook and pull through, yarn over

hook and pull through 2 loops as for d.c., 1 tr. into same st. (another cl. completed), 23 cls., hook through last of back and first of second sleeve, complete cl. as before then work other side to match: 177 sts. and 88 cls. Work 1 row in patt. Now dec. thus on every alt. row and always working 1 row in patt. between each dec. row always turning with 1 ch.

Next row (3rd yoke row): 4 cl., (miss 3 sts., 7 cl.) 10 times, miss 3 sts., patt. 3 cl., 1 d.c.: 155 sts.

5th yoke row: 3 cl., (miss 3 sts., 6 cl.) 10 times, miss 3 sts., patt. to end, ending 1 d.c. in last st.: 133 sts.

7th yoke row: 2 cl., (miss 3 sts., 5 cl.) 10 times, patt. to end working 1 d.c. in last st.: 111 sts.

9th yoke row: 1 cl., (miss 3 sts., 4 cl.) 10 times, patt. to end working 1 d.c. in last st.: 89 sts.

11th yoke row: (miss 3 sts., 3 cl.) 10 times, patt. to end working 1 d.c. in last st.: 67 sts.

13th yoke row: (miss 3 sts., 2 cl.) 11 times, 1 d.c. in last st.

15th yoke row: 2 ch. instead of 1 turning ch., * 1 tr., 1 ch., miss 1 st.; rep. from * ending 1 tr. in last st.

This completes yoke, but do not cut yarn. Beg. with last loop on hook, work 3 rows d.c. along centre front edge, lower edge and along other front edge, working 3 d.c. into each of the 2 lower corners on both rows and turning with 1 ch. Fasten off. Work 6 rows of d.c. along wrist edge of each sleeve, always turning with 1 ch. Fasten off.

BONNET

Make 76 ch. and work in patt. as for Back: 75 sts. and 37 cl.
Work 22 rows straight, then always turning with 1 ch. shape top on every alt. row thus:

23rd row: 3 cl., (miss 3 sts., 7 cl.) 4 times, miss 3 sts., 1 cl. on next st., 1 d.c. on last st.: 65 sts.

25th row: 2 cl., (miss 3 sts., 6 cl.) 4 times, miss 3 sts., 1 cl. on next st., 1 d.c. on last st.: 55 sts.

27th row: 1 cl., (miss 3 sts., 5 cl.) 4 times, miss 3 sts., 1 cl., 1 d.c. in last st.: 45 sts.

29th row: (miss 3 sts., 4 cl.) 4 times, miss 3 sts., 1 cl., 1 d.c. in last st.: 35 sts.

31st row: (miss 3 sts., 3 cl.) 4 times, miss 2 sts., 1 d.c. in last st.: 25 sts. **33rd row:** (miss 3 sts., 1 cl.) to last st., 1 d.c. in st. Fasten off.

TO COMPLETE

Press work lightly with dry cloth and cool iron.
Coat. Join side and sleeve seams, then neatly join the 4 tiny armhole seams. Thread narrow ribbon through neck edge.
Bonnet. Sew back seam for about 2 in. from tip. Work 2 rows of d.c. along lower edge. Fold back brim for about 1½ in. and catch neatly in place. Work 1 row of d.c. round back neck edge. Sew on ribbon at each side.

Smockeasy dress
illustrated in colour on page 137

MATERIALS

5 (6, 7) balls Emu Tricel with Nylon in main shade, 1 ball in a contrast shade. Crochet hooks International Standard Sizes 4.00, 3.50, 3.00 and 2.50.

MEASUREMENTS

To fit chest size 24 (25, 26) in.

TENSION

7 sts. to 1 in. on No. 2.50 hook.

ABBREVIATIONS

See page 122; M., main; C., contrast.

BACK AND FRONT (make 2 pieces alike)
Bodice

With M. and No. 2.50 hook, make 90 (94, 98) ch.
Next row: 1 tr. in 6th ch. from hook, (1 ch., miss 1 ch., 1 tr. in next st.) to end.
Next row: 4 ch., 1 tr. in first tr., (1 ch., 1 tr. in next tr.) to end. Cont. to rep. last row until work is 2 (2½, 3) in.
Break yarn and rejoin at 5th (6th, 7th) tr. along, work to corresponding point at end of row, turn.
Cont. on these sts. till work is 2½ in. from beg. of armhole shaping.
Next row: work 4 ch., 1 tr. in first tr., (1 ch., 1 tr. in next tr.) 7 (8, 9) times, turn.
Work on this 'shoulder' until it is 2½ (2¾, 3) in.
Fasten off. Work second 'shoulder' to correspond.

Skirt

With M. and No. 3.00 hook, work along base of bodice making 44 (48, 52) d.c.
1st row: 5 ch., * miss 1 d.c., (2 tr., 2 ch., 2 tr.) into next d.c., 2 ch., miss 1 d.c., 1 tr. into next d.c., 2 ch.; rep. from * to last 4 sts., miss 1 d.c., (2 tr., 2 ch., 2 tr.) into next d.c., 2 ch., miss 1 d.c., 1 tr. into last d.c.
2nd row: 5 ch., * (2 tr., 2 ch., 2 tr.) into centre of first group, 2 ch., 1 tr. into single tr., 2 ch.; rep. from * to last 4 sts., (2 tr., 2 ch., 2 tr.) into centre of group, 2 ch., 1 tr. into single tr.
Now rep. last row until skirt is 2 in., change to No. 3.50 hook for next 2 in., and then to No. 4.00 hook and cont. until skirt is 9½ (10¾, 12) in. Fasten off.

TO COMPLETE

Join shoulder seams and side seams of dress.

Bodice Trim

With C. and No. 2.50 hook, work round neck and armhole edges as follows:
1st round: work all round evenly in d.c. making a multiple of 4 sts.
Next round: 1 ch., * 1 d.c. into next 4 d.c., 3 ch., sl.st. into 3rd ch. from hook; rep. from * all round.

Hem Edging

With C. and No. 2.50 hook work a picot edge as follows:
* 2 d.c. into 2 ch., 1 d.c. into each of 2 tr., then in 2 ch.sp. work (1 d.c., 3 ch., sl.st. into 3rd ch. from hook, 1 d.c.), 1 d.c. into

each of 2 tr., 2 d.c. into 2 ch., 1 d.c. into single tr.; rep. from *
to end, finishing 1 d.c. into top of ch. Fasten off.

Smocking

With No. 2.50 hook and C., work smocking over dress front
bodice, following chart and instructions below, and working
in the following sequence:
1st row: chain stitch.
2nd-6th rows: zig-zag stitch.
7th-8th rows: feather stitch.
9th-13th rows: zig-zag stitch.
14th row: chain stitch.
If required, further rows of chain stitch or another row of feather
stitch can be worked above and below this block for the two
larger sizes.

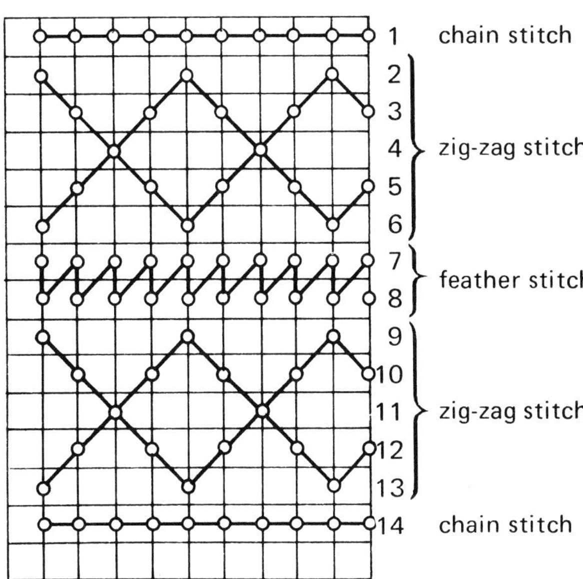

Smocking chart

1 square = 1 hole in the crochet

TO WORK SMOCKEASY CROCHET

Smockeasy is worked over the treble section of the garment.
When following the chart always work from right to left keeping
yarn to right side of work. All stitches are worked over the
surface by putting the crochet hook under a complete treble
and pulling yarn through, following the lines on the chart and
working in the correct colour. Each square on the chart represents
one hole in the crochet.

The Stitches

Chain stitch: 1 d.c., 1 ch. over each tr.
Zig-zag stitch: 1 d.c., 2 ch., moving from right to left.
Feather stitch: this is worked over 2 rows in the following
way: 1 d.c. (from right to left) over first tr. in first row, 1 ch., 1 d.c.
(from left to right) over first tr., in row above, * 1 ch., 1 d.c.
(from right to left) over 2nd tr. in first row, 1 ch., 1 d.c. (from
left to right) over 2nd tr. in row above; rep. from * to end, working
over each tr. in the correct sequence.

Three-colour play suit

illustrated in colour on page 141

MATERIALS

4 (4, 5) 50-gr. balls Patons Promise in main shade, and 1 ball
in each of two contrasting shades. Crochet hooks International
Standard Sizes 3.00 and 4.00. A 6-in. (7-in., 8-in.) zip fastener.
A 2-in. buckle.

MEASUREMENTS

To fit chest size 23 (26, 29) in.; length from top of shoulders
18 (20, 22) in.

TENSION

8½ sts. and 12 rows to 2 in. over d.c. on No. 4.00 hook.

ABBREVIATIONS

See page 122; M., main shade; C., contrast shade; dec. 1 on
d.c. rows, decrease 1 stitch on double crochet rows as follows:
(draw loop through next st.) twice, y.o.h., and draw through
all 3 loops on hook; dec. 1 on h.tr. rows, decrease 1 stitch on
half treble rows as follows: y.o.h., draw loop through next st.,
y.o.h., draw loop through 2 loops, y.o.h., draw loop through
next st., y.o.h., draw loop through all 4 loops on hook.
*Note. The turning ch. counts as 1 st., the first st. being missed
on every row unless otherwise stated.*

STRIPE PATTERN

1st row: join 1st C. in first st., and work 2 ch., 1 h.tr. in each
rem. st. to end. Break 1st C.
2nd row: join 2nd C. in first st., and work 1 ch., 1 d.c. in each
rem. st. to end, turn with 2 ch.
3rd row: 1 h.tr. in each st. to end, turn with 1 ch.
4th row: 1 d.c. in each st. to end.
Break 2nd C.
5th row: join 1st C. in first st. and work 2 ch., 1 h.tr. in each
remaining st. to end.
Break 1st C.
These 5 rows form stripe patt.

LEFT LEG

With No. 4.00 hook and M., make 75 (77, 79) ch.
Foundation row (right side): 1 d.c. in 2nd ch. from hook,
1 d.c. in each remaining ch., turn with 1 ch.: 74 (76, 78) sts.
1st row: 1 d.c. in each st. to end, turn with 1 ch.
2nd row: 2 d.c. in next st., 1 d.c. in each st. to last 2 sts., 2 d.c.
in next st., 1 d.c. in last st., turn with 1 ch.
Rep. first and 2nd rows once more, then first row again,
omitting turning ch. on last row: 78 (80, 82) sts.
Fasten off.

RIGHT LEG

Work as for Left Leg.

MAIN PART

With right side facing, leaving first 7 sts. of Right Leg free, join
1st C. to next st. and work 2 ch., dec. 1, 1 h.tr. in each st. to last
3 sts., leave these 3 sts. unworked and continue across Left
Leg as follows: leaving first 3 sts. free, work 1 h.tr. in each st.
to last 10 sts., dec. 1, 1 h.tr. in next st., turn: 134 (138, 142) sts.
Break 1st C.
Next row: as 2nd row of stripe patt.
Next row: dec. 1, 1 h.tr. in each st. to last 3 sts., dec. 1, 1 h.tr.,
turn with 1 ch.
Next row: as 4th row of stripe patt.
Next row: join 1st C. in first st. and work 2 ch., dec. 1, 1 h.tr.
in each st. to last 3 sts., dec. 1, 1 h.tr. in next st.: 130 (134, 138)
sts.
Break 1st C.
Next row: join M. in first st. and work 1 ch., 1 d.c. in each st.
to end, turn with 1 ch.
Next row: 14 (14, 15) d.c., (dec. 1, 31 (32, 33) d.c.) 3 times,
dec. 1, d.c. to end, turn with 1 ch.
Work 2 (3, 4) rows straight in d.c.
Next row: 13 (14, 14) d.c., (dec. 1, 30 (31, 32) d.c.) 3 times,
dec. 1, d.c. to end, turn with 1 ch.
Work 2 (3, 4) rows straight in d.c.
Next row: 13 (13, 14) d.c., (dec. 1, 29 (30, 31) d.c.) 3 times,
dec. 1, d.c. to end, turn with 1 ch.: 118 (122, 126) sts.
Next row: 1 d.c. in each st. to end, turn.
Break M.

continued on page 142

Little girls' dresses have effective colour contrasting.

Three-colour play suit (see page 139).

Shape Front Opening

Next row: leaving first 3 sts. free, join 1st C. to next st. and work 2 ch., 1 h.tr. in each st. to last 3 sts., turn: 112 (116, 120) sts.
Break 1st C.
Work 4 rows stripe patt., starting with a 2nd row.
Next row: join M. in first st. and work 1 ch., 1 d.c. in each st. to end, turn with 1 ch.
Next row: 10 d.c., (dec. 1, 28 (29, 30) d.c.) 3 times, dec. 1, d.c. to end, turn with 1 ch.: 108 (112, 116) sts.
Work 2 (3, 4) rows straight in d.c.
Next row: 9 d.c., (dec. 1, 27 (28, 29) d.c.) 3 times, dec. 1, d.c. to end, turn with 1 ch.
Work 2 (3, 4) rows straight in d.c.
Next row: 9 d.c., (dec. 1, 26 (27, 28) d.c.) 3 times, dec. 1, d.c. to end, turn with 1 ch.: 100 (104, 108) sts.
Work 3 rows straight in d.c., omitting turning ch. at end of last row.
Break M. (2 extra rows in M. have been worked here for position of Belt).
Work 5 rows stripe patt.
1st size only. Join in M. and work 9 rows d.c., omitting turning ch. on last row.
Work 5 rows stripe patt.
Join in M. and work 5 rows d.c.
2nd and 3rd sizes only. Join in M. and work (5, 6) rows straight in d.c.
Next row: (12, 13) d.c., (2 d.c. in next st., (25, 26) d.c.) 3 times, 2 d.c. in next st., d.c. to end, turn with 1 ch.: (108, 112) sts.
Work (3, 4) rows straight in d.c.
Next row: (12, 13) d.c., (2 d.c. in next st., (26, 27) d.c.) 3 times, 2 d.c. in next st., d.c. to end, turn with 1 ch.: (112, 116) sts.
Next row: 1 d.c. in each st. to end, turn.
Break M.
Work 5 rows stripe patt.
Join in M. and work 1 row in d.c.
2nd size only. Work 6 rows more in d.c.
3rd size only. Next row: 14 d.c., (2 d.c. in next st., 28 d.c.) 3 times, 2 d.c. in next st., d.c. to end, turn with 1 ch.
Work 3 rows straight in d.c.
Next row: 14 d.c., (2 d.c. in next st., 29 d.c.) 3 times, d.c. to end, turn with 1 ch.: 124 sts.
Work 3 rows straight in d.c.
All sizes. Divide for right front and shape as follows:
Next row: dec. 1, 18 (21, 24) d.c., dec. 1, 1 d.c., turn with 1 ch.: 22 (25, 28) sts.
Next row: 1 d.c. in each st. to end, turn with 1 ch.
Next row: dec. 1, 16 (19, 22) d.c., dec. 1, 1 d.c., turn with 1 ch.
Next row: 1 d.c. in each st. to end, turn.
Break M. Work 5 rows stripe patt. Join in M. and work 1 row in d.c.
Dec. 1 st. at each end as before on next and every following 3rd (4th, 5th) row until 14 (17, 20) sts. remain.
Next row: 1 d.c. in each st. to end, turn.
Break M. Work 5 rows stripe patt.
Join in M. and work 1 row in d.c.
Next row: dec. 1, 8 (11, 14) d.c., dec. 1, 1 d.c., turn with 1 ch.: 12 (15, 18) sts.
Work 4 (6, 8) rows straight in d.c., omitting turning ch. at end of last row.

Shape Shoulder

Next row: sl.st. over 4 (5, 6) sts., d.c. to end, turn with 1 ch.
Next row: 3 (4, 5) d.c., 4 (5, 6) sl.st.
Fasten off.

Left Front

With right side facing, join M. to 24th (27th, 30th) st. from end and work 1 ch., dec. 1, 18 (21, 24) d.c., dec. 1, 1 d.c.: 22 (25, 28) sts.
Complete to match Right Front reversing shapings.

Back

With right side facing, leaving 2 sts. free at underarm, join M. to next st. and work 1 ch., dec. 1, 42 (48, 54) d.c., dec. 1, 1 d.c., turn with 1 ch.: 46 (52, 58) sts.
Next row: in d.c. to end, turn with 1 ch.
Next row: dec. 1, 1 d.c. in each st. to last 3 sts., dec. 1, 1 d.c., turn with 1 ch.
Next row: in d.c. to end, turn with 1 ch.
Break M. Work 5 rows stripe patt. Join in M. and work 1 row d.c.
Dec. 1 st. at each end as before on next and every following 3rd (4th, 5th) row until 38 (44, 50) sts. remain.
Next row: in d.c. to end, turn. Break M.
Next row: join 1st C. in first st. and work 2 ch., 13 (16, 19) h.tr., turn.
Break 1st C. Work 4 rows stripe patt., starting with a 2nd row. Join in M. and work 1 row d.c.
Next row: dec. 1, 1 d.c. in each st. to last 3 sts., dec. 1, 1 d.c., turn with 1 ch.
Work 4 (6, 8) rows straight in d.c.

Shape Shoulder

Next row: d.c. to last 4 (5, 6) sts., turn.
Next row: sl.st. over 4 (5, 6) sts., 1 d.c. in each st. to end.
Fasten off.
With right side facing, leaving 10 sts. free, join in 1st C. to next st. and work 2 ch., 1 h.tr. in each st. to end.
Complete to match first side reversing shapings.

TO COMPLETE

Block each piece by pinning out round edges and press lightly using a warm iron and slightly damp cloth.
Join shoulder, leg and crutch seams, join front seam to opening.
Using 1st C. work a running stitch through each 3rd row of stripe patt.

Armhole Borders

With right side facing, No. 3.00 hook and M., start at underarm and work 1 row d.c. all round armhole, turn with 1 ch.
Work 4 rows more in d.c., omitting ch. at end of last row.
Fasten off.

Front Border

With right side facing, No. 3.00 hook and M., start at base of opening on Right Front and work in d.c. up Right Front, round neck and down Left Front, turn with 1 ch.
Work 4 rows more in d.c. omitting ch. at end of last row.
Fasten off.

Leg Borders

With right side facing, No. 3.00 hook and M., work 1 round d.c. all round leg working into remaining loop of starting ch.
Fasten off. Neatly join armhole borders. Stitch front borders to base of opening. Press seams. Sew zip in position.

BELT

With No. 4.00 hook and M., make 8 ch.
1st row: 1 d.c. in 2nd ch. from hook, 1 d.c. in each st. to end, turn with 1 ch.: 7 sts.
2nd row: 1 d.c. in each st. to end, turn with 1 ch.
Rep. last row until Belt measures 29 (32, 35) in. or required length, when slightly stretched.
Dec. 1 st. at each end of next 3 rows.
Fasten off.
With No. 3.00 hook and M., work 1 round d.c. all round Belt, working 1 d.c., 1 ch., 1 d.c. at corners.
Fasten off. Attach buckle.

Belt Tabs (make 4 alike)

With No. 3.00 hook and M., make 13 ch.
1st row: 1 d.c. in 2nd ch. from hook, 1 d.c. in each remaining ch., 1 d.c., 1 ch., 1 d.c. into row end, work 1 d.c. in each remaining ch. loop of starting ch., 1 d.c., 1 ch., 1 d.c. into row end, join with a sl.st. Fasten off. Attach 2 tabs to wide strip of M. approximately 3 in. from opening. Sew remaining tabs at back to correspond.

WOMEN

Pink and white beach set
illustrated in colour on page 144

MATERIALS. For cape: 5 (6, 6) balls Wendy Invitation Cotton in main shade and 7 (8, 8) balls in a contrasting shade (or any mediumweight cotton to give tension indicated below). One crochet hook International Standard Size 3.00. 1½ yards cord. **For bikini:** 5 (5, 7) balls Wendy Invitation Cotton in main shade and 1 ball in contrasting shade. One crochet hook International Standard Size 3.00. Waist length narrow elastic. Two hooks and eyes.

MEASUREMENTS. To fit bust size 32 (34, 36) in. and hip size 34 (36, 38) in.; length of Cape 20½ in.

TENSION. 10 sts. to 1½ in. and 5 rows to 1¾ in. over Cape patt.; 5 sts. to 1 in. over d.c.

ABBREVIATIONS. See page 122; M., main shade; C., contrasting shade.

CAPE (worked from top downwards)
Note. This garment can also be worn as a skirt if preferred.
With C. commence with 194 (209, 224) ch.
Foundation row: 1 tr. into the 3rd ch. from hook, 1 tr. into next ch., * miss 3 ch., 2 tr., 2 ch. and 2 tr. into next ch., miss 3 ch., 1 tr. into each of next 3 ch.; rep. from * to end.
Patt. row: 2 ch., 1 tr. into each of next 2 tr., 2 tr., 2 ch. and 2 tr. into 2 ch. sp., * 3 tr. into next gr. of tr., 2 tr., 2 ch. and 2 tr. into next 2 ch. sp.; rep. from * ending with 1 tr. into each of last 2 tr., 1 tr. into top of turning ch. Rep. last row once.
Now start to inc.: where there is an uneven number of tr. in the gr. work 2 tr. into the centre one; where there is an even number work 1 extra tr. through the centre of gr.
For size 32 only. Next row: patt., inc. 1 tr. in the 2nd, 5th, 8th, 10th, 11th, 13th, 16th and 19th tr. grs.
For sizes 34 and 36 only. Next row: patt., inc. 1 tr. in the 2nd (3rd) and every foll. 3rd gr.
For all sizes. Keeping the tr. grs. correct work 1 more row. Change to M. Now work 5 rows in each colour alternately and at the same time cont. to inc. as follows, working the incs. on the first row of each colour change.
For size 32 only. On next and every foll. alt. inc. row, inc. 1 tr. in the 2nd, 5th, 8th, 13th, 16th, 19th grs. only. On other inc. rows inc. as before.
For sizes 34 and 36 only. Inc. on same grs. as first inc. row.
For all sizes. Cont. to inc. until there are 12 trs. in the inc. grs. Work 5 rows straight in C. Fasten off.

Border. With C. and right side facing, beg. at top of left front edge and into each stripe down the side work 3 tr. to centre row, then into centre row work 2 tr., 2 ch. and 2 tr., then work 3 more tr. to end of stripe. Cont. to lower edge, then into the corner work 2 tr., 2 ch. and 2 tr., then cont. along lower edge working the 12 tr. grs. as before, work the second corner in the same way, then cont. up the 2nd side as for the first.
Work 4 more rows in patt. Fasten off.

To Make Up. Press with a warm iron over a damp cloth. Thread cord through the patt. holes at the top. Tie each end of cord 3 in. from the end and fringe out to form a tassel.

BIKINI BRIEFS
FRONT
With M., commence with 15 ch.
1st row: miss first ch., 1 d.c. into each of next 14 ch., 1 ch.; turn.
Patt. row: 1 d.c. into 2nd st., 1 d.c. into each st. to end, 1 ch., turn.
Rep. patt. row 12 times more.
Now inc. 1 st. (by working 2 d.c. into the same st.) at each end of the next and every foll. 3rd row until there are 22 sts.
Inc. 1 d.c. at each end of the next and every foll. row until there are 36 (40, 44) sts. ending last row with 4 ch.
Next row: 1 d.c. into 2nd ch. from hook, 1 d.c. into each of next 2 ch., patt. to end, 4 ch.; turn.
Rep. last row 5 times more ending last row with 5 ch.
Next row: 1 d.c. into 2nd ch. from hook, 1 d.c. into each of next 3 ch., patt. to end, 5 ch.; turn.
Work straight for 3½ in. in d.c.
Rep. last row once ending with 1 ch. Fasten off.

BACK
Return to the 14 ch. at the beg. of Front. Join M. and work 6 rows of d.c. along other edge of ch. Cont. in d.c., inc. 1 d.c. at each end of every row until there are 42 (46, 50) d.c. Inc. 1 d.c. at each end of every alt. row until there are 62 (66, 70) d.c.
Work straight in d.c. for 3½ in. Fasten off.

TO COMPLETE
Sides. With M., work 22 d.c. along one straight 3½ in. side edge of Back.
Next row: 2 ch., 1 tr. into 2nd st., * miss 3 d.c., 2 tr., 1 ch. and 2 tr. into next d.c., miss 3 d.c., 1 tr. into each of next 3 d.c.; rep. from * once.
Rep. the last row 4 times more. Fasten off.
Work other side of Back and sides of Front in same way.

Leg Borders. With M. work 112 (122, 132) d.c. round one leg edge.
With C. work 2 rows in patt. as for the sides. Fasten off. Work round other leg edge in same way.

To Make Up. Press with a warm iron over a damp cloth. Join side seams. Put elastic round waist and hold in place with herringbone casing.

BRA
CUPS (make 2 alike)
With M. commence with 4 ch. and join into a circle with a s.s.
1st round: 8 d.c. into the circle, s.s. into the first d.c., 1 ch.; turn and work in the opposite direction (beg. every round in this way).
Next round: 2 d.c. into 2nd d.c., * 1 d.c. into next d.c., 2 d.c. into next d.c.: rep. from * to end, s.s. into first d.c., 1 ch.; turn: 12 d.c.
Next round: 1 d.c. into 2nd d.c., * 2 d.c. into next d.c., 1 d.c. into each of next 2 d.c.; rep. from * twice, 2 d.c. into last d.c., s.s. into first d.c., 1 ch.; turn: 16 d.c.

continued on page 146

Pink/white beach set—wrap-around skirt doubles as cape (see page 143).

Another attractive bikini.

Cont. to inc. 4 d.c. in every round, working these between the incs. of the round before until there are 80 (88, 96) d.c.
Next row: work 14 (16, 18) d.c.; turn.
Work on these d.c. only, working 1 d.c. fewer at each end of every row until only 2 d.c. are worked. Fasten off.

TO COMPLETE

Back Strap and Joining Cups. With M. make 36 (38, 40) ch., then work 8 (9, 10) d.c. along one side of the triangle part of first Cup, work 18 (20, 22) d.c. round edge of circle part of first Cup, count 18 (20, 22) d.c. round circle part of 2nd Cup counting from the triangle, then work from this part round to triangle working 1 d.c. into each d.c., work 8 (9, 10) d.c. along side of triangle, then make 36 (38, 40) ch. Work 6 rows in d.c. across all sts. including the ch. Fasten off.

Neck Strap. Join M. with a s.s. to one Cup at the 14th (16th, 18th) d.c. from free side of triangle, make 98 ch., s.s. into the 14th (16th, 18th) d.c. from the triangle on the 2nd Cup, s.s. into next d.c. towards the centre, turn; 1 d.c. into each ch., s.s. into next d.c. towards the centre of first Cup; turn.
Rep. last row 5 times more, reading d.c. for ch. on strap. Fasten off.
Borders. With C. beg. at one end of back strap, join with 2 ch., 1 tr. into each of the next 2 d.c., *miss 3 d.c., 2 tr., 2 ch. and 2 tr. into next d.c., miss 3 ch., 1 tr. into each of the next 3 d.c.; rep. from * working round outer edge of first cup, neck strap and 2nd cup, and along other back strap, 1 ch.; turn.
Next row: 1 tr. into each of the 3 tr. of gr., and 2 tr., 2 ch. and 2 tr. into each 2 ch. sp. along row, ending with 3 tr. at the end of strap. Fasten off.
Join C. to centre of V then working round inner edge of cups and neck strap, work 1 tr. in centre, * miss 3 d.c., 2 tr., 2 ch. and 2 tr. into next d.c., miss 3 d.c., 1 tr. into each of next 3 d.c.; rep. from *, for size 32 only missing 2 d.c. instead of 3 at the join of strap, for size 34 only missing 4 d.c. instead of 3 at the join of strap, for size 36 only missing 1 d.c. instead of 3 at the join of strap, ending with a s.s. at the centre of V. Fasten off.
To Make Up. Press with a warm iron over a damp cloth. Sew 2 hooks and eyes to the ends of back strap.

Gold bathing costume
illustrated in colour on page 148

MATERIALS
5 oz. Twilleys Goldfingering. One crochet hook International Standard Size 2.50.

MEASUREMENTS
To fit bust size 34/36 in.

TENSION
6 tr. to 1 in.

ABBREVIATIONS
See page 122.

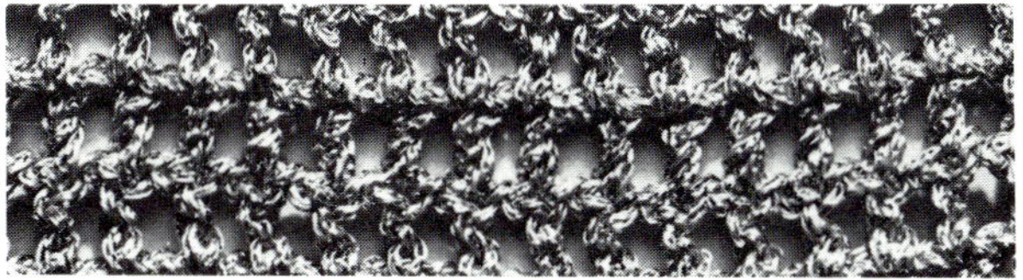

PANTS
Commence with yarn round finger to form a ring.
1st round: 3 ch., 15 tr. into ring, sl.st. into 3rd of 3 ch.
2nd round: 4 ch., * 1 tr. into next tr., 1 ch.; rep. from * sl.st. into 3rd of 4 ch.
3rd round: 3 ch., * 2 tr. into next sp., 1 tr. into next tr., into next sp. work 1 tr., 1 ch., 1 tr. (a 'V' st. formed), 1 tr. into next tr., 2 tr. into next sp., 1 tr. into next tr., 1 ch., 1 tr. into next tr.; rep. from * omitting last tr. of last rep., sl.st. into 3rd of 3 ch.
4th round: 3 ch., * 1 tr. into each of next 4 tr., a V st. into next V st., 1 tr. into each of next 5 ch., 2 ch., 1 tr. into next tr.; rep. from * omitting last tr. of last rep., sl.st. into 3rd of 3 ch.
5th round: 3 ch., * 1 tr. into each of next 5 tr., a V st. into next V st., 1 tr. into each of next 6 tr., 3 ch., 1 tr. into next tr.; rep. from * omitting last tr. of last rep., sl.st. into 3rd of 3 ch.
6th round: 4 ch., miss next tr., * 1 tr. into each of next 5 tr., a V st. into next V st., 1 tr. into next 5 tr., 1 ch., miss next tr., 1 tr. into next tr., (1 ch., 1 tr.) twice into next sp., 1 ch., 1 tr. into next tr., 1 ch., miss next tr.; rep. from * omitting last tr. and ch. at end of last rep., sl.st. into 3rd of 4 ch.
7th round: 4 ch., * 1 tr. into next tr., 1 ch., miss next tr., 1 tr. into next tr., 1 ch., 1 tr. into each of next 3 tr., a V st. into next V st., 1 tr. into each of next 3 tr., 1 ch., 1 tr. into next tr., 1 ch., miss next tr., (1 tr. into next tr., 1 ch) 5 times, miss next tr.; rep. from * omitting last tr. and ch. at end of last rep., sl.st. into 3rd of 4 ch., fasten off.
8th round: attach thread to a V st., 3 ch., * 1 tr. into next tr., 1 ch., 1 tr. into next tr., 1 ch., miss next tr., (1 tr. into next tr., 1 ch.) 10 times, miss next tr., 1 tr. into next tr., 1 ch., 1 tr. into next tr., a V st. into next V st.: rep. from * twice omitting last tr. at end of last rep., turn.
9th row: 3 ch., miss first tr., (1 tr. into next tr., 1 ch.) 12 times, miss next tr., 1 tr. into next tr., 1 ch., 6 tr. into next V st., 1 ch., 1 tr. into next tr., 1 ch., miss next tr., (1 tr. into next tr., 1 ch.) 3 times, (1 d.c. into next tr., 1 ch.) 6 times, (1 tr. into next tr., 1 ch.) 3 times, miss next tr., 1 tr. into next tr., 1 ch., 6 tr. into next V st., 1 ch., 1 tr. into next tr., miss next tr., 1 ch., into each tr. work 1 tr., 1 ch. to within last V. st., 1 tr. into V st., turn.
** **10th row:** 3 ch., miss first 2 tr., into each tr. work 1 tr., 1 ch. until 6 tr. group is reached, 1 tr. into centre sp. of next 6 tr. group, miss 2 tr., 1 d.tr. into next tr., turn.
11th row: 3 ch., miss first tr., into each tr. work 1 tr., 1 ch. to within last 2 sp., 1 tr. into next tr., turn.
12th row: 4 ch., into each tr. work 1 tr., 1 ch., 1 tr. into 3rd of 4 ch., turn.
13th row: 4 ch., miss first tr., into each tr. work 1 tr., 1 ch. to within last 3 sp., 1 tr., into next tr., 1 ch., 1 tr. into next tr., turn.
Rep. last 2 rows until only six 1 ch.sp. remain, then work 12th row twice more. Fasten off. **

Second Side
Work to correspond with first side attaching yarn to 3rd of 4 ch. and working from ** to ** of first side.

Crutch
1st row: mark centre of sp. of crutch, attach yarn to 4th tr. before marked sp., 4 ch., (1 tr. into next tr., 1 ch.) 6 times, 1 tr. into next tr., turn.
Work 12th row 4 times. Fasten off.
Make a 2nd piece the same, and then join side and crutch seams.

BRA
Yarn round finger to form a ring.
1st round: 3 ch., 11 tr. into ring.
2nd-5th rounds: same as for 2nd to 5th rounds of pants.
6th row: 4 ch., miss first tr., 1 tr. into each of next 5 tr., 1 V st. into next V st., patt. to within last V st., 1 V st. into last V st., 1 tr. into each of next 5 tr., miss next tr., 1 tr. into next tr., turn.
7th row: 1 sl.st. into first tr., 3 ch., (miss next tr., 1 tr. into next tr., 1 ch.) twice, 1 V st. into next V st., patt. to within last V st., 1 V st. into next V st., (1 ch., miss next tr., 1 tr. into next tr.) twice, miss next tr., 1 tr. into next tr., turn.
8th row: 3 ch., miss first 2 tr., 1 tr. into next tr., 1 ch., 1 tr. into next V st., patt. to within last V st., 1 tr. into next V st., 1 ch., miss next tr., 1 tr. into each of next 2 tr., turn.
9th row: 3 ch., miss first 2 tr., 1 tr. into next tr., 1 ch., patt. to within turning ch., turn.

Strap
1st row: 4 ch., miss first tr., (1 tr. into next tr., 1 ch.) twice, 1 tr. into next tr., turn.
Rep. 12th row of pants 11 times. Fasten off.

Second Half
Work as first half until strap is reached. Fasten off.

Strap
1st row: with right side facing attach yarn to 4th tr. from beg. of last rep., then work as first row of first strap, turn.
Complete as first strap. Fasten off.
Join 2 halves by sewing three 1 ch.sp. together.

BODY SECTION
1st round: with right side facing attach yarn to first tr. from centre back of pants, 4 ch., 1 tr., 1 ch. into each row-end all round, 1 tr. into same place as join, turn: 109 sp. altogether. Work 12th row of pants 11 times (adjust length here if necessary).
13th row: 1 sl.st. into each of first 10 sts., patt. to within last 5 sp., turn.
14th row: 1 sl.st. into each of first 6 sts., patt. to within last 3 sp., turn.
Rep. last row twice more.
17th row: 1 sl.st. into each of first 2 sts., patt. to within last sp., turn.
Rep. last row 7 times more, then work 12th row of pants 6 times. Fasten off.

TO COMPLETE
Sew bra to top of body section.

Edging
1st round: with right side facing attach yarn to centre back, then work d.c. evenly round, 1 d.c. into first d.c.
2nd round: work d.c. evenly round making 3 d.c. into corners and missing 2 d.c. where the 2 halves of the bra were joined together.

Straps
Using double thickness of yarn attach yarn to top of bra and work 18 in. of chain, sl.st. into top of other bra cup. Fasten off.
Attach yarn to top corner of back and work a chain 10 in. long. Fasten off. Repeat at other side.

Above: *gold bathing costume (see page 147).*

Opposite: *Reversible and peaked berets (see page 150).*

Reversible beret
illustrated in colour on page 149

MATERIALS
2 oz. Hayfield Gaylon Double Knitting in each of two contrasting shades. One crochet hook International Standard Size 5.00. Short length shirring elastic.

MEASUREMENTS
To fit an average size head.

TENSION
6½ tr. to 2 in.

ABBREVIATIONS
See page 122; A, first shade; B, 2nd shade.

TO MAKE
First Side
With A commence with 6 ch. and join with sl.st. to form a ring.
1st round: 3 ch., 11 tr. into ring, sl.st. to 3rd of 3 ch.: 12 sts.
2nd round: 3 ch., 1 tr. into same st., 2 tr. into each st. to end, sl.st. to 3rd of 3 ch.: 24 sts.
3rd round: 4 ch., * 1 tr. into next tr., 1 ch.; rep. from * to end, sl.st. to 3rd of 4 ch.
4th round: as 3rd round.
5th round: sl.st. into first ch.sp., * 4 ch., 1 d.c. into next ch.sp.; rep. from * to end, 4 ch., sl.st. to beg. of round.
6th round: sl.st. to centre of ch.loop, * 4 ch., 1 d.c. into centre of next ch. loop; rep. from * to end, 4 ch., 1 d.c. into centre of first ch.loop.
7th round: as 6th round.
8th round: as 6th round.
9th round: as 6th round but work 5 ch. instead of 4 ch.
10th round: as 9th round.
11th round: as 9th round.
12th round: as 9th round, but work 6 ch. instead of 5 ch.
13th round: as 12th round.
14th round: as 12th round but work 7 ch. instead of 6 ch.
15th round: as 14th round.
16th round: as 12th round.
17th round: as 9th round.
18th round: as 6th round.
19th round: as 18th round.
20th round: as 6th round but work 3 ch. instead of 4 ch.
21st round: as 20th round.
Fasten off.

Second Side
With B, work as first side.

TO COMPLETE
Insert one side of the beret inside the other and secure at crown. With crochet hook and either A or B, insert hook through ch. loops on outer edges of both sides of beret and work 1 d.c. and 1 ch. into each loop all round. Fasten off. Thread 2 strands shirring elastic round edge of beret.

Peaked beret
illustrated in colour on page 149

MATERIALS
4 oz. Hayfield Gaylon Double Knitting. One crochet hook International Standard Size 5.00.

MEASUREMENTS
To fit an average size head.

TENSION
6½ tr. to 2 in.

ABBREVIATIONS
See page 122.

TO MAKE
Commence with 6 ch. and join with sl.st. to form a ring.
1st round: 3 ch., 11 tr. into ring, sl.st. to 3rd of 3 ch.: 12 sts.
2nd round: 3 ch., 1 tr. into same st., 2 tr. into each st. to end, sl.st. to 3rd of 3 ch.: 24 sts.
3rd round: 1 tr. into each tr.sp. to end, sl.st. to first tr.: 24 sts.
4th round: * 1 tr. into first tr.sp., 2 tr. into next tr.sp.; rep. from * to end, sl.st. to first tr.: 36 sts.
5th round: 1 tr. into each tr. sp. to end, sl.st. to first tr.
6th round: * 1 tr. into each of first 2 tr.sps., 2 tr. into next tr.sp.; rep. from * to end, sl.st. to first tr.
7th round: as 6th round but work 3 tr. between each inc.
8th round: as 5th round.
9th round: as 6th round but work 4 tr. between each inc.
10th round: as 5th round.
11th round: as 6th round but work 5 tr. between each inc.
12th round: as 5th round.
13th round: as 6th round but work 6 tr. between each inc.: 96 sts.
14th round: as 5th round.
15th round: as 5th round.
16th round: * 1 tr. into each of next 7 tr.sps., miss 1 tr.sp.; rep. from * to end, sl.st. to first tr.: 84 sts.
17th round: as 5th round.
18th round: as 5th round.
19th round: as 16th round but work 6 tr. between each dec.
20th round: as 5th round.
21st round: as 16th round, but work 5 tr. between each dec.: 60 sts.
22nd round: as 5th round.
23rd round: as 5th round.
24th round: 1 h.tr. into each st. to end, sl.st. to first h.tr.
25th round: as 24th round.
26th round: as 24th round.
Fasten off.
Fold last 3 rounds to wrong side to form an inside band.
Rejoin yarn and work 1 round of d.c. along folded edge to hold band in place.

Peak
Next row: sl.st. over 10 sts., 1 d.c. into next st., * 2 d.c. into next d.c., 1 d.c. into next d.c.; rep. from * 17 times; turn.
Next row: sl.st. over 2 sts., 1 d.c. into each st. to last 2 sts.; turn.
Rep. last row 9 times. Fasten off.

TO COMPLETE
Beg. at centre back, work 1 round of d.c. round back edge and peak. Fasten off.

Tunic sweater
illustrated in colour on page 152

MATERIALS
30 (31, 31) oz. Lee Target Loch Isle Double Knitting wool. One crochet hook International Standard Size 3.50. A 9-in. zip fastener. A 2-in. buckle.

MEASUREMENTS
To fit bust size 36 (38, 40) in.; length 29 in.; sleeve seam 17 in.

TENSION
6 sts. and 5½ rows to 1 in. over Pattern A, with No. 3.50 hook.

ABBREVIATIONS
See page 122.

PATTERN A (all main parts are worked in this patt.)
1st row: 1 d.c. in the first st. of last row, * 1 ch., miss 1 st., 1 d.c. in foll. st.; rep. from * to end.
2nd row: 1 ch. to turn; in every d.c. of row below, work 1 d.c., 1 ch. between each d.c.
The 2nd row forms the patt. Repeat it throughout.

PATTERN B (pocket, neckband and sleeve welts are worked in this patt.)
1st row: miss 1 ch., 1 d.c. in 2nd and 3rd ch., * 1 tr. in next ch., 1 tr. in next ch., 1 d.c. in next ch., 1 d.c. in next ch.; rep. from * to end.
2nd row: 1 ch. to turn; on the d.c. of last row work d.c., for every tr. work a ch. and miss the tr.
3rd row: 1 ch. to turn; on the d.c. of last row work d.c., round each tr. of first row work as follows in sculptured tr.: (always keeping the 2 ch. of the previous row at back of the work) y.o.h. and insert hook from front round the back of the tr. below, y.o.h. and pull through and work the tr. in the usual way.
4th row: as 2nd row.
5th row: as 3rd row, working the sculptured tr. round the sculptured tr. of the 3rd row.
The 4th and 5th rows form Pattern B.

BACK
Make 115 (121, 127) ch. and begin Pattern A. Work straight for 4 in. Dec. 1 st. at both ends of next and every foll. 30th row until 109 (115, 121) sts. remain. Work straight until Back measures 21½ in. from beg.

Divide for Zip
Next row: work across 54 (57, 60) sts. to centre back, turn and work this side first.

**Shape Armhole
Sl.st. across 4 (5, 6) sts. at armhole edge once, work to centre.
Next row: work to armhole.
Next row: sl.st. across 2 sts. at armhole edge, work to centre.
Next row: work to armhole.
Rep. last 2 rows 3 times more. Work on 42 (44, 46) sts. until armhole measures 7 (7½, 8) in. from beg., ending at armhole edge.

Shape Shoulder
Next row: sl.st. across 8 (8, 9) sts., work to neck edge.
Next row: work to end.
Next row: sl.st. across 8 (9, 9) sts., work to end.
Next row: work to end.
Next row: sl.st. across 9 sts., work 17 (18, 19) sts. for half of back of neck. Fasten off. **
Rejoin yarn at inner edge and work from ** to **, reversing all shapings.

FRONT
Work as for Back until 109 (115, 121) sts. remain. Work straight until Front matches Back to beg. of armhole.

Shape Armholes
Next row: sl.st. across 4 (5, 6) sts., work to last 4 (5, 6) sts., turn, leaving them unworked.
Next row: work across in patt.
3rd row: sl.st. across 2 sts., work to last 2 sts., turn, leaving them unworked.
4th row: work to end.
Rep. last 2 rows 3 times more. Work on 84 (88, 92) sts. until armhole measure 5 (5½, 6) in. from beg. of shaping.

Shape Neck
Next row: work across 36 (37, 38) sts., turn and work this side first.
***Dec. 1 st. at neck edge (by either sl.st. across or leaving it unworked) on foll. 11 rows. At the same time when armhole

matches Back to shoulder, shape shoulder as follows:
Sl.st. on alt. rows beg. at armhole edge across 8 (8, 9) sts. once, 8 (9, 9) sts. once, and 9 sts. once. Fasten off. ***
Count centre 12 (14, 16) sts. and leave them unworked. Rejoin yarn next to them and work from *** to ***, reversing shapings.

POCKET
Make 31 ch. and work in Pattern B for 5½ in. Fasten off.

SLEEVES (make 2 alike)
Make 43 ch. and work in Pattern B for 5½ in. Begin Pattern A and inc. 23 sts. evenly across first row of pattern to 65 sts. Cont. in Pattern B, inc. 1 st. at both ends of every 5th (5th, 4th) row until there are 85 (87, 89) sts. on the sleeve. Work straight until sleeve measure 17 in. from beg.

Shape Top
Next row: sl.st. across 4 (5, 6) sts., work to last 4 (5, 6) sts., turn, leaving them unworked. **Next row:** work to end.
3rd row: sl.st. across 3 sts., work to last 3 sts., turn, leaving them unworked.
4th row: work to end.
Rep. 3rd and 4th rows 7 times more.
19th row: sl.st. across 4 sts., work to last 4 sts., turn.
20th row: work to end.
21st row: sl.st. across 5 sts., work to last 5 sts.
Fasten off, leaving 11 sts. at top of sleeve.

BELT
Make 13 ch. and work in Pattern A for 38 (40, 42) in.
Fasten off.

TO COMPLETE
Join shoulder seams.

Neckband
With right side of work facing, work 58 (63, 68) d.c. around neck.
Next row: 1 ch. to turn; work d.c., then beg. Pattern B as follows: * 3 d.c., 2 sculptured tr.; rep from * to last 3 sts., 3 d.c. Work in this way for 3 rows. Now work 4 rows and work 2 d.c. only between the 2 sculptured tr. Work 1 row d.c. up and down the zip opening. Fasten off.

To Make Up
Press pieces on wrong side under a damp cloth, using a moderate iron. Join side and sleeve seams. Set in sleeves. Sew pocket to right half of front, 2½ in. above lower edge. Set in zip. Sew buckle to belt. Press all seams.

Tunic sweater (see page 150).

Cotton jumper with lacy-patterned sleeves and neckband (see page 154).   153

Cotton jumper – in six sizes
illustrated in colour on page 153

MATERIALS
9 (10, 10, 11, 12, 12) oz. Twilleys Lyscordet cotton yarn. One crochet hook International Standard Size 3.00. A 4-in. zip fastener.

MEASUREMENTS
To fit bust size 32 (34, 36, 38, 40, 42) in.; length 21 (21, 22, 22, 23, 23) in.; sleeve seam 2 in.

TENSION
6 tr. to 1 in.

ABBREVIATIONS
See page 122

FRONT
Make 85 (91, 97, 103, 109, 115) ch.
1st row: 1 tr. in 3rd ch. from hook, (1 tr. in next ch.) to end: 84 (90, 96, 102, 108, 114) sts.
Next row: 2 ch., 1 tr. in 2nd tr., (1 tr. in next tr.) to end. Working in tr. in this way, inc. 1 tr. each end of every 5th row until there are 8 incs. at each side: 100 (106, 112, 118, 124, 130) sts. Cont. until work measures 14 (14, 14½, 14½, 15, 15) in. from beg.

Armhole Shaping
Next row: sl.st. across first 8 (9, 10, 11, 12, 13) tr., 2 ch., 1 tr. in 2nd tr., 1 tr. in each tr. to last 8 (9, 10, 11, 12, 13) sts., turn.
Next row: sl.st. across first tr., 2 ch., 1 tr. in 2nd tr., 1 tr. in each tr. to last st., turn.
Work 1 row. Rep. last 2 rows twice more: 78 (82, 86, 90, 94, 98) sts. Cont. straight in tr. until work measures 19½ (19½, 20½, 20½, 21½, 21½) in. from beg.

Neck Shaping
Next row: work 28 (30, 32, 34, 36, 38), turn. Work on these sts. only.
Next row: sl.st. across first 2 tr., 2 ch., 1 tr. in 2nd tr., tr. to end.
Work 1 row straight. Rep. last 2 rows once more then dec. row again. Fasten off. Leave centre 22 sts., rejoin yarn to rem. 28 (30, 32, 34, 36, 38) sts. and tr. to end.
Next row: tr. to last 2 sts., turn.
Work 1 row. Rep. last 2 rows once more then dec. row again. Fasten off.

BACK
Work as Front until work measures 18 (18, 19, 19, 20, 20) in. from beg.

Back dividing row: work 39 (41, 43, 45, 47, 49), turn. Work on these sts. only until work measures 21 (21, 22, 22, 23, 23) in. from beg. Fasten off. Complete other side to match.

SLEEVES (make 2 alike)
Make 76 (76, 81, 81, 85, 85) ch.
1st row: 1 d.c. in 2nd ch. from hook, (1 d.c. in next ch.) to end: 75 (75, 80, 80, 84, 84) sts.
Next row: 1 ch., 1 d.c. in each d.c. to end.
Rep. last row twice more.
Next row: 1 ch., 1 d.c. in each of first 3 (3, 5, 5, 3, 3) d.c., (2 d.c. in next d.c., 1 d.c. in each of next 2 d.c.) to end: 99 (99, 105, 105, 111, 111) sts.
Now patt. thus:
Foundation row: 1 ch., 1 d.c. in each of first 2 d.c., (miss 2 d.c., 5 tr. in next d.c., miss 2 d.c., 1 d.c. in next d.c.) to last st., 1 d.c. in last d.c.
1st patt. row: 2 ch., 1 tr. in 2nd d.c., (2 ch., 1 d.c. in centre of 5 tr., 2 ch., 1 tr. in next d.c.) to last st., 1 tr. in last d.c.
2nd patt. row: 1 ch., 1 d.c. in each of first 2 tr., (5 tr. in next d.c., 1 d.c. in next tr.) to last st., 1 d.c. in last tr.
These 2 rows form the patt.
Work 6 rows more in patt.
Next row: sl.st. across first complete patt. (6 sts.), patt. to last complete patt., turn. Work 1 row straight. Rep. last 2 rows 5 (5, 6, 6, 7, 7) times more. Fasten off.

TO COMPLETE
Join shoulders. Work across 17 sts. in d.c. at left side of back neck, work 13 d.c. down left side of front neck, work in d.c. across 22 sts. at centre front, 12 d.c. up right side of front neck then work in d.c. across 17 sts. at right side of back neck: 81 sts. Now work foundation patt. row as for Sleeves, then rep. first and 2nd patt. rows of Sleeves twice. Fasten off. Do not press. Set in sleeves. Join side and sleeve seams. Work 1 row d.c. round back opening, then sew in zip fastener. Press seams.

Pillbox hat and sweater
also illustrated in colour on page 156

MATERIALS. 9 (9, 10) balls Wendy Invitation Cotton in main shade and 3 balls in a contrasting shade (or any medium-weight cotton to give tension indicated below). One crochet hook International Standard Size 2.50. Small quantity buckram. ½ yard lining material. One 4-in. zip fastener.

MEASUREMENTS. Hat: to fit head size 22 in. **Sweater:** to fit bust size 34 (36, 38) in.; length 17 (17½, 18) in.

TENSION. 6½ sts. and 6 rows to 1 in. over rounds of d.c.

ABBREVIATIONS. See page 122; dec. 1, leaving last loop of each on hook work next 2 sts., y.o.h. and draw through all 3 loops on hook; M., main shade; C., contrasting shade.

Note. When working crochet in 2 colours is it essential that the 2nd half of the preceding stitch should be worked in the colour of the next stitch, otherwise the effect will be patchy i.e. when working 2 black sts. followed by 2 white, the first half of the 2nd st. must be worked in black and the 2nd half of this st. in white. The 4th st. must be worked with the first half white and the 2nd half black.

HAT
With M. commence with 6 ch. and join into a ring with s.s.
1st round: 12 d.c. into ring, s.s. into first d.c.
2nd round: * 2 d.c. into each of next 2 sts., 1 d.c. into next st.; rep. from * twice, 2 d.c. into each of next 3 sts., s.s. into first d.c.: 21 sts.
3rd round: * 1 d.c. into each of next 2 sts., 2 d.c. into next

st.; rep. from * 6 times, s.s. into first d c.: 28 sts.
4th round: * 1 d.c. into each of next 3 sts., 2 d.c. into next st.; rep. from * 6 times, s.s. into first d.c.: 35 sts.
5th round: * 1 d.c. into each of next 4 sts., 2 d.c. into next st.; rep. from * 6 times, s.s. into first d.c.: 42 sts.
Cont. inc. 7 sts. every round in this way, working 1 more st. between incs. each time, until there are 168 sts.
Next round: * 1 d.c. into each of next 83 sts., 2 d.c. into next st.; rep. from * once, s.s. into first d.c.: 170 sts.
Next round: work in d.c.
Change to C. and work 3 rounds straight in d.c.
Now work in M. and C. in rounds of d.c.
1st round: * 1 C., 9 M.; rep. from * 16 times, s.s. to first d.c.
2nd round: * 2 C., 7 M., 1 C.; rep. from * 16 times, s.s. to first d.c.
3rd round: * 3 C., 5 M., 1 C.; rep. from * 16 times, s.s. to first d.c.
4th round: * 4 C., 3 M., 2 C.; rep. from * 16 times, s.s. to first d.c.
5th round: * 5 C., 1 M., 4 C.; rep. from * 16 times, s.s. to first d.c.
6th round: as 4th round.
7th round: as 3rd round.
8th round: as 2nd round.
9th round: as first round.
10th round: with C. to end.
11th to 19th rounds: as first to 9th rounds.
20th round: as 10th round.
21st round: with C., * 1 d.c. into each of next 6 d.c., dec. 1 d.c. over next 2 d.c.; rep. from * 20 times, 1 d.c. into each of last 2 d.c., s.s. into first d.c.
22nd round: with C., * 1 d.c. into each of next 5 d.c., dec. 1 d.c. over next 2 d.c.; rep. from * 20 times, 1 d.c. into each of last 2 d.c., s.s. into first d.c.

SWEATER
MAIN PIECE
With C. commence with 191 (201, 211) ch.
1st row: 1 d.c. into 2nd ch. from hook, 1 d.c. into each ch. to end: 190 (200, 210) d.c.
Break yarn, rejoin at beg. of row and work 1 row in d.c. with C. Rep. this row. Now work 19 rows in patt. as for lower part of Hat (brim), breaking yarn at end of every row and rejoining at beg. Then work 3 rows in C. in same way.
Now change to M. and work a row of d.c. and join the 2 ends of row with a s.s. Place a marker of contrasting coloured thread at join and at opposite side of work. Now work in rounds in d.c. On next round work twice into st. on either side of each marker (thus inc. 4 sts.), then work 2 rows straight. Rep. these 3 rows 11 times more: 238 (248, 258) sts.

Shape Armholes. Next round: work to within 5 sts. of first marker; turn then work 5 ch., 1 d.c. into 4th st. from hook 21 (22, 23) times; turn.
Next row: sl. st. to centre of first ch.-loop, 5 ch., 1 d.c. into next space to end of row. Rep. this row until there are 19 (19, 19) patts.
Work straight in this patt. until work measures 14 (14½, 15) in. from beg.

Shape Neck. Patt. to within 1½ in. of centre (7 patts.); turn and sl. st. to centre of first ch.-loop, (5 ch., 1 d.c. into next space) to end of row. Turn and patt. across row to centre of last ch.-loop, turn, sl.st. to centre of ch.-loop then patt. back. Rep. last 2 rows twice more. Fasten off. Work up second shoulder to match, reversing shapings.
Now rejoin cotton to 5 sts. beyond marker and d.c. to within 2 sts. of 2nd marker, then work in patt. as for first half of sweater, which was for back, but in this case working only 6 rows in patt. Now shape for neck exactly as for back and when the 8 rows of shaping are completed work up straight until you have worked 25 rows of this openwork patt. and patt. matches back exactly. Fasten off and work second shoulder to match. Slip st. shoulders together.

TO COMPLETE
Press work under damp cloth.

Edgings. With C. work 80 d.c. all round one armhole then work 3 more rounds in d.c., dec. 2 sts. at bottom of armhole on 2nd and 4th rounds. Fasten off. Work round second armhole in same way. With C. work 70 d.c. round back of neck and 100 d.c. round front of neck. Work 1 further round in d.c. with C. Cont. in rounds of d.c. as follows.
1st round: * 1 C., 9 M.; rep. from * 16 times.
2nd round: * 3 C., 7 M., rep. from * 16 times.
3rd round: * 5 C., 5 M.; rep. from * 16 times.
4th round: * 7 C., 3 M.; rep. from * 16 times.
5th round: * 3 C., with C. dec. 1 st. over next 2 sts., 4 C., 1 M.; rep. from * 16 times.
6th round: with C. to end.
7th round: with C., * 1 d.c. into each of next 8 d.c., dec. 1 st. over next 2 sts.; rep. from * 16 times.
Press these edgings. Insert zip in side opening. Press.

To Make Up Hat. Press well under damp cloth. Cut a piece of buckram about 3 in. deep — or desired depth — and length to fit head and join into a ring. Cut a length of lining material about 1 in. longer and a circle of lining material to fit crown of hat. St. circle of lining in place to inside of hat. Slip st. buckram inside brim of hat firmly, then join lining strip into a ring, and slip st. to inside of Hat over buckram, turning in raw edges of lining.

White lacy-patterned dress
illustrated on page 157

MATERIALS
17 (18) oz. Lister Lavenda 4-ply Wool. Crochet hooks International Standard Sizes 2.50 and 3.00 (3.00 and 3.50). Six medium buttons.

MEASUREMENTS
To fit bust size 32/34 (36/38) in.; hip size 34/36 (38/40) in.; length from top of shoulder 36 (38) in. (adjustable).

TENSION
1 patt. to 2¼ in., and 6 tr. to 1 in. on No. 3.00 hook.
1 patt. to 2½ in., and 11 tr. to 2 in. on No. 3.50 hook.

continued on page 158

156   *Specially for holidays—two-colour crochet top with matching pillbox hat. Instructions on page 154.*

White lacy-patterned dress (see page 155).

ABBREVIATIONS

See page 122; dec. 1 tr., decrease 1 treble, by working next 2 tr., leaving last loop on hook each time, y.o.h., and draw through 3 loops tog., thus dec. 1 tr.

BACK

With No. 2.50 (3.00) hook make 132 ch.
1st row (right side): 1 d.c. in 2nd ch. from hook, 1 d.c. in each remaining ch.: 131 d.c.
2nd row: 1 d.c. in each d.c.
Repeat 2nd row twice.
Change to No. 3.00 (3.50) hook and commence patt.
1st patt. row: 3 ch., miss first 2 d.c., 1 tr. in next d.c., * miss 1 d.c., 1 ch., 1 tr. in next d.c.; rep. from * to end, 3 ch., turn (these to count as first tr. and ch.).
2nd patt. row: miss first tr. and ch., 1 tr. in next tr., * miss 1 tr., 5 ch., 1 d.tr. in next tr., 1 d.tr. in each of next 3 tr., miss 1 tr., 5 ch., 1 tr. in next tr., 1 ch., 1 tr. in next tr.; rep. from * to end, 3 ch., turn.
3rd row: miss first tr. and ch., 1 tr. in next tr., * 5 ch., 1 d.c. in d.tr., 1 d.c. in each of next 3 d.tr., 5 ch., 1 tr. in next tr., 1 ch., 1 tr. in next tr.; rep. from * to end, 3 ch., turn.
4th row: miss first tr. and ch., 1 tr. in next tr., * 5 ch., 1 d.c., 1 d.c. in each of next 3 d.c., 5 ch., 1 tr. in next tr., 1 ch., 1 tr. in next tr.; rep. from * to end, 3 ch., turn.
5th row: as 4th row.
6th row: miss first tr. and ch., 1 tr. in next tr., * 3 ch., 1 d.tr. in next d.c., 1 ch., 1 d.tr. in each of next 3 d.c., 3 ch., 1 tr. in next tr., 1 ch., 1 tr. in next tr.; rep. from * to end, 3 ch., turn.
7th row: miss first tr. and ch., 1 tr. in next tr., * 1 ch., 1 tr. in 2nd of 3 ch., (1 ch., 1 tr. in next d.tr.) 4 times, 1 ch., 1 tr. in 2nd of 3 ch., (1 ch., 1 tr. in next tr.) twice; rep. from * to end.
The 2nd–7th rows inclusive form the patt. Cont. until 10 patts. are complete, ending with a 7th row. (Skirt length may be adjusted at this point but must finish on a 7th row of patt.)
Work a 2 ch. turn at end of last row.

Commence Bodice

1st row (wrong side facing): (working into front loop only, leaving back loop to form a ridge on right side) miss first tr. and ch., * (1 tr. in next tr., 1 tr. in ch., 1 tr. in next tr., miss next ch.) 3 times, (1 tr. in next tr., 1 tr. in next ch.) twice; rep. from * to end, 2 ch., turn: 105 tr.
2nd row: 1 tr. in each tr. to end, 2 ch., turn.
The 2nd row forms the patt. Cont. in patt. until bodice measures 9 (10) in.

Shape Armhole

1st row (right side facing): sl.st. over 6 tr., patt. to last 6 tr., 2 ch., turn.
2nd row: (dec. 1 tr.) twice (see Abbreviations), patt. to last 5 tr., (dec. 1 tr.) twice, 1 tr. in end tr.
Repeat 2nd row 3 times: 77 tr.
Cont. without shaping until bodice measures 15 (16½) in.

Shape Neck

1st row: patt. 15, dec. 1 tr. in next tr., 2 ch., turn.
2nd row: dec. 1 tr., patt. to end. Fasten off.
Miss centre 41 tr., and rejoin yarn to next tr.
1st row: 1 tr. in this tr., dec. 1 tr., patt. to end.
2nd row: patt. to last 3 tr., dec. 1 tr., 1 tr. in end tr. Fasten off.

FRONT

Work Skirt section exactly as given for Back, ending with a 7th row of patt.

Commence Bodice

1st row (wrong side facing): (working into front loop only) miss first tr. and ch., * (1 tr. in next tr., 1 tr. in ch., 1 tr. in next tr., miss next ch.) 3 times, (1 tr. in next tr., 1 tr. in next ch.) twice; rep. from * 3 times more, 2 ch., turn: 53 tr.
2nd row: 1 tr. in each tr. to end, 2 ch., turn.
Cont. in patt. until bodice measures 9 (10) in.

Shape Armhole

1st row (right side facing): sl.st. over 6 tr., patt. to end, 2 ch., turn.
2nd row: patt. to last 5 tr., (dec. 1 tr.) twice, 1 tr. in end tr., 2 ch., turn.
3rd row: (dec. 1 tr.) twice, patt. to end.
Rep. 2nd and 3rd rows once: 39 tr.
Cont. without shaping until Bodice measures 11½ (13) in.

Shape Neck

1st row (right side facing): patt. to last 15 tr., dec. 1 tr., 1 tr. in next tr., 2 ch., turn.
2nd row: dec. 1 tr., patt. to end, 2 ch., turn.
3rd row: patt. to last 3 tr., dec. 1 tr., 1 tr. in end tr.
Rep. 2nd and 3rd rows until 16 tr. remain.
Cont. without shaping until work measures same as Back to shoulders. Fasten off.
Rejoin yarn to centre.
1st row: 1 tr. in ch., * (1 tr. in next tr., 1 tr. in ch., 1 tr. in next tr., miss next ch.) 3 times, (1 tr. in next tr., 1 tr. in next ch.) twice; rep. from * 3 times, 2 ch., turn: 53 tr.
2nd row: 1 tr. in each tr. to end, 2 ch., turn.
Cont. in patt. until bodice measures 9 (10) in.

Shape Armhole

1st row (right side facing): patt. to last 6 tr., 2 ch., turn.
2nd row: (dec. 1 tr.) twice, patt. to end, 2 ch., turn.
3rd row: patt. to last 5 tr., (dec. 1 tr.) twice, 1 tr. in end tr., 2 ch., turn.
Rep. 2nd and 3rd rows once: 39 tr. Cont. without shaping until bodice measures 11½ (13) in.

Shape Neck

1st row (right side facing): sl.st. over 12 tr., 1 tr. in next tr., dec. 1 tr., patt. to end.
2nd row: patt. to last 3 tr., dec. 1 tr., 1 tr. in end tr., 2 ch., turn.
3rd row: dec. 1 tr., patt. to end, 2 ch., turn.
Rep. 2nd and 3rd rows until 16 tr. remain.
Cont. without shaping until work measures same as Back to shoulders.
Fasten off.

SLEEVES (make 2 alike)

With No. 2.50 (3.00) hook make 84 ch.
1st row: 1 d.c. in 2nd ch. from hook, 1 d.c. in each rem. ch.: 83 d.c.
2nd row: 1 d.c. in each d.c.
Change to No. 3.00 (3.50) hook and work 2 patts. as for Back ending with a 6th patt. row.

Shape Top

1st row: sl.st. over 6 sts., patt. to last 6 sts., 3 ch., turn. Cont. in patt., dec. 2 sts. at each end of every row until 10 sts. rem. Fasten off.

TO COMPLETE

Press each piece carefully. Sew side and shoulder seams. Sew in sleeves.

Edging

With No. 3.00 hook and commencing at lower edge of right front work 2 rows d.c. along front edge, working 6 buttonholes evenly along 2nd row. For each buttonhole work 2 ch., miss 2 d.c., 1 d.c. in next d.c. Break off yarn.
Now commencing at right side seam work 1 row d.c. all round edge of bodice — i.e. work into loops on right side across right front edge, up right front, round neck, down left front edge, across loops at left front and across loops at back.
2nd round: * 1 d.c. in first d.c., miss 2 d.c., 6 tr. in next d.c., miss 2 d.c.; rep. from * all round, sl.st. into first d.c. to complete round. Fasten off.
Press all seams. Sew on buttons to correspond with buttonholes.

Button-through dress
illustrated in colour on page 160

MATERIALS
25 (27, 29) oz. Emu Double Knitting Crochet Wool. Crochet hooks International Standard Sizes 3.00, 3.50, 4.00 and 4.50. Eight medium buttons.

MEASUREMENTS
To fit bust size 34 (36, 38) in.; length 41 in. approx.

TENSION
9 tr. to 2 in.

ABBREVIATIONS
See page 122.

WAISTBAND
With No. 4.00 hook make 13 ch. and work 1 d.c. into 2nd ch. from hook, then 1 d.c. to end: 12 d.c.; 1 ch., turn.
Next row: work 1 d.c. into back loop of each d.c. to end, 1 ch., turn.
Rep. this row 119 (130, 141) times.

BODICE
Change to No. 3.00 hook and work 1 d.c. into top edge of each row along the waistband: 120 (131, 142) d.c., then 3 ch., turn. Cont. as follows:
** **1st row:** 1 tr. into each of next 2 d.c., * miss 2 d.c., 1 ch., 2 tr., 1 ch., 2 tr. into next st., miss 2 d.c., 1 ch., then 1 tr. into each of next 5 (6, 7) d.c.; rep. from * to end, finishing 3 tr. instead of 5 (6, 7) tr., 3 ch., turn.
2nd row: 1 tr. into each of next 2 tr., * 1 ch., 2 tr., 1 ch., 2 tr. into centre ch. of gr., 1 ch., then 1 tr. into each of next 5 (6, 7) tr.; rep. from * to end, finishing 3 tr. instead of 5 (6, 7) tr., 3 ch., turn.
3rd row: 1 tr. into each of next 2 tr., * 1 ch., 1 d.c. loosely into the sp. 2 rows below, 3 ch., 2 tr., 1 ch., 2 tr. into next centre ch. of 3 ch., 1 d.c. loosely into the sp. 2 rows below, 1 ch., 1 tr. into each of next 5 (6, 7) tr.; rep. from * to end, finishing with 3 tr. instead of 5 (6, 7) tr., 3 ch., turn. **
Next row: as 2nd row.
Next row: as 2nd row.
Next row: as 3rd row.
Change to No. 3.50 hook and work last 3 rows twice. Change to No. 4.00 hook and work last 3 rows twice.
Next 2 rows: as 2nd row.

Shape Armholes and Divide for Fronts and Back
Next row: 1 tr. into each of next 2 tr., * 1 ch., 1 d.c. loosely into the sp. 2 rows below, 3 ch., 2 tr., 1 ch., 2 tr. into next gr., 3 ch., 1 d.c. loosely into the sp. 2 rows below, 1 ch., 1 tr. into each of next 5 (6, 7) tr.; rep. from * once, 1 ch., 1 d.c. loosely into sp. 2 rows below, 3 ch., 2 tr. into gr., 1 ch., turn.
Next row: 1 tr. into each of next 5 (6, 7) tr., patt. as 2nd row to end.
Next row: as 2nd row, but with 5 (6, 7) tr. instead of 3 tr. at armhole edge.
Work 3 rows in patt. with extra tr. at armhole edge. Rep. last 3 rows twice, then 2nd row once omitting 3 ch. on last row.

Shape Neck
Next row: sl.st. to first gr., 3 ch., 1 tr. in gr., 1 ch., patt. to end, turn.
Next row: patt. to last tr. panel, 1 tr. into each of 5 (6, 7) tr., 1 ch., 1 d.c. loosely into 2 rows below, turn.
Next row: sl.st. into first tr., patt. to end.
Next row: patt. to end, 3 ch., turn.
Next row: sl.st. over next 2 tr., patt. to end. Fasten off.
Rejoin yarn to work across back bodice by missing the 5 (6, 7) tr. panel, and join yarn at next gr., 3 ch., 1 tr. into same sp., 3 ch., 1 d.c. loosely into sp. 2 rows below, 1 ch., patt. to 4th gr. from other edge and work 2 tr. into this gr., 1 ch., turn.

Next row: as 2nd row of front armhole shaping, ending with 1 tr. into each of next 5 (6, 7) tr., 1 ch., sl.st. into first tr. of 2 tr. gr. of previous row, 3 ch., turn.
Work 17 rows in patt. with tr. blocks each side of armhole.
Next row: sl.st. over first 5 (6, 7) tr., * 3 ch., 1 d.c. in next gr., 3 ch., 1 tr. into next 5 (6, 7) tr.; rep. from * twice, 3 ch., 1 d.c. into next gr., 3 ch., sl.st. to next tr. Fasten off.
Work other side to match first side, reversing shapings. Join shoulders.

SKIRT
With No. 3.00 hook and wrong side of work facing, rejoin yarn at lower edge of waistband and work 1 d.c. into each row along the waistband: 120 (131, 142) d.c.
Rep. from ** to ** of bodice patt. once. Change to No. 3.50 hook and work 3 rows in patt.
Inc. row: as 2nd row but work 2 tr. into the first and last tr. of each 5 (6, 7) tr. panel and 2 tr. into the 3rd tr. from front edge and 2 tr. into the first tr. of the last 3 tr. in row at opposite edge. There are now 4 tr. in panel at each edge, and 7 (8, 9) in other panels.
Work 5 rows in patt. with extra tr. in panels.
Change to No. 4.00 hook. *** Work 3 more rows.
Inc. row: inc. as before so that there are now 5 tr. at each edge and 9 (10, 11) tr. in each panel. Work 5 rows in the new patt. ***
Work from *** to *** twice, then change to No. 4.50 hook and work from *** to *** once, then work 3 more rows in patt.
Next row: work an inc. row as before so that there are now 9 tr. at each edge and 17 (18, 19) in each panel. Work 2 more rows in patt.
Next row: * 1 tr. into each tr. of panel, 3 ch., 1 d.c. into centre ch. of gr., 3 ch.; rep. from * to end, finishing 1 tr. into each of last 9 tr. Now work a row of d.c. into each tr. and ch. to end, then work 4 rows of d.c. on d.c. working into back of loops. Fasten off.

TO COMPLETE
Neck Edging
With right side of work facing, and No. 3.50 hook, join yarn at neck edge and work 56 (60, 65) d.c. evenly round neck, 1 ch., turn. Work 5 rows of d.c. on d.c. working into back of loops. Fasten off.

Left Front Border
With No. 4.00 hook make 8 ch. and work in d.c. working into back of loops, with 1 ch. to turn each row, until border is long enough when slightly stretched to reach up left front. Fasten off.
Place pins on border as a guide for buttonholes, the first one about 1 in. from top, the 2nd about 12 in. from lower edge, and 6 more at equal intervals between.

Right Front Border
Work to match Left Front Border, working buttonholes at pin positions as follows: 3 d.c., miss 2 d.c., 2 ch., d.c. to next buttonhole position. In the following row work in d.c. over d.c. and ch.

Armhole Borders
Make 2 more strips in a similar way as for Left Front Border. Sew borders in position. Sew on buttons to correspond with buttonholes. Lightly press.

A pair of pretty belts—the brown-based belt has embroidery worked on it in cross stitch; the reversible hipster belt is made up of motifs on one side, a plain-coloured continuous strip on the other (see page 162).
Opposite: *button-through dress (see page 159).*

Reversible hipster belt
illustrated in colour on page 161

MATERIALS
3 oz. Hayfield Gaylon Double Knitting in cream (or any other main shade, as wished), 1 oz. in each of four contrasting colours. One crochet hook International Standard Size 4.50.

MEASUREMENTS
Finished belt, excluding centre front fastening, measures 33 in. long, 5 in. wide.

TENSION
One motif measures $4\frac{1}{2}$ in. square.

ABBREVIATIONS
See page 122.

TO MAKE
With first contrast shade, make 8 ch., and join into a ring with sl.st.

1st round: 6 ch., (1 tr., 3 ch.) 7 times into ring, sl.st. to join.
2nd round: join in 2nd contrast shade and work 2 ch., 3 tr., 2 ch. into first sp., * 4 tr., 2 ch. into next sp.; rep. from * to end of round, sl.st. to join.
3rd round: with first contrast shade, 3 ch., 5 tr., 1 ch. into first sp., * 6 tr., 3 ch. into next sp., 6 tr., 1 ch. into next sp.; rep. from * to end of round, sl.st. to join.
4th round: with 2nd contrast shade, 2 ch., 1 tr., 3 ch., 2 tr. into 3 ch.sp. at corner, * 3 ch. 1 d.c. between 3rd and 4th tr. in next group, 3 ch., 1 d.c. into 1 ch.sp., 3 ch., 1 d.c. between 3rd and 4th tr. of next group, 3 ch., (2 tr., 3 ch., 2 tr.) into 3 ch.sp. at corner; rep. from * 3 times and from * excluding instructions in brackets once more, sl.st. to join. Fasten off.
Make 2 more motifs with first and 2nd contrast shades, then make 4 motifs with 3rd and 4th contrast shades.

Reverse Side of Belt
With cream (or main shade chosen) make 18 ch.
1st row: 1 d.c. in 2nd ch. from hook, 1 d.c. in each ch. to end of row.
2nd row: 2 ch., 1 d.c. in each d.c. to end of row. Continue working each row in d.c. until belt measures 32 in. Fasten off.

TO COMPLETE
Press the motifs, and press the long strip in main shade. Join the motifs into a long strip, alternating colours, and using cream (or main shade) yarn to join the motifs. Place motif strip to plain strip, wrong sides together, and with cream (or main shade) yarn work d.c. all round edges to join the strips together.
Next row: 4 ch., 1 sl.st. into same st., sl.st. over 3 sts., 4 ch., 1 sl.st. into same st. as last sl.st. Continue in this way all round the edges of belt. Fasten off.
Make 3 crochet chains with cream (or main shade) yarn, each 15 in. long. Thread these through 3 of the loops down each end of belt, and tie ends of each chain in a bow, to form centre front fastening.

Embroidered belt
illustrated in colour on page 161

MATERIALS
3 oz. Hayfield Gaylon Double Knitting in main shade, oddments in each of five different shades for the embroidery. One crochet hook International Standard Size 3.00. Piece of canvas, $4\frac{1}{2}$ in. by $25\frac{1}{2}$ in., for stiffening. Piece of lining fabric, $4\frac{1}{2}$ in. by $25\frac{1}{2}$ in.

MEASUREMENTS
Finished belt measures just over $4\frac{1}{2}$ in. by $25\frac{1}{2}$ in.

TENSION
5 sts. and 5 rows to 1 in.

ABBREVIATIONS
See page 122; M., main shade.

TO MAKE
With M., make 26 ch.
1st row: 1 h.tr. in 3rd ch. from hook, 1 h.tr. in each ch. to end of row.
2nd row: 2 ch., 1 h.tr. in each h.tr. to end of row.
Repeat 2nd row until work measures 26 in. Fasten off.

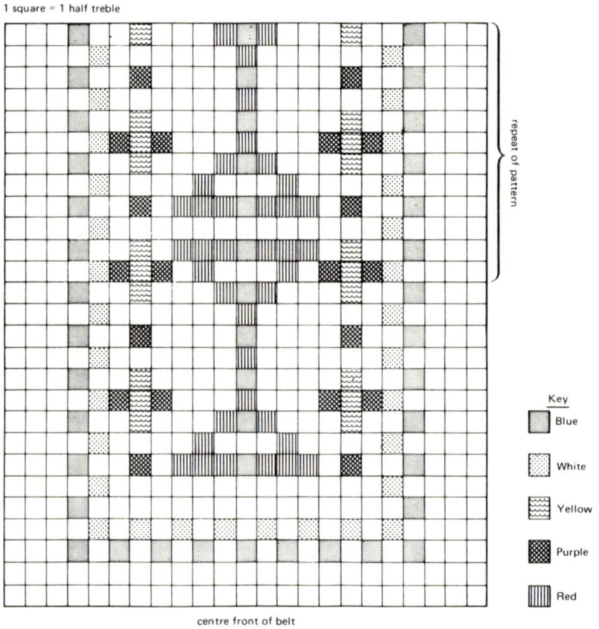

To Work Embroidery
Using contrast shades as wished, embroider pattern on belt in cross stitch, following above for position of the blocks of cross stitch. One square on the chart represents 1 h.tr. on the crocheted fabric.

TO COMPLETE
Place canvas stiffening centrally against wrong side of belt, and then place lining on top of canvas, wrong side of lining facing the canvas. Baste in place, then turn over edges of crochet to wrong side of belt and stitch neatly all the way round.
With one of the contrast shades, work 2 rows of crochet at each end of belt to make lace-up holes, as follows:
1st row: 4 ch., * miss next st., 1 tr., 1 ch. in next st.; rep. from * to end of row.
2nd row: 2 ch., 1 d.c. in each sp. and each tr. to end of row. Fasten off.
Working with 2 other contrast shades together, make a crocheted chain 44 in. long, and lace this through alternate holes, to fasten belt at centre front.

Suit and beret

illustrated in colour on page 164

MATERIALS

20 (22) oz. Emu Scotch 4-ply in green, 3 (4) oz. in dark green, 2 oz. in white. Crochet hooks International Standard Sizes 3.00, 4.50 and 5.00. A waist length of elastic, 1 in. wide. Five small buttons.

MEASUREMENTS

To fit bust size 32/34 (36/38) in.; hip size 34/36 (38/40) in.; centre back length of jacket 21 (22½) in.; sleeve seam 18 (18½) in.; skirt length at side seam 19 (20) in.

TENSION

15 rows and 12 sts. to 3 in. on No. 5.00 hook.

ABBREVIATIONS

See page 122; G., green; D.G., dark green; W., white.

JACKET LEFT FRONT

With No. 5.00 hook and G., make 38 (42) ch.
1st row: miss first 2 ch., d.c. into next ch., d.c. to end: 36 (40) sts.
Cont. to work in d.c. on these sts., dec. 1 st. on side edge only every 5th (6th) row 4 times in all: 32 (36) sts.
Work 24 rows in d.c. without shaping.
Next row: inc. 1 st. at side edge.
Inc. 1 st. at side edge on every foll. 10th row twice, then cont. straight for another 5 (7) rows: 35 (39) sts.

Shape Armhole and Neck

Next row: sl.st. across 5 sts., d.c. to 3rd st. from end, d.c. 2 sts. tog., d.c. in last st. Place coloured thread on this last st. to mark it.
Next row: work in patt., dec. 1 st. at armhole edge.
Work 1 row in patt.
Next row: dec. 1 st. on neck and armhole edges.
Cont. to dec. 1 st. every alt. row on armhole, and 1 st. every 3rd row on neck edge until 10 rows have been worked from start of armhole and neck shaping. **
No further shaping for armhole is now required, but cont. to dec. at neck edge as before 11 (13) more times.
Work 1 row straight: 10 (12) sts.

Shape Shoulder

Next row: sl.st. across 2 (3) sts., d.c. to end, turn, d.c. 6, turn, sl.st. across 2 sts., d.c. 4. Fasten off.

JACKET RIGHT FRONT

Work as for Jacket Left Front, reversing all shapings.

JACKET BACK

With No. 5.00 hook and G., make 78 (86) ch. Work as for Jacket Left Front as far as armhole and neck shaping, but shaping on both side edges (instead of just one): 74 (82) sts.

Shape Armhole

*** Work armhole shaping as given for Jacket Left Front as far as **, working shaping at both ends of work, and omitting the neck shaping given for Front. *** Work straight for 30 (36) rows: 54 (62) sts.

Shape Neck

Next row: d.c. 20 (22), turn, sl.st. across 2 sts., d.c. to end.
Next row: d.c. 16 (18), turn, sl.st. across 2 sts., d.c. to end.
Next row: shape shoulders as given for Front, and cont. to dec. 2 sts. each row on neck edge.
Last 2 rows: sl.st. across 2 sts. on neck, d.c. 6, turn, sl.st. 2, d.c. 4. Fasten off.
Fasten yarn to 20th (22nd) st. from end of row and complete second shoulder to match first, reversing shapings.

JACKET SLEEVES (make 2 alike)

With No. 4.50 hook and D.G., make 34 (42) ch.
1st row: miss 2 ch., d.c. to end.
Work 8 more rows in d.c. Change to W., and work 2 rows.
Change to No. 5.00 hook and G., and cont. in patt., inc. 1 st. at each end of next and every foll. 10th row 7 times.
Work 4 (10) more rows straight: 48 (56) sts.

Shape Top

Work shaping as given for Jacket Back, from *** to ***: 28 (36) sts. Dec. 1 st. each end of every 3rd row 6 times, then dec. 1 st. each end of every alt. row 3 (5) times: 10 (14) sts. Fasten off.

TO COMPLETE JACKET

Sew shoulder and side seams. Sew sleeve seams.

Sleeve Edgings

With No. 4.50 hook and W., work 2 rows of d.c. round lower edge of each sleeve.

Front Borders

With No. 4.50 hook and W., join yarn to lower edge of centre front edge on jacket left front, 3 d.c. on st. at this corner edge, working up centre front, miss 1 st., * d.c. into each of next 2 d.c., miss 1 st.; rep. from * to coloured thread marker: 50 (55) sts. worked. Continuing up shaped edge of front neck, d.c. into each row end: 48 (50) sts. worked on shaped neck edge. Continuing round back neck, d.c. into each row end or st.: 34 (38) sts. worked on back neck edge. Work d.c. down shaped edge of right front, as for left front, and down straight centre front edge of right front, work 2 d.c. into corner st. at lower edge. Work 148 (164) d.c. evenly across lower edge of jacket, to beg. of round. Work 2 d.c. into last st. to turn corner, sl.st. to first st. of first round.
Next round: with W., work as for first round to first marker, work 2 d.c. into next st., work in d.c. to 2nd marker, and work 2 d.c. into next st., work to end of round, working 2 d.c. into corner sts. at centre fronts as before.
Rep. this shaping at marker points every alt. round, thus inc. 1 st. at each hem corner on every round and 1 st. at each marker point every alt. round.
Next round: change to D.G., and patt. right round.
Next round: still working in patt., and shaping at corner and marker points, shape neck as follows: work to marker, d.c. into each of next 12 (16) sts., then dec. 10 sts. in next 100 sts. as follows: d.c. 4, d.c. 2 tog., (d.c. 8, d.c. 2 tog.) 9 times, d.c. 4, d.c. 12 (16) to next marker, work in patt. to end of round. In the 4th round of D.G., work to first marker, d.c. 8 (12), dec. 10 sts. in next 100 as before, d.c. 8 (12) to second marker; now form buttonholes: 2 ch., miss 2 sts., (d.c. 10 (11), 2 ch., miss 2 sts.) 4 times, d.c. 3 (4).
In the 5th round of D.G., work d.c. into each of ch. worked for buttonholes in previous round.
In the 6th round of D.G., work neck shaping between markers as follows: d.c. 4 (8), dec. 10 sts. in next 100 as before, d.c. 4 (8).
8th round of D.G.: d.c. 0 (4), dec. 10 sts. in 100 sts. between markers as before, d.c. 0 (4).
Work 1 more row of D.G. without shaping.
Next row: change to W., and work as 2nd row of W. before.
Next row: in W., d.c. all round, with no extra sts.

To Make Up

Sew sleeves into armholes. Sew on buttons to left front to correspond with buttonholes worked in right front.

SKIRT FRONT AND BACK (make 2 pieces alike)

With No. 4.50 hook and D.G., make 82 (98) ch.
Work border in D.G. and W. as given for Sleeves.
Change to No. 5.00 hook and G., and work 13 rows in patt., dec. 1 st. at each end of next and every foll. 14 rows 4 times. Then dec. 1 st. each end of every foll. 4th row 5 (7) times: 62 (70) sts. Fasten off.

continued on page 164

Suit and beret (see page 163).

TO COMPLETE SKIRT

Join side seams, matching rows carefully.
With No. 4.50 hook and W., work 2 rows of d.c. round hem edge.
Fasten off.

Waistband

With No. 4.50 hook and G., work 5 rows of d.c., then work 2 rounds of tr. Turn band of tr. to inside of skirt and sl.st. each tr. st. to first d.c. row of waistband to form a casing. Fasten off, and thread elastic through this casing, joining ends of elastic together.

BERET

With No. 4.50 hook and G., make a ch. of 4, and join into a ring with sl.st.

1st round: work 2 d.c. into each ch. on ring, sl.st. to join.

Next round: work 2 d.c. into each d.c. of previous round, sl.st. to join.

Next round: 1 d.c. into each d.c., sl.st. to join.

Next round: * 2 d.c. into first d.c., 1 d.c. into next d.c.; rep. from * to end, sl.st. to join.

Next round: 1 d.c. into each d.c., sl.st. to join.

Rep. last 2 rounds 3 times for first size. For second size, rep. last 2 rounds 3 times, then on next round inc. 1 st. every 9 sts., and then work 1 more round without inc.

Both sizes. D.c. 22 (26) rounds on 81 (90) sts.

Border

With No. 4.50 hook and W., work in d.c. for 2 rounds, then change to D.G. and work 7 rounds of d.c.

Next round: dec. 1 st. every 9 sts.

Next round: d.c. 72 (81) sts.

Change to W., and work 2 rounds d.c. fairly tightly. Fasten off.

TO COMPLETE BERET

Darn in all ends. Press very lightly over a damp cloth on the wrong side. Fill beret with crumpled tissue paper while still damp to obtain rounded shape.

A smart trouser suit that is quick and easy to crochet—see page 166 for instructions.

Red trouser suit
illustrated in colour on page 165

MATERIALS. For top: 17 (18, 19) 20-gram balls Patons Brilliante 4 ply (or any 4 ply to give tension as indicated below); 5 medium buttons. **For trousers:** 23 (24, 25) 20-gram balls Patons Brilliante 4 ply (or any 4 ply to give tension as indicated below); waist length of elastic. **For both:** crochet hooks International Standard Sizes 3.00 and 3.50.

MEASUREMENTS. To fit bust sizes 32 (34, 36) in.; hip size 34 (36, 38) in.; length of top 30 (30½, 31) in.; inside leg seam of trousers 28 (28½, 29) in.

TENSION. 11 sts. and 10 rows to 2 in. with No. 3.50 hook.

ABBREVIATIONS. See page 122.

TOP
BACK
With No. 3.00 hook, make 116 (122, 128) ch. **
Foundation row (right side): 1 d.c. in 2nd ch. from hook, 1 d.c. in each ch. to end, turn: 115 (121, 127) sts.
Next row: 1 d.c. in first st., 1 d.c. in each st. to end, turn.
Rep. this row twice more.
Change to No. 3.50 hook and work in patt. as follows:
1st row: 3 ch., miss first 2 sts., 1 h.tr. in next st., * 1 ch., miss next st., 1 h.tr. in next st., rep. from * to end, turn.
2nd row: 1 d.c. in first st., * 1 d.tr. in next ch. sp., 1 d.c. in next h.tr., rep. from * to end, working last d.c. in 2nd of 3 ch., turn.
These 2 rows form patt.
Work straight in patt. until Back measures 3 in. from start, ending with a 2nd patt. row. **
Dec. row: 3 ch., miss first 2 sts., 1 h.tr. in next st., (1 ch., miss next st., 1 h.tr. in next st.) 8 times, 1 ch., miss next 3 sts., 1 h.tr. in next st., patt. to last 22 sts., 1 ch., miss 3 sts., 1 h.tr. in next st., patt. to end: 111 (117, 123) sts.
Work 13 rows straight in patt.
Work dec. row again: 107 (113, 119) sts.
Rep. last 14 rows twice more: 99 (105, 111) sts.
Work 7 rows straight.
Work dec. row again.
Rep. last 8 rows once more: 91 (97, 103) sts.
Work straight in patt. on these sts. until Back measures 23 in. from start, ending with right side facing.
Keeping continuity of patt., shape armholes as follows:
1st row: s.s. across 4 sts., patt. to last 4 sts., turn.
2nd row: in patt.
3rd row: s.s. across 2 sts., patt. to last 2 sts., turn.
Rep. 2nd and 3rd rows until 59 (61, 63) sts. remain.
Work straight until Back measures 30 (30½, 31) in.
Fasten off.

RIGHT FRONT
With No. 3.00 hook, make 58 (60, 64) ch. and work as Back from ** to **: 57 (59, 63) sts.
Dec. row: patt. to last 22 sts., 1 ch., miss next 3 sts., 1 h.tr. in next st., patt. to end: 55 (57, 61) sts.
Work 13 rows straight.
Work dec. row again: 53 (55, 59) sts.
Rep. last 14 rows twice more: 49 (51, 55) sts.
Work 7 rows straight.
Work dec. row again.
Rep. last 8 rows once more: 45 (47, 51) sts.
Work straight on these sts. until Front measures same as Back to start of armhole shaping, ending with right side facing.
Keeping continuity of patt., shape armhole as follows:
1st row: patt. to last 4 sts., turn.
2nd row: in patt.
3rd row: patt. to last 2 sts., turn.
Rep. 2nd and 3rd rows until 29 (29, 31) sts. remain.
Work 7 (5, 5) rows straight.

Shape Neck. Next row: s.s. across 10 sts., patt. to end.
Next row: in patt.
Next row: s.s. across 2 sts., patt. to end.
Rep. last 2 rows until 11 sts. remain.
Work straight until Front measures same as Back.
Fasten off.

LEFT FRONT
Work as for Right Front, reversing all shapings.

TO COMPLETE
Block out to shape and press very lightly using a cool iron and dry cloth. Join shoulder seams.

Front Border. With right side facing and No. 3.00 hook, work in d.c. up right front edge, round neck and down left front edge, turn and work 3 rows more in d.c., inc. or dec. where necessary to ensure Border lies flat.
Fasten off.
Work buttonloops on Right Front as follows:
To make a loop: join in yarn 3 in. down from neck edge and make 6 ch., miss 4 sts., s.s. in next st., turn, work 7 d.c. in 6 ch. sp., s.s. to main border.
Fasten off.
Make 4 more loops, leaving 4 in. between each one.
Armhole Border. With right side facing for first row and No. 3.00 hook, work 5 rows d.c. as for front border.
Join side seams and armhole borders.
Press seams only.
Attach buttons.

TROUSERS
RIGHT LEG
With No. 3.50 hook, make 113 (119, 125) ch. and work foundation row as on Back of Top: 112 (118, 124) sts.
Work 3 rows more in d.c.
Next row: 3 ch. to form first st., miss first st., * 1 tr. in next st., rep. from * to end, turn.
Rep. this row until work measures 25½ (26, 26½) in. from start, ending with right side facing.
Inc. row: 3 ch., 1 tr. in first st., work to last st., 2 tr. in last st., turn: 114 (120, 126) sts.
Next row: in tr.
Rep. these 2 rows 3 times more: 120 (126, 132) sts.
Shape Top. 1st row: s.s. across 2 sts., work to last 2 sts., turn.
2nd row: s.s. across first st., work to last but 1 st., turn.
Rep. 2nd row until 100 (106, 112) sts. remain.
Work 1 row straight.
Now keep front edge straight and dec. at back edge only (end of next row, beg. of next row on Left Leg) on next and every following alt. row until 89 (94, 99) sts. remain.
Work 2 rows straight (1 row on Left Leg), thus ending at back edge.
Change to No. 3.00 hook and shape back as follows:
1st row: 1 d.c. in next 60 (65, 70) sts., turn.
2nd and every alt. row: in d.c. to end, turn.
3rd row: 1 d.c. in next 48 (52, 56) sts., turn.
5th row: 1 d.c. in next 36 (39, 42) sts., turn.
7th row: 1 d.c. in next 24 (26, 28) sts., turn.
9th row: 1 d.c. in next 12 (13, 14) sts., turn.
11th row: in d.c. across all sts.
Work 10 rows straight in d.c.
Fasten off.

LEFT LEG
Work as for Right Leg reversing all shapings.

TO COMPLETE
Press using a cool iron and dry cloth.
Join front, back and leg seams.
Make herringbone casing at waist for elastic. Insert elastic.
Join ends. Press seams.

Lace-up motif waistcoat

illustrated in colour on page 168

MATERIALS

5 (5, 6) oz. Hayfield Gaylon Double Knitting in main shade, 1 (2, 2) oz. in each of four contrasting shades. One crochet hook International Standard Size 4.00 (4.50, 5.00).

MEASUREMENTS

To fit bust size 34 (36, 38) in.

TENSION

One motif measures $4\frac{1}{2}$ in. square.

ABBREVIATIONS

See page 122; M., main shade; C., contrast shade.

TO MAKE

Motif

With 1st C., make 8 ch., and join into a ring with sl.st.

1st round: 6 ch., work (1 tr., 3 ch.) 7 times into ring, sl.st. to join.

2nd round: join in 2nd C. and work 2 ch., 3 tr., 2 ch. into first sp., * 4 tr., 2 ch. into next sp.; rep. from * to end of round, sl.st. to join.

3rd round: with 1st C., 2 ch., 5 tr., 1 ch. into first sp., * 6 tr., 3 ch. into next sp., 6 tr., 1 ch. into next sp.; rep. from * to end, sl.st. to join.

4th round: with 2nd C., 2 ch., 1 tr., 3 ch., 2 tr. into 3 ch.sp. at corner, * 3 ch., 1 d.c. between 3rd and 4th tr. of next gr., 3 ch., 1 d.c. into 1 ch.sp., 3 ch., 1 d.c. between 3rd and 4th tr. of next gr., 3 ch., (2 tr., 3 ch., 2 tr.) into 3 ch.sp. at corner; rep. from * 3 times and from * excluding instructions in brackets once more, sl.st. to join.

Fasten off.

Make 7 more motifs in 1st and 2nd C., then make 8 more using 3rd and 4th C., then make 7 more using M. only.

TO COMPLETE

Join alternate C. squares to make 2 strips each with 8 squares, then join 2 strips of 2 squares each in M., and one strip of 3 squares in M.

Take the strip of 3 M. squares (this will form centre back of waistcoat), rejoin yarn and work 19 tr. across one short edge (this will be top edge), 3 ch., turn.

1st row: 1 tr. in next 2 tr., * 1 ch., miss next tr., 1 tr. in next 3 tr.; rep. from * to end of row, 4 ch., turn.

2nd row: miss next tr., * 1 ch., 1 tr. in next tr., 1 tr. in ch.sp., 1 tr. in next tr., 1 ch.; rep. from * to end of row ending with 1 tr. in 3rd of the 4 turning ch., 3 ch., turn.

3rd row: as first row. Fasten off. This completes the centre back panel.

Fold one strip of C. motifs in half, and join one strip of 2 M. motifs to the 2 bottom squares at each end, thus giving the effect of side, back and front with armhole shaping.

Join the other strip of C. motifs to the other strip of 2 M. motifs in a similar way.

Round the long side of the C. strips work 1 row in tr. then the first row of the 3 tr., 1 ch. patt. as for centre back panel.

Join both side pieces to the centre back panel. The waistcoat is now assembled.

With M., rejoin yarn at bottom of front opening and working up centre front, work the 2 rows of 3 tr., 1 ch. as far as top of 2nd square (counting from lower edge). Fasten off. Repeat along other centre front edge.

Work 1 row of tr., then 1 row of d.c. all round outer edges and armholes. With 3 strands of yarn in 3 different C. shades, make a chain 2 yd. long. Lace up front of waistcoat, then curl each end of ch. round and stitch in place to make a flat circle approx. 1 in. in diameter. Stitch firmly to hold circle in place.

Striped scarf and hat

illustrated in colour on page 169

MATERIALS

For scarf: 7 balls (20 gr. each) Robin Super Crimp Bri-Nylon D.K. in main shade, and 5 balls in each of two contrasting shades plus 3 extra balls in main shade if fringe is required. **For hat:** 1 ball of same yarn in main shade, and 1 ball in each of two contrasting shades. **For both:** one crochet hook International Standard Size 4.00.

MEASUREMENTS

Scarf: width 18 in.; length (excluding fringe) 118 in.

Hat: to fit an average size head.

TENSION

2 patts. to $1\frac{1}{4}$ in. approx.

ABBREVIATIONS

See page 122; M., main shade; C., contrast shade.

SCARF

With No. 4.00 hook and M., commence with 122 ch.

Foundation row: 1 d.c. into 2nd ch. from hook, * 5 ch., miss 3 ch., 1 d.c. into next ch.; rep. from * to end, 3 ch., turn. Continue in patt.

1st row: 1 d.c. into centre ch. of first 5 ch. loop, * 5 ch., 1 d.c. into centre ch. of next 5 ch. loop; rep. from * ending 2 ch., 1 tr. into last d.c., 1 ch.; turn.

2nd row: 1 d.c. into tr., * 5 ch., 1 d.c. into centre ch. of next 5 ch. loop; rep. from * ending 5 ch., 1 d.c. into 3rd of 3 turning ch., 3 ch.; turn.

These 2 rows form the patt.

Work 4 more rows.

7th row: as first row; break M. and join 1st C. by drawing a ch. through loop on hook; turn.

Continue in stripes.

Work 6 rows in 1st C., 6 rows in 2nd C., and 8 rows in M., joining new colours as in 7th row. Rep. these 20 rows until Scarf measures 118 in. or required length, ending with an M. stripe, and working last row as follows:

Last row: 1 d.c. into centre ch. of first 5 ch. loop, * 3 ch., 1 d.c. into centre ch. of next 5 ch. loop; rep. from * ending 2 ch., 1 tr. into last d.c. Fasten off.

Sew in ends.

Fringe

Using 8 strands of M. yarn 14 in. long for each tassel work a fringe along narrow edges of scarf, working a tassel into each ch. loop as follows: insert hook into loop, double yarn strands and pull doubled end through loop then pull yarn ends through doubled end. Trim.

continued on page 170

Lace-up motif waistcoat (see page 167).

Striped scarf and hat (see page 167).

HAT

With No. 4.00 hook and 2nd C., commence with 6 ch. and join with sl.st. to form a ring.

1st round: * 5 ch., 1 d.c. into ring; rep. from * 4 times.

2nd round: sl.st. over first 2 ch. of 5 ch. loop, work 1 d.c., 5 ch. and 1 d.c. into next ch., * 5 ch., work 1 d.c., 5 ch. and 1 d.c. into centre ch. of next 5 ch. loop; rep. from * ending 5 ch., 1 d.c. into first d.c.

3rd round: sl.st. over first 2 ch. of 5 ch. loop, 1 d.c. into next ch., * 5 ch., 1 d.c. into centre ch. of next 5 ch. loop; rep. from * ending 5 ch., 1 d.c. into first d.c.

4th round: sl.st. over first 2 ch. of 5 ch. loop, work 1 d.c., 5 ch. and 1 d.c. into next ch., * 5 ch., 1 d.c. into centre ch. of next 5 ch. loop, 5 ch., work 1 d.c., 5 ch. and 1 d.c. into centre ch. of foll. 5 ch. loop; rep. from * ending 5 ch., 1 d.c. into centre ch. of last 5 ch. loop, 5 ch., 1 d.c. into first d.c.

5th and 6th rounds: as 3rd round.

Break 2nd C.

7th round: join 1st C. to centre ch. of next 5 ch. loop with a d.c., * 5 ch., 1 d.c. into centre ch. of next 5 ch. loop, 5 ch., 1 d.c. into centre ch. of foll. 5 ch. loop, 5 ch., work 1 d.c., 5 ch. and 1 d.c. into centre ch. of next 5 ch. loop; rep. from * ending 5 ch., work 1 d.c., 5 ch. and 1 d.c. into first d.c.

8th round: as 3rd round.

9th round: sl.st. over first 2 ch. of 5 ch. loop, 1 d.c. into next ch., * 5 ch., work 1 d.c. and 5 ch. into centre ch. of each of next three 5 ch. loops, work 1 d.c., 5 ch. and 1 d.c. into centre ch. of next 5 ch. loop; rep. from * ending work 1 d.c., 5 ch. and 1 d.c. into first d.c.

10th, 11th and 12th rounds: as 3rd round.

Break 1st C.

13th round: join M. to centre ch. of next 5 ch. loop with a d.c., * 5 ch, 1 d.c. into centre ch. of next 5 ch. loop; rep. from * ending 5 ch., 1 d.c. into first d.c.

14th–19th rounds: as 3rd round.

20th round: sl.st. over first 2 ch. of 5 ch. loop, 1 d.c. into next ch., * 3 ch., 1 d.c. into centre ch. of next 5 ch. loop; rep. from * ending 3 ch., 1 d.c. into first d.c.

Fasten off. Sew in ends.

Long fringed cover-up

illustrated in colour on page 172

MATERIALS

18 oz. Hayfield Gaylon Double Knitting in main shade, 1 oz. each in seven contrasting shades for fringe. Crochet hooks International Standard Sizes 4.50 and 4.00.

MEASUREMENTS

The cover-up is loose fitting so should comfortably fit any average size up to 38 in. bust; length 46 in.

TENSION

4 tr. and 2 rows measure 1 in.

ABBREVIATIONS

See page 122; M., main shade.

BACK

With No. 4.50 hook and M., make 73 ch.

1st row: 1 tr. into 3rd ch. from hook (this stands for first tr. of every row); work 1 tr. into each ch. to end of row.

2nd row: 1 tr. into each tr. of previous row.

Work 46 rows straight in tr.

Next 4 rows: dec. 1 st. at each end of the row for waist.

Work straight until work measures 33 in.

Shape for Armholes

Next row: sl.st. over 4 sts., work to last 4 tr., turn with 3 ch.

Cont. to dec. 1 st. at each end of every alt. row until there are 43 tr. Cont. straight until 20 rows have been worked from beg. of armhole. Fasten off.

FRONTS (as work is reversible, make 2 pieces alike – i.e. no need to reverse shapings for second piece)

With No. 4.50 hook and M., make 39 ch.

1st row: 1 tr. into 3rd ch. from hook (this stands for first tr. of every row), work 1 tr. into each ch. to end of row.

2nd row: 1 tr. into each tr. of previous row.

Work 46 rows straight in tr.

Next 4 rows: dec. 1 st. at one end of each row for waist. Work straight until work measures same as Back to start of armhole shaping.

Shape for Armhole and Neck

Next row: sl.st. over 4 tr. at armhole edge, work to end of row. Dec. 1 st. at armhole edge on every alt. row, making 6 decs. in all. At the same time dec. at centre front edge on every row until you have 12 tr.

Cont. on these 12 tr. till you have worked 20 rows from beg. of armhole shaping. Fasten off.

TO COMPLETE

Press with slightly damp cloth. Join shoulder and underarm seams.

Borders

With No. 4.00 hook and M., and starting at lower corner of centre front edge, work 4 rows of d.c. round all edges.

Work a similar border round each armhole.

To Make Fringe

To make each individual tassel in the fringe, cut 1 strand in each of the 7 contrast shades, each strand 8 in. long. Place the strands together, double them, and working on right side of garment pull loop end of strands through the crochet fabric, take cut ends of strands down through the loop and pull tight. Work tassels on each front as follows: start tassels on the 4th row of tr. up from lower edge, and make first tassel on first tr. at centre front edge; make another tassel on every 4th tr. across row, until 7 tassels in all have been worked.

Work similar rows of tassels on every 3rd row of tr. up front of garment. Gradually reduce number of tassels at edge nearest side seam until you have only 3 tassels in the row at waist level. Increase tassels gradually after this point so that at top of fronts entire area of crocheted fabric is filled with tassels.

Work 5 rows of tassels across back yoke of garment, working rows of tassels on every 3rd row of tr. patt. as before.

Flower-motif mat

Motif waistcoat

illustrated in colour on page 173

MATERIALS. 6 balls Hayfield Beaulon 4-ply in main shade, 2 balls in each of first and 2nd contrasting shades and 1 ball in each of 3rd and 4th contrasting shades (or any 4-ply yarn to give tension indicated below). One crochet hook International Standard Size 4.00. Four medium buttons.

MEASUREMENTS. To fit bust size 34 in.; length 27 in.

TENSION. 1 motif measures 4 in. square.

ABBREVIATIONS. See page 122; M., main shade; A., first contrasting shade; B., 2nd contrasting shade; C., 3rd contrasting shade; D., 4th contrasting shade.

FULL SQUARES (make 22 in D., A. and M. and 18 in C., B. and M.)
With D. commence with 8 ch. and s.s. to first ch. to form a ring.
1st round: 3 ch., leaving last loop of each on hook work 2 d.tr., y.o.h. and drawn through all 3 loops on hook, 5 ch., * leaving last loop of each on hook work 3 d.tr., y.o.h. and draw through all 4 loops (1 cl. made), 5 ch.; rep. from * 6 times, s.s. to beg. of round: 8 petals.
Break D. and change to A.
2nd round: into each of the 8 5-ch. loops work 1 d.c., 1 h.tr., 1 tr., 1 d.tr., 1 ch., 1 d.tr., 1 tr., 1 h.tr., 1 d.c. Break A. and change to M.
3rd round: join yarn to centre ch. of petal point with an s.s., * 4 ch., 1 d.tr. in between the 2 d.c. of previous row, 4 ch., 1 d.c. into centre ch. of next petal point; rep. from * all round.
4th round: 2 ch., 3 tr. into 4-ch. loop, 4 tr. into next 4-ch. loop, 3 ch. to form corner, * 4 tr. into each of next 4 4-ch. loops, 3 ch.; rep. from * twice, 4 tr. into each of next 2 4-ch. loops, s.s. to beg. of round.
Fasten off.

HALF SQUARES (make 8 in C., B. and M. and 1 in D., A. and M.)
With C. commence with 8 ch. and s.s. to form a ring.
1st row: 6 ch., * 1 cl. of 3 d.tr., 5 ch.; rep. from * twice, 1 cl. of 3 d.tr., 6 ch., s.s. into ring. Change to B.

2nd row: join yarn to 3rd ch. of first 6 of first row, 4 ch., 1 tr., 1 h.tr., 1 d.c. into loop, * into each 5-ch. loop work 1 d.c., 1 h.tr., 1 tr., 1 d.tr., 1 ch., 1 d.tr., 1 tr., 1 h.tr., 1 d.c; into last loop work 1 d.c., 1 h.tr., 1 tr. and 1 d.tr. Fasten off. Change to M.
3rd row: 1 d.c. into 4th ch. of 2nd row, * 4-ch., 1 d.tr. between 2 d.c. of 2nd row, 4 ch., 1 d.c. into petal point; rep. from * 3 times, working last d.c. into top of d.tr. Fasten off.
4th row: join M. with an s.s. into 2nd 4-ch. loop of 3rd row, 3 ch., 3 tr. into loop, 4 tr. into each of next 2 4-ch. loops, 3 ch., 4 tr. into each of next 4 4-ch. loops, 3 ch., work 4 tr. down side of d.tr. of 2nd row, work 4 tr. into last 3 ch. of first row, work 4 tr. into centre ring, work 4 tr. into first 3 ch. of first row, work 4 tr. into first 4 ch. of 2nd row, 3 ch., 4 tr. into next 4-ch. loop of 3rd row, 3 ch., s.s. to 3rd ch. of first set of 4 tr. Fasten off.

TO COMPLETE

Join squares and half squares as shown in diagram below. Join side seams.

With M. work 2 rows of d.c. round each armhole and round neck, front and lower edge. Link each pair of buttons with a crochet ch., 2 in. long, and use to fasten centre front edges of waistcoat, at points of motifs.

1 = Pink and Viola
2 = Blue and Turquoise

Long fringed cover-up (see page 170).

Evening skirt and blouse

illustrated in colour on page 176

MATERIALS

For blouse: 16 (17, 18, 19) balls Robin Tricel-Nylon Double Knitting. Twelve medium buttons.
For skirt: 15 (16, 17, 18) balls Robin Tricel-Nylon Double Knitting and 16 (17, 18, 19) balls Robin Camilla Crêpe Double Knitting in a contrasting colour. A waist length of elastic, 1 in. wide.
For both: crochet hooks International Standard Sizes 3.00, 4.00, 4.50 and 5.00.

MEASUREMENTS

To fit bust size 32 (34, 36, 38) in.; hip size 34 (36, 38, 40) in.; skirt length 39½ in.

TENSION

9 tr. to 2 in. and 6 rows to 2½ in. on No. 4.00 hook with Tricel-Nylon Double Knitting; 6 tr. and 3 rows to 2 in. on No. 5.00 hook with Tricel-Nylon and Camilla Crêpe together.

ABBREVIATIONS

See page 122; dec. 1, decrease 1 tr. by inserting hook into next st., draw through loop, insert hook into next st. and draw through loop, insert hook into next st. and draw through loop, (y.r.h., draw through 2 loops) twice.

BLOUSE BACK

With No. 4.00 hook and Tricel-Nylon Double Knitting make 80 (84, 90, 94) ch.
Foundation row: work 1 tr. into 3rd ch. from hook, 1 tr. into each ch. to end, 2 ch., turn.
Work 1 tr. into each tr. and turn each row with 2 ch. until work measures 15 in. from beg.; do not work ch. to turn on last row.

Shape Armholes

Next row: sl. st. over 4 (5, 5, 6) sts., 1 d.c., work in tr. to last 5 (6, 6, 7) sts., 1 d.c., no ch. to turn.
Next row: sl.st. over 2 sts., 1 d.c., work in tr. to last 3 sts., 1 d.c., no ch. to turn.
Rep. the last row 2 (2, 3, 3) times more, 2 ch. to turn on last row. Now work straight until armhole measures 7 (7½, 8, 8½) in., no ch. to turn.

Shape Shoulder

Next row: sl.st. over 9 sts., 1 d.c., work to last 10 sts., 1 d.c., no ch. to turn.
Next row: sl.st. over 9 (9, 10, 10) sts., 1 d.c., work to last 10 (10, 11, 11) sts., 1 d.c. Fasten off.

BLOUSE LEFT FRONT

With No. 4.00 hook and Tricel-Nylon Double Knitting make 73 (77, 83, 87) ch. Work foundation row and 1 row of treble as Back.
Shape Front
Dec. 1 tr. at front edge on every row until the same number of rows as Back to armhole have been worked ending at side edge.

Shape Armhole

1st row: sl.st. over 4 (5, 5, 6) sts., 1 d.c., work in tr., dec, last st.
2nd row: dec. 1, work to last 3 sts., 1 d.c., no ch. to turn.
3rd row: sl.st. over 2 sts., 1 d.c., work to end, dec. last st.
1st and 2nd sizes. Work 2nd row again.
3rd and 4th sizes. Work 2nd and 3rd rows again.
All sizes. 2 ch., turn.
Keeping side edge straight, dec. 1 st. at front edge on every row to 18 (18, 19, 19) sts. Then work straight until the same number of rows as Back to shoulder have been worked ending at side edge, no ch. to turn on last row.

Shape Shoulder

Sl.st. over 9 sts., 1 d.c., work to end. Fasten off.

continued on page 174

Motif waistcoat (see page 171).

BLOUSE RIGHT FRONT
Work to match Left Front reversing shapings.

BLOUSE SLEEVES (make 2 alike)
With No. 4.00 hook and Tricel-Nylon Double Knitting make 62 (64, 66, 68) ch. and work as back to 18 in. from beg.

Shape Armholes
Next row: sl.st. over 4 (5, 5, 6) sts., 1 d.c., work to last 5 (6, 6, 7) sts., 1 d.c., no ch. to turn.
Next row: sl.st. over 2 sts., 1 d.c., work to last 3 sts., 1 d.c., no ch. to turn.
Rep. the last row 4 times more.
Dec. 1 st. at each end of the next 4 (4, 5, 5) rows.
Fasten off.

BLOUSE CUFFS (make 2 alike)
With No. 3.00 hook and Tricel-Nylon Double Knitting make 40 (40, 42, 42) ch.
Work 1 d.c. into 2nd ch. from hook, 1 d.c. into each ch. to end, 1 ch., turn.
Now work in d.c. to 4½ in. from beg. Now work 2 rows d.c. all round cuff but on the 2nd row make loops on side edge for 6 buttons.

BLOUSE TIE
With No. 3.00 hook and Tricel-Nylon Double Knitting make 254 (275, 292, 309) ch. and work in patt. as cuff to 2 in. from beg. Fasten off.
With 63 ch. make another tie in the same way.

TO COMPLETE BLOUSE
Lightly press all parts on wrong side using a warm iron over a damp cloth.
Join shoulder, side and sleeve seams.
With No. 3.00 hook work 2 rows d.c. evenly on each front edge and round back neck. Easing fullness round back and sides, pin long tie to lower edge of blouse beg. at edge of left front and ending at right front edge with 11 in. of tie free for fastening. Sew tie into place. Sew short tie to left front about 2 in. from side edge. Beg. at centre of sleeve edge and sew cuff to edge of sleeve easing fullness. Set sleeves into armhole gathering fullness at shoulder. Press seams as before, sew on buttons.

SKIRT BACK AND FRONT (make 2 pieces alike)
With No. 5.00 hook and using one strand of Tricel-Nylon Double Knitting and one strand of Camilla Crêpe tog., make 66 (70, 72, 76) ch.
Foundation row: 1 tr. into 3rd ch. from hook, 1 tr. into each ch. to end, 2 ch., turn.
Now work 5 in. in tr., turning each row with 2 ch. Cont. in tr. dec. 1 tr. at each end of the next row and at 5-in. intervals to 52 (56, 58, 62) tr. Change to No. 4.50 hook and work straight to 34 in. from beg.
Work 6 rows dec. 1 st. at each end of the first, 3rd and 5th rows. Change to No. 4.00 hook and work straight to 39 in. from beg. Fasten off.

TO COMPLETE SKIRT
Press work lightly on wrong side using cool iron over a dry cloth. Join side seams. Press as before. Join elastic and sew inside waist using a herringbone casing stitch.

Golden party sweater
illustrated in colour on page 177

MATERIALS
10 balls Lister Bel Air Starspun 4-ply Knitting. Crochet hooks International Standard Sizes 3.00, 2.50 and 4.00.

MEASUREMENTS
To fit bust size 34/36 (38/40) in.; length 21 in.; sleeve seam 3 in.

TENSION
1 rep. (of 18 sts.) to 3 in. and 9 rows to 3 in.

ABBREVIATIONS
See page 122; 1 bobble, make bobble as follows: 1 tr. around tr. 4 times, y.o.h. and pull yarn through, yarn over hook and pull through all 9 loops, 1 chain on top of bobble to close it; gr., group (of 3 tr. together).

THE PATTERN
1st row: 3 ch. to turn, in 4th ch. work 1 tr., miss 2 ch., 3 tr. in next ch., miss 2 ch., 3 tr. in next ch., miss 2 ch., * 1 bobble in next ch., (miss 2 ch., 3 tr. in next ch.) 5 times, miss 2 ch.; rep. from * to end, finishing with 1 bobble in next ch., (miss 2 ch., 3 tr. in next ch.) twice, miss 2 ch., 2 tr. in last ch.
2nd row: 3 ch. to turn, 3 tr. between the first 2 tr. of row and next gr. of 3 tr., 3 tr. between next 2 groups, 1 bobble between group and bobble, * 1 bobble between bobble and group, (1 group between 2 groups) 4 times, 1 bobble between last group and bobble; rep. from * to end, finishing with 2 groups, work 1 single tr. in turning ch. of row below.
3rd row: 3 ch. to turn, 1 tr. in 3rd ch. from hook, 1 group between the 2 groups below, 1 bobble between group and bobble, * 1 group between 2 bobbles, 1 bobble between bobble and group, (1 group between groups) 3 times, 1 bobble between group and bobble; rep. from * to end, finishing with 1 group, then 2 tr. into turning ch.
4th row: 3 ch. to turn, 1 group between 2 tr. and first group, * 1 bobble, 2 groups, 1 bobble, 2 groups; rep. from * to end, finishing with 1 bobble, 1 group, 1 tr. in turning ch. of last row.
5th row: 3 ch. to turn, 1 tr. in 3rd ch. from hook, 1 bobble between first group and bobble, * 3 groups, 1 bobble, 1 group, 1 bobble; rep. from * to end, finishing with 3 groups, 1 bobble, 2 tr. in turning ch.
6th row: 3 ch. to turn, 1 bobble between 2 tr. and bobble, *

4 groups, 1 bobble, 1 bobble; rep. from * to end, finishing with 4 groups, 1 bobble, 1 tr. in turning ch.
7th row: 1 bobble on single tr., * 5 groups, 1 bobble; rep. from * to end.
8th row: as 6th row.
9th row: as 5th row.
10th row: as 4th row.
11th row: as 3rd row.
12th row: as 2nd row.
13th row: 3 ch. to turn, 1 tr. in 3rd ch. from hook, 2 groups, * 1 bobble, 5 groups; rep. from * to end, finishing with 1 bobble, 2 groups, 2 tr. in turning ch.
The 2nd-13th rows inclusive form the patt.

BACK
With No. 2.50 hook, make 108 ch. and begin patt.
Work straight for 3 in. Change to No. 3.00 hook and work straight for 6 in. more.
Size 38/40 only. Change to No. 3.50 hook and cont. until Back measures 14½ in. from beg.
Size 34/36 only. Cont. with No. 3.00 hook until Back measures 14½ in. from beg.

Shape Armholes (all sizes)

Sl.st. across 2 groups (or bobbles), work to last 2 groups, turn and leave them unworked.
Next row: work to end.
Next row: sl.st. across 1 group (or bobble), work to within 1 group, turn.
Next row: work to end.
Repeat last 2 rows twice more. Work straight on 26 groups (or bobbles) remaining until armhole measures 7 (7½) in. from beg.

Shape Shoulders

Next row: sl.st. across 3 groups, work to last 3 groups, turn and work 1 row straight.
3rd row: sl.st. across 4 groups, work to last 4 groups, sl.st. to end across 4 groups, leaving 12 groups for back of neck.

FRONT

Work as for Back until first row of armhole shaping has been worked (there are 32 groups, or bobbles, on work).

Shape Neck

Next row: work across 13 groups, turn and work this side first. ** Now dec. (by leaving unworked or sl.st. across) 1 group (or bobble) at neck edge on next 3 rows, at the same time dec. 1 group at armhole edge on alt. rows 3 times. Work on 7 groups until armhole matches back to shoulder.

Shape Shoulder

Sl.st. across 3 groups at armhole edge, work to end.
Next row: work to armhole.
Next row: sl.st. across 4 groups.
Fasten off. **
Leave 6 groups (or bobbles) at centre front free.
Rejoin yarn next to them and work across 13 groups to end. Now work from ** to **, reversing all shapings.

SLEEVES (make 2 alike)

With No. 3.00 hook make 72 ch. and work in patt. on these 4 patt. repeats for approx. 3 in., ending with same patt. row as Back to armhole.

Shape Top

1st row: sl.st. across 1 group (or bobble), work to last group, turn.
2nd row: work to end across 22 groups.
3rd row: sl.st. across 1 group, work to within 1 group, turn.
4th row: work to end.
Repeat last 2 rows 3 times more until 14 groups (or bobbles) remain.
11th row: sl.st. across 1 group, work to within 1 group, turn, leaving it unworked. Repeat 11th row 3 times more.
Fasten off, leaving 6 groups (or bobbles) for top of sleeves.

TO COMPLETE

Join shoulder seams.

Neck Edging

With right side of work facing, work 1 row of d.c. around neck edge.
Next row: 3 ch. to turn, * 1 bobble on 3rd st. from hook, miss 2 sts.; rep. from * all round neck. Work 1 row d.c. holding neck in and missing a few sts. Fasten off.

To Make Up

Join sleeve and side seams. Sew in sleeves. Work around sleeve and lower edge as follows:
1st row: d.c.
Next row: 3 ch., * 1 bobble on 3rd st. from hook, miss 2 sts.; rep. from * to end.
Work 1 more row d.c.
Fasten off. Press seams on wrong side under a damp cloth, using a cool iron.

Laced long dress

illustrated in colour on page 180

MATERIALS. 19 balls Lister Bel Air Starspun in main shade and 2 balls in a contrasting shade (or any mediumweight glitter yarn to give tension indicated below). Crochet hooks International Standard Sizes 3.50, 3.00 and 4.00.

MEASUREMENTS. To fit bust size 34 (36, 38) in.; length 50 in.; length of sleeve seam 17 in.

TENSION. 6 tr to 1 in. and 7 rows to 2¼ in. with No. 3.00 hook.

ABBREVIATIONS. See page 122; dec. 1 tr., work 2 tr. leaving last loop of each on hook, y.o.h. and draw through all 3 loops; M., main shade; C., contrasting shade.

BACK (worked from top downwards)
With No. 3.00 hook and M. commence with 73 (77, 81) ch.
1st row (right side): 1 tr. in 3rd ch. from hook, 1 tr. in to each ch. to end, 2 ch. (to stand as first tr. on next row); turn: 72 (76, 80) tr.
2nd row: 1 tr. into 2nd tr., 1 tr. into each tr. to end, 2 ch.; turn.
The last row forms the patt.
Rep. 2nd row 16 times.

Shape Armhole. 1st row: 1 tr. into first tr. (inc. made), 2 tr. into next tr., patt. to last 2 tr., 2 tr. into each of last 2 tr., 2 ch.; turn.
Rep. last row 6 times.
8th row: 1 tr. into first tr., 2 tr. into each of next 1 (2, 3) tr., patt. to last 2 (3, 4) tr., 2 tr. into each of last 2 (3, 4) tr., 2 ch.; turn: 104 (110, 116) tr.
Cont. straight in patt. until work measures 15 in.
With No. 3.50 hook, cont. straight until work measures 22 in.
With No. 4.00 hook cont. straight until work measures 50 in. or required length. Fasten off.

continued on page 178

Evening skirt and blouse (see page 173).

Golden party sweater (see page 174).   177

FRONT (worked from top downwards)
Left Front. With No. 3.00 hook and M. commence with
21 (23, 25) ch.
1st row: 1 tr. into 3rd ch. from hook, 1 tr. into each ch. to
end, 2 ch.; turn: 20 (22, 24) tr.
2nd row: 1 tr. into 2nd tr., 1 tr. into each tr. to last tr., 2 tr.
into last tr., 2 ch.; turn.
3rd row: 1 tr. into first tr., 1 tr. into each tr. to end, 2 ch.;
turn.
Rep. 2nd and 3rd rows 7 times: 36 (38, 40) tr. Work 1 row.

Shape Armhole. 1st row: patt to last 2 tr., 2 tr. into each of
last 2 tr., 2 ch.; turn.
2nd row: 1 tr. into first tr., 2 tr. into next tr., patt. to end, 2
ch.; turn.
Rep. last 2 rows twice, then first of them again.
8th row: 1 tr. into first tr., 2 tr. into each of next 1 (2, 3) tr.,
patt. to end, 2 ch.; turn: 52 (55, 58) tr.
Cont. straight in patt. until work measures 15 in. ending with a
wrong-side row.

Right Front. With No. 3.00 hook and M. commence with
21 (23, 25) ch.
1st row: 1 tr. into 3rd ch. from hook 1 tr. into each ch. to end,
2 ch.; turn: 20 (22, 24) tr.
2nd row: 1 tr. into first tr., 1 tr. into each tr. to end, 2 ch.; turn.
3rd row: 1 tr. into each tr. to last tr., 2 tr. into last tr., 2 ch.;
turn.
Rep. 2nd and 3rd rows 7 times: 36 (38, 40) tr. Work 1 row.

Shape Armhole. 1st row: 1 tr. into first tr., 2 tr. into next
tr., patt. to end, 2 ch.; turn.
2nd row: patt. to last 2 tr., 2 tr. into each of last 2 tr., 2 ch.;
turn.
Rep. last 2 rows twice, then first of them again.
8th row: patt. to last 2 (3, 4) tr., 2 tr. into each of last 2 (3, 4)
tr., 2 ch.; turn: 52 (55, 58) tr.
Cont. straight in patt. until work measures same as left front.

Join Fronts. With No. 3.50 hook and right side facing, patt.
across 52 (55, 58) tr. of right front, then patt. across 52 (55,
58) tr. of left front, 2 ch.; turn: 104 (110, 116) tr.
Now complete to correspond with Back.

SLEEVES (make 2 alike)
With No. 3.00 hook and M., commence with 49 (51, 53) ch.
Work 6 rows in patt. as given for Back, inc. 1 tr. at each end of
3rd and 6th rows. Cont. to inc. at each end of every 3rd row
until there are 72 (76, 80) tr. Work in foll. stripe patt.
4 rows in C.
2 rows in M.
4 rows in C.
6 rows in M.
These 16 rows form stripe patt.
Keeping continuity of stripe patt. cont. straight after incs.
until Sleeve measures 17 in. Cont. in patt.

Shape Top. 1st row: dec. 1 tr. 2 (3, 4) times, patt. to last
5 (7, 9) tr., dec. 1 tr. 2 (3, 4) times, 1 tr. into last tr., 2 ch.; turn.
2nd row: dec. 1 tr. twice, patt. to last 5 tr., dec. 1 tr. twice,
1 tr. into last tr., 2 ch.; turn.
Rep. last row 6 times.
Next row: dec. 1 tr., patt. to last 3 tr., dec. 1 tr., 1 tr. into last
tr., 2 ch.; turn.
Rep. last row 7 times.
Fasten off.

TO COMPLETE
Press each piece carefully. Sew shoulder seams, then side and
sleeve seams. Sew in Sleeves. With No. 3.00 hook and M.,
work 1 row of d.c. round each cuff and lower and neck edges.
With C., make a crochet chain 30 in. long. Thread between tr.
down front edge of each Front to form a laced effect as shown
in photograph on page 180. Press all seams.

Long pink dress
illustrated in colour on page 181

MATERIALS
31 (32, 33, 34) balls (23.25 gr. each) Wendy Courtelle Crêpe
4-ply. Crochet hooks International Standard Sizes 3.00, 3.50,
and 2.50. Eighteen small buttons.

MEASUREMENTS
To fit bust size 34 (36, 38, 40) in.; sleeve seam 17½ in.; length
from shoulder 56 in.

TENSION
4 patts. measure 4½ in.

ABBREVIATIONS
See page 122.
*Note. This patt. is worked from the neckline downwards so can
be adjusted to any length. Allow one ball of given yarn more
or less for every 2 in. of adjustment required.*

BACK
With No. 3.00 hook, make 80 (88, 96, 104) ch. plus 2 ch. to
turn. Work 8 d.c., miss 3 ch., 3 h.tr., 2 ch., 3 h.tr. in next ch.,
miss 3 ch., 1 h.tr. in next ch., * miss 3 ch., 3 tr., 2 ch., 3 tr. (1
group) in next ch., miss 3 ch., 1 tr. in next ch.; rep. from *
4 (5, 6, 7) times, miss 3 ch., 1 gr. in next ch., miss 3 ch., 1 h.tr.
in next ch., miss 3 ch., 3 h.tr., 2 ch., 3 h.tr. in next ch., miss
3 ch., 9 d.c.
Next row: 3 ch., turn, miss 3 ch., 1 gr. in next st., miss 3 ch.,
1 tr. in next st., * 1 gr. in next 2 ch.sp., 1 tr. in single tr.; rep.
from * 7 (8, 9, 10) times, 1 gr. in next 2 ch.sp., 1 tr. in first
d.c., miss 3 ch., 1 gr. in next st., miss 3 ch., 1 tr. in last st.
Pattern row: 3 ch., turn, * 1 gr. in next 2 ch.sp., 1 tr. in single
tr.; rep. from * across row ending 1 tr. in last st.: 10 (11, 12, 13)
patts.
Rep. this row 10 times.

Shape Armholes
1st row: 4 ch., turn, 3 tr. into st. at base of ch., patt. across
row ending 3 tr. and 1 d.tr. into last st.
2nd row: 4 ch., turn, 1 gr. into first tr., patt. across row ending
1 gr. into last st., 1 d.tr. into same st.
Repeat these 2 rows once more: 14 (15, 16, 17) patts. Cont. in
patt. till work measures 5½ in. from armhole.
1st waist row: 3 ch., turn, make grs. of 2 tr., 2 ch., 2 tr., 1 tr.
into single tr. Rep. this row once.
2nd waist row: 3 ch., turn, make grs. of 2 tr., 1 ch., 2 tr., 1
tr. into single tr. Rep. this row 3 times.
3rd waist row: change to No. 2.50 hook and rep. 2nd waist
row 4 times. Change to No. 3.00 hook and work 2nd waist
row for 2 rows and first waist row for 2 rows. Then work main
patt. for 4 rows.
1st inc. row: 4 ch., turn, * 1 gr. in next 2 ch.sp., 1 ch., 1 tr.
into single tr., 1 ch.; rep. from * across row ending 1 ch., 1 tr.
into last st.
Rep. this row 11 times.
2nd inc. row: 4 ch., turn, * 1 gr. into next 2 ch. sp., 1 ch., 2
tr. into single tr., 1 ch.; rep. from * across row.
Next row: 4 ch., turn, * 1 gr. into 2 ch.sp., 1 ch., 1 tr. into
each tr., 1 ch.; rep. from * across row ending 1 ch., 1 tr. into
last st. Rep. this row 10 times.
3rd inc. row: 4 ch., turn, * 1 gr. into next 2 ch.sp., 1 ch., 1
tr. into tr., 1 ch., 1 tr. into tr., 1 ch.; rep. from * across row
ending 1 ch., 1 tr. into last st.
Rep. this row 11 times.
4th inc. row: 5 ch., turn, * 1 gr. in 2 ch.sp., 2 ch., 1 tr., 1 ch.,
1 tr., 2 ch.; rep. from * across row ending 2 ch., 1 tr. into last
st. Rep. this row 13 times.
5th inc. row: as before but work 2 ch. between the single tr.
and 3 ch. in the centre of the groups.
6th inc. row: change to No. 3.50 hook and work the same
row until work measures 56 in. (or desired length) from the
shoulder. Fasten off.

LEFT FRONT

With No. 3.00 hook make 33 (33, 41, 41) ch.

1st row : into 5th ch. from hook, work 3 tr., miss 3 ch., * 1 tr. in next ch., miss 3 ch., 1 gr. in next ch., miss 3 ch.; rep. from * 0 (0, once, once), 1 tr. in next ch., miss 3 ch., 3 h.tr., 2 ch., 3 h.tr. in next ch., miss 3 ch., d.c. into each of next 9 ch.

2nd row : 3 ch., turn, miss 3 d.c., 1 gr. in next d.c., miss 3 ch., 1 tr. in next d.c., patt. across row ending 3 tr., 1 ch., 1 tr. into last sp.

Pattern row : 4 ch., turn, 3 tr. into first sp., patt. to end: 3½ (3½, 4½, 4½) patts.

** Shape Neck

Sizes 34 and 38 only. Working the extra sts. into the patt. inc. by 1 tr. at the end of next and every alt. row for 19 rows, and at the same time when 10 rows from ** have been worked, shape the armhole (see below).

Sizes 36 and 40 only. Working the extra sts. into the patt. inc. by 1 tr. at the end of next and every alt. row for 10 rows, then every row for 9 rows, and at the same time when 10 rows from ** have been worked, shape the armhole.

Shape Armhole (all sizes)

1st row : 4 ch., turn, 3 tr. into st. at base of ch., patt. across row.

2nd row : patt. to end, into turning ch.sp. work 1 gr. then 1 d.tr. into 3rd of turning ch.

Rep. these 2 rows once.

Cont. straight at side edge and inc. as given at neck edge till there are 7 (7½, 8, 8½) patts.

When work measures 5½ in. from armhole, complete as given for Back.

RIGHT FRONT

With No. 3.00 hook make 30 (30, 38, 38) ch.

1st row : d.c. in 3rd ch. from hook, 1 d.c. in next 8 ch., miss 3 ch., 3 h.tr., 2 ch., 3 h.tr. in next ch., * miss 3 ch., 1 tr. in next ch., miss 3 ch., 1 gr. in next ch.; rep. from * 0 (0, once, once) miss 3 ch., 1 tr. in next ch., miss 3 ch., 3 tr., 1 ch., 1 tr. in last st.

2nd row : 4 ch., turn, 3 tr. in sp. under hook, patt. to 9 d.c., 1 tr. in first d.c., miss 3 ch., 1 gr. in next d.c., miss 3 ch., 1 tr. in last st.: 3½ (3½, 4½, 4½) patts.

Work 1 row.

** Shape Neck

At beg. of next row, work incs. as given for Left Front, and when 10 rows from ** have been worked, shape armhole as follows.

Shape Armhole

1st row : patt. to end of row, work 3 tr. and 1 d.tr. into top of turning ch.

2nd row : 4 ch., turn, work 1 gr. into top of d.tr., patt. to end.

Rep. these 2 rows once.

Complete to match Left Front.

SLEEVES (make 2 alike)

With No. 3.00 hook make 27 ch.

Work 1 gr. into 7th ch. from hook, miss 3 ch., 1 tr. in next ch., * miss 3 ch., 1 gr. in next ch., miss 3 ch., 1 tr. into next ch.; rep. from *: 3 patts.

Work first and 2nd rows of back armhole shaping (making turning ch. and d.tr. quite loose) until 11 patts. have been completed.

Work 2 rows straight.

Now dec. by working 1 tr. less at both ends of every row for 9 rows: 7 patts. and 1 half gr. at each end.

Cont. straight till sleeve measures 7 in. from armhole. Change to patt. as for first waist row for 2 rows, with No. 2.50 hook work 2nd waist row for 2 rows.

With No. 3.00 hook work first waist row for 2 rows.

Work main patt. for 4 rows then work 2 rows each of the 6 inc. rows as given for the Back cont. the last row until sleeve measures 17½ in. from armhole.

TO COMPLETE

Sew shoulder seams.

Front and Neck Bands

With No. 3.00 hook and starting at lower edge of Right Front, join yarn to front and work 1 row of tr. along right front, around neck and along left front working 2 tr. to every row. Work another row of tr.

Starting at top of straight edge of right front, mark places for 9 pairs of buttonholes with 4 tr. between 2 holes then 10 tr. to next hole. Work 1 row d.c. working 1 ch. and missing 1 st. where marked. Work 2 more rows of tr. Fasten off.

To Make Up

Set in sleeves. Stitch side and sleeve seams matching patterns. Press lightly with a cool, dry iron.

Sew on buttons to correspond with buttonholes.

Bolero and skirt

illustrated in colour on page 181

MATERIALS

8 (9) 50-gr. balls Pingouin Classique Crylor in light blue, and 1 ball each in red, yellow, green and black. One crochet hook International Standard Size 4.00 (4.50). A waist length of elastic, ¾ in. wide.

MEASUREMENTS

To fit bust size 32/34 (36/38) in., and hip size 34/36 (38/40) in.; length of skirt 37½ (38) in.; length of bolero 16 (17) in.

TENSION

4 tr.gr. to approx. 2¾ in. with No. 4.00 hook, and 4 tr.gr. to approx. 3 in. with No. 4.50 hook.

ABBREVIATIONS

See page 122; B., blue; R., red; Y., yellow; G., green; Bl., black.

Note. For the first size use No. 4.00 hook throughout; for the second size use No. 4.50 hook throughout.

BOLERO

With B., make 109 ch. loosely.

Foundation row : 2 tr. into 4th ch. from hook, * 1 ch., miss 2 ch., 3 tr. into next ch.; rep. from * to end: 36 tr.gr.

1st patt. row : 4 ch., * 3 tr. into next sp., 1 ch.; rep. from * until 1 tr.gr. remains, 1 tr. into turning ch.

2nd patt. row : 3 ch., 2 tr. into first sp., * 1 ch., 3 tr. into next sp.; rep. from * working last 3 tr. into end sp.

These 2 rows form patt. Rep. them 5 times, then rep. first row again.

Divide for Armholes

Next row : 3 ch., 2 tr. into first sp., * 1 ch., 3 tr. into next sp., rep. from * 3 times more, turn and continue straight on these 5 tr.gr. until armhole measures approx. 7½ in.
Fasten off.

Leave the next 6 tr.gr. free for first armhole and rejoin yarn into next sp. (between 6th and 7th tr.gr.), 3 ch., 2 tr. into same sp., * 1 ch., 3 tr. into next sp.; rep. from * 14 times, turn and work on these 16 tr.gr. Cont. straight until armhole measures approx. 7½ in. Fasten off.

Leave the next 6 tr.gr. free for second armhole and rejoin yarn into next sp., 3 ch., 2 tr. into same sp., patt. to end. Cont. straight on these 5 tr.gr. until armhole measures 7½ in.
Fasten off.

Small Motifs

With G., make 5 ch., and join into ring with sl.st.

1st round : 3 ch., 2 tr. into ring, (1 ch., 3 tr. into ring) 3 times, 1 ch., sl.st. to top of 3rd ch. Fasten off.

continued on page 182

Laced long dress (see page 175).

Bolero and skirt (see page 179) and long button-up dress in pink (see page 178).   181

2nd round: join R. into a 1 ch.sp., (3 ch., 2 tr., 2 ch., 3 tr.) all into same sp., * 1 ch., (3 tr., 2 ch., 3 tr.) all into next sp.; rep. from * twice more, 1 ch., sl.st. to top of 3rd ch. Fasten off.

3rd round: join Y. to a corner sp., 3 ch., in same sp. work 2 tr., 2 ch. and 3 tr., 1 ch., 3 tr. in next sp., * 1 ch., into next sp. work 3 tr., 2 ch. and 3 tr., 1 ch., 3 tr. in next sp.; rep. from * twice more, 1 ch., sl.st. to top of 3rd ch. Fasten off.

4th round: with Bl., work 1 row of d.c. all round motif, working 1 d.c. into every tr. and into every 1 ch.sp. and 2 d.c. into corner spaces. Fasten off.

Work another 8 motifs as above. Now work 8 motifs as follows: use Y. for making 5 ch. and first round, B. for 2nd round, R. for 3rd round, and Bl. for 4th round.

HALF MOTIF (make 2 alike)

With Y., make 5 ch. and join into a ring with sl.st.

1st row: with Y., 4 ch., 3 tr. into ring, 1 ch., 3 tr. into ring, 1 ch., 1 tr. into ring. Fasten off.

2nd row: join B. into top of 4th ch. at beg of last row, 4 ch., 3 tr. into same sp., 1 ch., (3 tr., 2 ch., 3 tr.) into next sp., 1 ch., 3 tr. into last sp., 1 ch., 1 tr. into same sp. Fasten off.

3rd row: join R. into top of 4th ch. at beg. of last row, 4 ch., 3 tr. into same sp., 1 ch., 3 tr. into next sp., 1 ch., (3 tr., 2 ch., 3 tr.) into next sp., (1 ch., 3 tr. into next sp.) twice, 1 ch., 1 tr. into same sp. Fasten off.

4th round: join Bl. into top of 3rd ch. and work a round of d.c. all round motif.
Fasten off.

SKIRT

Large Motif

With Y., make 5 ch., and join into ring with sl.st.

1st round: with Y., 3 ch. for first tr., 2 tr. into ring, (1 ch., 3 tr. into ring) 3 times, 1 ch., sl.st. to top of 3rd ch.

2nd round: with Y., sl.st. into next sp., (3 ch., 2 tr., 2 ch., 3 tr.) all into same sp., * 1 ch., (3 tr., 2 ch., 3 tr.) all into next sp.; rep. from * twice more, 1 ch., sl.st. to top of 3rd ch. Fasten off.

3rd round: join B. to a corner sp., 3 ch., in same sp. work (2 tr., 2 ch., 3 tr.), 1 ch., 3 tr. in next sp., * 1 ch., (3 tr., 2 ch., 3 tr.) all into next sp., 1 ch., 3 tr. in next sp.; rep. from * twice more, 1 ch., sl.st. to top of 3rd ch.

4th round: with B., sl.st. into next sp., 3 ch., in same sp. work (2 tr., 2 ch., 3 tr.), * 1 ch., (3 tr. in 1 ch.sp., 1 ch.) twice, (3 tr., 2 ch., 3 tr.) all into next sp.; rep. from * twice more, 1 ch., (3 tr. in 1 ch.sp., 1 ch.) twice, sl.st. to top of 3rd ch. Fasten off.

5th round: join R. to a corner sp. and work as for 4th round, but work the (3 tr. into 1 ch.sp., 1 ch.) 3 times instead of twice.

6th round: join Y. to a corner sp. and work as for 4th round, but work the (3tr. into 1 ch.sp., 1 ch.) 4 times.

7th round: join Bl. to a corner sp. and work as for 4th round, but work the (3 tr. into 1 ch.sp., 1 ch.) 5 times. Fasten off.
Work another 3 motifs as above. Now work 4 motifs thus: use G. for making 5 ch. and first 2 rounds, R. for 3rd and 4th rounds, Y. for 5th round, B. for 6th round, and Bl. for 7th round.

Fill-in Triangles (make 16 alike)

With B., make 5 ch., and join into a ring with sl.st.

1st row: 4 ch., 3 tr. into ring, 1 ch., 1 tr. into ring, turn.

2nd row: 4 ch., 3 tr. into first sp., 1 ch., 3 tr. into end sp., 1 ch., 1 tr. into same sp., turn.

3rd row: 4 ch., 3 tr. into first sp., 1 ch., 3 tr. into next sp., 1 ch., 3 tr. into end sp., 1 ch., 1 tr. into same sp., turn.

4th row: 4 ch., 3 tr. into first sp., (1 ch., 3 tr. into next sp.) twice, 1 ch., 3 tr. into end sp., 1 ch., 1 tr. into same sp., turn.

5th row: as 4th row, but rep. between brackets 3 times.

6th row: as 4th row, but rep. between brackets 4 times.

7th row: as 4th row, but rep. between brackets 5 times.

8th row: as 4th row, but rep. between brackets 6 times.

9th row: 3 ch., 2 tr. into first sp., (1 ch., 3 tr. into next sp.) 7 times, 3 tr. into end sp. Fasten off.

Join large motifs at corners as shown in diagram, alternating colours, to form a ring. Then sew in fill-in triangles at each side.

Next round: join B. into a 2-ch. sp. at top of one motif, 4 ch., * (3 tr. into next 1 ch.sp. of fill-in triangle, 1 ch.) 8 times, 3 tr. into 2 ch.sp. of next motif, 1 ch.; rep. from * twice, (3 tr. into next 1 ch.sp. of fill-in triangle, 1 ch.) 8 times, 1 tr. into 2 ch.sp. of next motif and mark this tr. with a thread (for side decreasings), work along second side of skirt in a similar way, ending with 1 ch., sl.st. into top of 3rd of 4 ch. and again mark this last st. with a thread as before. Now dec. thus:

1st round: sl.st. into first sp., 3 ch., 1 tr. into same sp., (1 ch., 3 tr. into next sp.) to within 1 sp. before first marked tr., 2 tr. into sp. before single tr., 2 tr. into sp. after single tr., (1 ch., 3 tr. into next sp.) to within 1 sp. before second marked tr., 2 tr. into sp. before single tr., sl.st. into top of 3rd ch.

2nd round: sl.st. into first sp., 3 ch., 2 tr. into same sp., (1 ch., 3 tr. into next sp.) to end, (working over the 4 tr. at side edge as over a tr.gr.), 1 ch., sl.st. into top of 3rd ch.

3rd round: turn and work a sl.st. into last sp. just worked, 4 ch., turn work again, (3 tr. into next sp., 1 ch.) to sp. above first marked tr., 1 tr. into sp. above marked tr., 1 ch., (3 tr. into next sp., 1 ch.) to end, sl.st. to top of 3rd of 4 ch.

Rep. last 3 rounds 16 times, then rep. first round again. For first size only, work 1 round straight.

Next row: work 1 d.c. into each tr. of previous round and 1 d.c. into each sp. Turn and work another 5 rows of d.c. Fasten off. Join ends of border.

Lower Border

With B., work 2 (1) rounds of patt., (3 tr. into each sp. and work 1 ch. between each tr.gr. as before) along lower edge of skirt. Fasten off. Join any two of the contrasting colours and work another 2 rounds of patt. Fasten off.

TO COMPLETE

Press very lightly with a cool iron.

Bolero. Join motifs as shown in diagram, alternating colours. Join shoulder seams, then sew border to main part ending about ½ (¾) in. below shoulder seams. With Bl., work a row of d.c. along lower, front and neck edges.

With B., work 2 rows of d.c. round armhole edges. Press seams and edgings very lightly.

Skirt. Join elastic into ring and sew inside waist with herringbone casing stitch.

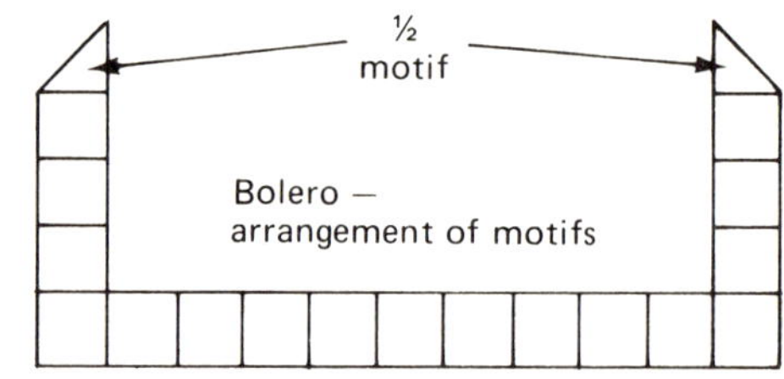

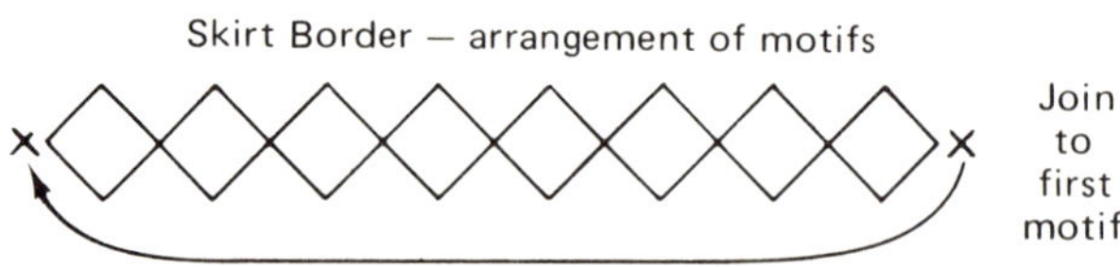

Embroidery, in simple terms, means merely the addition of ornament to a plain fabric. So a flimsy pocket handkerchief with a buttonhole stitch edging is an embroidery; so too is a dramatic abstract wall hanging intricately embellished with surface stitchery, beads, pebbles and bits of ironmongery! Between these two extremes is a vast range of design possibilities, both practical and decorative, traditional and modern.

For a modest outlay, you can buy a few coloured threads, a needle and a piece of fabric, and immediately set to work, to experiment with stitches and techniques, and find out which type of embroidery will suit you: the mathematical precision of counted-thread work where stitches and designs are determined by the mesh of the fabric itself; the diversity of free embroidery where almost anything is possible, from lifelike needlework 'paintings' to classic monograms and initials; the timelessness of canvas work where wonderful rich colour effects are possible, beautiful traditional patterns worked entirely in tent stitch, and modern designs combining literally dozens of different stitches in the one piece of work.

Part 1

FREE EMBROIDERY

There is a tremendous scope for expression in design in this work – a child will find pleasure in working a simple outline embroidery in stem stitch; an experienced embroiderer will be challenged to produce a mammoth and intricate wall hanging with an abstract design; yet another may prefer to depict a pictorial subject, painstakingly and laboriously picking out every detail in a different stitch and colour. All are free embroideries worked on plain backgrounds, the stitches being used to form any shape or size or area as wished.

EQUIPMENT
Needles

The ideal needle for embroidery work should pierce the fabric easily and make a large enough hole for the thread to pull through the fabric smoothly. The thread should also move through the eye of the needle freely. Never use a crooked needle for this will make a crooked stitch.

Sharps are ordinary sewing needles which are used in embroidery with mercerised cotton thread or a single strand of stranded cotton.

Crewel needles are long and sharp and have large eyes. They are used with most embroidery threads – stranded cotton, *coton à broder,* pearl cotton No. 5 and No. 8. Choose a size with a large eye, such as No. 5, when working with six strands of stranded cotton or with pearl cotton No. 5.

Chenille needles are also sharp and have large eyes, but they are slightly shorter then crewel needles. Use the No. 19 size with soft embroidery thread or tapestry wool.

Tapestry needles are used for canvas work and also for counted-thread embroidery on coarse fabrics. A tapestry needle has a blunt end and so is useful for lacing or whipping stitches, too.

Threads

Stranded cotton. This is a shiny, twisted thread. It has six strands which can be untwisted so as many or as few as liked can be used, depending on the embroidery being worked. It is suitable for most types of embroidery.

Pearl cotton is available in two thicknesses, No. 5 and No. 8. It is a smooth, corded thread used for all types of embroidery, but most often for counted-thread work.

Coton à broder is a very twisted, shiny thread, suitable for drawn-thread and drawn-fabric work and cutwork.

Soft embroidery thread is a thick, matt cotton used in most types of embroidery.

Tapestry wool is firm, twisted, woollen yarn, which can be used in ordinary embroidery as well as canvas work.

All these threads are available in a good range of colours. In addition you may find it useful to have basting cotton, a range of mercerised cotton, some metal threads – gold and silver – in different thicknesses and to collect odds and ends of knitting yarns.

If you will want to wash your embroidery a lot, it is best to match yarn and fabric – cotton yarn on cotton fabric, for instance, and make sure your thread is colour fast. Always cut embroidery threads – never break them. Do not use too long a length at a time as it may fray. If it is a twisted thread, make sure it remains twisted during work.

Above: *a 19th-century Chinese embroidered
panel, worked mainly in satin stitch.*

184

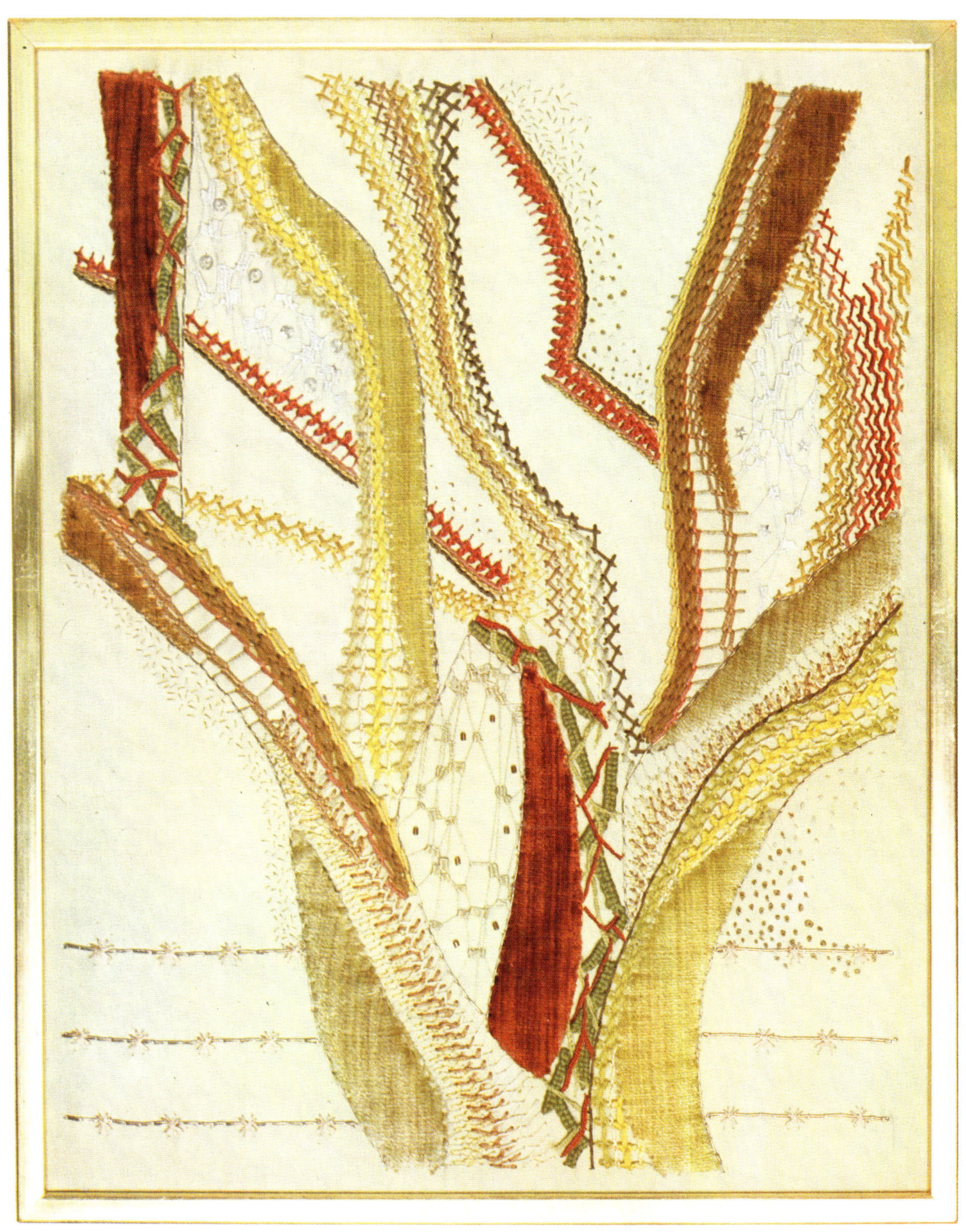

Above: *'Branches', an embroidered picture
worked on a gold silk background in wools, soft
and stranded cotton, raffia, metal threads and
beads, with applied strips of furnishing velvet.*

Fabrics

Almost any fabric can be embroidered, but the stitches and design should be chosen to suit the material. Do not waste your efforts on embroidering a cheap fabric which will not last long. For counted-thread work a fabric with an even weave must be used. Evenweave linen is inexpensive and is a very good choice for beginners, too, for either free-style or counted-thread work, as regular stitches can be made easily, right from the start.

Frames

All large embroideries should be worked in a frame, and so should most small ones, particularly if a delicate fabric is being used or if there are areas with a lot of stitches. There are two basic types of frame: the Swiss, or tambour, frame and the slate frame. The tambour frame consists of two hoops, one slightly larger than the other. The fabric is placed over the smaller hoop, then the larger hoop is placed over the fabric so that it holds it taut. Some of these frames have a screw for tightening the outer hoop and some have a stand or clamp so the frame can be placed on a table. If a very fine fabric is being used, it is a good idea to have a piece of muslin or tissue between hoop and fabric.

The slate frame is rectangular and consists of two parallel horizontal bars. Each bar has a length of tape nailed along it. The fabric to be embroidered is sewn to the tape. The side pieces are then slotted into the bars and secured so that they hold the fabric taut. The fabric is laced to these side pieces with strong thread; if a very fine fabric is used, the sides of the fabric should first have strips of tape sewn to them and then the tape is laced to the side pieces of the frame.

Thimble

A metal one is preferable.

Scissors

You will need a large pair for cutting fabrics and a small pointed pair for cutting thread.

Also useful

In addition pins and pounce are needed for transferring designs (see below), a clean white cloth is needed for wrapping the embroidery in while it is not being worked, an iron, ironing board and pressing cloth will be required for pressing the work and a sewing machine is useful for finishing off a piece or making it up into its finished form.

TRANSFERRING
Purchased transfers

There are two types of embroidery transfers – single impression which are used once only, and multi-print which can be used up to eight times: the thinner the fabric the more often can the transfer be used. Cut any lettering away from the transfer and keep aside. Heat iron to fairly hot (wool) temperature for a single impression transfer or hot (cotton) temperature for a multi-print transfer. On a spare piece of fabric test the heat of the iron by placing the cut-away lettering face downwards on the fabric, running the iron over it for a few seconds, then peeling off the transfer. If a good impression has been obtained, place the main transfer in position on the fabric and secure with pins. Apply iron for a few seconds, then lift the corner of the design to make sure the design has transferred properly. If it has not, iron over it again. Make sure you do not move either the transfer or the fabric or the impression will smudge. If on testing the lettering a good impression is not obtained, set the iron a little hotter.

Pouncing

Pricking and pouncing is the traditional method of putting a design on to fabric, and usually considered to be the best one. Trace the design you wish to use on to tracing paper and place tracing paper on a thickly folded piece of spare material. With a needle, prick holes at $\frac{1}{2}$ in. intervals all along lines of design. Place pricked tracing over fabric to be used for embroidery, and hold in place with weights – make sure it is not in a draught. Take a small, tightly-rolled piece of fabric – about the size of a finger – and dip it in pounce (powdered charcoal) for a light-coloured fabric or powdered chalk for a dark one. Dab rolled fabric over holes so a little pounce or chalk falls through each hole on to fabric. When whole design has been worked over, remove tracing paper and go over lines with a very fine paint brush and water-colour paint or waterproof Indian ink.

Tracing

A design can be traced direct on to transparent material. Use a fine paint brush and water-colour paint or waterproof Indian ink.

Basting

If a very thick material is being used, the basting method is more satisfactory than the prick and pounce method. Trace design on to tracing paper then place tracing paper over fabric to be used; pin in place. Using a basting thread to contrast with fabric colour, work small running stitches over all the lines of the design through paper and fabric. When complete, carefully tear away tracing paper. Remove basting stitches as soon as possible when working the design.

STITCHES

Back stitch

Work from right to left. Bring thread through on stitch line a little to left of the point where you wish stitching to begin. Take a small stitch backwards, bringing needle out again the same distance ahead of the starting point. This stitch can be laced, if wished.

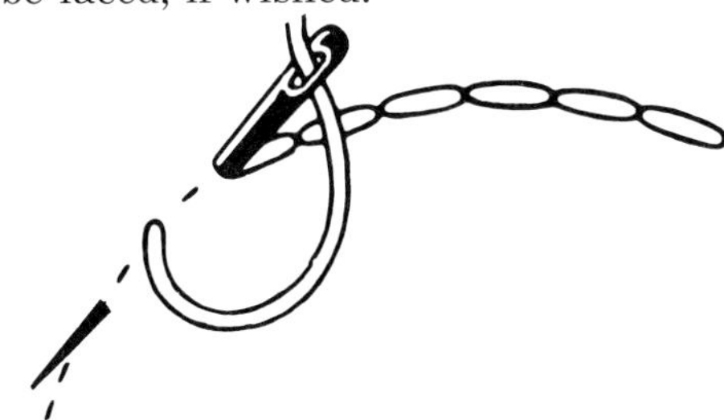

Blanket and buttonhole stitches

These stitches are worked in a similar way, but blanket (diagram 1) has open stitches while in buttonhole (diagram 2) they are closed. Work from left to right. Bring needle through on lower line, insert at upper line and, holding thread down with left thumb, take a straight downward stitch over thread.

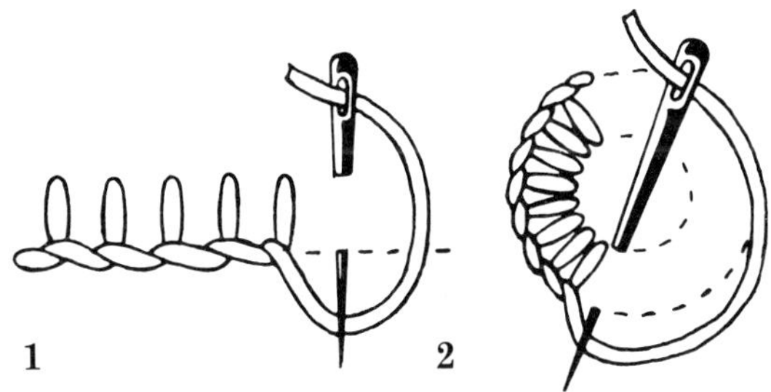

Bullion knot

Bring needle through at left side of point where bullion knot is to appear, then take a small stitch back to the right bringing needle through again at starting point, but without pulling it fully through fabric. Twist thread round needle point as many times as required for length of stitch (about eight times gives a satisfactory stitch) and hold coil with left thumb. Pull needle through. Take it back to the right again, insert and pull fairly tightly so knot lies flat.

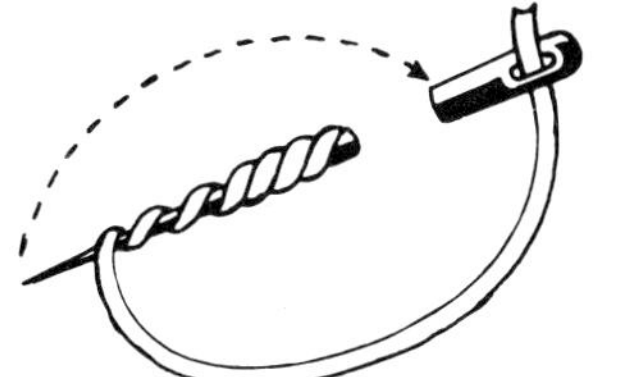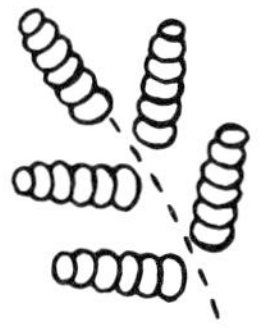

Cable stitch

This stitch is worked from left to right. Bring the needle through on the line of the design, and insert a little to the right on the line, and bring out to the left at the midway point of the stitch, with the thread below the needle (diagram 1). Work the next stitch in a similar way but with the thread above the needle (diagram 2). Continue in this way, alternating the position of the thread. This stitch may also be worked in counted-thread embroidery on an evenweave fabric.

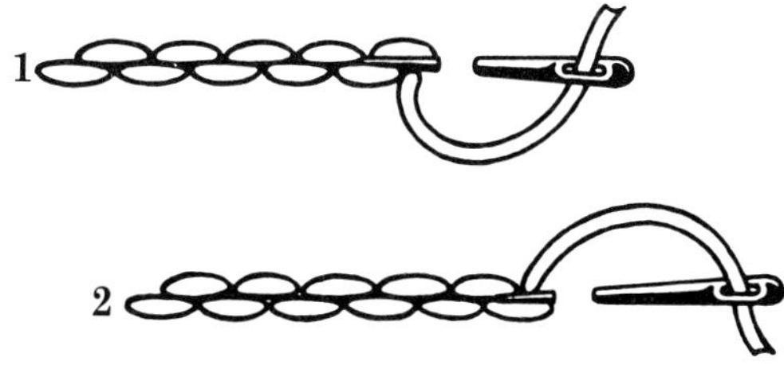

Chain stitch

Bring thread out at top of stitch line, make a loop and hold down with left thumb. Insert needle at starting point again and bring out a short distance down stitch line, with thread under needle point. Continue in this way.

Detached chain stitch
or daisy stitch

This is worked in a similar way as chain stitch, but each loop is tied with a vertical stitch.

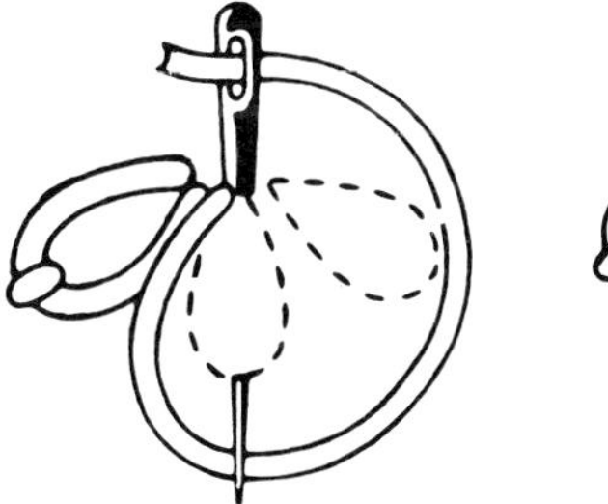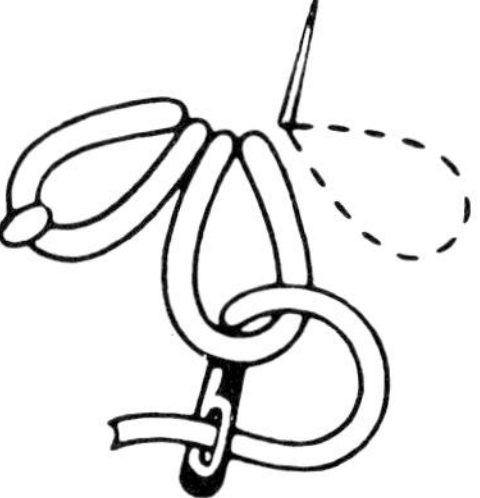

A little embroidery can pretty-up a functional garment like this beach coat.

Open chain stitch

Bring thread through at A and hold down with left thumb. Insert needle at B and bring out again at C, with needle point above thread. Leave loop fairly loose and insert needle inside loop at D.

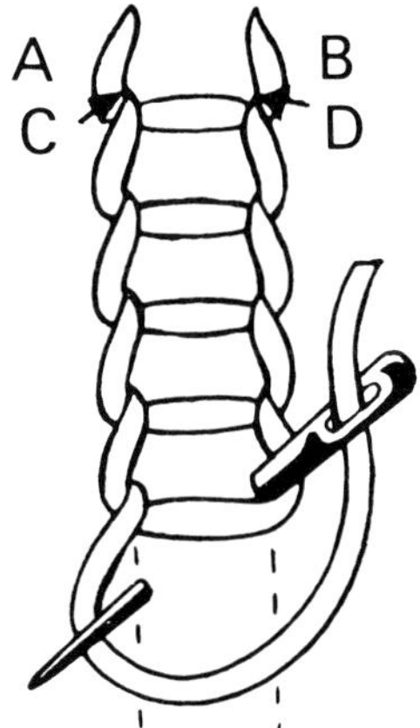

Chevron stitch

Bring the needle through on the lower line at the left side of work, and insert a little to the right on the same line. Take a small stitch to the left emerging at the midway point of the stitch being made. Insert the needle on the upper line a little to the right, and take a small stitch to the left, as shown in diagram 1. Insert the needle again on the same line a little to the right and take a small stitch to the left, emerging at centre as in diagram 2. Continue to work in this way alternately on the upper and lower lines.

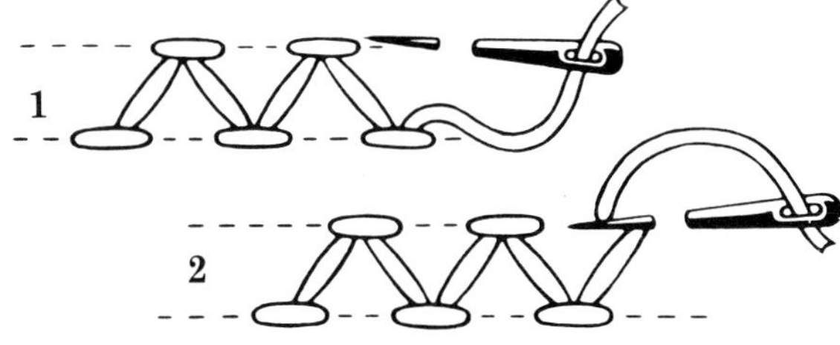

Couching

Bring thread to be couched through from back to front of fabric and lay it along stitch line. With couching thread (usually a thinner one) make tiny stitches over other thread at regular intervals to hold it firmly in place.

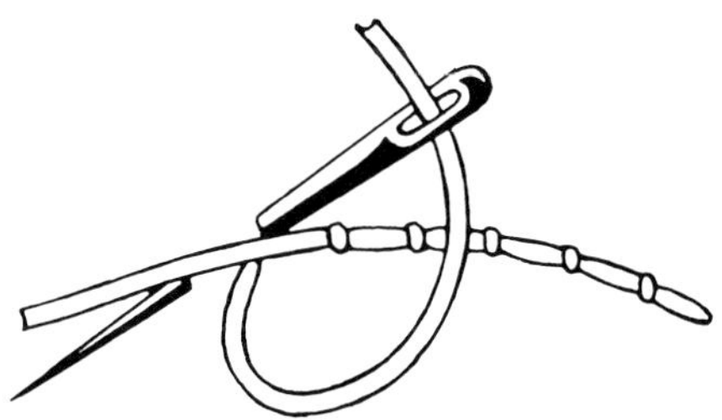

Cretan stitch

Bring needle through just above the centre of the space to be filled at left side. With thread to right, insert needle at lower edge and bring out just below centre with needle point above

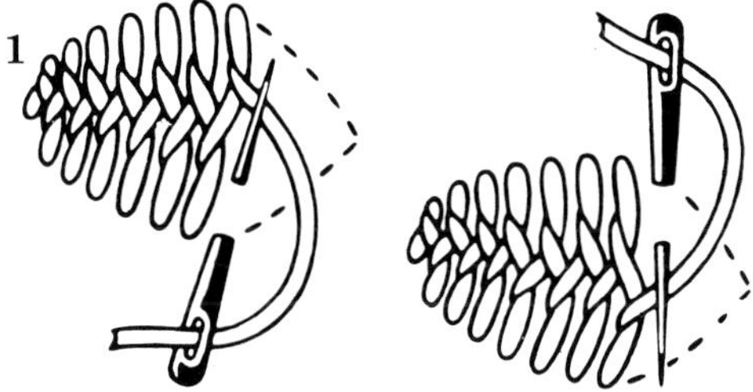

thread (diagram 1). With thread to right again, insert needle at top edge and bring out just above centre, with needle point over thread. This stitch can also be worked open (diagram 2).

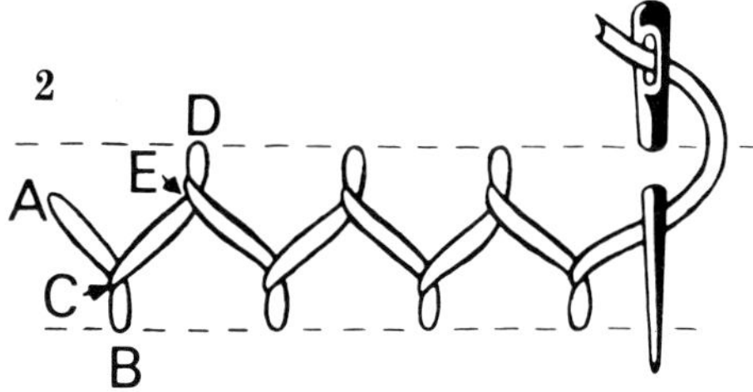

Double knot stitch

Bring the needle through at A on diagram 1. Take a small stitch across the line at B. Pass the needle downwards under the surface stitch just made, without piercing the fabric, as at C. With the thread under the needle, pass the needle again under the first stitch at D. Pull the thread through to form a knot. The knots should be spaced evenly and closely to obtain a beaded effect.

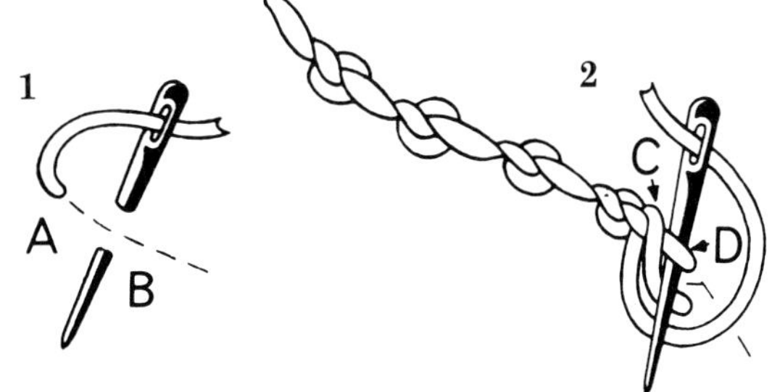

Feather stitch

Bring needle out at top of stitch line. Holding thread down with left thumb, insert needle a

little to the right and bring out above thread a short distance down in the centre. Insert to the left and bring out above thread a little lower down (diagram 1). Double feather stitch has two stitches to the right and two to the left (diagram 2).

Fern stitch

This consists of three straight stitches (see page 192) of equal length radiating from the same central point. Bring needle through at A and make a straight stitch to B. Bring the needle through again at A and make another straight stitch to C. Repeat once more at D and bring the needle through at E to begin the next three radiating stitches. The central stitch follows the line of the design. This stitch may also be used in counted-thread embroidery on evenweave fabric.

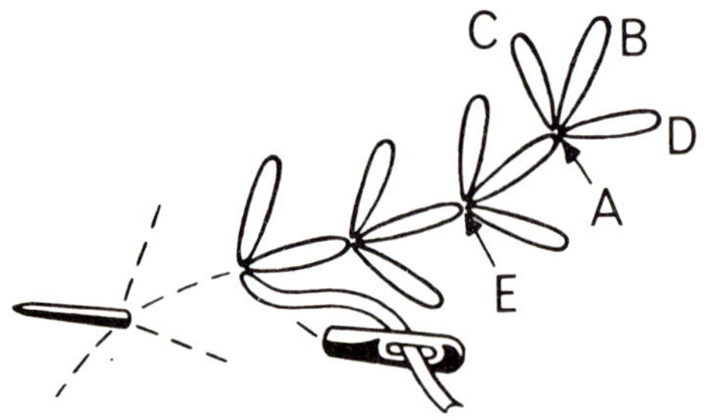

Fly stitch

Begin at top of stitch line and bring needle through a little to the left. Holding thread down with left thumb, insert needle an equal distance to the right of stitch line and bring out again on stitch line a short distance down. Make a short vertical stitch downwards, then bring needle out ready for next stitch. This stitch can be worked in rows or individually. When a single stitch is being made the vertical stitch is very tiny.

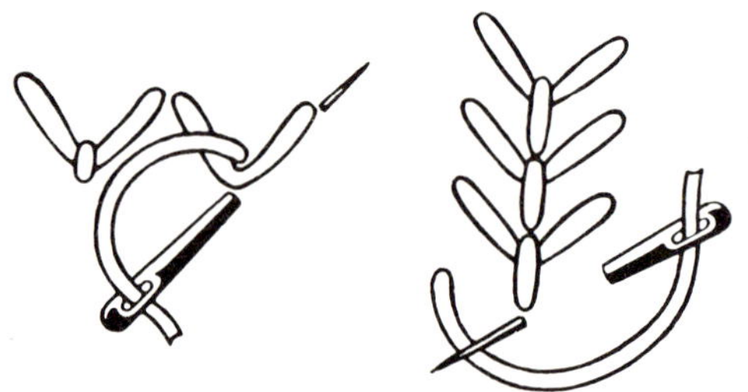

French knot

Bring needle through fabric and hold thread down with left thumb. Twist thread twice round

needle. Still holding thread firmly turn needle and insert close to starting point. Pull tightly.

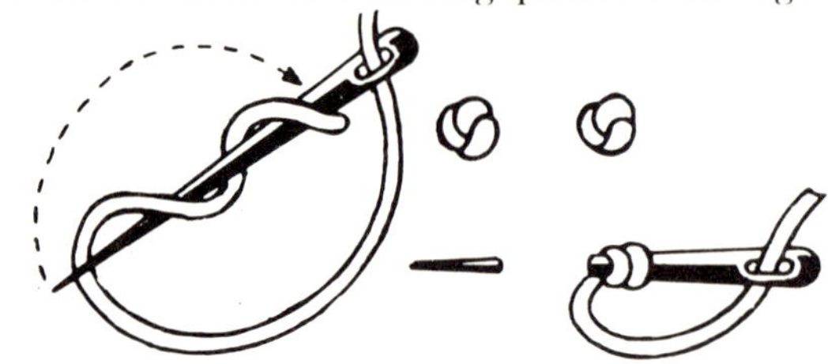

Herringbone stitch

Work from left to right. Bring needle out at bottom of area where stitching is to appear. Insert at top and to the right, take a small stitch to the left then insert back at bottom. Ideally the stitch taken up by the needle should be the same length as the space between stitches.

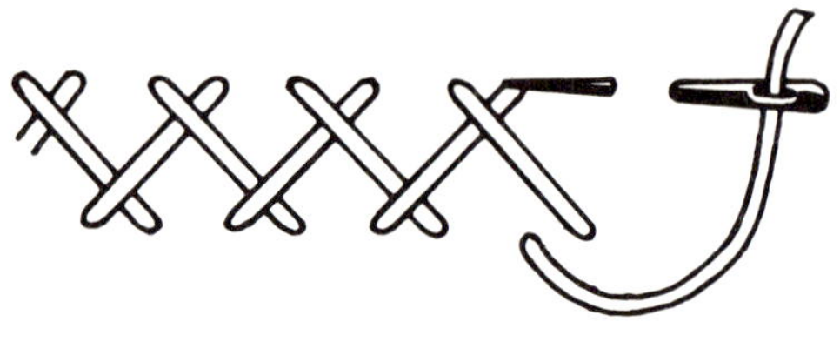

Long and short stitch

This form of satin stitch is so named as all the stitches are of varying lengths. It is often used to fill a shape which is too large or too irregular to be covered by satin stitch. It is also used to achieve a shaded effect. In the first row the stitches are alternately long and short and closely follow the outline of the shape. The stitches in the following rows are worked to achieve a smooth appearance.

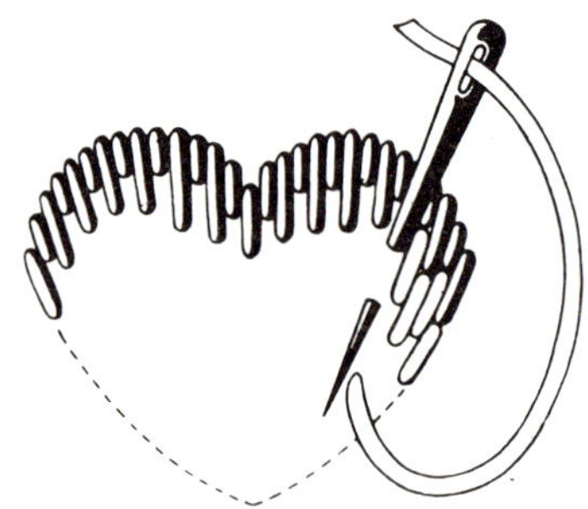

Overcast stitch

Work from left to right. Bring needle through just below stitch line and insert it just above. Bring it out again just below stitch line a little to the right. Continue in this way, following stitch line and working stitches close together.

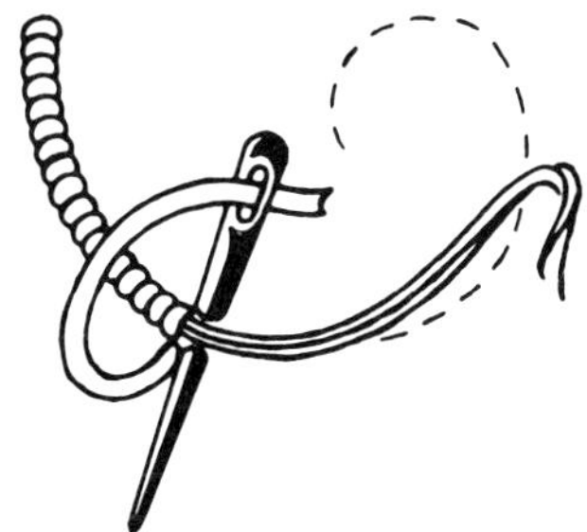

Pekinese stitch

Work back stitch in the usual way (see page 187), then interlace with toning or contrasting thread. The stitch is shown open in the diagram but the loops should be pulled slightly when working.

Running stitch

Work from right to left. Bring needle through on stitch line and take it over three or four threads of the fabric then under one or two threads. Continue in this way, keeping all the same length, and all the spaces the same. This stitch can be threaded in the same way as for back stitch.

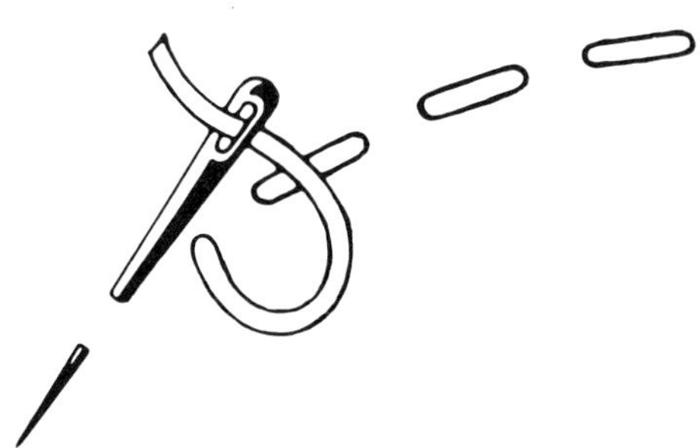

Satin stitch
illustrated at top of next column

Work straight stitches (see page 192) close together across space to be filled, bringing needle out for each new stitch only a thread of the fabric beyond previous stitch so you get a solid shape of stitching.

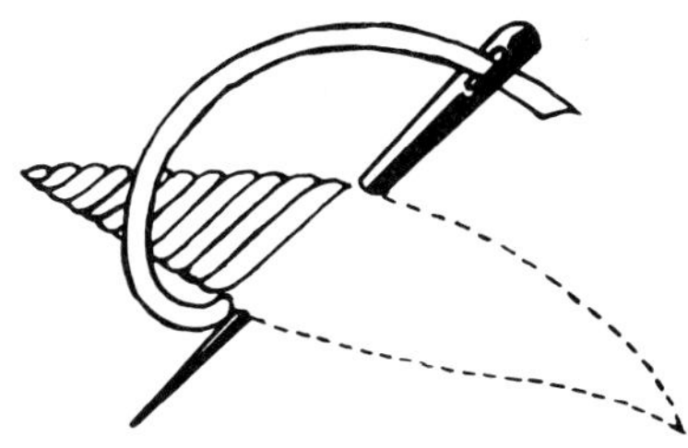

Satin stitch, padded

This is often used for working monograms and initials, when a slightly raised, well-padded surface is required. Outline the design first of all with small running stitches, then work chain stitches to cover the area completely – begin the chain stitches just inside line of running stitches and work in towards the centre. Finally cover the area with satin stitches, worked close together and all slanting in the same direction.

Split stitch

Bring the needle through at left-hand side of work. Make a small stitch over the line of the design, piercing the working thread with the needle, as shown in the diagram below.

Stem stitch

Work from left to right. Bring needle out on stitch line then insert a little way along and slightly below line. Bring needle up a little way back just above stitch line. Continue in this way.

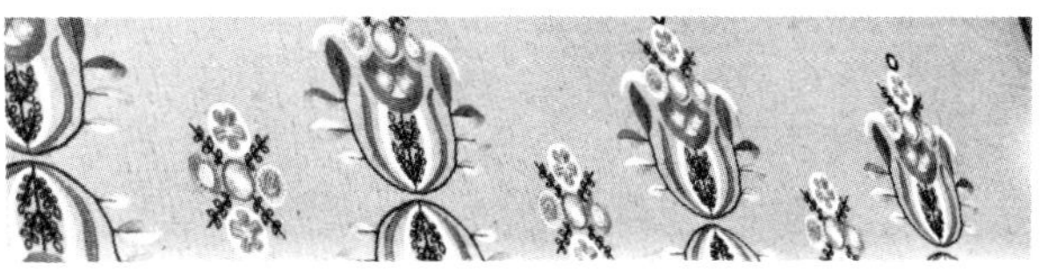

Motifs for an embroidered bedspread, worked mainly in stem, chain and satin stitch, and French knots.

Above: *sample of couching and flat (free embroidery) stitch worked on canvas.*

Machine embroidery

Straight stitch

Bring needle through at bottom of stitch area, insert at top then bring out at bottom of next stitch. Continue in this way. Straight stitches can be worked to form any shape or fill any area.

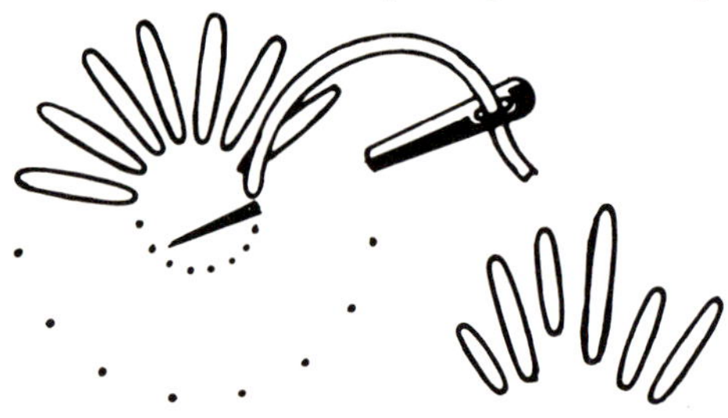

SHADOW WORK

This is a delicate and pleasing form of embroidery, particularly effective for children's party dresses, and fragile dressing-table mats, although it can be used for many other purposes too. As the name suggests the embroidery appears in 'shadow' – this is achieved by using transparent fabric and working the stitching on the wrong side of the fabric. Closed herringbone stitch is always used for this work, but if wished the work can be highlighted with further stitching detail by working directly on to the right side of the fabric.

Stem, back, satin, straight stitches, and French knots, are the stitches most often combined with shadow work, and are usually worked on the right side of the fabric.

To work shadow work stitch

This can either be worked on the right side of fabric as a double back stitch, or on the wrong side of fabric as closed herringbone stitch. Diagram 1 shows the double back stitch version: a small back stitch is worked alternately on each side of the traced double lines (the dotted lines on the diagram show the formation of the thread on the wrong side of the fabric). The colour of the thread appears delicately through the fabric. Diagram 2 shows the stitch worked on the wrong side of the fabric as a closed herringbone stitch with no spaces left between the stitches. Both methods achieve the same result.

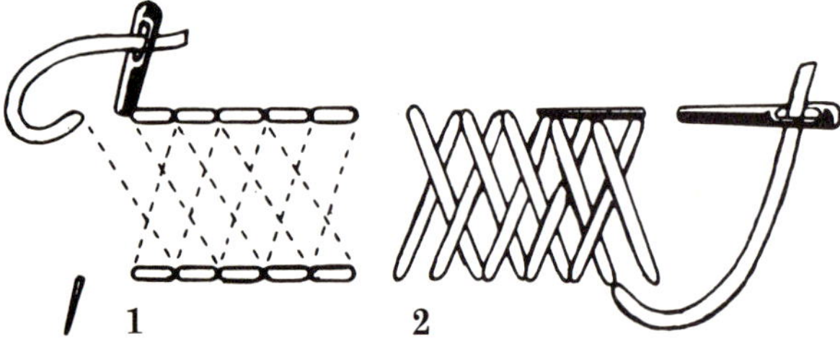

A pretty shadow work pattern worked on a ground of pale blue organdie.

CUTWORK

This is a specialised type of free embroidery in which flowers, leaves and figures are surrounded by buttonhole stitch, sometimes joined by bars and then certain areas of the fabric are cut away to give a lace-like effect. Sometimes surface stitchery is added to enhance the embroidery.

A fairly firm linen or similar fabric should be used for cutwork – if the fabric is too flimsy it will be difficult to cut away areas cleanly. And a small pair of well-sharpened, pointed scissors will be required.

Begin by transferring your design in any of the usual ways. Work a double line of running stitches round outline of design to emphasise and strengthen it. Now work buttonhole stitch closely over the edge of the outline of the design, having the 'head' of the buttonhole stitch at the edge which will be cut. Finally when all the design has been stitched, trim away the unwanted areas of fabric. Work on the right side of fabric, and take care not to snip the stitches as you cut.

Buttonhole stitch bars

These bars occur frequently in conventional cutwork and in Richelieu work. Make a row of running stitches between the double lines of the design as a padding for the buttonhole stitch. Where a single line bar is required, take a thread across the space and back. securing with a small stitch and buttonhole stitch closely over the loose threads without picking up any of the fabric (diagram 1). Buttonhole stitch round the shape, keeping the looped edges of the stitch to the inside, then cut away the fabric from behind the bar and round the inside of the shape. Where a double line or a broad bar is required between shapes, or sometimes for stems of flowers when the fabric is to be cut away on each side, make a row of running stitches along the centre, then buttonhole stitch along one side spacing the stitches slightly. Buttonhole stitch along the other side into the spaces left by the first row. The fabric is then cut away close to the buttonhole stitch leaving a strong broad bar (diagram 2).

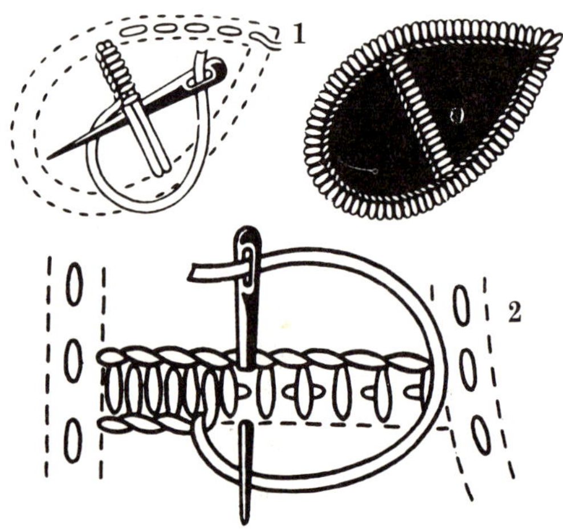

THE PATTERNS

Tissue holder

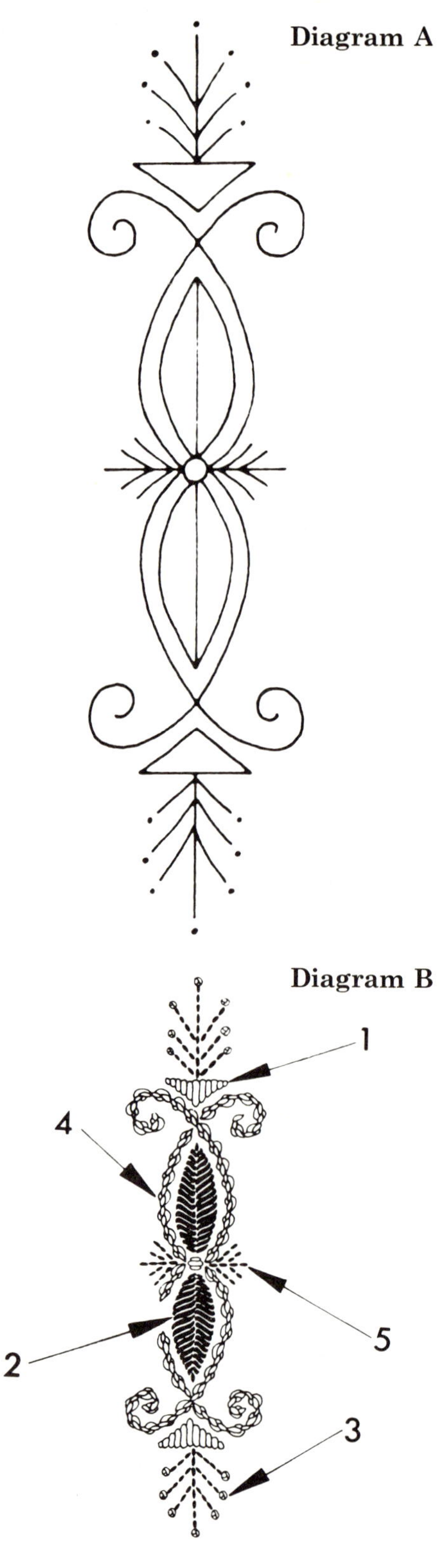

MATERIALS

Of Clark's Anchor Pearl Cotton No. 8 — one 10-gram ball each Gorse Yellow 0301/442 and Black 0403 *or* of Clark's Anchor Stranded Cotton (USA J. & P. Coats Deluxe Six Strand Floss) — 1 skein each Gorse Yellow 0301/442 and Black 0403. Piece of green poplin, or other suitable fabric, 6 in. by $7\frac{1}{4}$ in. A 6-in. square of non-woven iron-on interfacing. A Milward 'Gold Seal' crewel needle No. 6.

STITCHES

Satin; French knots; double knot; back.

DIAGRAMS *(see opposite)*

Diagram A gives one complete motif in actual size.
Diagram B gives a guide to the stitches and colours used throughout the design.

TO MAKE

Note. If using stranded cotton, then use 3 strands throughout.

With one long side of fabric facing, trace the motif as given in diagram A centrally on to fabric, $\frac{5}{8}$ in. from one side edge. Repeat at other end of fabric. Work embroidery, following diagram B and stitch and colour key. Unnumbered parts on diagram B are worked in the same stitch and colour as the numbered parts most similar to them.

TO COMPLETE

Press embroidery on the wrong side. Turn in $\frac{1}{2}$ in. on side edges and press. Iron interfacing centrally on to wrong side, overlapping turned-in edges. Fold sides to the centre, right sides together, and machine stitch $\frac{1}{4}$ in. from raw edges. Turn right side out.

Brighten up a pair of old nylons.

Traditional floral embroidered pictures. Wild Rose **(left)** *and Apple Blossom; Penelope Designs.*

A fine white linen tablecloth with a circular pattern of cutwork embroidery.

Diagram A

Shadow work cheval set

MATERIALS
Of Clark's Anchor Stranded Cotton (USA J. & P. Coats Deluxe Six Strand Floss) – 2 skeins Cyclamen 088, 1 skein Moss Green 0267. $\frac{1}{2}$ yd. white organdie or other similar transparent fabric, 36 in. wide. A Milward 'Gold Seal' crewel needle No. 7.

STITCHES
Shadow work stitch (see page 16); stem; satin; French knots; blanket; back.

DIAGRAMS
Diagram A gives the complete motif in actual size.
Diagram B (see opposite page) gives a guide to the stitches and thread colours used throughout the design.

TO MAKE
Note. Use 3 strands of cotton throughout.
Cut one piece from fabric, 11 in. by 21 in., and two pieces each $8\frac{1}{2}$ in. square. With one long side of large piece facing, trace motif as given in diagram A on to bottom left-hand corner, $1\frac{1}{2}$ in. from side edge and $1\frac{3}{4}$ in. from lower edge. Trace motif at right-hand corner to correspond. Trace the flower head centrally on to each square of fabric, omitting stem and leaves and tracing one more small motif between petals to complete the design.
Work embroidery, following diagram B and stitch and colour key. Unnumbered parts on diagram B are worked in the same stitch and colour as the numbered parts most similar to them.

TO COMPLETE
Press embroidery on the wrong side. Turn in $\frac{1}{4}$-in. hems on all edges of each mat, and slipstitch neatly in place.

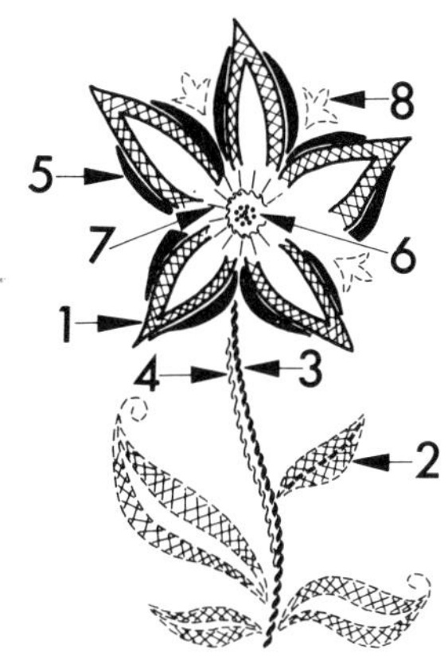

Diagram B

STITCH AND COLOUR KEY
1	Cyclamen	Shadow work stitch
2	Moss Green	Shadow work stitch
3	Cyclamen	Stem stitch
4	Moss Green	Stem stitch
5	Cyclamen	Satin stitch
6	Cyclamen	French knots
7	Moss Green	Blanket stitch
8	Moss Green	Back stitch

Cutwork trolley cloth

MATERIALS
Of Clark's Anchor Pearl Cotton No. 8 — one 10-gram ball each Pale Geranium 08/734, Mid Geranium 011/382, Mid Moss Green 0266/789, Dark Moss Green 0268/954, and Gorse Yellow 0301/442. $\frac{5}{8}$ yd. fine white embroidery linen, 36 in. wide. A Milward 'Gold Seal' crewel needle No. 6.

STITCHES
Buttonhole; stem; satin.

DIAGRAMS *(see page 200)*
Diagram A gives one complete motif of the design in actual size.
Diagram B gives a guide to the stitches and thread colours used throughout the design.

TO MAKE
Cut one piece from fabric, 28 in. by 20 in. Fold fabric across the centre both ways and crease lightly. With one short side of fabric facing, trace motif as given in diagram A on to right-hand side of fabric, 9 in. below widthwise fold. The large broken line on the diagram indicates the lengthwise fold, and should coincide with your fold line. To complete short side, turn fabric and omitting double side lines, trace left-hand side to correspond. The small broken line on the diagram indicates the position and outline of the start of the second motif. Trace other short side of fabric in a similar way, then join up double lines at the side edges. Work embroidery, following diagram B and stitch and colour key. Unnumbered parts on diagram B are worked in the same stitch and colour as the numbered parts most similar to them.

TO COMPLETE
Press embroidery on the wrong side. Cut away all sections marked 'X' on diagram A, and trim away surplus fabric round the outside edge, using small, sharp-pointed scissors. Cut from the wrong side, taking care not to snip stitches.

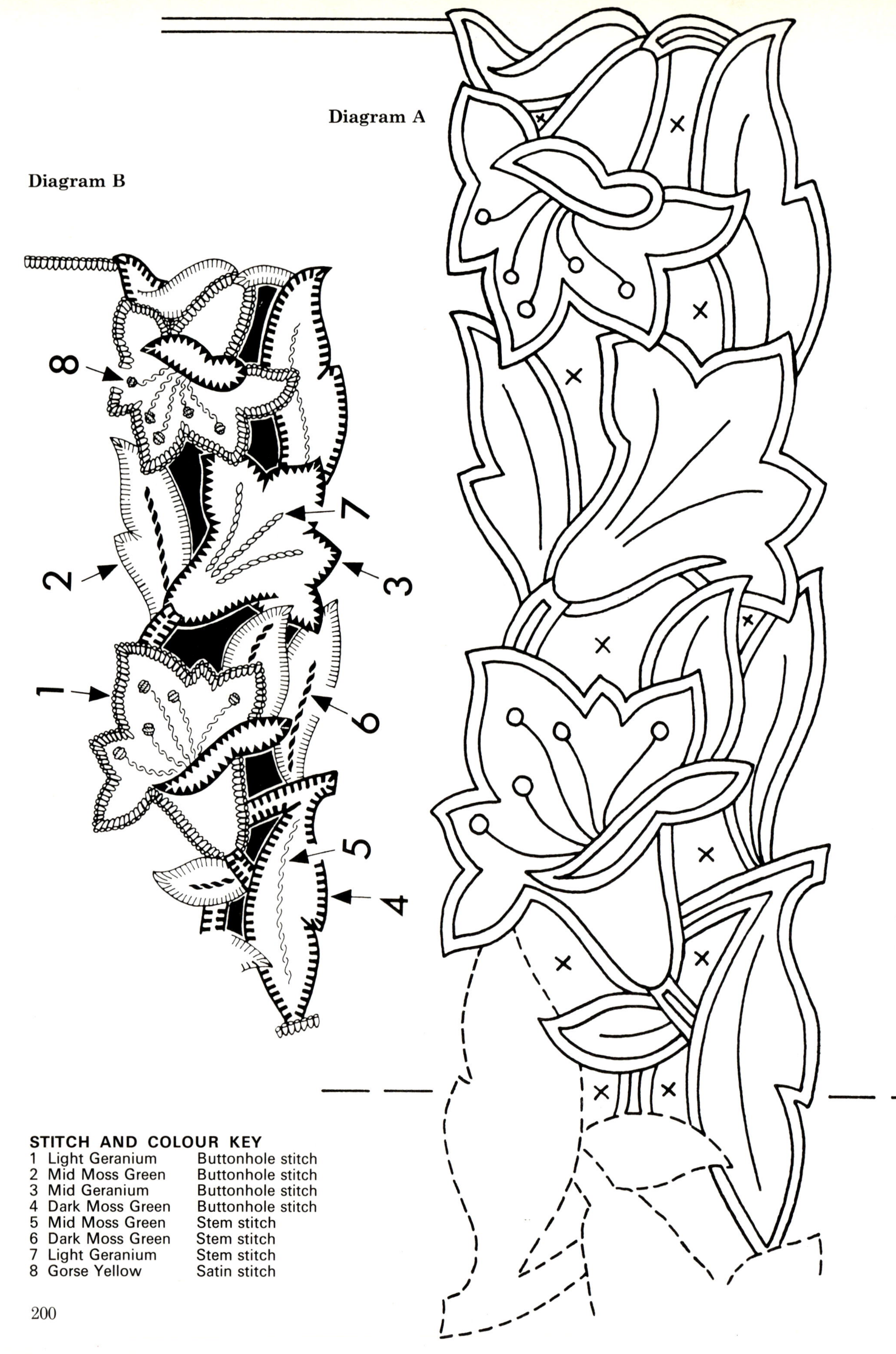

STITCH AND COLOUR KEY
1 Light Geranium   Buttonhole stitch
2 Mid Moss Green   Buttonhole stitch
3 Mid Geranium   Buttonhole stitch
4 Dark Moss Green   Buttonhole stitch
5 Mid Moss Green   Stem stitch
6 Dark Moss Green   Stem stitch
7 Light Geranium   Stem stitch
8 Gorse Yellow   Satin stitch

A traditional counted-thread design worked in satin and back stitch.

COUNTED-THREAD EMBROIDERY

The principal difference between free-style embroidery and counted-thread work is that in free-style work the design must be drawn on to the fabric by tracing or some other suitable method; in counted-thread embroidery this is not necessary. A design is formed by worked stitches over specific numbers of the threads of the fabric. For this reason it is necessary to use an evenweave fabric in which warp and weft threads are clearly defined and easy to count. Most counted-thread designs are presented in chart form, with each line on the chart representing one thread of your fabric. Stitches are then indicated on the chart to cover different numbers of threads.

Many traditional styles of embroidery, including cross stitch, drawn-fabric and drawn-thread work, as well as innumerable national embroideries, are based on count-thread work.

Before embarking on any counted-thread design, it is essential to prepare your fabric very carefully. As the entire design is based on the accurate counting out of fabric threads, if you miscount by even one or two threads, the result will be an out-of-true and unbalanced design.

Beginners should start with a very coarse mesh fabric, in which fabric threads are easy to see and to count. From this you can progress to finer meshes and more intricate designs. Evenweave linen, net, huckaback and hessian (burlap) are all suitable fabrics to use.

Begin by cutting your fabric to the size required, remembering to allow extra for hems or seams. Machine stitch or oversew along cut edges to prevent them fraying. Now work lines of basting stitches lengthwise and widthwise across the exact centre of the fabric. These lines will act as a guide when placing the design. As a further guide it is a good idea to mark out threads in groups of ten or eight along the top and down one side of the fabric. Take basting stitches alternately over then under each group.

STITCHES TO USE

Many traditional forms of counted-thread embroidery will use only one or sometimes two stitches throughout the whole design. Others are created from a variety of different stitches. The following is a selection of general-purpose counted-thread stitches – others which relate to specific techniques are described under the appropriate heading. There are also a number of free-style stitches which can be adapted for use in counted-thread work – for instance, cable, fern, chevron, fly, double knot and Pekinese (see Part 1 for these stitches). And most of the stitches used in needlepoint tapestry (see Part 3) can also be used for counted-thread work on evenweave fabric. In most cases however where a canvas stitch is worked over only one or two threads of canvas, it will be worked over several threads of fabric.

Back stitch

Stitches should be worked over a regular number of threads throughout a design. Bring needle out on the right-hand side of work two threads (or the required number) to the left of the fabric edge. Take a backward stitch over this number of threads and bring the needle through two threads in front of the previous stitch. Continue in this way, always returning the needle in a backward stitch into the same place where it last emerged.

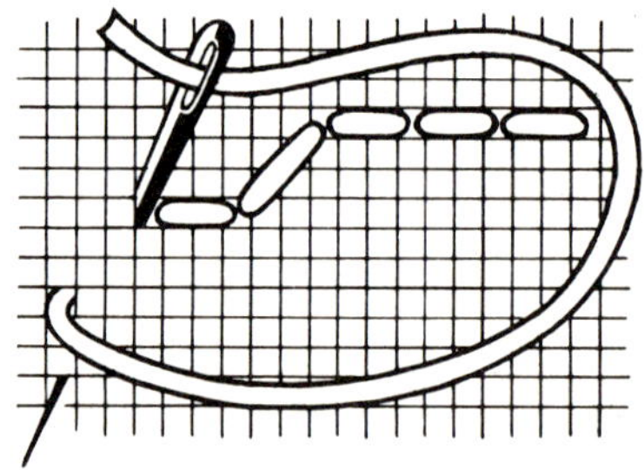

Back stitch, whipped

Work back stitch first, as described above, then with another thread in the needle whip over each back stitch without entering the fabric.

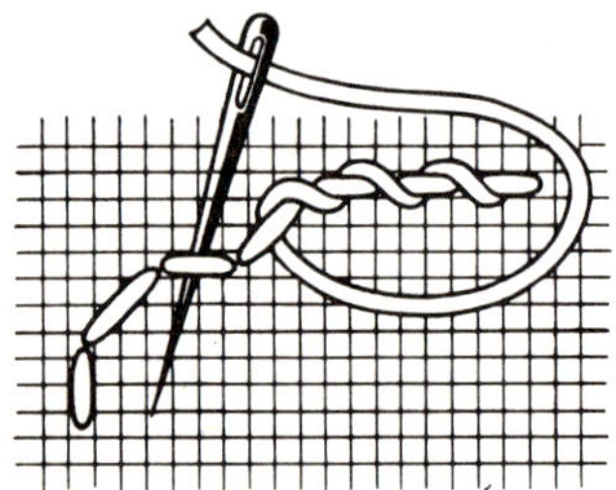

Darning

The simple darning stitch forms the basis for a number of decorative embroidery styles. Usually a design will be worked entirely in darning

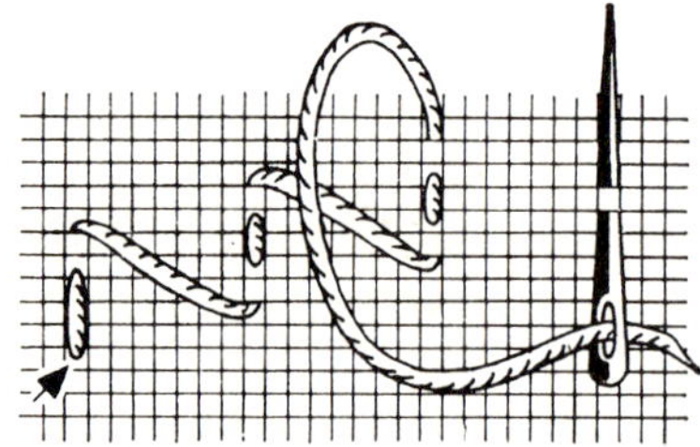

stitches, although the length of the individual stitches may vary according to the requirements of the design. Work from right to left, or left to right, in rows, weaving thread over and under the required number of threads. The diagram shows one arrangement of darning stitches frequently found in Swedish darning designs.

Diagonal raised band

This stitch is worked diagonally from lower right to top left corner. Bring needle out at the arrow on diagram 1. Insert four threads up (A) and bring out two threads down and two threads to the left (B). Continue in this way to the end of the row. Diagram 2 shows the second stage in working the band. After completing the last stitch at the end of the first (upward) row, bring the needle through as if to commence a further stitch. Take the needle horizontally across the last stitch worked and insert four threads to the right (C). Bring needle through two threads down, and two to the left (D). Continue to the end of the row. Pull all stitches firmly.

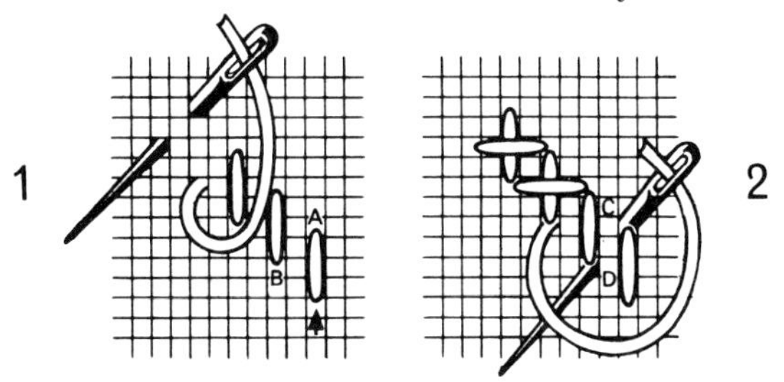

Holbein or double running stitch

Work a row of running stitches (see page 191) with the spaces between stitches the same length as the stitches themselves. Work a return journey of running stitches, filling in the gaps left on the first row. This gives a continuous line of even stitches.

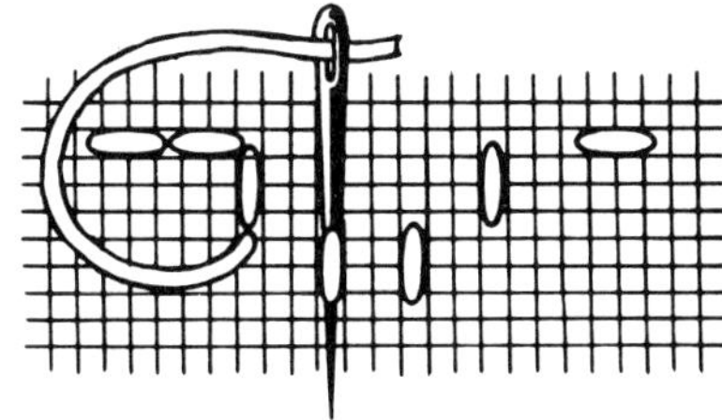

Mosaic filling

Work four blocks of satin stitches to form a square, with an equal number of stitches in each block and worked over an equal number of

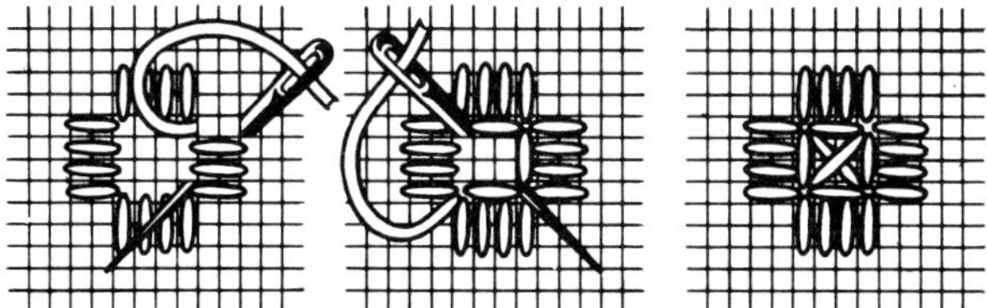

threads. Bring the needle from the last stitch through to the right-hand corner of the inner square. Work a four-sided stitch (see page 210) within the satin stitch blocks, bringing the needle out at the starting point. Now work a basic cross stitch (see below) in the centre.

Satin stitch

Another free-style stitch which can be used in counted-thread designs. Work from right to left, or left to right. The number of threads over which the stitches are worked may vary depending upon the effect desired. When satin stitch is worked in counted-thread designs, it is often termed counted satin stitch. It forms the basis for several different national styles of embroidery.

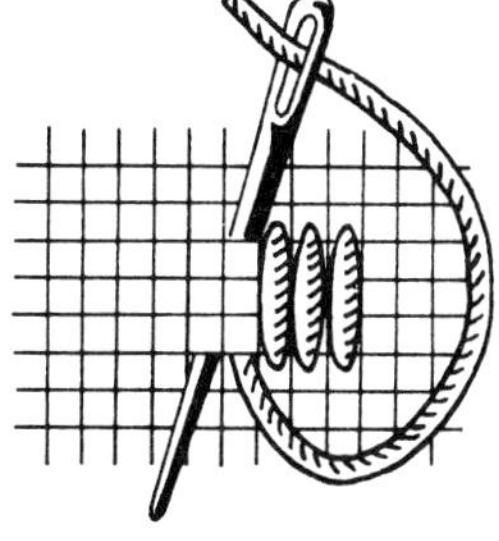

Straight stitch

Single stitches are worked over two threads. The stitches may be horizontal, vertical or diagonal.

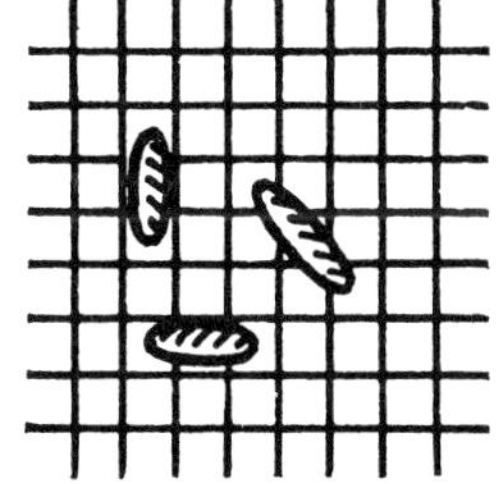

CROSS STITCH WORK

Cross stitch can be used in free, counted-thread and canvas embroidery, but as it is the basis for so many traditional embroidery styles, and the stitch itself has so many variations, cross stitch work has in a way become a technique in itself.

Some beautiful examples of cross stitch work have been found in peasant embroideries throughout the world; some are worked in wonderfully vivid colours, others are delicate and muted. Often a design is worked entirely in cross stitch only, but the stitch can be effectively combined with one or two other counted-thread stitches – for instance, in Assisi and Roumanian work (see pages 211 and 213) where it is combined with Holbein stitch.

Sampler worked in cross and Holbein stitches.

Swedish darning trolley set.

To work the basic cross stitch

When working cross stitch on canvas, in order not to distort the canvas threads, each complete cross must be completed before moving to the next. But on evenweave fabric, where there is no danger of distortion, it is possible to work cross stitch in rows; bring needle out at bottom right edge of row. Insert four threads up and four threads to the left (or number of threads over which you are working the cross) and bring out again four threads down. Insert four threads up and four threads to the left then work this half of each cross all along row. On the return journey work second arm of each cross to complete the stitch.

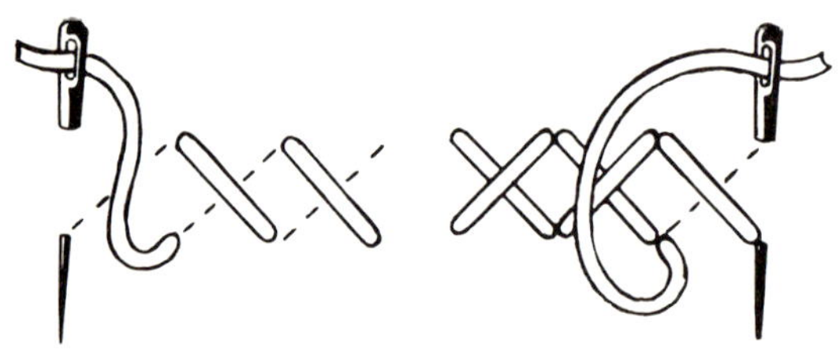

Variations on the basic cross

Double cross Work basic cross stitch then bring needle out four threads down and two vertical threads to the left. Insert needle four threads up and bring out two threads to the left and two horizontal threads down. Complete stitch by inserting needle four threads to the right and bring out two threads down and four threads to the left in readiness for the next stitch.

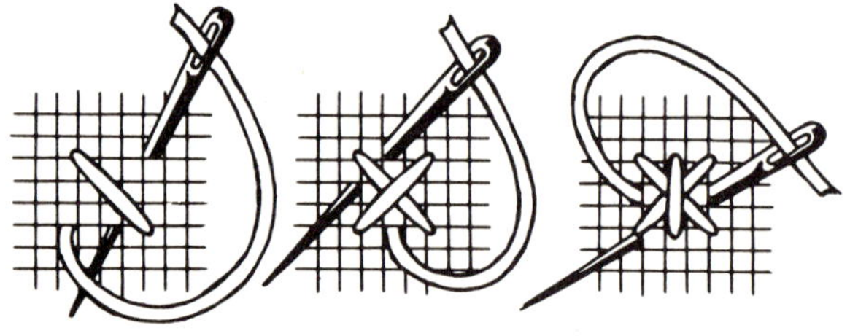

Double straight cross This consists of a straight cross stitch worked over four horizontal and four vertical threads, with a basic cross stitch worked over the centre of the straight cross over two horizontal and two vertical threads.

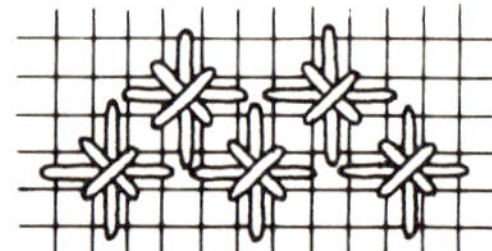

Long-legged cross Work from left to right. Work the second arm over double the number of threads of the other arm – e.g. work the first arm over eight threads, the second over four.

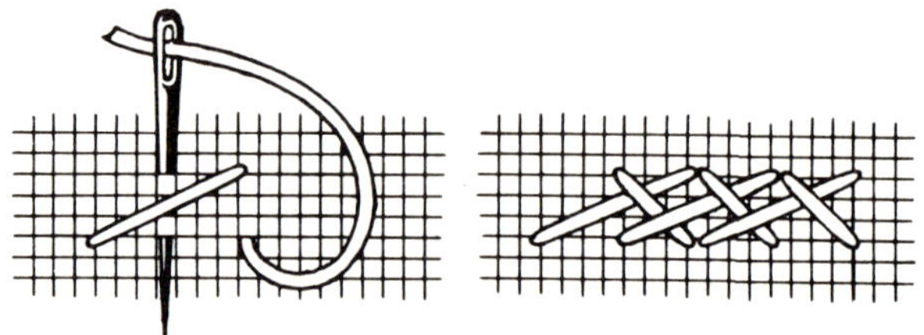

Oblong cross This is an 'oblong' version of the basic cross stitch. Stitches are worked over four horizontal and two vertical threads.

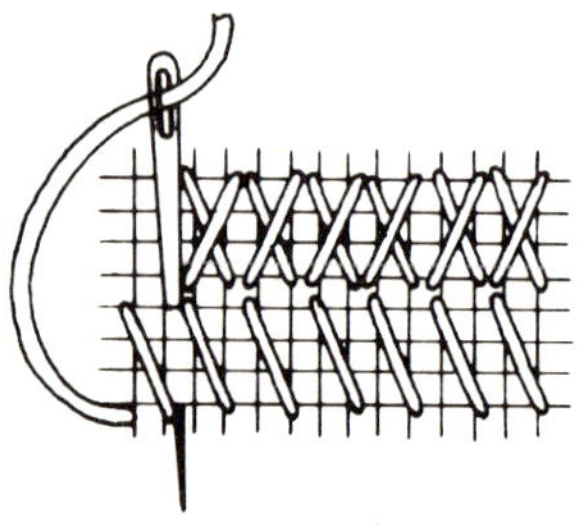

Straight or upright cross This is usually worked over two horizontal and two vertical threads. A straight vertical stitch is crossed by a straight horizontal stitch. Rows of straight cross stitches should be worked between each other to give an interlocked appearance.

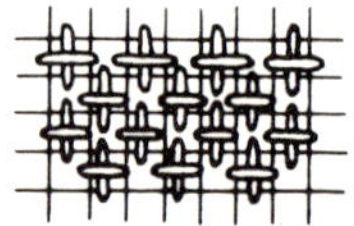

See also **rice stitch** (page 223) and **smyrna cross stitch** (page 223).

DRAWN-THREAD WORK

In this type of embroidery, threads are withdrawn from the fabric and then embroidery is worked over the edges of the space of the withdrawn threads. Decorative stitches may also be worked over the loose threads which are left when the

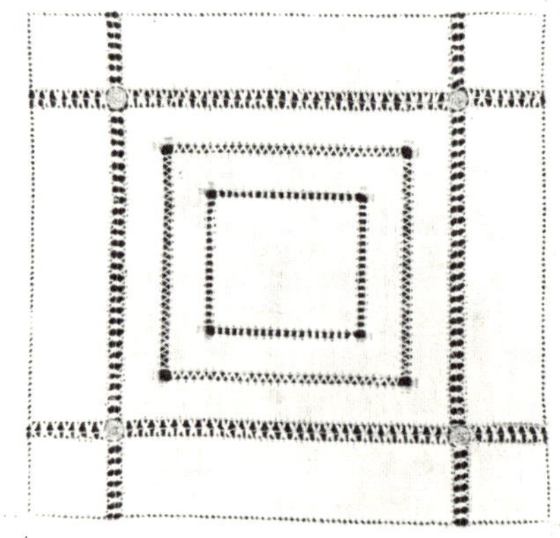

Linen mat with hemstitched insertions.

warp and weft threads are withdrawn. This is one of the easiest and most ancient forms of open-work embroidery, and the foundation of lace. The drawn-thread technique is often used to create a decorative hem.

Basic hemstitch

Measure required depth of hem, plus the turnings and withdraw required number of threads. Do not withdraw the threads right across fabric, but only to form a square or rectangle. Cut threads at the centre and withdraw gradually outwards on each side to within the hem measurement leaving a sufficient length of thread at corners in order to darn the ends invisibly. Turn back the hem to the space of the drawn threads, mitre corners and baste. Bring the working thread out two threads down from the space of drawn threads through the folded hem at right-hand side, pass the needle behind four loose threads, bringing needle out two threads down through all the folds of the hem in readiness for next stitch. The number of threads may be varied to suit the fabric or design.

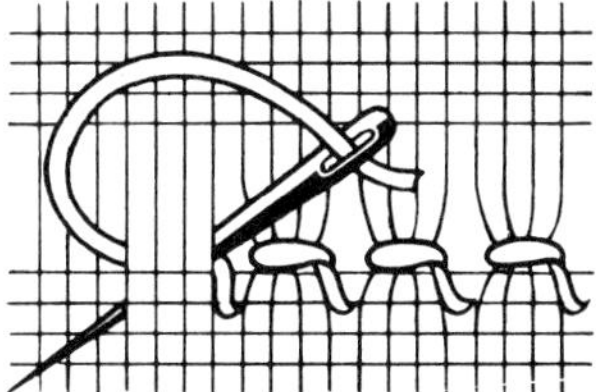

Ladder hemstitch

In this the basic hemstitch is worked along both edges of the spaces of drawn threads.

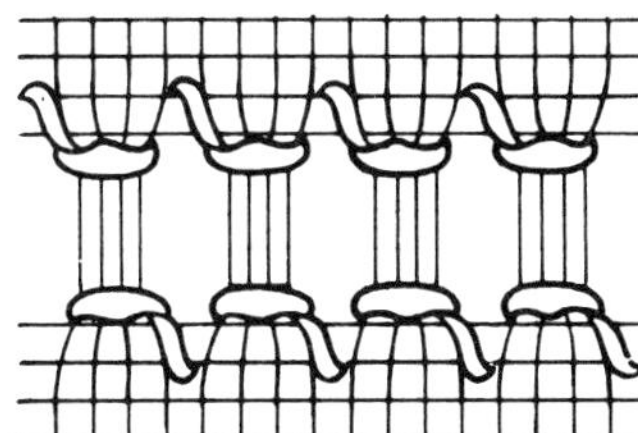

Zigzag hemstitch

This is similar to ladder hemstitch but there must be an even number of threads in each group of loose threads caught together in the first row. In the second row, the groups are divided in half, so that each group is composed of half the number of threads from one group and half from the adjacent group. A half group starts and ends the second row.

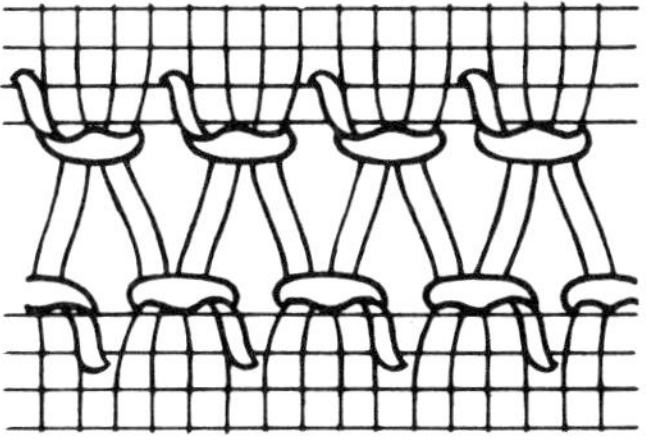

Diamond hemstitch

Withdraw threads from the fabric for the required width, miss six threads and withdraw another band of the same number of threads. Bring needle out four loose threads to the left. Working on band of threads not withdrawn, from right to left, bring needle through four threads to the left and three threads down. Insert needle four threads to the right, bring out at starting point, insert three threads down and bring out four threads to the left. Insert four threads to the right and bring back out four threads to the left. Insert three threads up. Continue in this way to the end of the row, and finish off thread by securing neatly on wrong side of embroidery. Turn fabric and work back along row forming diamond shapes as shown in diagram 2.

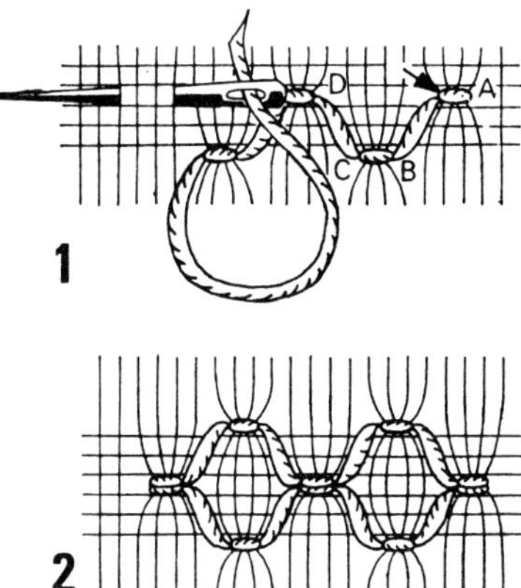

Double (or Italian) hemstitch

Withdraw threads from the fabric for the required width, miss the same number of threads and withdraw another band of the same number of threads. Bring the needle out four (or less) loose threads to the left in the top band of drawn threads, pass the needle behind the four threads, bringing it out where the thread first emerged. Pass the needle down over the fabric and under four loose threads in the lower band of drawn threads; pass the needle over the same four threads and under the fabric bringing it out four threads to the left in the top band of drawn threads. These two movements are worked throughout. The free edges of the drawn-thread spaces can be hemstitched in the usual way.

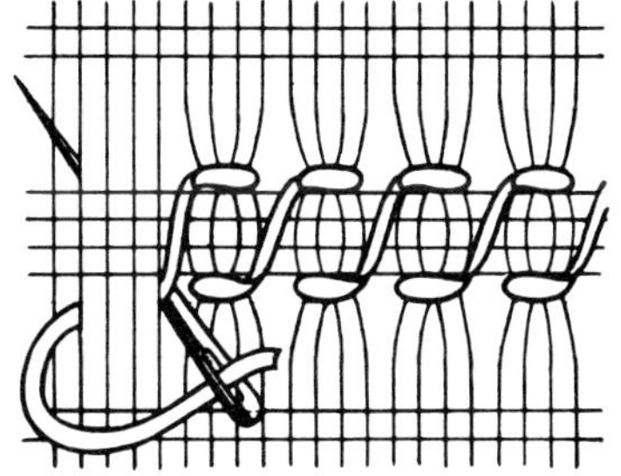

Tablecloth embroidered with a traditional Hardanger design.

208

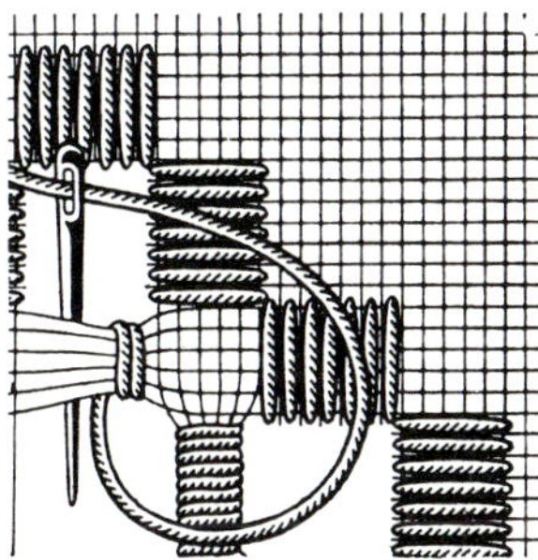

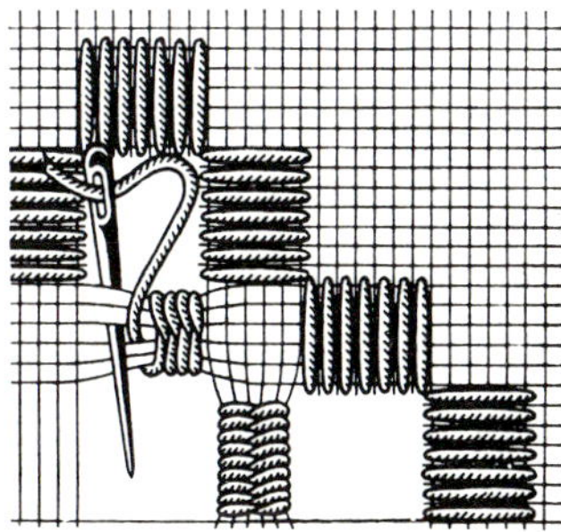

An Austrian cushion in cross and back stitch.

Overcast bars

Withdraw the number of threads required from the fabric and separate the loose threads into bars by overcasting firmly over these threads as many times as necessary to cover the group of threads completely.

Woven bars

Withdraw an even number of threads from the fabric and separate the loose threads into bars by weaving over and under an even number of threads until the threads are completely covered.

DRAWN-FABRIC WORK

This creates a similar open-work appearance to drawn-thread work, but no threads are withdrawn from the fabric – instead, groups of threads are pulled together by stitching. The actual stitching is not the main feature of the work – it is the open pattern formed on the fabric by the pulling together of the threads. The stitches are worked over a regular number of threads, and the working thread is always pulled firmly with each needle movement so that an open-work effect is achieved. Although drawn-fabric work looks fragile, because no threads are withdrawn the embroidery remains strong and durable. The following are a few drawn-thread stitches.

Four-sided stitch

This stitch is worked from right to left, and can be used as a border or a filling. Bring the needle through at the arrow on diagram 1, insert the needle four threads up, bring it through four threads down and four to the left, insert at starting point and bring out four threads up and four to the left. Insert needle at A on diagram and bring out at B. Continue in this way to the end of the row or close the end for a single four-sided stitch. Turn the fabric round for next and each successive row and work in a similar way. Pull all stitches firmly.

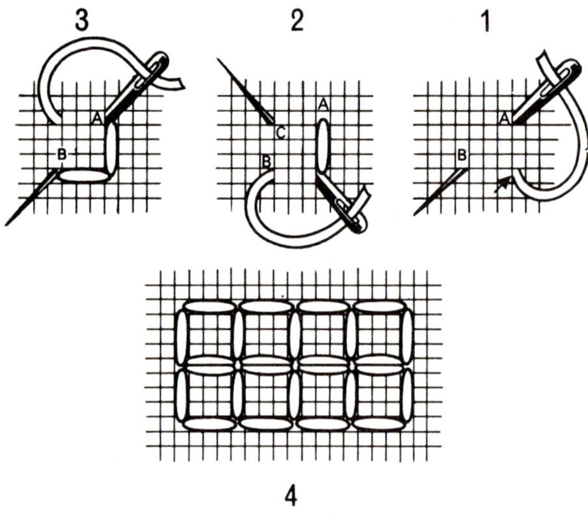

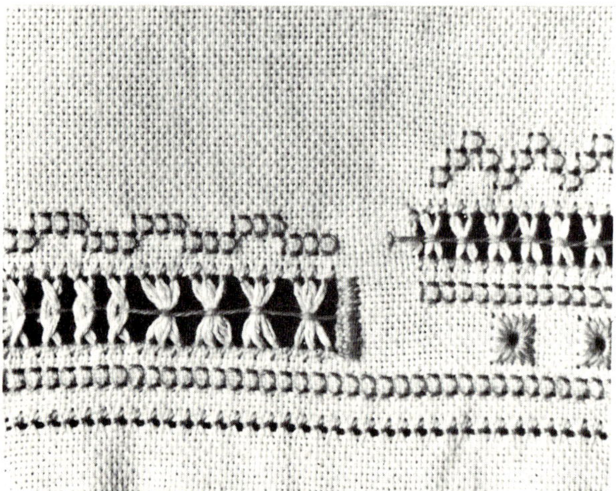

Pin stitch

This stitch can also be used in drawn-thread work and for outlining appliqué work. For a hem edge, bring the needle through the folded hem at A on diagram 1, insert the needle at B and bring out at C; insert once more at B and bring out at C. Insert again at B, bring out through the folded hem at D. Continue in this way to the end of the row. Pull all stitches firmly.

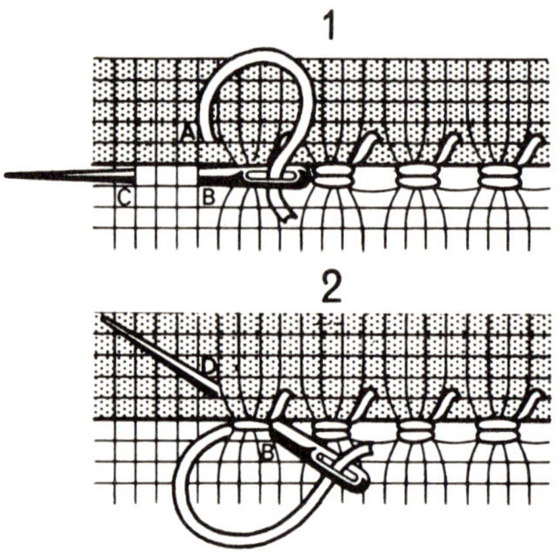

Punch stitch

Work two straight stitches into same place over four threads, then bring the needle out four threads down and four threads to the left in readiness for the next stitch. Work along the row in this way. Turn the fabric for next and each successive row. Diagram 2 shows the squares completed by turning the fabric sideways and working in a similar way.

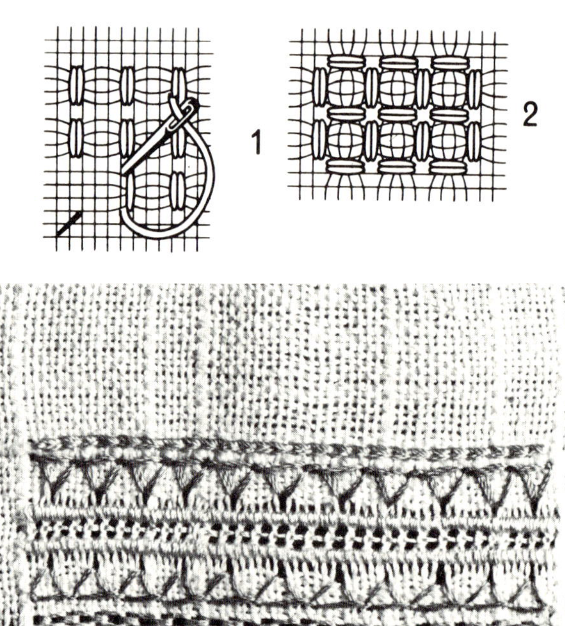

Above and right: samples showing a combination of drawn-thread and drawn-fabric stitches.

Ringed back stitch

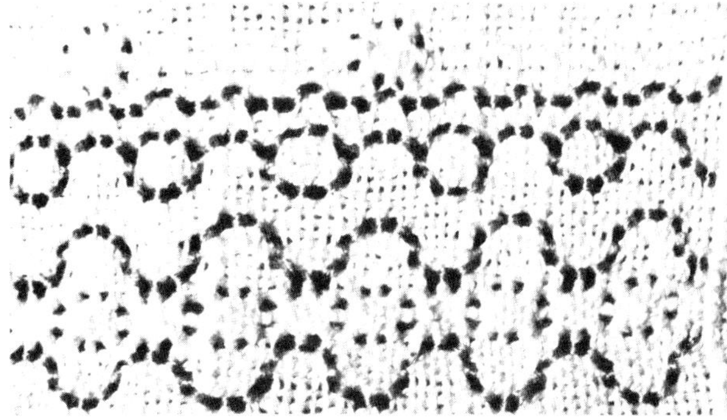

Work from right to left. Bring needle through and insert three threads down, bring it through six threads up and three threads to the left, insert it at starting point, bring it through three threads down and six to the left, insert three threads to the right. Continue working back stitches in this way to make half rings, as shown in diagram. Turn the fabric round for the second row and work in a similar way to complete the rings. All connecting stitches are worked into the same holes.

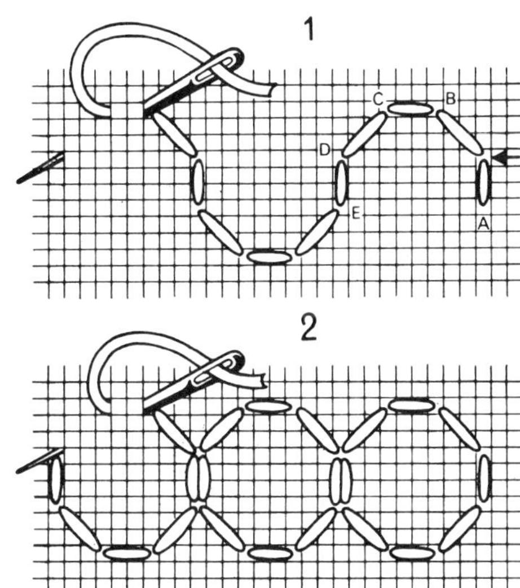

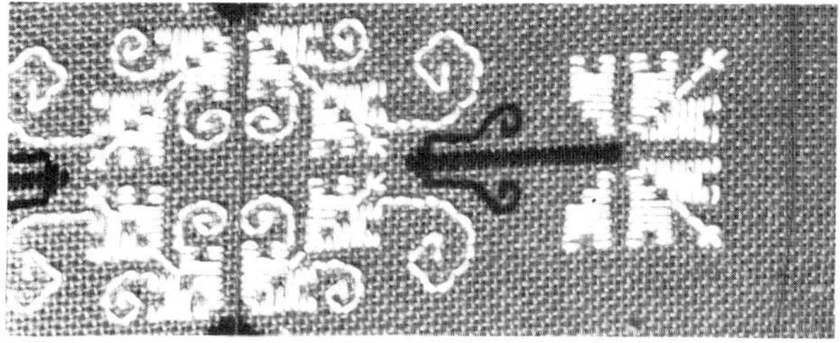

Motif used in traditional Scandinavian embroideries.

Three-sided stitch

Work from right to left. Bring the needle through at A (diagram 1) and take two stitches from A to B over four threads of the fabric; bring the needle through at A and take two stitches from A to B over four threads of fabric. Bring the needle through at A and take two stitches from A to C (four threads up from A and two to the right). Bring the needle through at D (diagram 2), four threads to the left, take two stitches from D to C, bring the needle through at D. Take two stitches from D to A (diagram 3). Bring the needle through at E (diagram 4), four threads to the left. Diagram 5 shows a corner turning. Pull all stitches firmly.

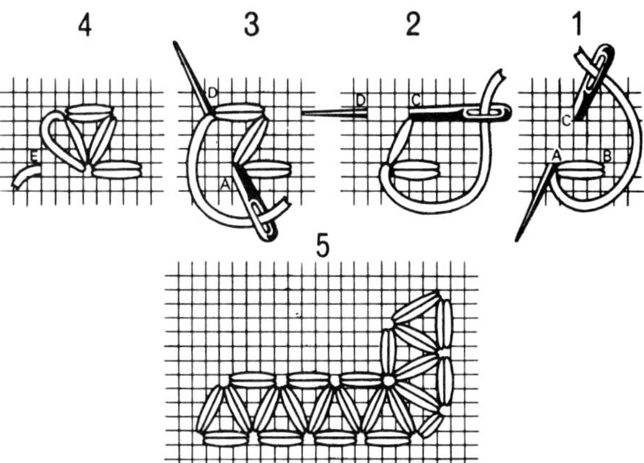

SOME NATIONAL COUNTED-THREAD EMBROIDERY STYLES

Assisi

This is worked in cross and Holbein stitches. It differs from normal cross stitch designs in that the background is stitched, and the pattern motifs left plain. The design is first outlined with Holbein stitch, then the background filled in with cross stitch.

Blackwork

Often known as Spanish blackwork because the embroidery is reputed to have originated in Spain. Traditionally designs are based on floral motifs from Spanish medieval architecture and engravings, and are stitched with black thread on white linen. Stitches used include back stitch, whipped back stitch and cross stitch. Modern blackwork designs can be worked with coloured threads and fabrics, with fairly simple natural forms as pattern motifs.

Hardanger

This embroidery comes from Norway, and is named after the Hardanger Fjord. Traditionally it is worked in white thread on coarse white linen. Satin stitches are worked in groups of an uneven number of stitches. When all the

Dutch-style apron with cross stitch embroidery—instructions start opposite.

Drawn-fabric runner (see page 214).

satin stitch blocks are complete, the fabric threads are cut and withdrawn as required. The loose threads are overcast or woven to form bars and various filling stitches worked within the spaces left by the drawn threads. Designs are usually geometric in character.

Hedebo

Hedebo embroidery, worked in white thread on white linen, is a traditional form of Danish needlework, and takes its name from the stretch of heath (*hede*) that lies between Copenhagen and Roskilde. Since time immemorial the peasants who lived there have spun and woven their own linen from the flax grown on their farms, and their pride in their home-made articles was very great. It was a natural development that they should ornament their garments with stitching. The idea of drawing out some of the threads and rearranging them with a needle and thread was their first attempt at Hedebo work. Eventually a beautiful tradition in cut and drawn-work was established. Design motifs are frequently outlined with chain stitch.

Rhodes

Also sometimes known as punch or punched embroidery. This is really drawn-fabric work in reverse, for the background only is worked in drawn-fabric stitches and the pattern motifs left clear. This creates solid shapes against an attractive net-like background.

Roumanian

This, like Assisi work, is worked in cross and Holbein stitches, but here the pattern motifs are in cross stitch, the background is left plain, and little decorative scrolls extending from the cross stitch motifs are worked in Holbein stitch.

THE PATTERNS

Cross stitch apron
illustrated in colour opposite

MATERIALS
Of Clark's Anchor Stranded Cotton (USA J. & P. Coats Deluxe Six Strand Floss) — 1 skein each Carnation 029, Rose Madder 055, Cyclamen 087, Electric Blue 0140, Saxe Blue 0147, Forest Green 0218, Emerald 0227, Buttercup 0295, Terra Cotta 0336, Cinnamon 0371, Snuff Brown 0374, White 0402, and Black 0403. ¾ yd. pale green mediumweight evenweave fabric, with 21 threads to 1 in., 59 in. or 54 in. wide. A Milward 'Gold Seal' tapestry needle No. 24.

STITCHES
Cross; back.

DIAGRAM *(see page 215)*
The diagram gives the complete design, showing the arrangement of the stitches on the threads of the fabric. Each background square on the diagram represents three threads of the fabric.

213

TO MAKE

Note. Use 3 strands of cotton throughout.
Cut fabric into sections as follows: one piece, 37½ in. by 19 in., for main skirt section; one piece, 19 in. by 6 in., for waistband; two pieces, each 21 in. by 6½ in., for ties; two pieces, each 7½ in. by 6½ in., for pockets. Mark an 11½-in. square with basting stitches centrally on to skirt section, 4¼ in. from lower edge. Mark the centre of this square both ways with basting stitches. The blank arrows on the diagram should coincide with your basting stitches. Begin embroidery centrally and work design as given in diagram following stitch and colour key. Each cross stitch is worked over three threads of the fabric, thus giving approximately seven crosses to 1 in.

Mark the centre of each pocket piece lengthwise with basting stitches. The large basket of flowers in the lower right-hand corner of the diagram is worked on each pocket. With one short side of fabric facing you, begin embroidery at the lower right-hand corner of the basket, 12 threads to the right of basting stitches and 1 in. from lower edge. Work the complete section of the design, following stitch and colour key.

TO COMPLETE

Press embroidery on the wrong side. Turn back ½-in. hems on short sides of apron skirt, and stitch in place. Turn back a 2-in. hem at lower edge and slipstitch in position. Turn back ½ in. on sides and lower edge of pockets and press; turn back a 1-in. hem along top edge, and slipstitch. Stitch pockets in position to skirt, 5¼ in. from sides and 3½ in. down from upper edge. Run two rows of gathering stitches along top edge of apron, making first row ⅜ in. from edge, and the second row ⅛ in. below this. Turn back ½ in. on short ends of waistband and press. Pull up gathers on skirt to fit waistband for approximately 5 in. at each side, leaving centre section flat. With right sides together, stitch waistband to skirt, ½ in. from edge. Fold waistband in half lengthwise and slipstitch in position on wrong side to line of stitching. Fold tie pieces in half lengthwise and machine stitch long sides and one short end ½ in. from edge. Turn to right side. Pleat raw ends to fit open ends of waistband, insert ties and sew neatly in position. Press.

STITCH AND COLOUR KEY

Cross stitch	Back stitch	
☒		– Carnation
∅		– Rose Madder
◩		– Cyclamen
◿		– Electric Blue
◉		– Saxe Blue
◎	ʃ	– Forest Green
⊠	♪	– Emerald
⊓		– Buttercup
C		– Terra Cotta
◪	ʃ	– Cinnamon
◸		– Snuff Brown
⊡		– White
■	⌐	– Black

Drawn-fabric runner
illustrated in colour on page 213

MATERIALS

5 skeins Clark's Anchor Stranded Cotton (USA J. & P. Coats Deluxe Sis Strand Floss) in Delphinium 0122. ½ yd. blue mediumweight evenweave fabric, with 21 threads to 1 in., 59 or 54 in. wide. A Milward 'Gold Seal' tapestry needle No. 23.

MEASUREMENTS

The finished size of the runner is 14 in. by 29 in.

STITCHES

Double faggot filling; satin.

DIAGRAMS

Diagram on page 216 gives a little over half of one motif, showing the arrangement of the stitches on the threads of the fabric. The background lines on the diagram represent the threads of the fabric.

Diagrams 1 and 2, below, show how to work double faggot filling stitch: bring the needle out at A (on Fig. 1), insert at B, bring out at A and insert again at B; bring out at C, insert at A, bring out at C and insert again at A; bring out at D; continue in this way for required number of times. Insert needle as shown in Fig. 1, turn fabric and work second row in a similar way. Turn fabric for each alternate row. Fig. 2 shows the worked corner section, alternate rows shown without shading. Pull each stitch firmly. The stitch may be worked over two fabric threads (as in this design) or over three fabric threads.

TO MAKE

Note. Use 3 strands of cotton for double faggot filling stitch, 4 strands for remainder of embroidery.
Cut a piece from fabric 16 in. by 31 in. Mark the centre both ways with basting stitches. The unnumbered black arrows on diagram on page 216 should coincide with the basting stitches worked on your fabric. With long side of fabric facing, begin the embroidery with double faggot filling stitch 8 threads to the left of the crossed basting stitches. Work section of the design as given in the diagram, following stitch key. Pull each stitch firmly, with the exception of satin stitch (number 2 on the stitch key). (*Note.* The drawing together of the fabric threads is not shown on the diagram in order to make the counting of the threads and method of working the stitches easier to follow.)

Complete remainder of motif to correspond with first half. Repeat the complete motif four more times on left half of fabric, then turn fabric and work other half in a similar way.

TO COMPLETE

Trim to finished size, plus ¾ in. for hem. Turn in hems on all edges, mitre the corners and slipstitch.

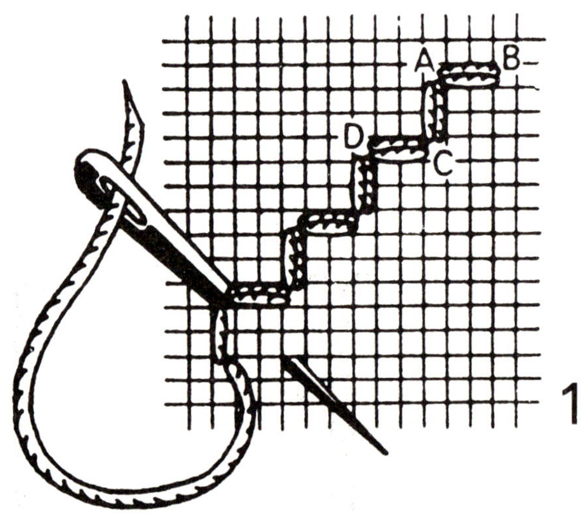

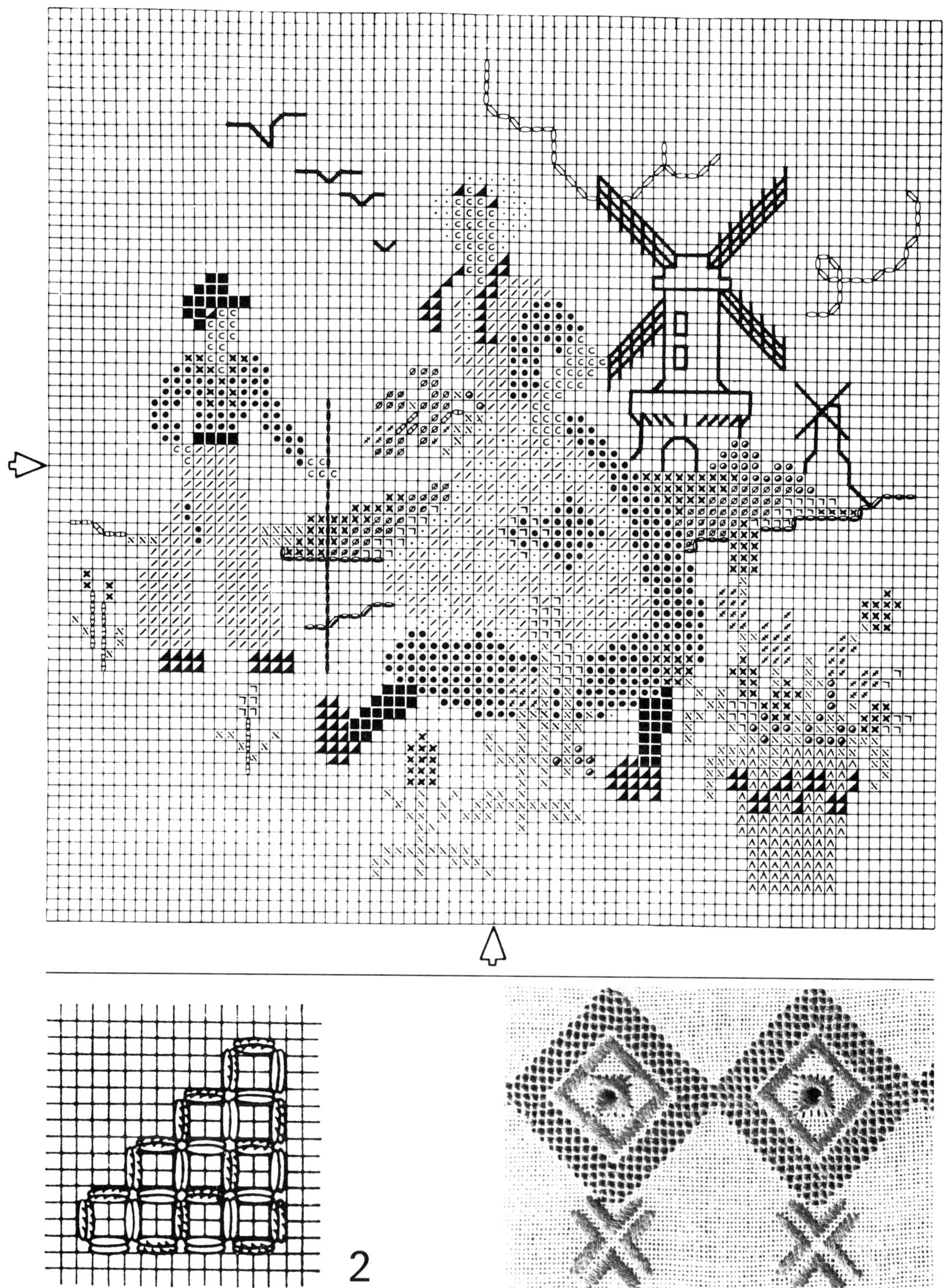

2

STITCH KEY
1 Double faggot filling stitch
2 Satin stitch
3 Satin stitch square

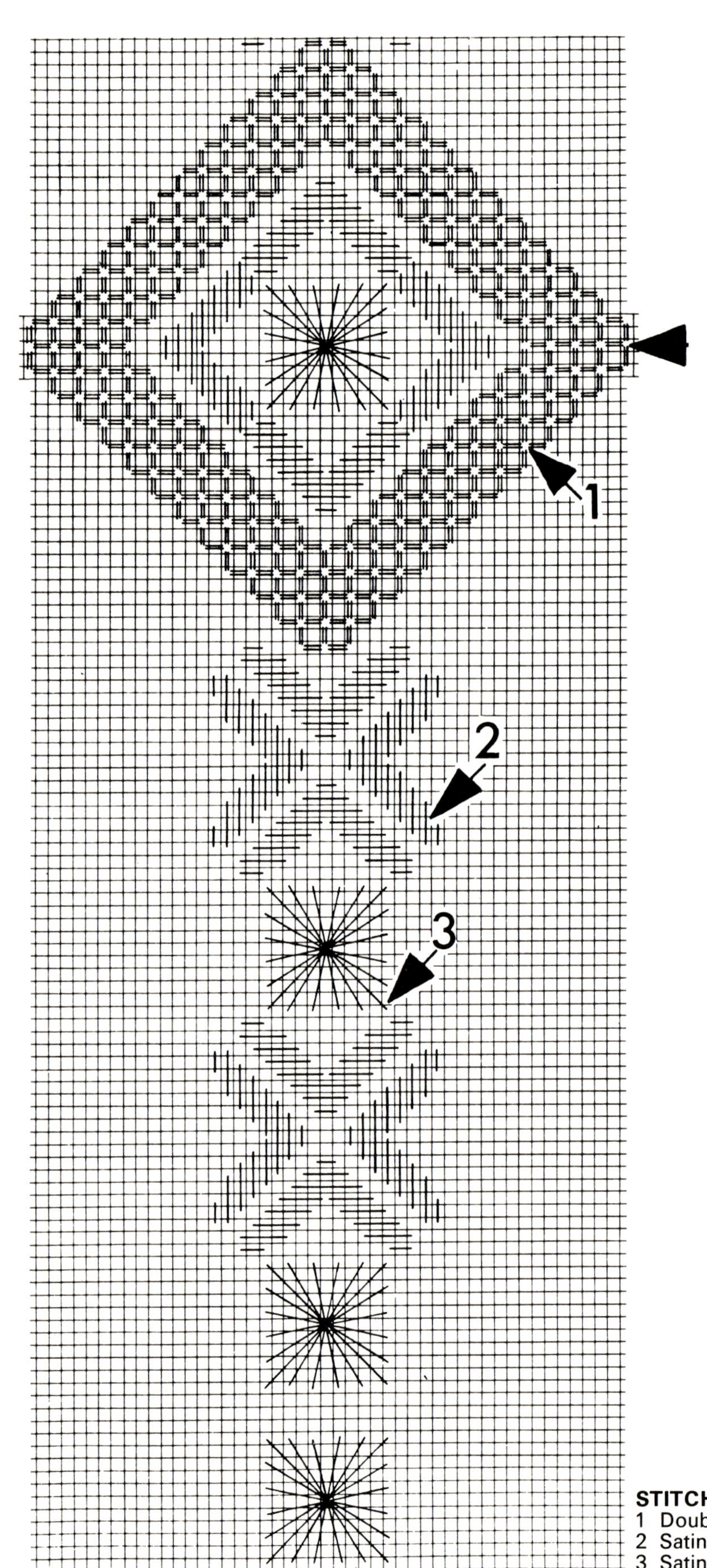

216

Part 3—

NEEDLEPOINT TAPESTRY

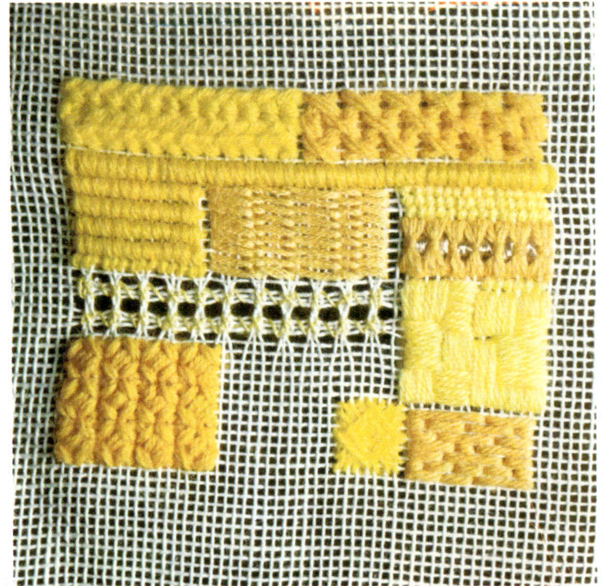

Above: *sample showing a selection of different needlepoint tapestry stitches.*

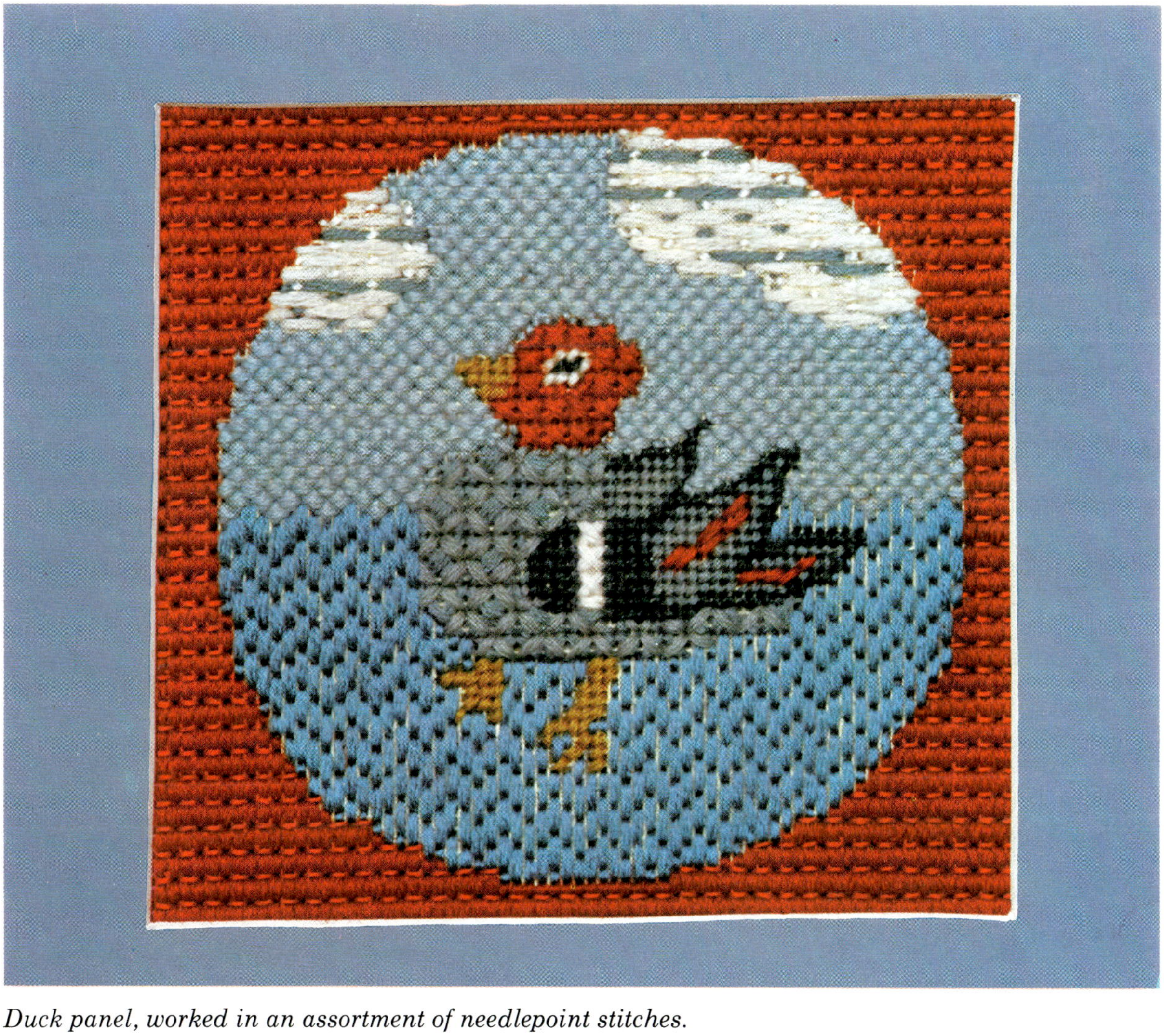

Duck panel, worked in an assortment of needlepoint stitches.

Needlepoint tapestry is, strictly speaking, not tapestry at all – for the word really means a woven fabric – but is embroidery on a canvas ground. When the embroidery is worked entirely in either tent or gobelin stitch, the effect thus achieved is similar to a woven tapestry, hence the name. But there is a great deal more to needlepoint besides these two traditional stitches: in fact there are dozens of interesting, attractive stitches which can be used, and once an understanding of the craft has been acquired it is possible to invent new stitches. Build up an extensive stitch vocabulary, learn to use threads and colours as an artist uses paints, and you will be able to create all manner of fascinating textures and effects.

EQUIPMENT

The basic equipment for needlepoint tapestry consists of thread, canvas and a frame.

Yarns

Traditionally, only linen, wool and silk threads are used for tapestry work, but in fact a wide range of threads, natural and synthetic, can be most effectively used depending on the type of design being worked.

To begin with, however, stick to the conventional tapestry yarns: tapisserie wool (tapestry wool), crewel wool and stranded embroidery cottons. These are all good hardwearing threads which will withstand the long and constant wear usually demanded by designs made up in needlepoint.

Embroidery cottons and crewel wool can be used in single or multiple strands to suit the canvas mesh: tapisserie wool can only be used in a single strand.

When you become experienced in needlepoint you will no doubt want to experiment with unusual and novelty threads. These can be most successfully used, but whichever yarn you choose to use should never be finer than the threads of the canvas or the background canvas will show through your stitches.

Canvas

Most designs made in needlepoint have to withstand fairly hard wear – for instance, church kneelers, handbags, chair seats, cushions. For this reason, it is important to buy a good-quality canvas. If you work your embroidery correctly, there should be no canvas visible after the design is complete, but nevertheless the choice of a good canvas will give your work a much longer life, and often help to show your stitches to best effect.

Canvas is usually made either from cotton or linen: which you choose is a matter of personal preference, although linen is probably the more hardwearing of the two.

Canvases are available in a choice of double thread or single. In double-thread canvases, the warp and weft threads are arranged in pairs. For a beginner, a single-thread canvas is probably the best choice. Double-thread canvases can be used for detailed designs later where it is wished to use both tent stitch and trammed tent stitch in the same design.

Single and double-thread canvases are made in a range of mesh sizes, to suit different types of designs and different yarns. A wide mesh gives only a few threads or holes to the inch, and is useful for big scale work; a fine mesh has considerably more threads or holes to the inch and should be used for intricate designs.

Canvases are sold by their mesh size: in a single-thread canvas this size is given as the number of threads to the inch; in double-thread canvas this is given by the number of holes to the inch. Mesh sizes usually range from about 10 to 30 threads or holes to the inch, but there are even bigger mesh canvases available, with only 4 or 5 holes to the inch, known as rug canvas.

Needles

The ideal tapestry needle should pass through the canvas easily, without forcing the threads of the canvas apart and without splitting the threads. Sizes of tapestry needles range from 13 through to 24. The lower the number the bigger the needle, so for fine intricate work you would choose a No. 24 needle.

Frames

Many of the stitches used in needlepoint tapestry are diagonal stitches, and if a frame is not used to stretch and control your canvas, then the canvas will be pulled out of shape by the continual slant of stitches in the same direction. There are a number of straight stitches in needlepoint and if you intend to work a design using only these stitches, then a frame will not be necessary.

A round embroidery frame is not suitable for needlepoint work: only use a square or rectangular frame. A simple frame can be easily made by stretching the canvas tautly and pinning it to a wooden picture frame. However there are a number of different types of ready-made frames available if you wish to buy one.

Leader frame This is a simple rectangular frame which has to be supported at a comfortable working height in order to leave your hands free to stitch.

Floor frame Probably the most versatile frame of all. A free-standing, adjustable frame, which can be placed anywhere with work left in position on it.

Table frame A self-supported frame which can be placed on a table top. There are usually screw fittings to adjust the frame to give the slant required.

Travel frame Not recommended for everyday use, but useful if you want to carry your work around, and for small pieces of work. The total depth of this frame is only 12 in., so your work has to be rolled up and re-rolled each time you need a fresh piece of canvas to work on.

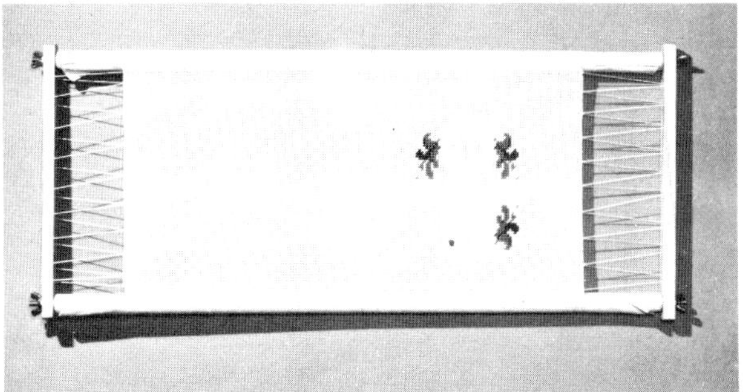

Also useful

Scissors, tape measure, pins and drawing pins, blotting paper for stretching the canvas, water-proof Indian ink for transferring designs to your canvas.

FRAMING-UP CANVAS

Most frames operate on a similar principle: two horizontal, parallel rollers are covered with webbing to which your canvas is attached. The rollers then slot or screw into wooden side struts. The sides of your canvas are laced to these struts.

The width of your canvas should never exceed the length of the webbing on the rollers of the frame.

Before fixing your canvas in position on the frame, you should cut your canvas to size – this should be the size of the finished embroidery plus at least 3 in. extra all round. Mark the centre points horizontally and vertically on your canvas with lines of basting stitches. Make $\frac{1}{2}$-in. turnings at top and bottom edges of canvas, and baste in place. Enclose these and the side edges with a length of 1-in. tape.

Now position canvas on your frame, and stitch top edge of canvas with overcasting stitches to top roller, bottom edge to bottom roller. Finally lace side edges of canvas to side struts of frame, using string or strong button thread. The lacing should be taken through the taped edge of canvas and then round the strut of frame, at regular intervals.

STITCHES

Many of the counted-thread stitches given on pages 202–211 can also successfully be used in needlepoint work, including cross stitch and its many variations. Also, the stitches given for Florentine embroidery (see page 235) are canvas embroidery stitches, so can be incorporated in any needlepoint design.

Brick stitch

This stitch is worked in rows alternately from the left and from the right. It is usually worked over four horizontal threads of the canvas, between alternate pairs of vertical threads. Bring needle through at lower point of each stitch and work stitch upwards. In the following row, stitches are worked in the spaces between stitches of previous row to give an interlocked 'brick' formation.

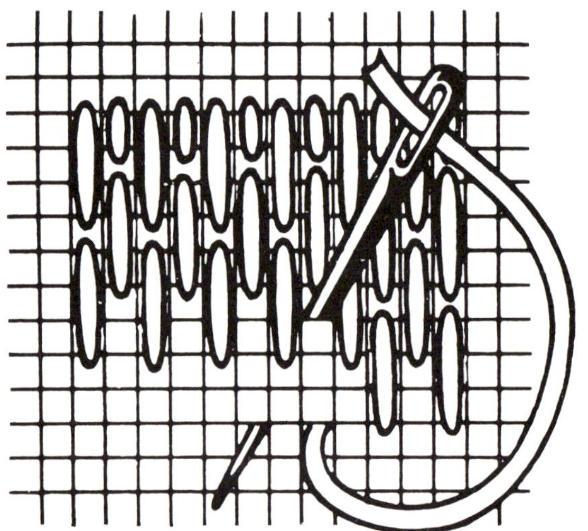

Above and opposite: *church kneelers embroidered in needlepoint tapestry stitches.*

Byzantine stitch

This is a diagonal stitch, worked in 'steps'. Bring needle through canvas and take a stitch four horizontal threads up and four vertical threads to the right. Continue in this way working from bottom right to top left, having six stitches to each step, and working each stitch over four horizontal and four vertical threads.

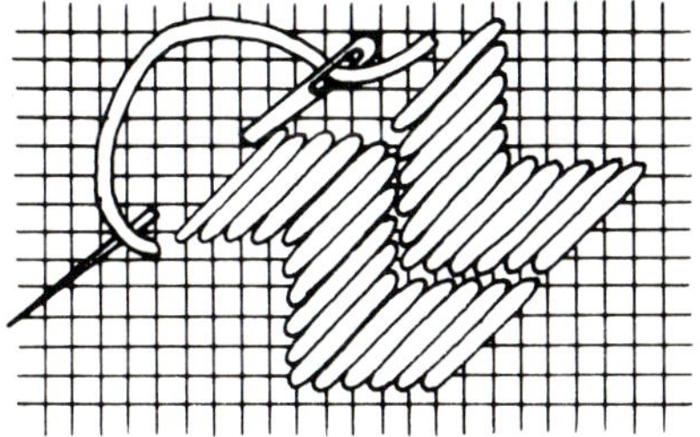

Diagonal stitch

Any stitch worked in a slanting direction across the canvas threads can be termed a diagonal stitch. In its traditional form however, each stitch is worked in turn over two, three, four and then three intersections of the canvas threads. Continue working in this sequence from top left to bottom right. In the following row, work stitches to fit exactly into the zigzag of previous row.

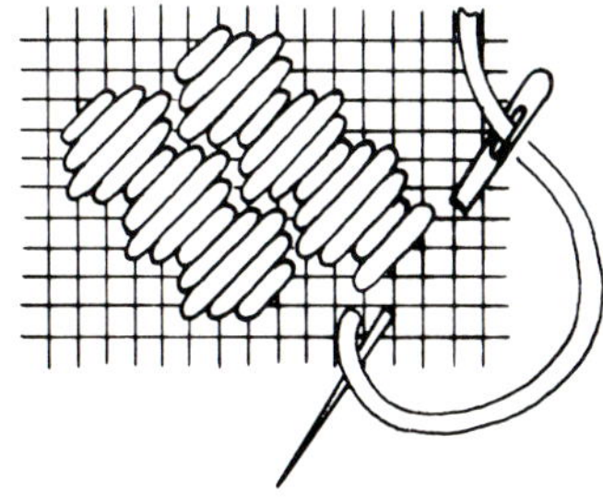

Chequer stitch

Groups of seven diagonal stitches, covering four horizontal and four vertical threads of the canvas, are alternated with groups of sixteen tent stitches also covering four horizontal and four vertical threads.

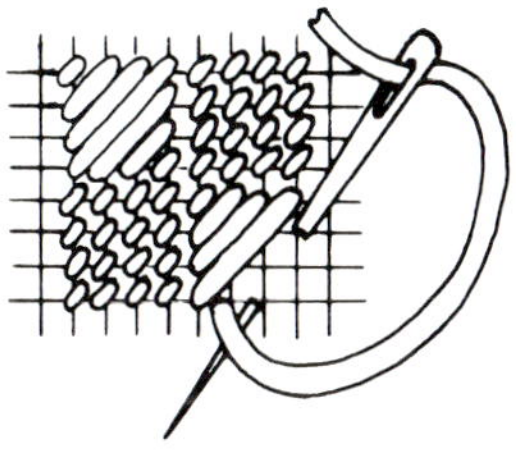

Fern stitch

Work from top to bottom. Bring needle through at top left-hand corner and take a diagonal stitch two vertical threads to the right and two horizontal threads down. Bring needle through one vertical thread to the left. Insert two vertical threads to the right, two horizontal threads up. Bring back out three threads to the left, one thread down. Continue in this way.

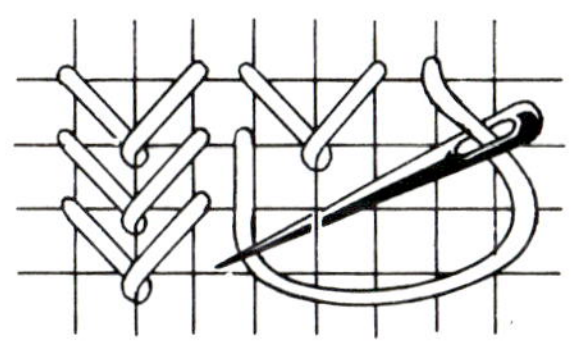

Cross stitch

See page 206 for the basic cross stitch, and its variations. When working cross stitch on canvas, in order to prevent distortion of the canvas, it is essential to complete each cross stitch separately before moving to the next. Work as follows: bring needle out at bottom right point of cross, insert four threads to the left and four threads up at top left point and bring out four threads down. Insert four threads up and four threads to the right.

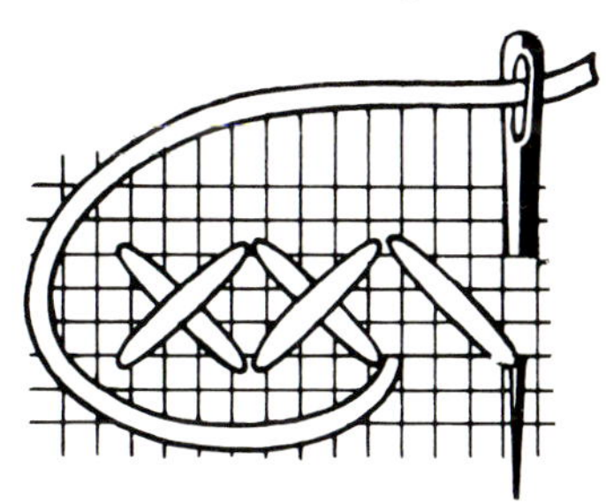

Sample showing eyelets and upright gobelin stitch.

Flat stitch

This is worked in blocks of diagonal stitches, each block consisting of five stitches and covering three horizontal threads and three vertical threads. Blocks of stitches slant alternately to the left and to the right.

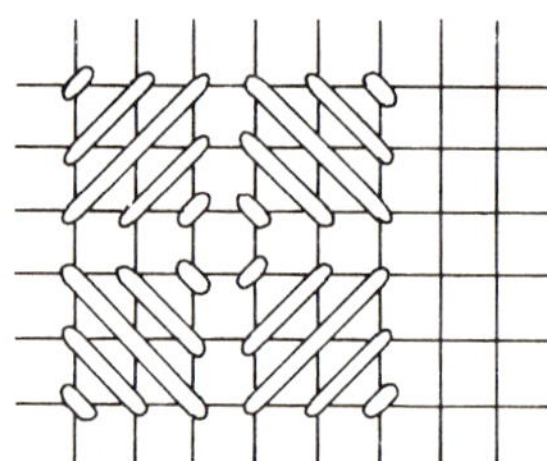

Gobelin stitch

Work in rows alternately from the left and from the right. In the first row, worked from left to right, work diagonal stitches across one vertical thread to the left and two horizontal threads down. Bring needle out two horizontal threads up and two vertical threads to the right. In the following row, needle is inserted from above downwards instead of upwards from below to give the same slant of stitch. See also **straight gobelin stitch** (page 238).

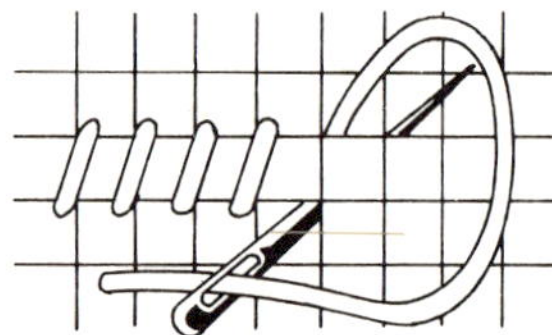

Half cross stitch

This is simply the first half of the complete basic cross stitch. It may be worked from left to right, or right to left.

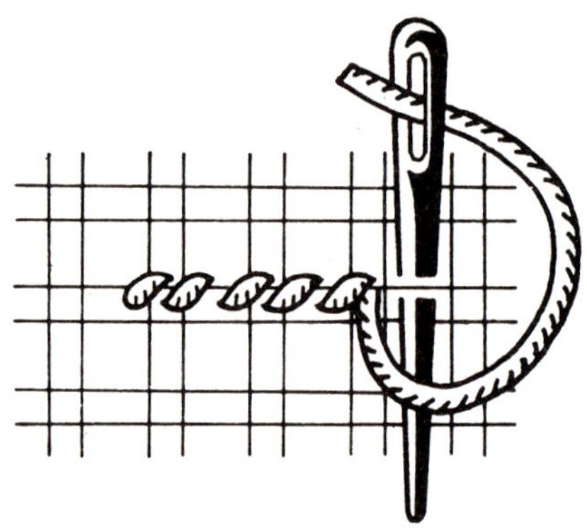

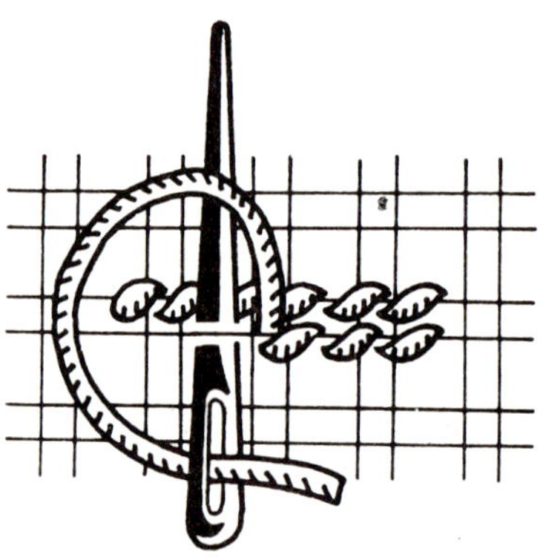

Jacquard stitch

This, like Byzantine stitch, is worked in diagonal rows from bottom right to top left, in steps of six stitches each. Rows of diagonal stitches worked over two horizontal and two vertical threads, are alternated with rows of tent stitch.

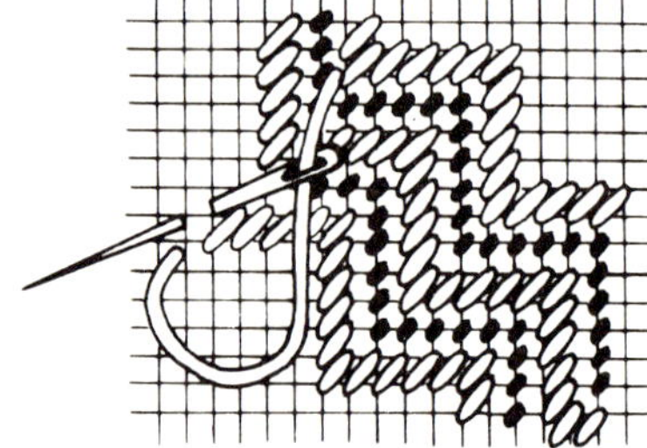

Knotted stitch

Work a diagonal stitch over three horizontal and one vertical threads, then work a small horizontal stitch over the centre of the diagonal stitch to tie it down. Work in rows, overlapping each row by one thread of the canvas.

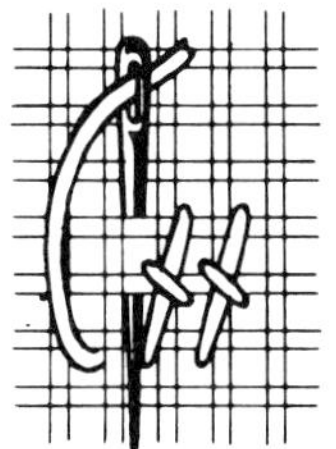 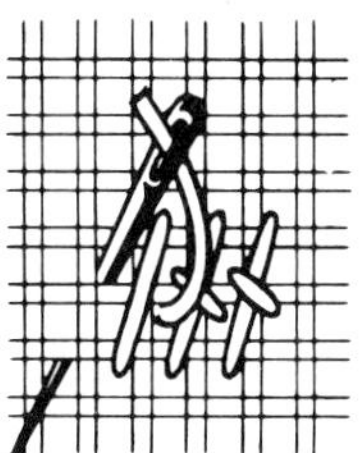 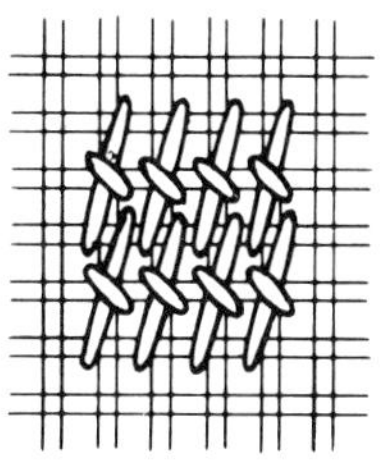

Parisian stitch

This is similar to Hungarian stitch (see page 238) and often confused with it. Work upright stitches alternately over one and then three horizontal threads. In the following row, stitches are worked in alternate sequence from the previous one so they interlock.

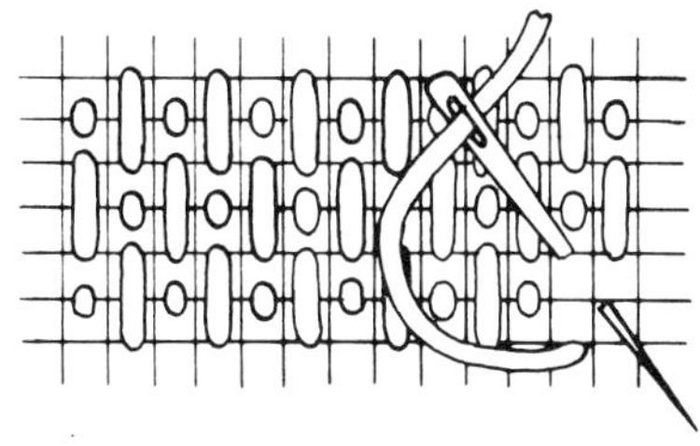

Rice stitch

In this a basic cross stitch is worked over four horizontal and four vertical threads, then a small straight stitch is worked over each corner of the basic cross. It is usual to work the crossed corner stitches in a contrasting yarn and colour to the basic cross.

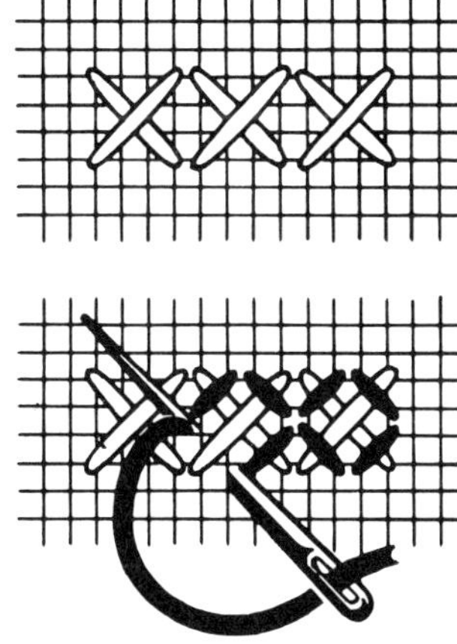

Satin stitch

This is a simple straight stitch, which may be horizontal or vertical, worked from right to left, or left to right, and over any number of threads as required.

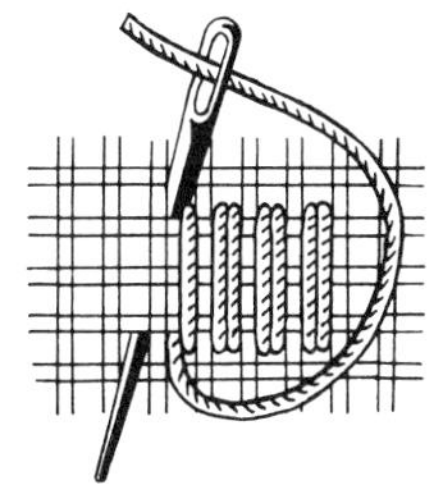

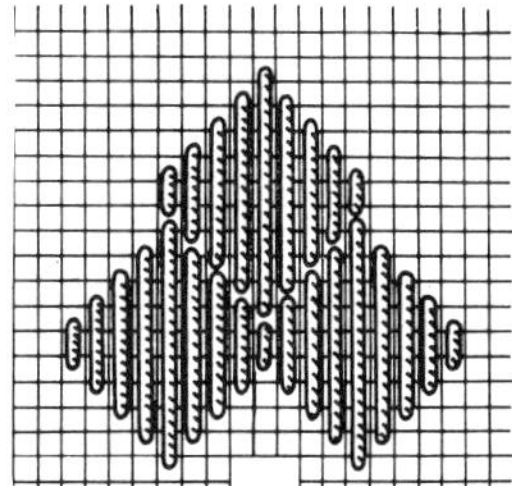

Scottish stitch

Blocks of five diagonal stitches covering three horizontal and three vertical threads of the canvas, are outlined with tent stitches, each worked over a single intersection of canvas threads.

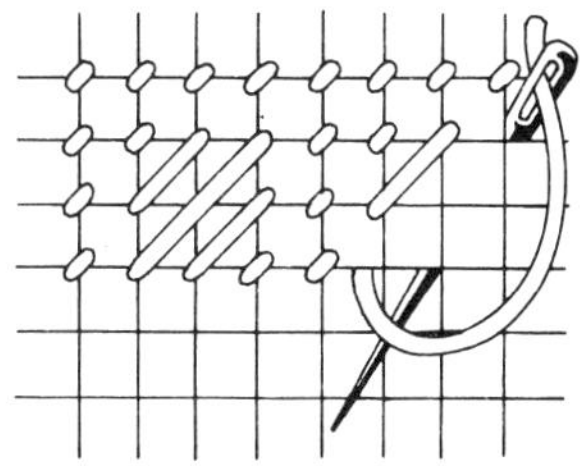

Smyrna cross stitch

Work a basic cross with a straight cross over it. A smyrna cross is usually worked over four by four threads.

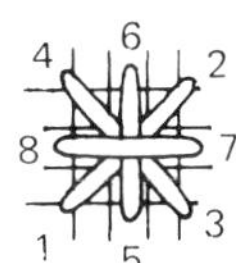

Tent stitch

Sometimes known as petit point stitch. It may be worked over single canvas, or if worked over double-thread canvas then the threads are opened up so each tent stitch is worked over a single intersection. Bring the needle out on the left-hand side of area where stitching is to appear on the top part of the first stitch. Pass the needle down over one horizontal thread and one vertical thread to the left. Bring it out one horizontal thread up and two vertical threads to the right. Continue in this way. In the following row, worked from right to left, the needle passes the crossed threads up and over, then under two threads. All stitches should slope in the same direction.

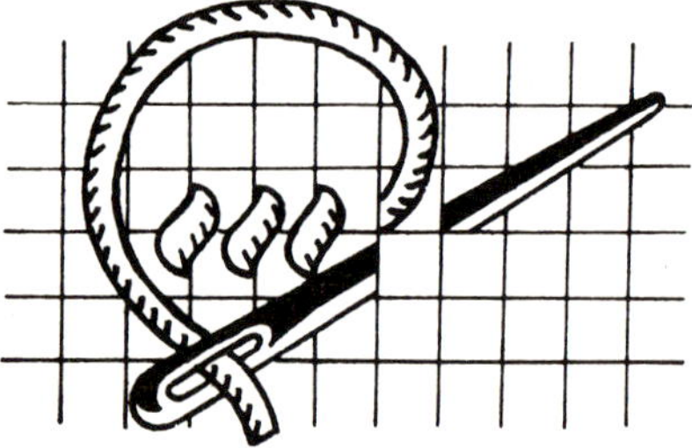

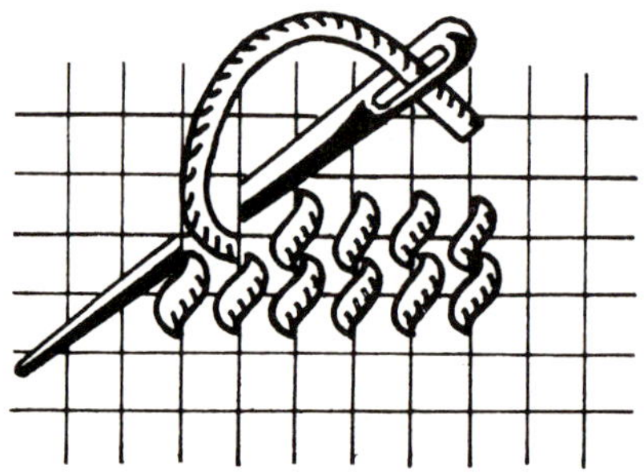

Above: *traditional tapestry bell-pull.*
Below: *geometric-patterned cushion, worked in satin stitch.*

Trammed tent stitch

This form of tent stitch gives a denser coverage to the canvas, and a richer appearance to your finished design. It must be worked on double-thread canvas. The stitch is sometimes known as gros point stitch. Bring needle through at a point where a pair of vertical threads cross a pair of horizontal threads, then take a straight horizontal stitch across work (the stitch should not be longer than five inches) from left to right. Pull needle through just below and to the left of the intersection. Work a tent stitch over the double-thread intersection of canvas threads and pull needle through on the lower line two double threads (vertical) to the left in readiness for the next stitch. Work tent stitches across the trammed stitch in this way, then bring needle out between a crossing of canvas threads on the line below and work another trammed stitch from left to right. Work tent stitches from right to left over this, as before. Continue in this way.

Another tapestry embroidered church kneeler, this time showing the Cross, one of the traditional symbols used on kneelers. The kneeler opposite shows another traditional symbol, the initials I.H.S., generally taken to be the initial letters of Iesus Hominum Salvator – Jesus Saviour of Man. The church kneeler is both functional and ornamental, and is becoming increasingly popular as a means of decorating churches, both traditional and modern. Needlepoint tapestry is the ideal technique for the making of kneelers, as it produces a firm, hardwearing fabric.

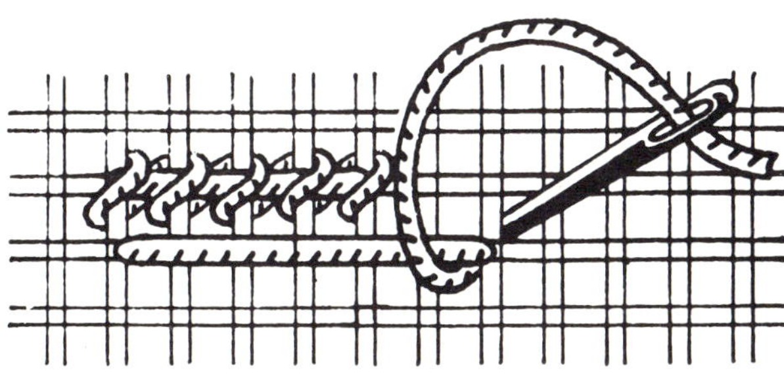

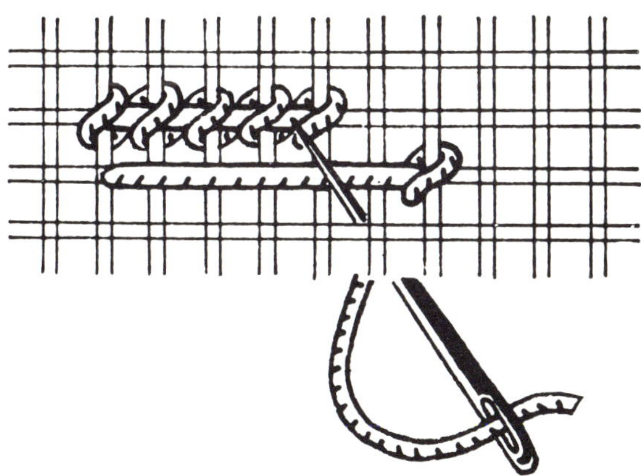

Trammed stitch, split

If it is wished to give dense coverage to your canvas work split trammed stitches over the canvas and then work the finished embroidery stitches over this tramming. Tramming should be worked in a similar colour and thread as the finished design. Bring needle through at a point where a pair of vertical threads of the canvas cross a pair of horizontal threads. Insert needle the required distance along (no longer than five inches) and bring through the canvas at a similar crossing of threads. Bring needle through one vertical thread to the left on the same line, through the stitch just made, thus forming a split stitch. Continue in this way.

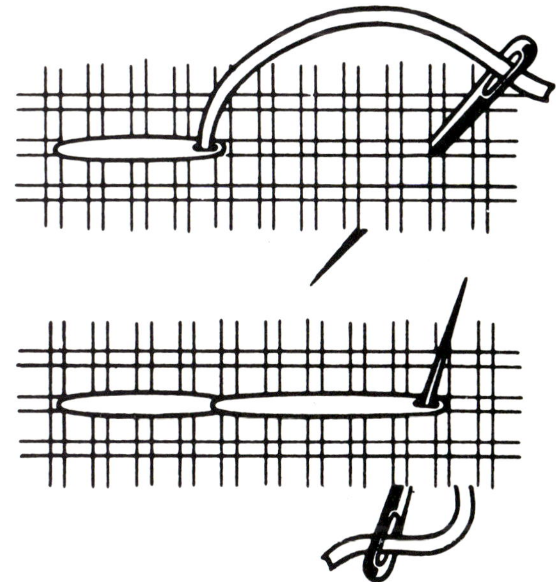

STRETCHING CANVAS

After your embroidery is complete, before making it up into the required finished item, the canvas should be stretched. This will compensate for any distortion caused by the pull of the stitches. Stretch the canvas in the following way: cover a flat wooden surface with a few sheets of damp blotting paper, and using a sponge soaked in cold water, thoroughly dampen the back of the embroidered canvas. Place canvas right side up, on the board over the damp blotting paper and using drawing pins carefully pin the canvas to the board, pinning the top edge first, then pulling opposite edge taut and pinning it. Pin side edges in a similar way. Canvas must be left until thoroughly dry and this can take up to two or even three weeks, depending on the weight of the canvas and threads. When canvas is completely dry, unpin from board and make up into finished article.

QUICK HINTS TO HELP

Never work with a thread longer than about sixteen inches as the constant friction of canvas against thread can fray it away in places.

If on completion of a design you find several small patches of canvas showing through, disguise these by working tent stitch or any suitable small stitch over the area.

It is normal to start in the centre of a design and work outwards. However, leaving the whole of the background area until last can be tedious.

It is therefore permissible to have several parts of a design being worked at the same time. Leave needles and threads in position ready for you to continue with whichever part of the design appeals to you at a particular time.

Try to keep the tension of your stitches even. It should be neither too loose nor too tight. Yarn should fill each hole of the canvas, and the stitches must cover the canvas completely and bed evenly together to form a smooth texture.

If your canvas is correctly stretched on the frame it is impossible to make any stitch in one movement: with right hand on top, insert the needle downwards through the canvas and pull the needle through with the left hand. With the left hand, push the needle upwards through the canvas and pull the needle up and out with the right hand.

THE PATTERNS
Heart-patterned belt
illustrated in colour on pages 228 and 229

MATERIALS
3 skeins tapestry wool in cream, 3 skeins crewel wool in dark blue, 2 skeins crewel wool in medium blue, 3 skeins crewel wool in red, and 1 skein stranded cotton in pink. Piece of single-thread tapestry canvas, with 14 threads to 1 in., to measure $8\frac{1}{2}$ in. wide, and the length of your waist size plus 12 in. A $2\frac{1}{2}$-in. buckle. Strip of belt backing to measure $3\frac{1}{2}$ in. wide, and the length of your waist size plus 7 in. A tapestry needle No. 18.

MEASUREMENTS
Finished belt should be the size of your waist plus 6 in. for ease of fit and buckle overlap; $2\frac{1}{2}$ in. wide.

STITCHES
Cross; straight gobelin (see page 238); back; straight cross; satin; tent; smyrna cross; Parisian; Hungarian (see page 238); double straight cross.

DIAGRAMS
Diagram A gives the pointed end of belt, the cross stitch border, one dividing bar, and the first heart panel.
Diagram B gives the second heart panel. **Diagram C** gives the third heart panel.
Each diagram shows the position of the various stitches, and the background lines represent the threads of the canvas.

TO MAKE
Mark centre of canvas lengthwise with basting stitches. Prepare canvas and frame-up.
Begin embroidery on the central basting stitches 3 in. down from one short end of canvas. Work the pointed tip of belt, the dividing bar and the first heart panel, as given in diagram A, first. The arrow on this diagram should coincide with your basting stitches. When the first heart panel is completed work another dividing bar followed by the second heart panel (diagram B), then work another dividing bar followed by the third heart panel (diagram C). Continue in this way working heart panels in rotation, always separating each with a dividing bar, and continuing double row of cross stitches down each side of work to form border. Continue until embroidery measures your waist size plus 6 in. (or length required).
Use threads and colours as follows, using 4 strands of crewel wool and 3 strands of cotton throughout (except for centre of first heart panel).

Border: dark blue crewel wool, cross stitches, each stitch worked over two horizontal and two vertical threads of the canvas.
Dividing bars: centre row of bar is worked in dark blue crewel wool, straight satin stitches worked in blocks of five horizontal stitches, four vertical stitches alternately, each block covering four horizontal, four vertical threads of the canvas. On either side of this centre row is worked a row of cross stitches in medium blue crewel wool, each stitch over four horizontal and four vertical threads of the canvas. Small back stitches are worked on either side of each cross, and between crosses, as indicated on diagram A.
Backgrounds: all worked in cream tapestry wool; in straight gobelin stitch, each stitch over two threads of the canvas, and arranged in alternate interlocking pattern, for first heart panel background; in Hungarian

continued on page 228

B
C
A

STITCH KEY

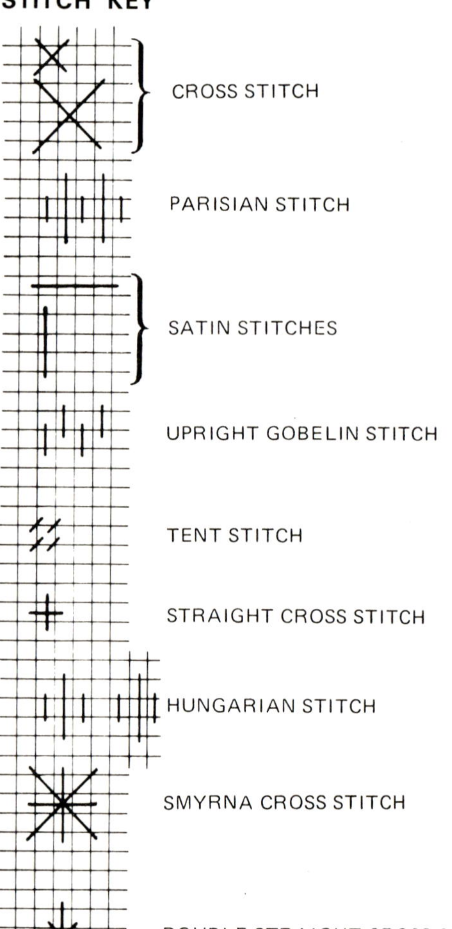

stitch, over four and two threads of the canvas, for second heart panel background; in Parisian stitch, over four and two threads of the canvas, for third heart panel background, and also background for pointed end section of belt.

First heart panel: heart is worked in red crewel wool in straight cross stitch, over two horizontal, two vertical threads of the canvas, with a centre section worked in six strands of pink stranded cotton in tent stitch.

Second heart panel: heart is worked in smyrna cross stitch, with red crewel wool for basic cross, pink stranded cotton for straight cross. Each complete stitch covers four horizontal, four vertical threads of the canvas.

Third heart panel: heart is worked in double straight cross stitch in red crewel wool, over four horizontal, four vertical threads of the canvas.

TO COMPLETE

Stretch canvas if necessary. Trim canvas to within 1 in. of embroidery. Press the unworked borders to back of belt and baste to hold in position. Take short straight end of belt over bar of buckle and baste. Cut one short end of backing fabric to pointed shape to match embroidery, plus $\frac{1}{2}$ in. for seam allowance. Turn in $\frac{1}{2}$-in. seam allowance round all edges of backing and place on embroidered strip, wrong sides together. Oversew neatly round edges.

Above and opposite: *heart-patterned belt (see page 226). Flower belt is appliqué work—see Part 7.*

Stool top

illustrated in colour on page 232

MATERIALS

Of Coats Anchor Tapisserie Wool (or any good-quality tapestry wool) — 20 skeins Peacock Blue 0170, 10 skeins Muscat Green 0281, 5 skeins White 0402, 3 skeins Mid Blue 0168, and 2 skeins Pale Blue 0158. $\frac{5}{8}$ yd. double-thread tapestry canvas, with 10 holes to 1 in., 27 in. wide. A Milward 'Gold Seal' tapestry needle No. 18. A stool with inset pad measuring approximately $23\frac{1}{2}$ in. by 15 in. Upholstery tacks or nails.

COLOUR KEY

◙	–	Pale Blue
◪	–	Mid Blue
⊡	–	Peacock Blue
◪	–	Muscat Green
☐	–	White

MEASUREMENTS
The finished stool top measures 23½ in. by 15 in.

STITCH
Trammed tent.

DIAGRAM *(see opposite)*
The diagram gives half the design. Each background square on the diagram represents the double threads of the canvas.

TO MAKE
Mark the centre of the canvas both ways with basting stitches, run between a pair of narrow double threads lengthwise and widthwise. Mark out total area of embroidery to fit stool pad. Prepare canvas and frame-up. With one long side of canvas facing you, begin embroidery centrally and work the half given in the diagram, following colour key. The design is worked throughout in trammed tent stitch. The blank arrows on the diagram should coincide with your basting stitches. To complete the embroidery, turn the diagram and work other half in a similar way.

TO COMPLETE
Stretch canvas if necessary. Place the embroidery right side up centrally on the stool pad, fold back the unworked border of canvas and secure in position on the underside with tacks or nails.

Owl design bell pull, worked on a medium mesh, single-thread canvas, in a variety of different stitches.

Satin stitch workbag
illustrated in colour on page 233

MATERIALS. Of Coats Anchor Tapisserie Wool (or any good-quality tapestry wool) — 31 skeins Dark Violet 0107, 5 skeins Cyclamen 085, 3 skeins each Pale Violet 0106 and Beige 0388. 1⅛ yd. double-thread tapestry canvas, 10 holes to 1 in., 27 in. wide. ½ yd. mediumweight lining fabric, 36 in. wide. ⅝ yd. mediumweight interfacing, 32 in. wide. A pair of wooden handles with 11¾-in. slots. A piece of cardboard 12 in. by 3 in. for base. A Milward 'Gold Seal' tapestry needle No. 19.

MEASUREMENTS. Finished bag measures 12½ in. long, 12 in. wide, 3 in. deep (at base).

DIAGRAMS (see page 234). **Diagram A** gives one half of the design. Each background square represents one block of 3 double satin stitches worked over 3 double threads of the canvas.
Diagram B gives a guide to the making-up of the finished embroidery. The numbers indicate the number of satin stitch blocks; the dotted lines indicate folds and seam lines.

TO MAKE
Mark the centre of canvas both ways with a line of basting stitches. Take stitches along a line of holes widthwise and between a pair of narrow double threads lengthwise. Prepare the canvas, and frame-up.
Begin the embroidery centrally, following diagram A and the colour key as given. The design is worked throughout in blocks of 3 double satin stitches, each pair of satin stitches worked over 3 double threads of the canvas. The arrows on diagram A should coincide with your basting stitches. Work the half given in diagram A first, then work other half to correspond.

TO COMPLETE
Trim canvas to within 1 in. from embroidery on all sides. Using this as a pattern, cut one piece each from interfacing and from lining fabric. Fold embroidered piece in half, wrong side out, matching up the horizontal rows of satin stitches carefully.
Stitch side seams as indicated in diagram B, commencing one block in from finished side edge. Fold, so that side seam lies centrally along base section and stitch across base sides. Turn to right side.
Make up interfacing and lining in a similar way. Lightly herringbone stitch cardboard in position to interfacing to form base. Insert in bag; trim the interfacing level with embroidery at gusset edges, sides and fold line at top; turn down seam allowance of canvas on gusset edges over interfacing, clip corners and stitch lightly.
Turn in sides of section to go through handle slots. Insert lining in bag; trim lining even with interfacing at fold line only. Turn down seam allowance level with gusset edges at both sides, clip corners and slipstitch.
Turn in seam allowance at sides of handle section and slipstitch, then slip handle over embroidered section, fold in half, turn in seam allowance and slipstitch securely.

Stool top in trammed tent stitch—instructions start on page 230.

Satin stitch work bag (see page 231).

COLOUR KEY

- ☒ Cyclamen
- ● Pale violet
- ◢ Dark violet
- ⊡ Beige

Diagram B

Diagram A

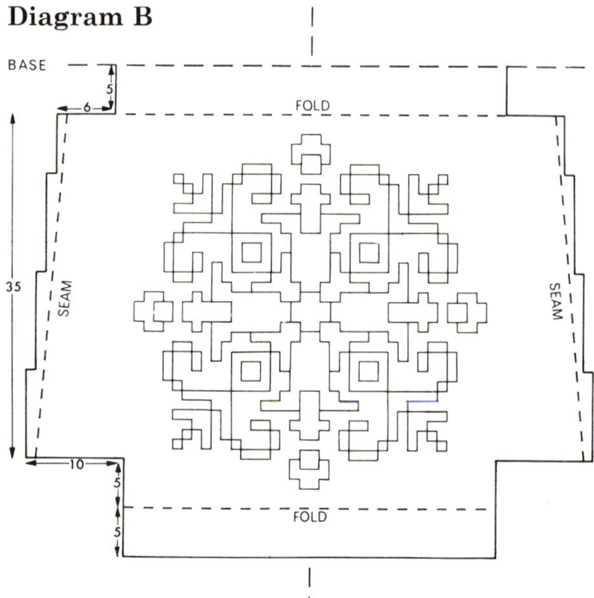

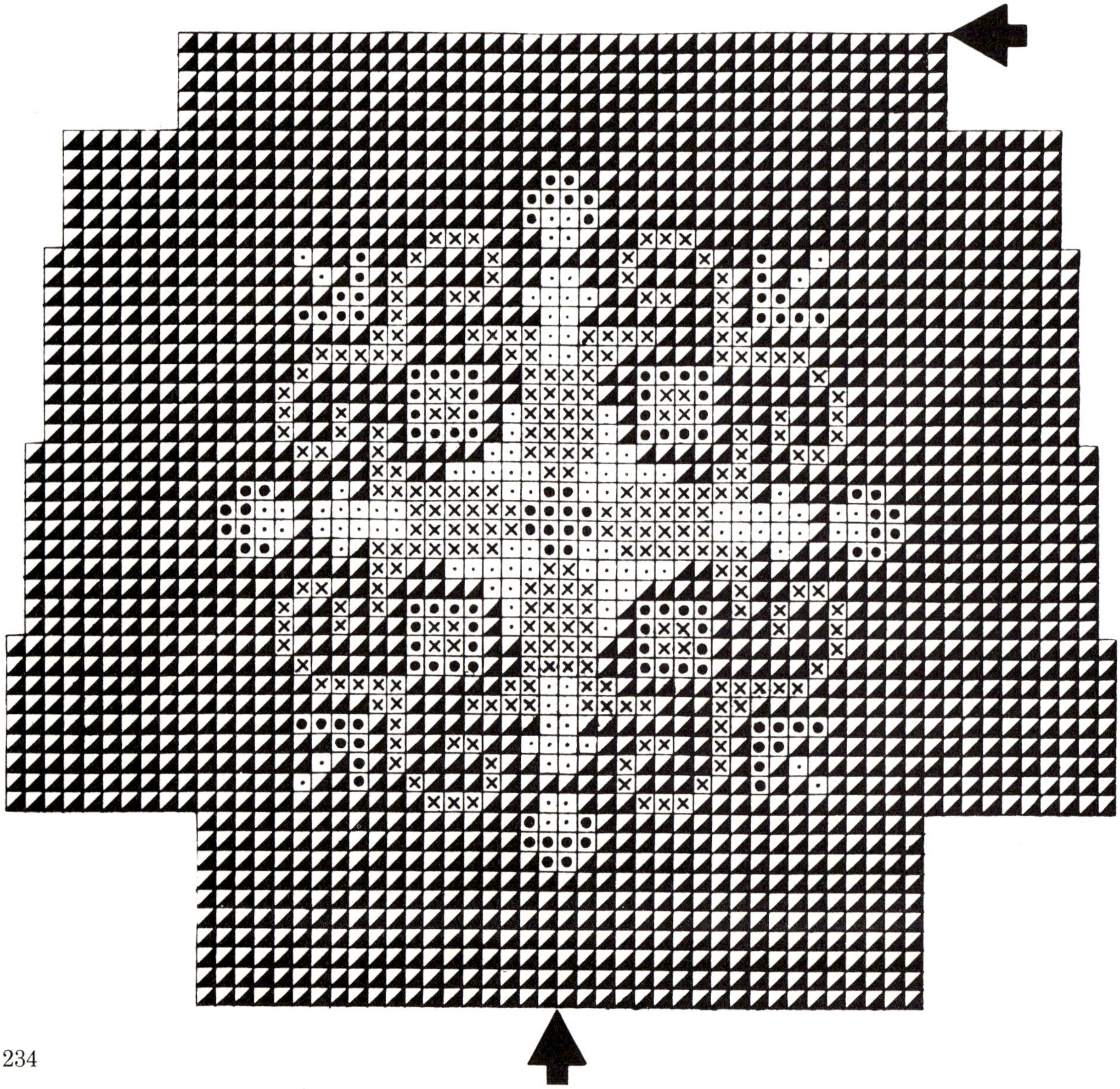

Part 4—
FLORENTINE EMBROIDERY

This is a traditional form of canvas embroidery (needlepoint) which can also be worked on evenweave linen. The technique is sometimes incorrectly called Bargello work, because there are some fine examples of Florentine embroidery to be seen in the Bargello Museum, Florence. The technique also includes Hungarian point, fianna or flame stitch. The latter name is derived from the flame-like points which occur frequently in a number of the patterns.

Florentine work, probably more than any other embroidery technique, makes marvellous use of colour. The basic principle of a Florentine design is to create a 'wave' or zigzag pattern of upright stitches, each line of stitching worked in a different colour. Traditionally graduated shades of the same colour are used, but in modern designs totally different colours can be used for each row. Colours can also change within rows.

In its simplest form, each step of the zigzag is formed by taking an upright vertical stitch over four horizontal threads of the canvas, and 'stepping' this stitch two horizontal threads above or below the previous stitch (see diagram and detailed instructions below). This is referred to as Florentine stitch in the 4:2 step. Alternatively, a 6:3 stepped zigzag can be worked, by taking each stitch over six horizontal threads, and stepping it three threads above or below the previous one.

Variations on this basic zigzag are endless: try varying the lengths of the individual stitches, the number of stitches worked in each step, and vary the depth of the wave itself – and you will create entirely new patterns. Curves can also be produced in this way, as well as the sharp traditional zigzag form. Usually Florentine patterns tend to be abstract, their interest lying in the vivid and dramatic use of colour, but the patterns can be representative as well – flowers, foliage and birds can all be 'drawn' in Florentine embroidery, once the principles of the techniques have been learned and understood.

Hungarian stitch is frequently combined with Florentine stitch (see below), and so are many other upright needlepoint stitches – e.g. brick and satin. These are useful for filling in areas of canvas which might otherwise be left unstitched when the main Florentine design is completed. As with all canvas embroideries, it is essential that the canvas is completely and smoothly covered by stitching.

MATERIALS

It is usual to work Florentine embroidery on single-thread canvas. Any size mesh, from 14 threads to 28 threads to the inch, may be used, although for first efforts a fairly coarse mesh will be easier to work with. An evenweave linen may, if preferred, be used (see note on evenweave fabrics on page 202).

Whichever type of canvas or fabric you choose, it is essential to choose the right yarn – with canvas, particularly, the yarn used should never be finer than the threads of the canvas mesh, and should fill each hole exactly, so the mesh of the canvas is completely covered in the finished design. Stranded cotton, tapestry or knitting wool, crewel wool and silk, are all suitable yarns. Novelty yarns – such as plastic raffia and metal threads – can also be used to good effect in a modern Florentine design. But experiment with a small sample first of all to see if the yarn suits your canvas, and is reasonably easy to work with. When working designs with a great number of colours, it is a good idea to keep a separate needle ready threaded with each colour.

As with other forms of canvas embroidery, needles should be chosen to suit canvas and thread (see page 218).

As all the stitches used in Florentine work are straight stitches, and there is therefore little danger of canvas distortion, it is not necessary to use a frame. To support a large piece of work as you stitch, roll down the canvas from the top as far as the part of the canvas you are working on. When you stop working, always roll up the canvas carefully. Never fold it.

STITCHES
The basic Florentine stitch

This stitch is usually worked in rows of different colours, to form an allover wave pattern. Stitches are straight and vertical, and can be worked over any number of canvas threads. They are stepped as shown in the diagram, below, to give a zigzag, or wave, of desired depth; the size of the wave may also be varied. A common version of the stitch is to work each vertical stitch over four horizontal threads, stepping each stitch up or down two threads at a time. This is known as the 4:2 step. Each row is an exact repetition of the previous one, so stitches fit together.

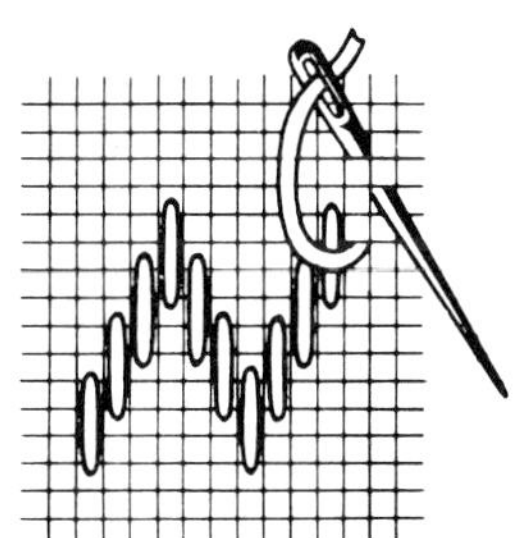 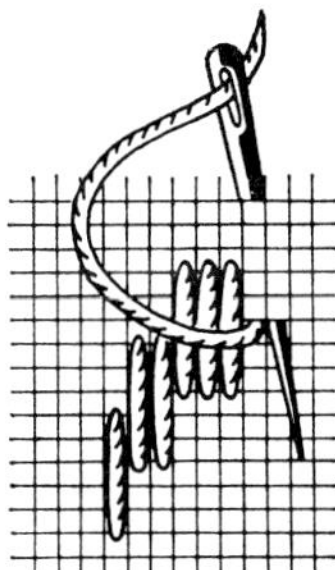

*Traditional Florentine patterns (see pages 238,
239 and 242). Top row, left to right: samples 1 and
2. Second line, left to right: samples 3 and 5.
Left: sample 4. Opposite: samples 6, 7 and 8 (the
three illustrations down left-hand side of page)
and sample 9, a traditional honeycomb pattern.*

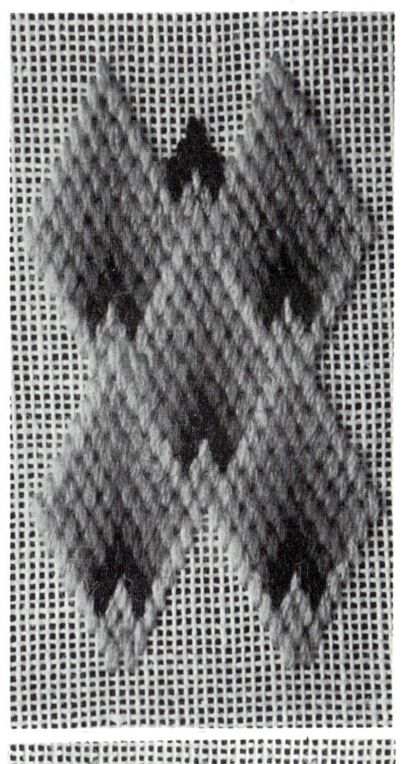

Hungarian stitch

This is worked in groups of three vertical stitches, each worked in turn over two, four and two horizontal threads; two vertical threads are left between each group, so stitches in the following row can be worked to give an interlocked pattern.

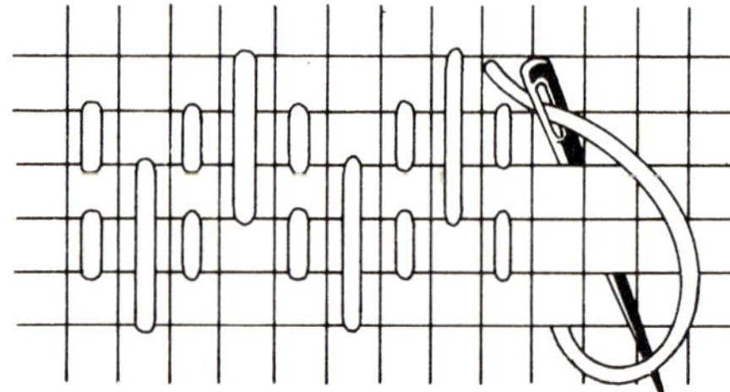

Hungarian ground

This is often used as a background filling in Florentine designs. Rows of basic Florentine stitches, worked in a 4:2 step, three stitches to each wave, are alternated with a row of small upright stitches. Each upright stitch is worked over two horizontal threads, and stitches are arranged in groups of four to form 'diamonds' fitting exactly between the rows of Florentine stitches.

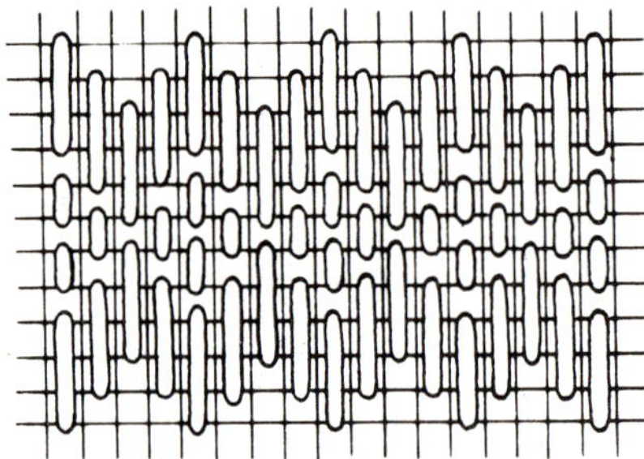

Straight gobelin

This is a useful stitch for filling in unstitched areas at the edges of the canvas. It consists of straight vertical stitches worked over two horizontal threads of the canvas. Work from right to left, or left to right. The stitch may also be worked in an alternate interlocking arrangement, similar to brick stitch (see page 220).

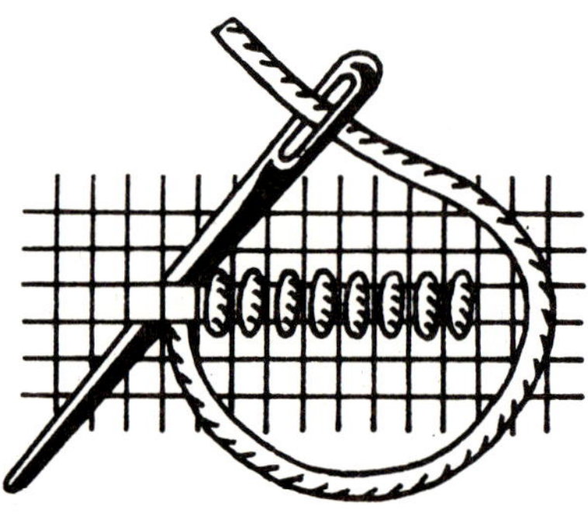

SOME TRADITIONAL FLORENTINE PATTERNS

illustrated on pages 236 and 237

The illustrated samples – with the exception of the basketweave pattern – have been worked on a single-thread canvas with a mesh size of 18 threads to the inch, with two strands of crewel wool, and a No. 24 needle. Where a design is accompanied by a chart, this will indicate the position and length of each stitch on the canvas. The background lines on the chart represent the threads of the canvas.

It is recommended that some of these 'sampler' patterns are worked first to help you become familiar with the Florentine technique, before trying any designs.

Sample 1

This is worked in five shades of blue, the same length stitch is used throughout, and the same step (the 4:2 step – i.e. each stitch worked over four threads of the canvas, stepped up or down by two threads each time), but there is a variable number of stitches in each step. Chart 1 opposite shows one row of the pattern, indicating the grouping of stitches, and the depth of the wave. Every row is worked alike, to fit into the previous row. Colours range from palest blue (1) through in numerical order to very dark blue (5). Work in the following colour sequence: a row in 5, followed by rows each in 4, 3, 2, 1, 2, 3 and 4. Continue to repeat this sequence to length required.

Sample 2

This is similar to sample 1 for this is also worked in the 4:2 step, with a variable number of stitches in each step, but the different arrangement of the stitches, the shallower wave, and the change of colours in each row, create an entirely new pattern. Each row is worked exactly as chart 2 opposite. Four shades of orange are used, three shades of green. Work in the following colour sequence (low numbers indicate lightest shades, high numbers dark shades): 1st row – orange 4; 2nd row – green 3 (first step only), orange 3 (seven steps), green 3 (last step); 3rd row – green 2 (first step), green 3 (second step), orange 2 (five steps), green 3 (one step), green 2 (last step); 4th row – green 1 (first step), green 2 (one step), green 3 (one step), orange 1 (three steps), green 3 (one step), green 2 (one step), green 1 (last step); 5th row – green 1 (two steps), green 2 (one step), green 3 (one step), orange 1 (one step), green 3 (one step), green 2 (one step), green 1 (two steps). As you work this pattern you will see two distinct motifs are formed – a circular motif from the shades of orange, and a smaller diamond motif of greens. Although each row is worked alike in the same sequence of stitches and steps, because of the colour changes within each row, you may find it easier to mark out the positions of the motifs on your canvas, then work in blocks of colour rather than complete rows.

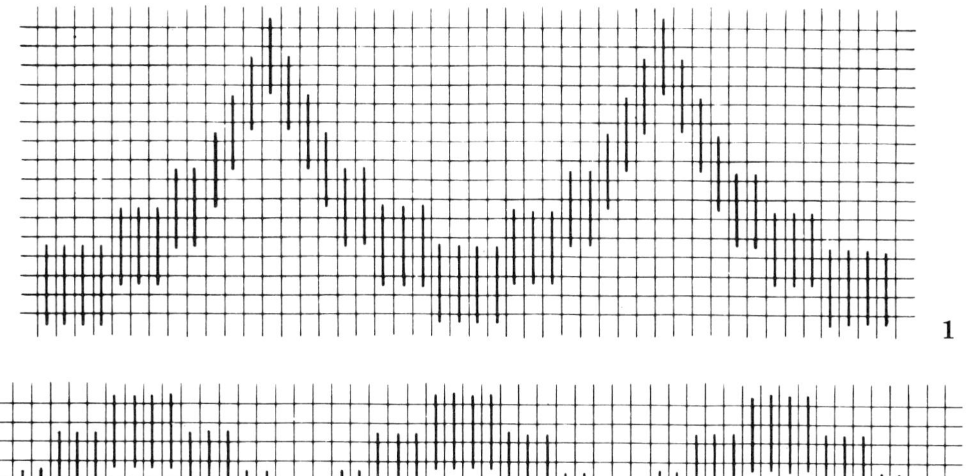

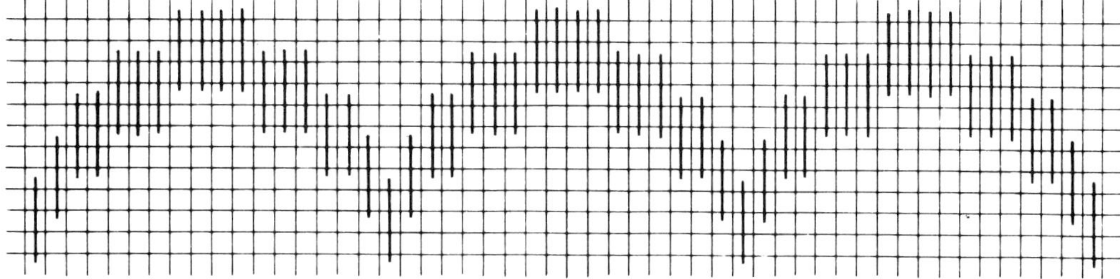

Sample 3

A sharper 'step', variable number of stitches in each step, and a steep wave, creates this angular zigzag pattern. Worked in the 6:1 step (i.e. each stitch is worked over six threads of the canvas, and each step overlaps previous step by only one thread each time), a block of stitches is worked at the base of each wave, then single stitches step up to top of wave. Each row is worked exactly as chart 3 below. Using four shades of purple and one of duck egg blue, work in the following colour sequence, one colour for each row: blue, purple 1, purple 2, purple 3, purple 4.

Sample 4

This shows another version of the pattern type given in sample 2. Again, by changing colours within each row, a distinct circular motif is formed, with diamonds between (only half diamonds are shown on our worked sample). This time, however, the wave (which creates the curve of the circle) is wider, and the circle has a symmetrical arrangement of colours. Each row is worked exactly as chart 4 on page 242. Colours range from cream in centre of circle, through pale peach, mid peach to brown on outside of circle, and from cream at outside of diamond, through pale peach to mid peach in centre of diamond.

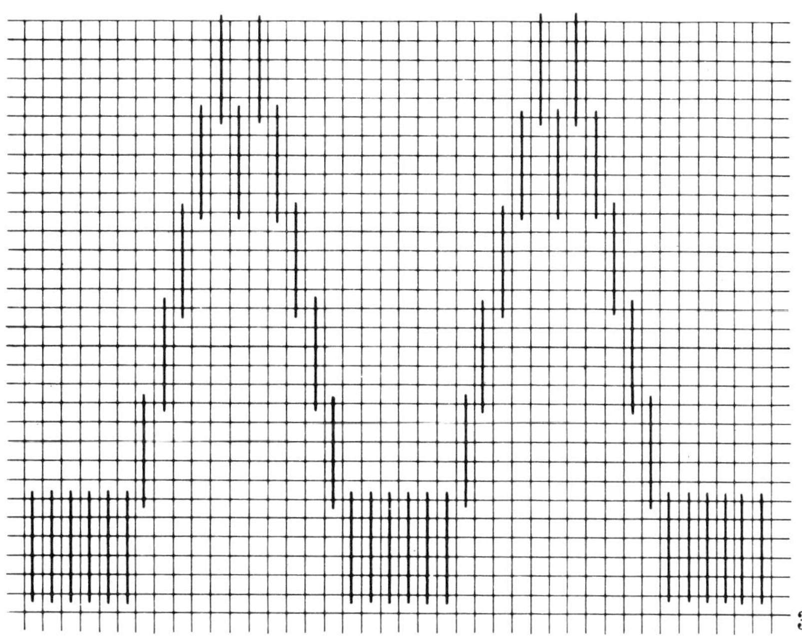

Above: *Florentine-embroidered cushion (6:1 step).* **Below:** *Florentine handbag and spectacle case.*

Trolley set (see page 242).

241

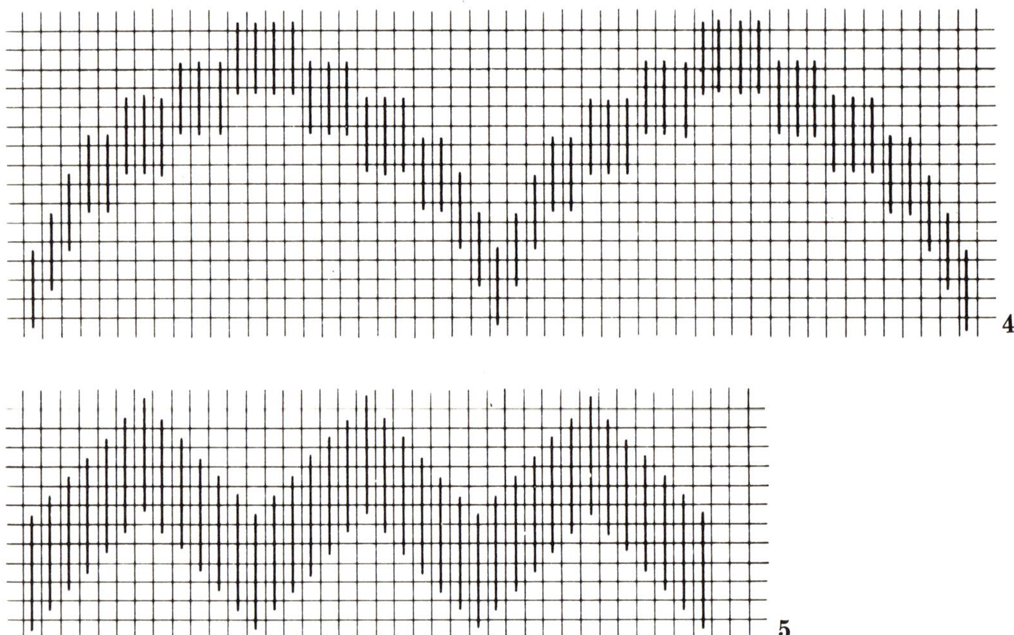

Sample 5

Chart 5 is a very regular pattern, with single stitches in the 6:5 step, seven steps to each wave, but by using four shades in each of two different colours, and changing colours within each row, an extremely effective colour pattern is created.

Samples 6, 7 and 8

These three patterns are all worked in the basic 4:2 Florentine step, but show how by altering the depth of each wave, and the colours used within each row, totally different patterns are created.

Sample 9

This is an example of the traditional basketweave pattern. The sample shown is worked on a single-thread canvas with a mesh of 24 threads to the inch. The pattern is worked in the basic 4:2 step, with two stitches to each step, eight steps to each wave. A very clever variation of colours in each row creates this intricate-looking 'plaid' pattern.

A PATTERN

Trolley set
illustrated in colour on page 241

MATERIALS (for two trolley cloths, four napkin rings)
Of Clark's Anchor Stranded Cotton (USA J. & P. Coats Deluxe Six Strand Floss) – 6 skeins each Mid Lilac 0105, and Dark Lilac 0106, 5 skeins each Violet 0102, and Parma Violet 0108, 4 skeins each Mid Magenta 062, Dark Magenta 064, and Old Rose 074. $\frac{3}{4}$ yd. blue mediumweight evenweight linen, with 21 threads to 1 in., 54 or 59 in. wide. A Milward 'Gold Seal' tapestry needle No. 21. $\frac{1}{8}$ yd. interfacing, 32 or 36 in. wide. Eight press fasteners.

MEASUREMENTS
The finished size of each trolley cloth is 18 in. by 24 in.; of each napkin ring $2\frac{1}{2}$ in. by $7\frac{1}{2}$ in.

STITCH
Florentine: worked in basic 4:2 step, with a variable number of stitches in each step.

DIAGRAM *(see opposite)*
The diagram gives a section of the design, showing the arrangement of the stitches on the threads of the fabric. The background lines on the diagram represent the threads of the fabric.

TO MAKE
Note. Use 6 strands of cotton throughout.
Cut two pieces from fabric, each $19\frac{1}{2}$ in. by $25\frac{1}{2}$ in., for the trolley cloths, and four pieces, each $6\frac{1}{2}$ in. by 9 in., for the napkin rings. Mark large pieces across the centre both ways with basting stitches. Mark small pieces across the centre lengthwise with basting stitches.

Trolley cloth
With one short side of fabric facing you, begin embroidery centrally 93 threads down from crossed basting stitches, and work section of design as given in the diagram. The blank arrow on the diagram should coincide with your lengthwise basting stitches. Each stitch is worked over four threads of the fabric; follow the colour key for thread colours. Repeat section once more to the right, then work left-hand side to correspond. Turn fabric and repeat on opposite short side.

Napkin ring
With one long side of fabric facing you, begin embroidery centrally at black arrow on diagram, $\frac{3}{4}$ in. in from right-hand side of fabric, and work four motifs along basting stitches.

TO COMPLETE
Press embroidery on the wrong side. Turn back and stitch $\frac{1}{2}$-in. hems on all edges of trolley cloths, mitre corners and slipstitch.
Cut four pieces from interfacing, each $2\frac{1}{2}$ in. by $7\frac{1}{2}$ in. Place an interfacing strip centrally on to wrong side of each napkin ring embroidery. Turn back seam allowance at short sides and stitch lightly to interfacing. Fold long sides towards centre, and slipstitch together. Slipstitch ends. Sew two press fasteners to each napkin ring to fasten.

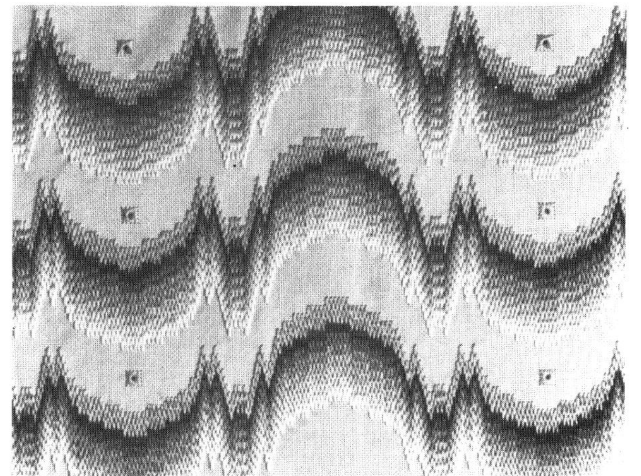

A traditional pattern worked on evenweave fabric.

COLOUR KEY

- Mid Magenta
- Dark Magenta
- Old Rose
- Violet
- Mid Lilac
- Dark Lilac
- Parma Violet

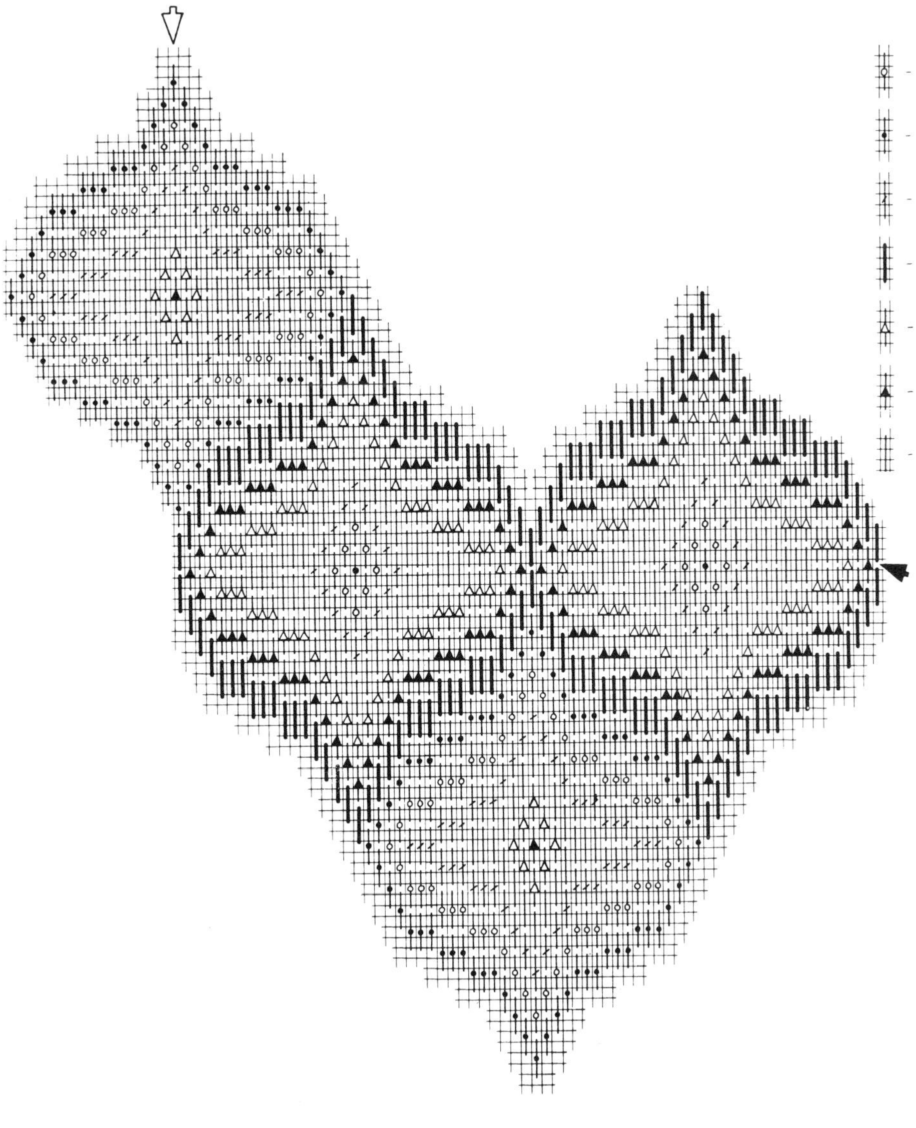

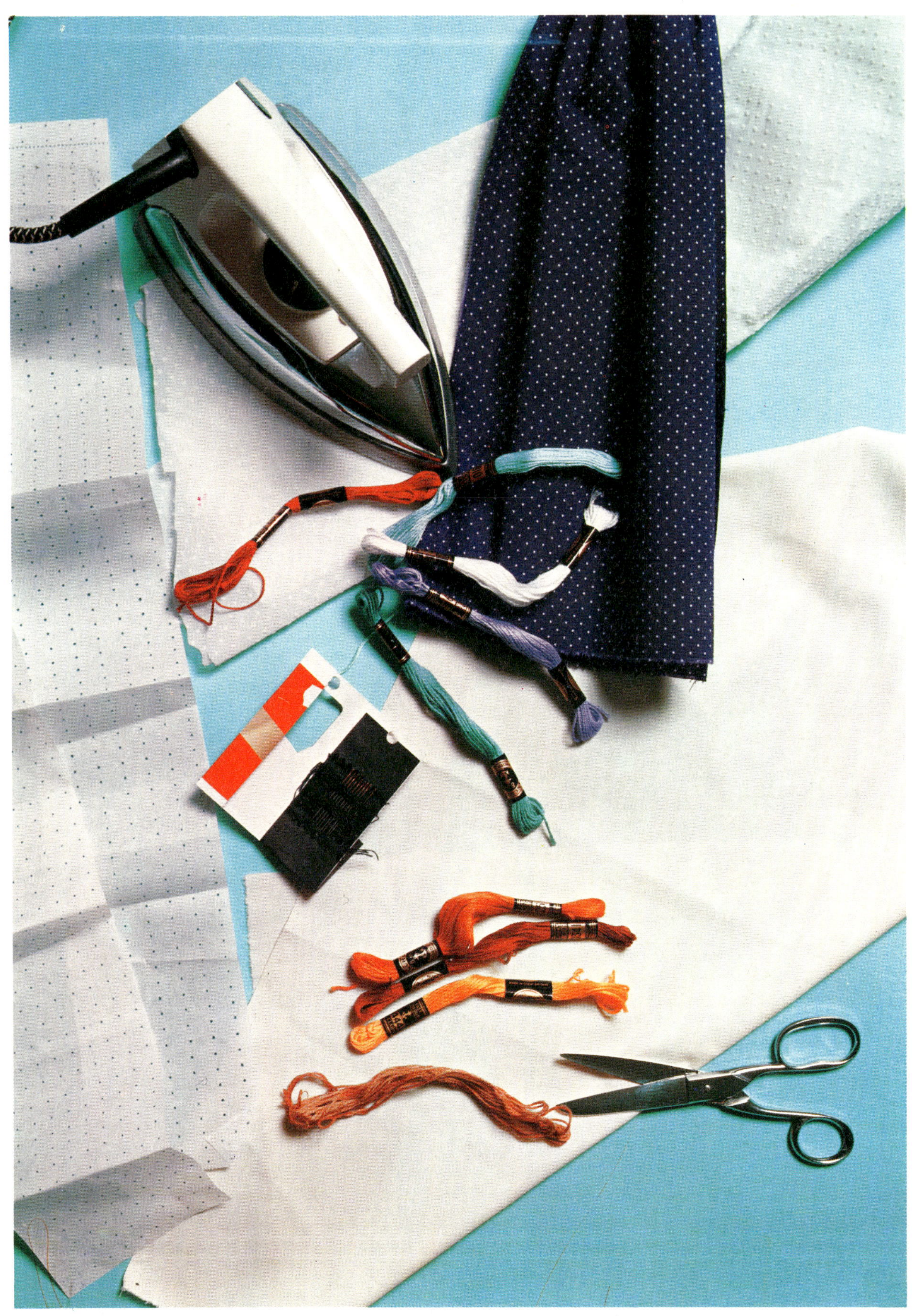

Part 5—
SMOCKING

Smocking was devised as 'a kind of needlework for holding gathers in place' and was originally used on the shiftlike garments worn by shepherds and agricultural workers. These 'smocks' were usually made of linen or homespun hemp, and they were rather like an elongated shirt or nightshirt. The gathers allowed freedom of movement without the garment looking too shapeless.

Apart from the embroidery which held the gathers in place, the smock was usually decorated on the yoke, collar and side to denote the occupation of the wearer. Thus gardeners would have flowers and leaves; shepherds had crooks, hurdles and sheep; wagoners and carters had cartwheels, whip lashes and reins; milkmaids had churns and butter pats; even gravediggers' smocks were decorated – usually with crosses!

Different districts had different coloured smocks, and some can still be seen today in museums. Usually the Sunday-best smock was in white or natural linen, worked in a self colour.

Nowadays smocking is used on all sorts of fabrics and for many types of garments: frocks, nightdresses and rompers for babies; party dresses for little girls; nightdresses and blouses for adults; cotton dresses for teenagers.

FABRICS AND THREADS

Almost any type of fabric can be smocked, such as voile, nylon, organza, lawn, fine cotton, poplin, silk, shantung, crêpe-de-chine, lingerie fabrics, gingham, and fine woollen fabrics. Heavier weights, such as linen, velvet and medium-weight woollen fabrics, can also be smocked successfully, but textured fabrics do not gather well. So choose your fabric according to the garment you wish to make.

If you are using a plain-coloured fabric, a smocking transfer will be needed to help you draw up the work evenly (these can be obtained from most needlework shops and good department stores). Many spotted, striped and checked fabrics can be drawn up without the use of a transfer, as the pattern on the fabric can be used as a guide. As smocking reduces the width of the fabric to approximately one third of its original size you will have to allow for this in your calculations when buying fabric.

The thread normally used for the embroidery is six-stranded embroidery cotton as this can be split to suit the weight of the fabric to be smocked. Two strands are used for light fabrics such as voile, nylon and organza, three strands for medium fabrics such as cotton and fine wools, and four strands for heavier fabrics like velvet or wool. Silk thread can be used to smock silk, shantung or crêpe-de-chine, and it is traditional to use linen thread to smock linen. Never use wool as this is too heavy and breaks too easily.

Colour depends on personal preference, but a very bright-coloured fabric such as scarlet looks most attractive smocked all in white. Pastel and white fabrics look effective smocked in a self colour or in a soft range of muted toning colours; patterned fabrics look best if the smocking complements the colours in the patterns.

PREPARING THE FABRIC

As smocking is worked on gathered fabric, it is essential the fabric is carefully and thoroughly prepared. The gathers must be uniform, and if the work is to have the necessary elasticity, the gathers should be made in the ratio of approximately $2\frac{1}{2}$:1 so allow at least two-and-a-half inches of fabric for every inch of finished smocking.

If you are working with plain fabric you will need to apply a smocking transfer first. This is like a normal embroidery transfer, but it consists only of rows of evenly-spaced dots, printed in blue or yellow. The yellow shows up well on dark fabrics – the blue is better for light-coloured fabrics. Select the size of transfer to suit your work – the larger the garment and heavier the fabric, the more widely spaced the dots should be.

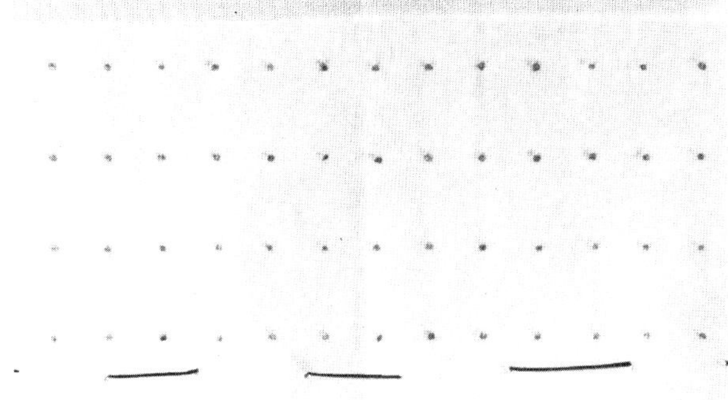

It may be necessary to cut a portion of the transfer off if it is too wide or deep for your fabric, or you may have to add on an extra piece.

The dots are transferred on to the *wrong* side of the fabric, and the work is gathered on the *wrong* side, then the smocking is worked on the gathers on the *right* side of the fabric. First, press the fabric, according to type, then position the transfer on your material – allow for seams and do not place it too near the selvedge (the work is gathered from selvedge to selvedge across the width of the fabric). Make sure the dots are in line with the weave of the material, then baste the transfer in position along the top. Iron over the transfer with a warm iron, or a cool one if the fabric is very delicate, or a synthetic. Then remove the transfer. If your fabric is spotted, checked or striped you may not need the transfer

and the fabric can be drawn up by counting out
regular points on the pattern, however it may
have to be gathered up on the right side if the
design is not printed on both sides of the fabric.

Having transferred the dots and removed the
transfer, start gathering up the work. Use a
strong thread of a suitable weight for the fabric
and a separate length for each line of gathering.
It is easier if you use a colour which contrasts
with your fabric. Each dot *must* be picked up in
the needle. Start at the right-hand side with a
knot and a back stitch to make it secure, then
put the needle in one side of every dot and bring it
out at the other, carry the thread to the next dot

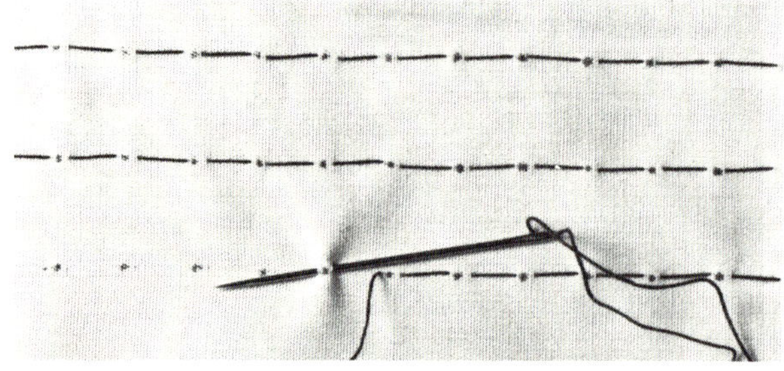

and continue to the end of the row, taking care
you put the needle in each side of the dot and not
through the middle. Leave the thread loose at the
left-hand side. When all the lines have been
threaded with the running thread, pull up the
work carefully to the required width. If you are
making very deep gathers, pull up a few at a time.
Tie the loose ends of the gathering threads in

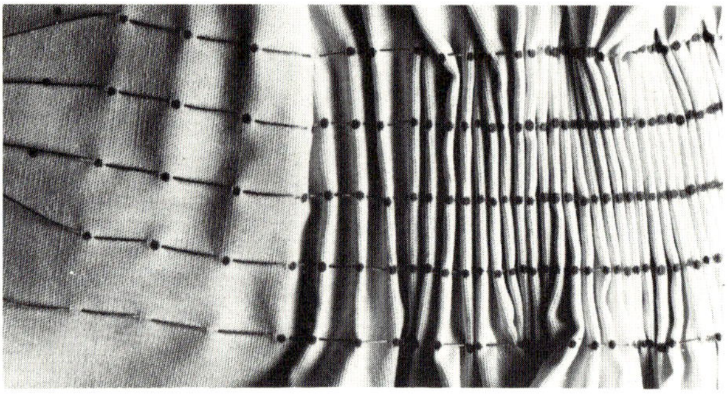

pairs, or if you prefer, the loose ends may be
secured by twisting them round pins. Turn the
work to the right side and even out the gathers.
The gathering threads are never removed until
all the work is complete.

The fabric is now ready to be smocked on the
right side, unless it is likely to fray badly. If so,
machine stitch or whip raw edges by hand first.
Before starting to smock, plan the design carefully; a true sense of balance between the different types of stitches should be maintained. Try
to avoid monotony by interspersing straight
stitches with those which form a diamond
pattern and do not overcrowd the work – never
be afraid to leave a blank line here and there.
Do not pull the smocking stitches too tightly
when working the design, otherwise you will
close up the pleats and lose the elasticity.

STITCHES

Cable stitch

Secure threads on first pleat at left-hand side.
This stitch is worked over two pleats by catching
up one pleat with the needle, the thread being
alternately above and below the needle.

Chevron stitch

This is sometimes known as **baby wave stitch,**
when worked in a single row, or **baby diamond
stitch,** when worked as two rows to form a
diamond pattern.

Work from left to right, as shown in diagram 1.
Begin with needle to the left of first pleat. Take
stitch straight across first and second pleats,
with thread below needle. Bring needle out to
left of second pleat, above stitch just made.
Keeping thread below needle, take next stitch
across third pleat but insert needle on gathering
line above. Bring needle out to left of third pleat.
With thread above needle, stitch over third and
fourth pleats, bringing needle out to left of fourth
pleat, below stitch. Now take thread back down
to lower line and stitch across fifth pleat, bring
needle out to the left of it. Continue in this way.
Diagram 2 shows a second row of chevron stitch
worked in reverse to form a diamond pattern.

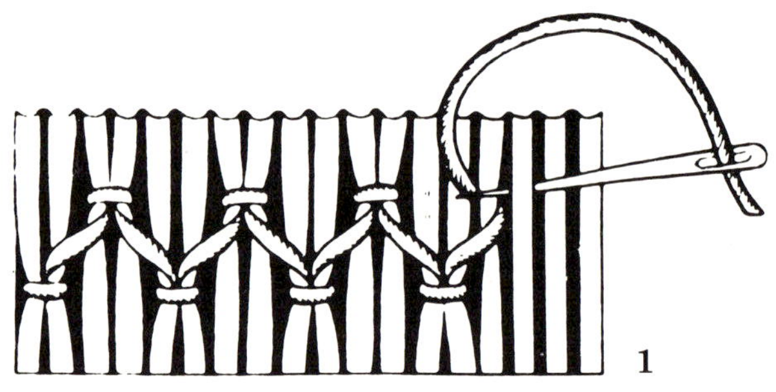

Double cable stitch

Work two rows of cable stitch close together, but for each stitch on the first row where the thread was above the needle work stitch immediately below it, on the second row, with the thread below the needle. Similarly for each stitch on the first row where the thread was below the needle, work the stitch below with the thread above the needle.

Honeycomb stitch

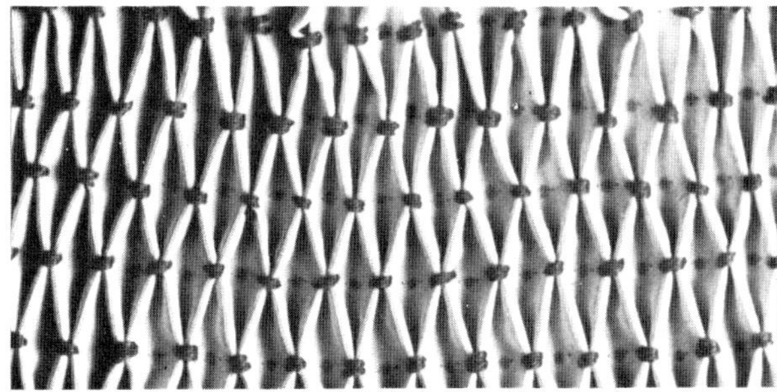

This smocking stitch is used where gathers have to be held together, but a definite design is not required. It also differs from other smocking stitches in that most of the thread is hidden in the folds of the fabric, and in fact only shows at the point where gathers are drawn together. Other smocking stitches are worked on the surface of the gathers. Traditionally, honeycomb stitch is worked with thread just a shade lighter or darker than the fabric, but it looks equally effective worked with a boldly contrasting thread – white fabric, for instance, looks attractive smocked with red thread, or cream fabric with orange. To work honeycomb stitch, bring needle through at the top line of first pleat and work a back stitch over it and second pleat, drawing them together. Work a second back stitch, then take needle down at the back of the second pleat to the lower line of gathering threads, bring it

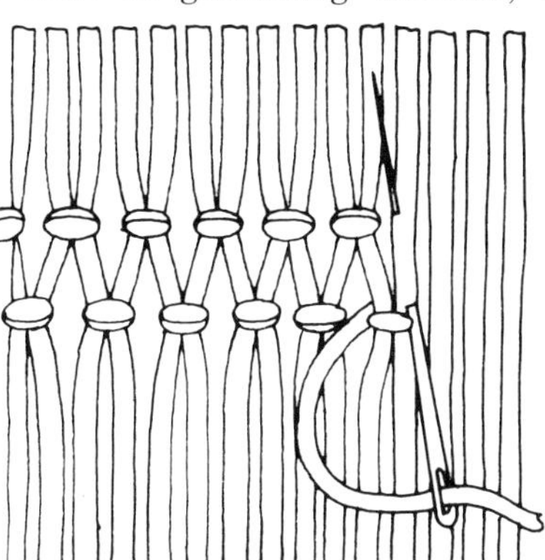

through and work another double back stitch this time over second and third pleats. Take needle up at the back of the third pleat to upper line and work a double back stitch over third and fourth pleats. Continue in this way. Always have the thread above the needle for the top level stitch, and below the needle for lower level stitch.

Mock chain stitch

This consists of one row of outline stitch worked close to one row of stem stitch to form a chain-like effect.

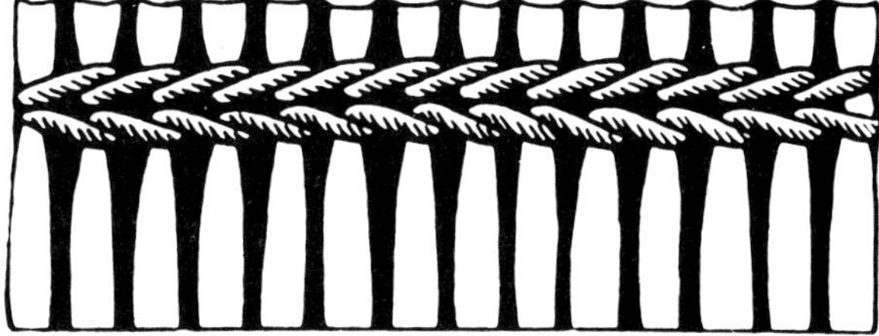

Outline stitch

Secure thread at left-hand side of work, and bring the needle through to the left of the first pleat. Pick up top of the next pleat, inserting the needle with a slight slant and having the thread above the needle. Continue in this way.

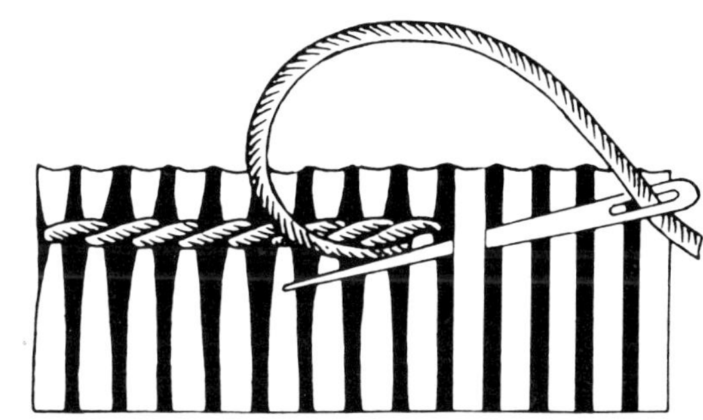

Stem stitch

Work from left to right, with the thread over two folds of fabric, but pick up only the top of one fold with the thread always kept below the needle.

Surface honeycomb stitch

This is sometimes known as **turret** or **vandyke stitch.** Bring the needle through on first pleat at lower level. Draw the needle horizontally through the second pleat keeping the thread below the needle. With the thread still below,

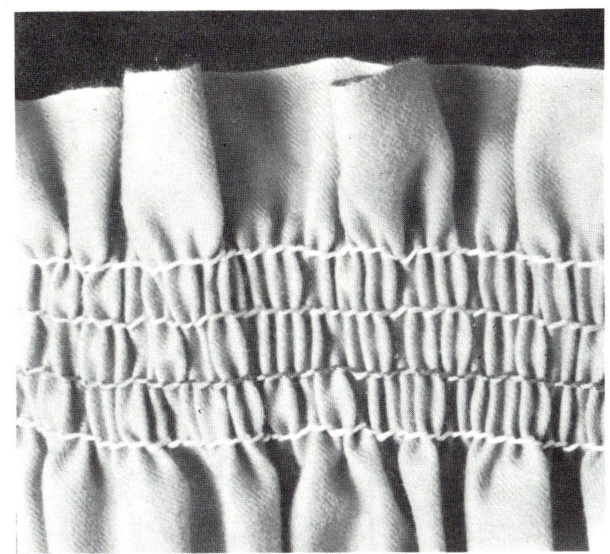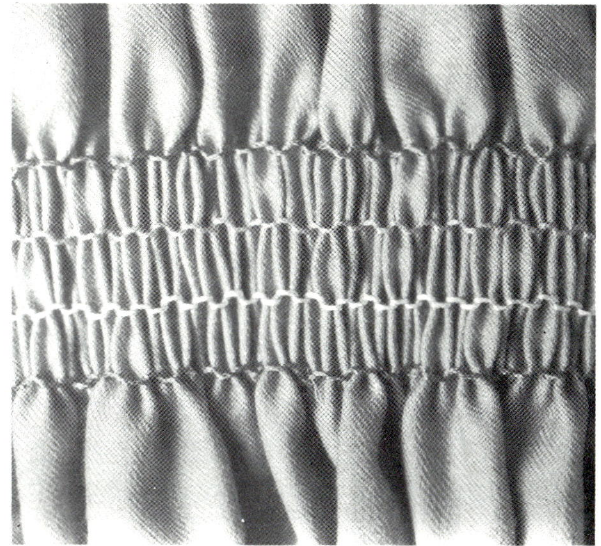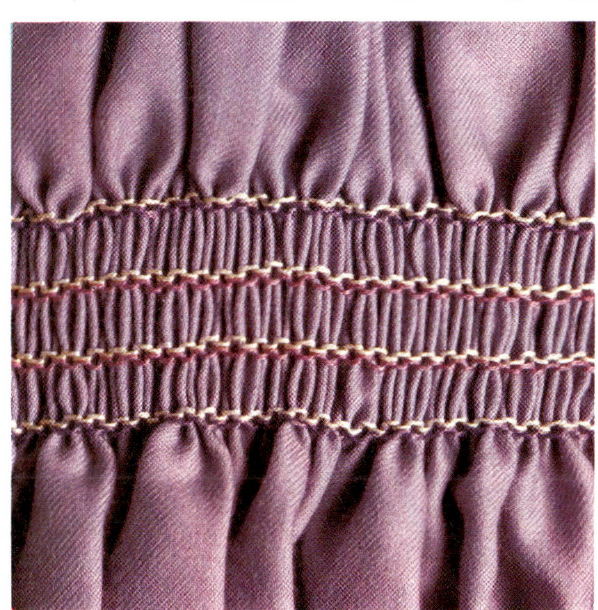

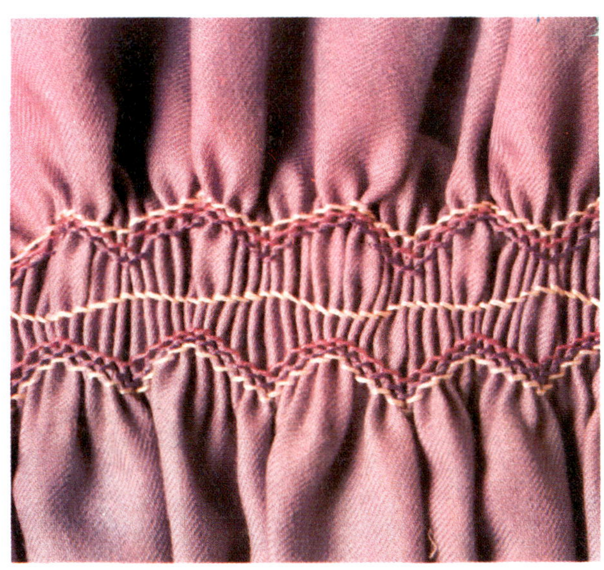

*Traditional smocking stitches (see page 250).
Top row, left to right: outline stitch; cable
stitch. Second row: double cable stitch. Left:
three rows of wave stitch, followed by a row of
outline stitch, followed by another three-row band
of wave stitch, with colours in reverse order to the
first band. Opposite: a sample showing how a
variety of different stitches can be effectively
combined in the same piece of work (see page 250
for working instructions).*

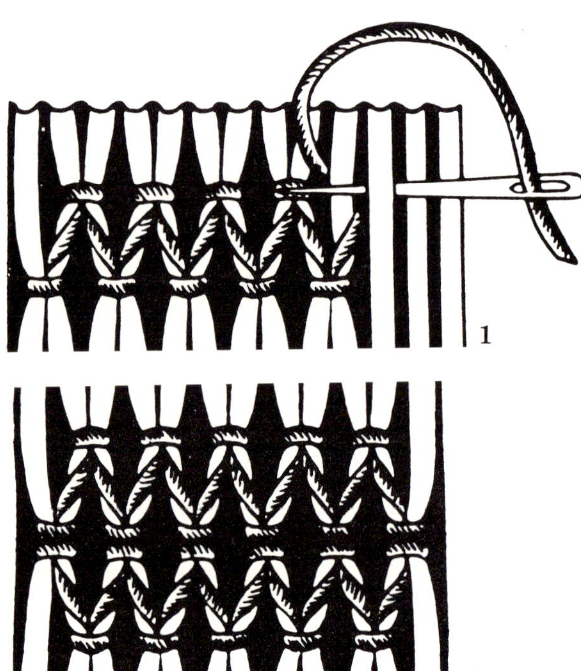

insert the needle horizontally through the same pleat on top level. With the thread above the needle, insert horizontally through third pleat on top level, and still with thread above, insert the needle through the same pleat on lower level. Continue in this way. Diagram 1 shows position of needle and thread when working stitch on top level; diagram 2 shows a second row of surface honeycomb stitch worked to form a diamond pattern.

Trellis stitch

This consists of two rows of wave stitch (see below), with the second row worked in reverse to form a diamond pattern.

Wave stitch

Work from left to right. Begin with needle to the left of first pleat. Take stitch straight across first and second pleats, with thread below needle. Bring needle out to left of second pleat above stitch just made. Continue in this way until sixth pleat is reached. Have thread above needle for this stitch and bring needle out to left of sixth pleat, just below stitch. Work downward slope to correspond with upward.

FINISHING THE WORK

It should not be necessary to press smocking, but if you feel the embroidery would be improved by a very light pressing, the finished work can be placed face down on an ironing board or thickly-padded table, place a damp cloth over the back of the smocking and pass a warm iron very lightly over it, but do not press flat.

Remove the gathering threads by cutting the knot and back stitch at the side of the work very carefully so as not to damage the fabric, then cut the tied ends (or remove pins) and draw out the gathering threads one by one. Take care not to drag at the gathering thread as it may be caught up in one or two places. The transfer dots may still be noticeable, but usually come out at the first washing.

When you wash the garment, treat it carefully. While the garment is still damp, pull the gathers firmly back into place, and if possible dry flat so the weight of the water does not pull the work out of shape. If necessary, place a damp cloth over the back of the smocking and pass a warm iron lightly over it. Never iron smocking flat.

If smocking becomes stretched with constant wear and washing, it is sometimes possible to restore the shape by whipping the back of the pleats with two or three rows of fine elastic thread.

SOME SAMPLES OF SMOCKING STITCHES
illustrated on pages 248 and 249

All our samples are worked in stranded embroidery cotton, using three strands of cotton. Samples 1–5 each show traditional stitches, suitable for use on any type of garment. Many of these may be combined in the one piece of work.

Sample 6 shows how a variety of stitches may effectively be combined in one piece of work. This is worked on a patterned soft wool fabric, with cream, pink, mauve, light and dark green threads. Stitches, from top to bottom, are as follows: cable stitch in cream; surface honeycomb stitch in pink; outline stitch in cream; cable stitch in light green; bars in dark green – this is simply oversewing two pleats together, by bringing the needle up from the wrong side of the fabric and then stitching over and over the pleats to the required depth; cable stitch in light green; chevron stitch in mauve; outline stitch in cream; two rows of wave stitch, one pink, one mauve; and finally a row of cable stitch in green.

CHILDREN'S DRESSES
Guide to thread quantities

Age	Rows of smocking	Skeins of cotton
1–2 years	11–13	4–5 skeins
3 years	13–15	6 skeins
4 years	17–21	8 skeins
5 years	23–25	9 skeins
6 years	26–27	10 skeins
7–8 years	29–31	12 skeins
9–10 years	31–33	14 skeins

A PATTERN

Smocked dress with sleeves

MATERIALS
Of Clark's Anchor Stranded Cotton (USA J. & P. Coats Deluxe Six Strand Floss) — 2 skeins Periwinkle 0119/606, 1 skein White 0402. Pattern for a child's dress suitable for smocking and preferably with a high, round neck and three-quarter length sleeves. Deep rose pink fine wool or other similar fabric — amount quoted in the pattern. A Milward 'Gold Seal' crewel needle No. 6.

STITCHES
Stem; chevron; cable; wave.

DIAGRAMS *(see page 252)*
Diagram A gives a guide to rows of gathers in actual size.
Diagram B shows a section of smocking which is repeated across the fabric. The dotted lines at the left-hand edge indicate the rows of gathers and show the placing of smocking stitches in relation to these rows. The broken vertical lines indicate the folds formed when the gathering threads are drawn up.

TO MAKE

Note. Use 3 strands of cotton throughout.
Cut out dress using paper pattern. Trace the dotted section as given in diagram A on to wrong side of bodice front section. ¾ in. in from top and side edges. Repeat section across width of fabric the number of times required for the dress size you are making, ending ¾ in. from other side.
Following instructions on page 246, gather work on wrong side, using a new thread for each line of dots. Draw up threads, easing gently to form pleats. Do not pull too tightly. Now work smocking stitches following diagram B and stitch and colour key. Do not pull stitches too tightly as the finished work must have elasticity.

TO COMPLETE

Place smocking on an ironing table wrong side up, and cover with a damp cloth. Pass a hot iron lightly over it — do not press. This sets the smocking. Remove all gathering threads and make up dress as instructed in the pattern.

Diagram A

252

Diagram B **Diagram C**

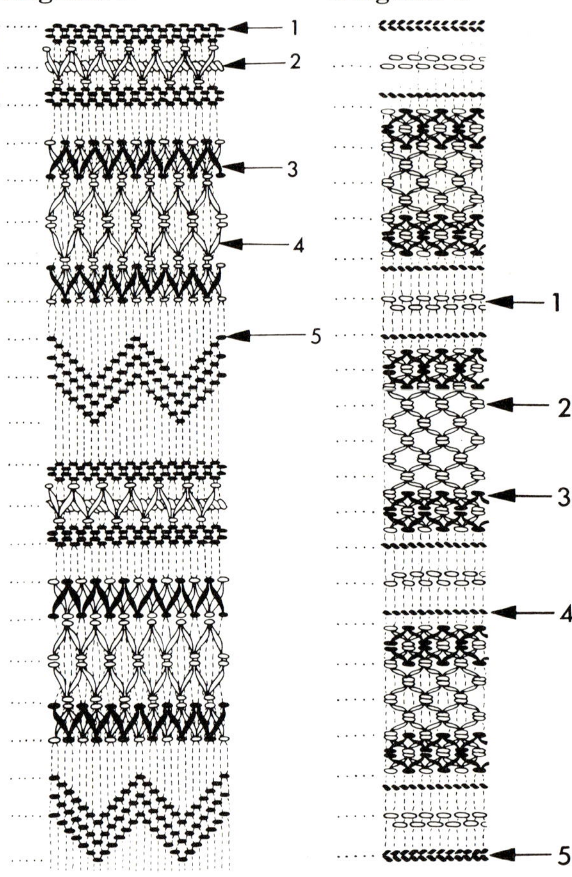

STITCH AND COLOUR KEY (B)
Dress with sleeves

1 Periwinkle   Cable stitch
2 White   Stem stitch
3 Periwinkle   Chevron stitch
4 White   Chevron stitch
5 Periwinkle   Wave stitch

STITCH AND COLOUR KEY (C)
Sleeveless dress

1 Cream   Cable stitch
2 Cream   Chevron stitch
3 Cornflower   Chevron stitch
4 Cornflower   Stem stitch
5 Cornflower   Mock chain stitch

PATCHWORK

Party stole has honeycomb patchwork borders and motifs.

A rag bag—plus needle and thread—are, in essence, the only raw materials necessary for the beautiful, traditional craft of patchwork. And no special stitches are needed either—just 'plain' sewing.

A beginner would do better to try out the more conventional geometric patchwork formulae first, and learn how to create pleasing designs with these shapes before moving to freer expressions.

FABRICS TO USE

Although most types of fabric – with the exception of very sheer and flimsy fabrics – can successfully be used for patchwork, the golden rule to remember is never to mix different weights of fabric in the same design. And if you are likely to want to wash the finished piece, then all the fabrics chosen should have similar washable finishes. Other fabrics which it is best to avoid are those which stretch out of shape easily, and those which fray.

The best fabrics are the 'stable', crisp ones: cotton is ideal especially as it is available in such a wide range of weights, textures and patterns. Linen is good too; some man-made fibres can be used successfully, but it is best not to combine them with natural fabrics. Velvet can give a wonderfully rich patchwork; wool and wool mixtures also are suitable, and pure silk, although it does need special care in the cutting and sewing, looks luxurious. Leather and suede are good for making patchwork belts, bags and waistcoats, and have the added advantage of not requiring paper shapes – the fabric is sufficiently stiff not to require this extra stabilising.

TEMPLATES

When patchwork first began to be designed on geometric lines, the shapes which were most used were those which could be easily produced by simple folding of the fabric – e.g. squares, rectangles and diamonds. But when patchwork became more complicated, and the traditional hexagonal shape was devised, it was not so easy to produce regular, even hexagons 'free hand', and so a template was invented: a rigid shape which was used as a pattern over and over again to cut out the fabric patches.

It is possible nowadays to buy plastic or metal templates in a variety of different shapes and sizes, but you can quite easily construct your own from strong, rigid card to suit your particular patchwork requirements. Ideally, for every shape you will have a pair of templates: a solid template, and a window template. The solid template gives the actual size and shape of finished patch; the window template is $\frac{1}{4}$ in. larger on all edges than the solid template, and has the centre area (equal to the solid template) removed. The solid template is used for cutting out the paper linings; the window template is used for cutting the fabric pieces – it can be moved around on the

fabric in order to select a pleasing area of pattern. The extra $\frac{1}{4}$ in. on all edges gives a sufficient allowance for turnings.

The best shapes to start with are the hexagon and the diamond, and a pair of templates for each of these shapes is on page 258. These can be traced off and used to make templates, or if you wish a larger or smaller shape then follow these outlines as guides. The diamond shape can be easily adapted to give a triangle shape if required.

To make a hexagon of a specific size you will need a pair of compasses with a pencil. Use the compasses to draw a circle with a radius equal to each side of the hexagon you wish to construct. Set the compass point anywhere on the circumference of the circle and keeping the same radius on the compasses, mark off a point on the circumference. Now place the compass point at this mark, and mark off another point on the circumference. Continue in this way until six marks have been made on the circumference. Use ruler and pencil to join these points together, and you have your hexagon shape. Cut it out carefully. This gives you a solid template. To make the matching window template, place the solid template on another piece of card and draw carefully round it. Remove solid template, draw another outline outside the first, $\frac{1}{4}$ in. from it all the way round. Cut out on this line, then carefully cut away the centre area.

Other popular traditional shapes: square, rectangle, scale or clamshell, pentagon, octagon, coffin and church window. Different shapes can be used in conjunction with each other to give different design motifs. Octagons used together create areas which have to be filled by squares. Before you start cutting patches from fabric, it is a good idea to cut a variety of paper patches and experiment with these to find an arrangement which pleases you.

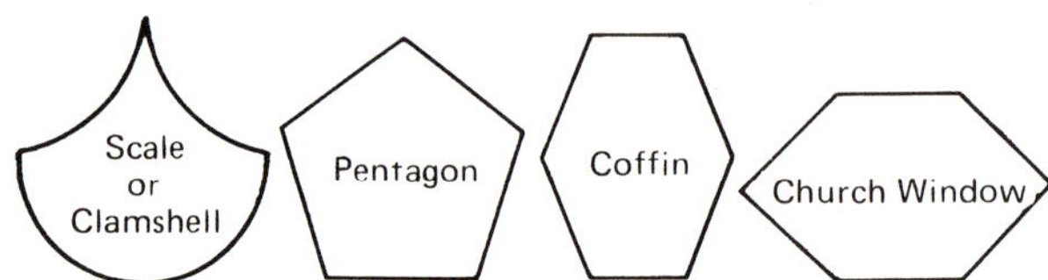

YOU WILL ALSO NEED . . .

Sewing needles and thread to suit the weight of fabrics being used. Pins – good-quality, steel ones are best as they will not mark the fabric. Scissors – two pairs: one for cutting out the fabric shapes, one for cutting the paper linings, both should be well-sharpened and pointed. Paper for making the linings – made do with whatever you can find in the house: old Christmas and birthday cards are ideal as they are fairly stiff. Tailor's chalk, a dressmaker's chalk pencil or an ordinary, well-sharpened lead pencil to mark out patchwork shapes on wrong side of fabric.

CONSTRUCTING A PATCHWORK FABRIC

Although most forms of embroidery depend for their finished effect on neat and careful sewing, with patchwork the primary requisite is accuracy. If each individual patch in a design is not absolutely symmetrical and identical to its neighbour the whole piece will appear 'amateurish' and slipshod. And accuracy begins with cutting the paper lining for each patch absolutely exactly to the right size and shape.

Just as different weights of fabrics should not be combined in a single piece of work, neither should different weights of paper linings. The papers are used to give crispness and stability to the fabric patches, so sewing is easier. The papers are in fact removed afterwards but even so if different weights and thicknesses of paper are used, this will show in the finished design – some fabric patches may appear a different size to others, puckering may appear in the sewing together, and working with different weights of lined patches will not be particularly easy.

If wished, patches may be lined with non-woven interfacing instead of paper, in which case it is not necessary to remove the linings afterwards.

Using your solid template, place it on the paper you are using for lining, and cut carefully round outside edges of template cutting as close to the edges as possible. Continue in this way to cut the number of paper linings required – linings can be cut from double thickness paper, but never try to cut more than two at once otherwise some are bound to be inaccurate.

When the paper linings are cut, use window template to cut fabric patches. If you are using a patterned fabric, move the template about on the right side of the fabric to find a pleasing area of pattern and then, on the wrong side of fabric, mark out the outline of the template, using chalk, chalk pencil or a lead pencil. Cut out on this line. Continue in this way to cut out the number of fabric patches required.

If you are not using a template (cutting squares or rectangles perhaps) then remember to add $\frac{1}{4}$ in. to all edges for turnings. The next step is to combine the fabric patches with their paper linings. Lay the fabric patch right side down on a clean flat surface, then place paper lining centrally on top of it. Fold down turnings on top of the paper, tucking in corners neatly and pin to hold in place. Now baste turnings in place, being sure to take basting stitches across tucked-in corners; remove pins.

To sew the lined patches together, place the first two patches right sides together, and using a thread to match or contrast with the fabric colour (or if you want to make a special feature of the stitching then use white or black thread) sew the patches together with a fine oversewing or edge-to-edge stitch. Take care not to catch papers in with the stitching. Continue to sew patches together to form design and shape required. If you are making a big or bulky item, then it is usually best to sew patches together in groups, then combine the groups later to avoid having a very heavy piece of work in progress for a long time.

FINISHING TOUCHES

When all your patches are sewn together, carefully remove basting, then press work on the wrong side using an iron setting to suit the fabrics. Now very carefully remove all the paper linings – if these are removed with care they can be kept and used again for another design.

It is usual to line the back of your finished patchwork with a plain-coloured fabric in a weight to suit the fabrics used for the patches. It is also possible to interline a patchwork design, and then work quilting on it to give a superb, quilted patchwork bedcover.

SOME TRADITIONAL PATCHWORK PATTERNS

The easiest design to start with is random patchwork which is, as the name suggests, a random arrangement of different colours and patterns. It is possible however to combine effectively a number of plain and patterned patches so design shapes of groups of patches are created. Or even in a random design by a careful arrangement of strong colours against muted colours the strong colours can be used to form highlights against a background.

After you have cut out your fabric patches, try arranging them on a flat surface, moving them around, and putting them in groups until you find a design arrangement which pleases you. Textures can also be effectively contrasted in patchwork – heavier fabrics such as corduroy and tweeds can be arranged to create an attractive and elegant design.

Hexagon or honeycomb. This is probably the most well-known patchwork pattern, and consists entirely of hexagon patches, arranged either in a random style, or grouped in different colours or patterns. See stole illustrated on page 253. Also see illustration on page 260.

One traditional arrangement is to surround a dark-coloured patch with six light ones (not necessarily all of same colour or pattern, but light in terms of colour effect). In the angles formed on the outside of the light patches, sew dark patches. Continue in this way.

Diamond. Also a very popular pattern. One effective arrangement is to alternate rows of dark-coloured diamonds with rows of light-coloured diamonds. Alternatively, four similar diamonds can be stitched together to form one

Elegant long skirt with jewel patchwork hem border (see below).

very large diamond; continue to arrange patches in groups of four then sew large diamonds together, alternating light and dark.

Mosaic. There are various forms of this traditional pattern. Each is derived from combining different patchwork shapes. One version uses squares and triangles; another uses two different sizes of church windows and squares. By arranging patches carefully in light and dark tones, a fascinating jewel-like pattern is produced.

Jewel. Another pattern using different shapes: squares, rectangles and split squares. To make the split squares (which forms the central 'jewel' part of the design) cut out a large square to size required from card. Now rule a line from the left-hand top corner to the right-hand bottom point. Rule another line horizontally across the centre. Cut down the diagonal line from the left-hand top corner to the centre of the square then cut across to the right on the horizontal line. The two pieces the square is now divided into will be the templates required for the split square. For each split square, combine a dark patch with a light one. Surround each side of the complete square with a rectangle of matching, plain-coloured, medium-toned fabric (to give the effect of a background colour). Fill in the remaining areas with small squares of assorted colours and patterns. The finished effect should give the appearance of large precious stones, set round with smaller ones, in a plain setting. Each of the large squares represents a cut stone with the light falling on it. See long skirt illustrated above.

Canadian or American patchwork. Also known as loghouse quilting, this pattern is traditionally made from several strips of ribbons, arranged to give the appearance of different kinds of wood formed into a succession of squares. The design can be simplified and worked from rectangles of fabric if wished.

Gardening apron, with patchwork flower motif (see page 258).

A PATTERN

Gardening apron
illustrated in colour on page 257

MATERIALS
1 yd. cotton fabric, 36 in. wide, in green (or colour preferred). Scraps of patterned cotton fabric for patchwork. Paper for linings. 1½ yd. cotton tape, 1 in. wide.

MEASUREMENTS
Finished apron (excluding tapes) measures 32 in. long and 24 in. wide (at widest point).

TO MAKE YOUR PATTERN
The diagram below gives the pattern you will need for the apron: 1 square on the diagram equals 1 inch. Mark out a large sheet of strong brown or white paper into 1-in. squares, then copy the pattern piece as given in the miniature diagram on to your full-size grid. Each of the squares on the miniature diagram represents one square on your paper. Copy the outlines and positions of lines, curves and angles in relation to the squares as accurately as possible. Cut out the pattern piece.

TO MAKE
Using your paper pattern, cut out the apron main piece from double thickness fabric, placing centre front edge of pattern on fabric fold as indicated. Turn in and stitch ½-in. hems on all raw edges of apron, and a 1-in. hem at lower edge.

Make patchwork
Below are the templates for diamond and hexagon shapes in actual size. Following the inner lines as a guide for the actual size template, and the outer lines as a guide for the window templates, construct your own templates from stiff card.
Using these templates, cut out ten diamond shapes (six will be used for flower petals, four for leaves) and one hexagon for flower centre. Use actual size template for cutting paper linings; window templates for fabric. Cut a strip of patterned cotton 16 in. long and 1½ in. wide for the flower stalk. Turn in and stitch a ¾-in. hem on all edges.

TO COMPLETE
Arrange shapes on apron to form flower. Baste and stitch in position. Press.

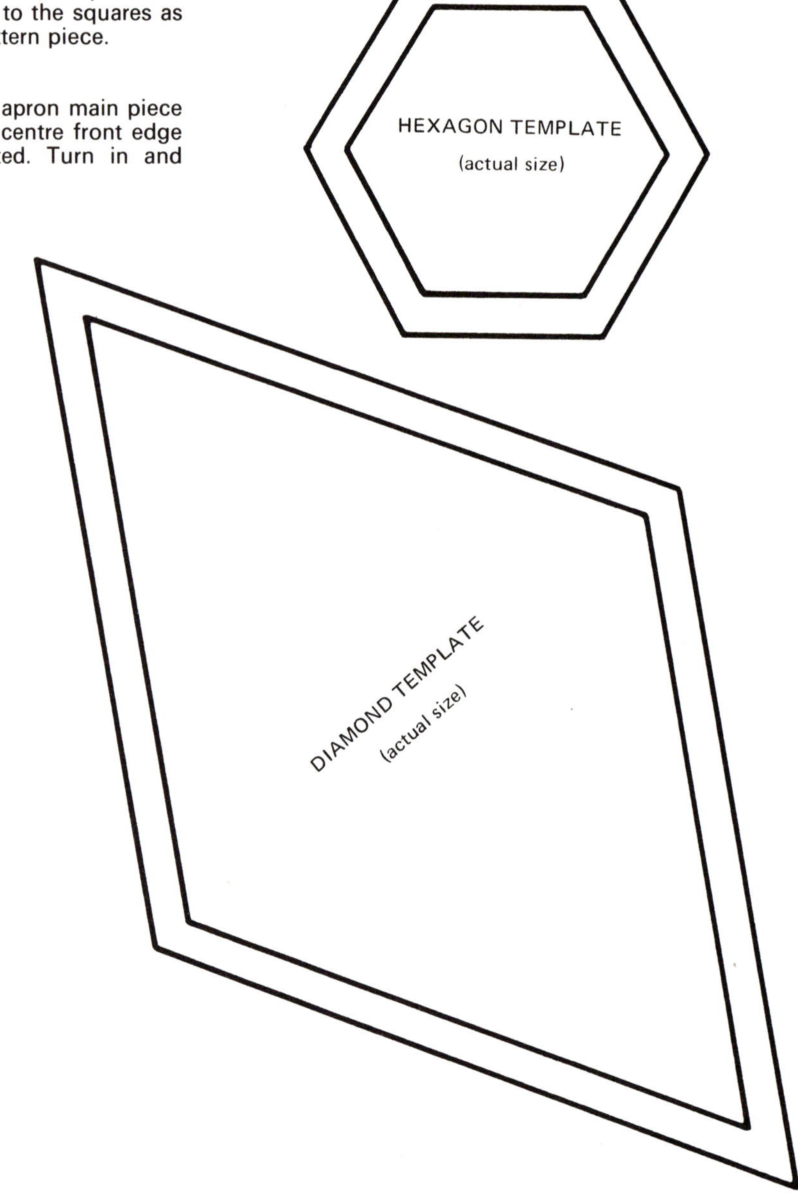

Part 7

APPLIQUÉ

Of all forms of decorative needlework, appliqué probably gives the greatest scope for original design. For this reason, beginners often shy away from the craft, preferring to work one of the more 'regimented' forms of embroidery where expression is of necessity controlled by a formalised stitching technique. And yet appliqué can be extremely simple, easy to work and still wonderfully effective.

Briefly, appliqué is created by 'applying' – hence, 'appliqué' – several fabrics to a background fabric. The applied fabrics are cut into decorative shapes and stitched in place to form a pleasing arrangement of colour and shape on the background fabric. Further interest can be added to the design with embroidery stitching used either to hold the fabric shapes in place, or merely as a surface decoration.

FABRICS

Most fabrics are suitable for background materials, depending on the sort of design you intend to create, and whether the background fabric is to be an important part of the design.

The applied fabrics again can be of many types but, as with the background fabric, they should not stretch or pucker easily, or be too bulky. Fabrics which do not fray easily are the easiest to work with – felt, plastic and leather are excellent as they are all fray-free fabrics. Other fabrics can have their edges treated in various ways (see below) to prevent fraying. In blind appliqué, the edges of all applied fabrics are turned under before the shapes are stitched to the background, so as non-fraying qualities are then not so important the choice of suitable fabrics is much wider.

THREADS

Thread can be synthetic, cotton, wool or silk depending on the fabrics being used in the design. The colour will depend on whether the stitching is to form a focal point of the design. If it is not,

YOU WILL ALSO NEED . . .

Needles to suit threads being used; good-quality rustless pins; basting thread; paper and pencil for trying out design ideas; scissors – one sharp pair for cutting out your fabric shapes, another for cutting threads; dressmaker's tracing paper, pounce, chalk, or watercolour paint and brush depending on which method you choose for transferring your designs to your background fabrics; iron-on interfacing (useful for giving extra 'body' to flimsy fabrics, and so prevent puckering); fabric glue (to treat edges of sheer fabrics); an embroidery frame, if you are working on an appliqué picture, or other large design, where it is imperative that the background fabric is kept taut.

WORKING METHODS

The first step in any appliqué is to plan your design. This is as important for a simple piece of work using only a single applied motif, as it is for a complex abstract picture. Try sketching out a rough idea of your design on a piece of paper first of all, so you can get some idea of the size and shape of the pieces you want, and their grouping and positions on the background. When you think you have established the sort of shapes you want to use – or even if you are still undecided – try cutting out shapes from paper and moving these about on your background fabric until you find a pleasing arrangement.

The next step is to transfer the design to your background. Again, even if it is only a simple design with one or two applied pieces, an accurate indication on your background of positions of the applied shapes will make working much easier. Designs can be transferred by any of the methods described on page 186. Alternatively, if you have used paper shapes to arrive at your design, then these may be pinned in place, and drawn round with watercolour paint, or with basting stitches.

If you are working on a picture, or large design, then mount background fabric on a frame – follow instructions for framing-up canvas on page 219, substituting the background fabric of your choice for the canvas. Small designs can be worked on a circular embroidery frame (see page 186).

PREPARING FABRICS

When you have established the shapes you want to use, cut them out from your fabrics – if you have used paper shapes as an initial guide, these again will come in useful for they can be used as paper patterns for cutting out fabrics. If you intend to turn in raw edges of the fabric shapes, then remember to add on an allowance for turnings to all edges – $\frac{1}{4}$ in. should be sufficient for most fabrics.

Another important point to remember when cutting out fabrics is that, if possible, the grain should run in the same direction when pieces are applied; the grain of the background fabric should also run in the same direction to avoid puckering. Ideally the grain should run downwards through all the fabrics but this may not always be possible. It is best in any case not to let yourself be too restricted by a slavish addiction to the grain-rule – otherwise the spontaneity of your design may suffer!

If the fabric is liable to fray and you are not turning in the edges, then it is advisable to oversew lightly round the edges of each shape. Alternatively, iron-on interfacing can be applied to the backs of the shapes, to give them extra

Above: *cushion cover worked in honeycomb patchwork (see Part 5, page 255). The hexagon patches are cut from plain and patterned cotton fabrics, and groups of patterned patches arranged to create separate design shapes. The dark green patches form a background framework for the pattern.*

Opposite: *some cheerful appliqué on a beach bag and a sun glasses case.*

stability; or a light coating of a fabric adhesive can be painted round the edges of the fabric, on the wrong side, and allowed to dry.

If you are working blind appliqué, run a line of machine stitching round your shape along the line where the turning is to be. This will give a clean, neat edge for turning. Clip into turnings carefully, especially on curved edges, then fold turnings to wrong side. Pin or baste to hold in place. Press if necessary.

ASSEMBLING YOUR DESIGN

Now arrange your prepared fabric shapes on your backing fabric, pin in place, then baste. If you have overlapping pieces, you can, if you wish, trim away the excess fabric from the underneath fabric, so the work does not become too bulky. Nets and similar fine transparent fabrics can be used to great effect either by partially overlapping other fabrics, or by laying a com-

plete piece of transparent fabric over the entire appliqué when other pieces are stitched in position.

When pinning pieces in place insert pins horizontally across work. When basting, take stitches slanting downwards in lines right across work. If you try to baste round each fabric shape, this tends to distort the piece and cause a 'bubble' to form in the centre. The best order to follow is to pin and subsequently baste the pieces which go at the back of the work first and work towards the front.

When basting is complete begin to stitch your fabric shapes to the background fabric. The type of stitching you use will depend on the design you are working, whether it needs to be securely fastened to withstand hard wear, and whether or not stitching is to form a decorative part of the finished design.

A straightforward stitching method is merely to take tiny, straight stitches through fabric and backing, always bringing needle up through the backing fabric, and taking it down into the applied fabric. For blind appliqué, stitch pieces in place with tiny slip stitches which will be virtually invisible in the finished design.

If the design will not have to withstand a lot of wear and tear, then various types of decorative stitching can be used to secure the applied shapes. For instance, a long piece of applied fabric (perhaps a length of lace or similar ornamental braid) could simply be secured by single stitches taken right across the width of the applied piece at regular intervals, using a thread to contrast or tone with the appliqué fabric. A circular motif could have small blanket or buttonhole stitches worked over its edge at evenly-spaced intervals.

When applied shapes are all stitched to the background fabric, further interest can if wished be added to the design by working decorative surface embroidery stitching. In one very old traditional appliqué technique, couched threads are worked round the edges of all applied pieces.

Other embroidery techniques and stitches which can be effectively used on appliqué designs are: padded satin stitch, split stitches, stem stitch, chain and detached chain stitches, French knots, cretan stitch, back stitches – and many more (see Part 1 for working instructions for these stitches). You will soon learn to recognise how a particular embroidery stitch can add interest to an appliqué design, and complement the fabric shapes and colours you have used. Beads, buttons, sequins and other small trimmings can also effectively be used.

Sometimes a design which appears somewhat weak when all the fabric shapes are stitched in place can be strengthened with the judicious use of surface stitching. On the other hand it is important to guard against overdoing a design . . . add too much, and you will end by overstating rather than understating a design idea.

If you have used a frame for your work, normally the only finishing necessary after removing basting stitches will be a light press on the wrong side. If there is slight puckering, then steam pressing should flatten out the piece. However, if the fabric is badly stretched out of true or puckered, then the whole piece will have to be thoroughly stretched. Follow instructions on page 225 for stretching canvas embroideries.

APPLIQUÉ TECHNIQUES

Inlaid appliqué. In this technique the design is worked out with great precision, then the shapes where fabrics are to be applied are cut away from the background material, and the applied fabrics carefully fitted into these holes. There is no overlap, and usually the point where the edges meet is covered with a couched thread or cord.

Whitework appliqué. As the name implies, white fabric shapes are applied to a white background fabric.

Decoupé appliqué. The principle in this work is similar to inlaid appliqué, with buttonhole or blanket stitches worked over the cut edges instead of couching.

San Blas appliqué. This technique which comes from the San Blas Islands, off Panama, is really a sort of appliqué in reverse for, instead of building up layers of fabrics, the design is created by cutting away areas of fabric. Usually worked in brightly-coloured plain cotton, the design starts with up to five or six layers of cotton placed together, and basted round the edges. Areas are then cut away to reveal the required colour beneath. Often the bottom layer of cloth is black, and in order to reach this ground colour it will be necessary in parts to cut through five layers of top fabrics.

Broderie suisse appliqué. In this, white cambric or muslin is used for the applied fabric, coloured satin or silk for the background. The muslin or cambric is first embroidered with chain stitch in a suitable pattern, and then shapes cut out and stitched in place to the background with open buttonhole or feather stitching.

Towelling motifs applied to a cotton ground.

A PATTERN

Blind appliqué border for a smock
illustrated in colour on page 264

MATERIALS
A suitable smock with yoke, in a natural calico or firm cotton fabric. Scraps of coloured cotton fabric (we used five different colours for our appliqué – bright pink, medium purple, dark purple, yellow and a pink and blue check). Transparent nylon sewing thread.

TO MAKE
The diagrams opposite give the templates you need in actual size. Using these as a guide, construct your own templates from stiff card. Using these templates, cut out fabric shapes as follows: 12 of shape A (bright pink); 12 of shape B (dark purple); 12 of shape C (checked fabric); 5 of shape D (yellow); 13 of shape E (medium purple). Turn in and baste ¼ in. round the edge of each shape. Press shapes flat.

There are two basic motifs in the border design: the

Star Motif formed from two A shapes and two B shapes; the Cross Motif formed from two C shapes, one D and one E. To arrange each Star Motif, first place the two B shapes to form an 'X' then place the two A shapes on top of the 'X' to form an upright cross, with its centre overlapping the centre of the 'X'.

To arrange each Cross Motif, first place the two C shapes to form an upright cross, then place the D shape exactly on centre of the cross, and then finally place the E shape exactly on the centre of the D shape.

Pin then baste a cross motif to the centre front of smock yoke, with a star motif on either side of the centre cross motif. Using nylon thread, and following method given opposite for stitching blind appliqué, stitch each motif to the smock.

Space the remaining four star motifs and four cross motifs evenly round hem of smock in an alternate pattern of crosses and stars. Baste then stitch in place. Stitch remaining E motifs between each cross and star motif round the hem of smock.

(Note. It may be necessary to have more or fewer motifs round hem of smock, depending on the width of the smock.)

CROSS MOTIF templates (actual size)

STAR MOTIF templates (actual size)

STAR MOTIF

CROSS MOTIF

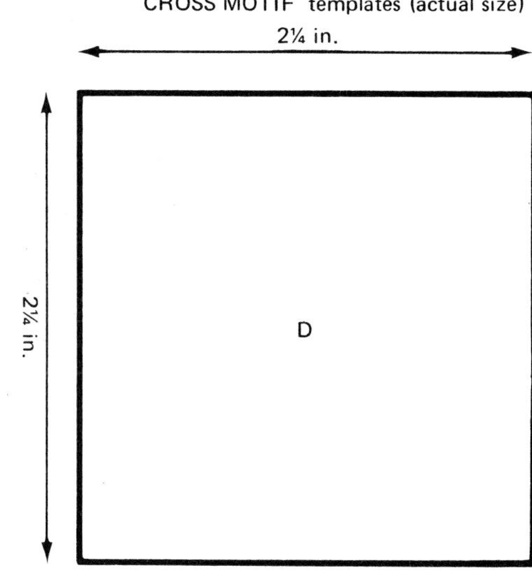

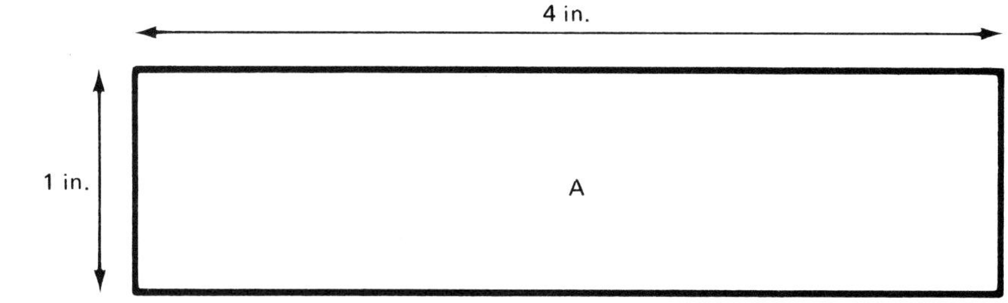

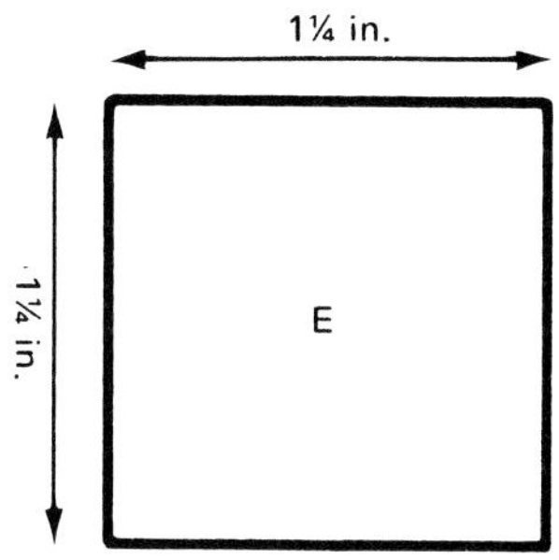

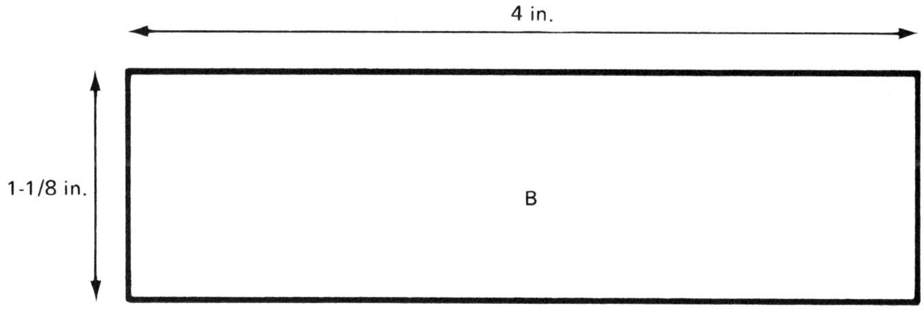

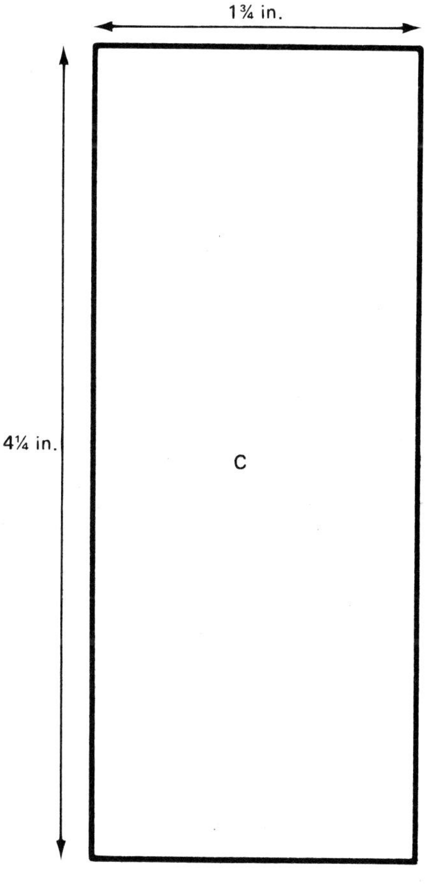

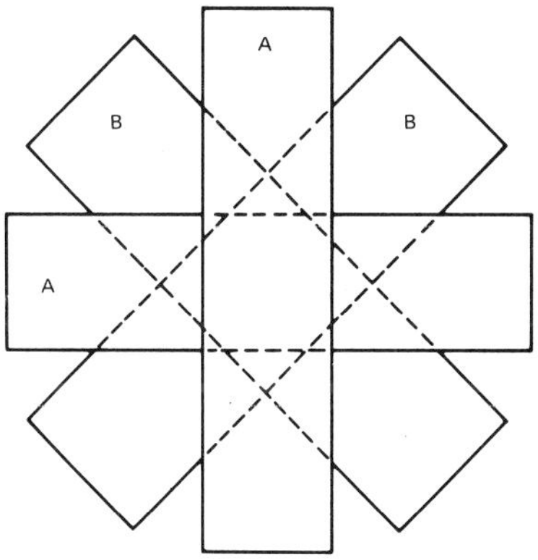

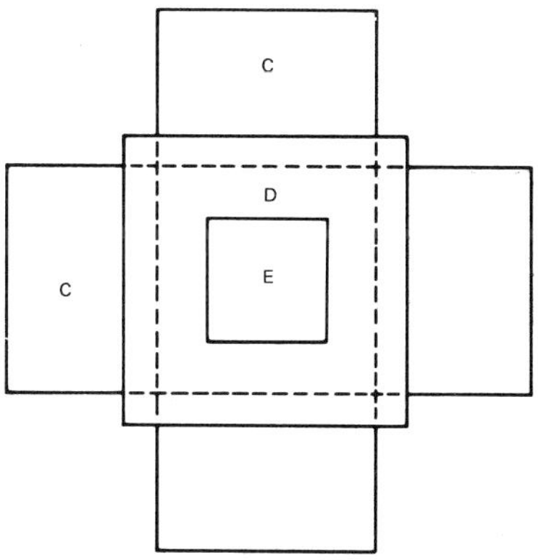

Blind appliqué border for a smock (see page 262).

Child's reversible jacket (see page 271).

Quilting is a decorative needlework which developed from a simple basic need to create a warm fabric: a layer of wool or cotton wadding was placed in between two layers of a suitable material. The stitching which held this 'sandwich' together had no more purpose originally than to prevent the filling from moving about. Then it was realised that as well as being practical, the stitching might just as well be decorative too, and so the many beautiful traditional quilting patterns were invented.

One usually thinks of quilting as a form of bedcovering – the word counterpane is derived from *contre-poinct,* a corruption of the French word for back stitch, or quilting stitch as it was also called – and perhaps for bedjackets and dressing-gowns. But the technique can equally effectively be used for attractive, heat-retaining tea and coffee cosies, for children's jackets and coats, for skirts, and all sorts of fashion accessories.

MATERIALS

If you are making an item in which both back and front will be seen then a similar 'outer' fabric should be used for both sides, but if the item is likely to be seen on the one side only, then inexpensive fabric can be used for the underside, provided it is similar in weight to the top fabric. Suitable fabrics for the top layer are satin, silk, dull satin crêpe-de-chine, and man-made fabrics which have a slightly lustrous quality – never use fabrics which are too shiny. Cotton can be used for the under layer, in a weight similar to the top fabric.

For fillings, a number of good synthetic fillings are available nowadays, or you can use cotton wadding, lamb's wool or cotton wool (the natural variety, not the medicated type sold by chemists). For thinner quilting – for a garment, for instance, where bulk is not required – then a lightweight interfacing fabric can be used. Alternatively, flannel or old, well-washed blankets are suitable.

Strong cotton, silk or synthetic thread (according to the fabric chosen) should be used in a

YOU ALSO NEED

Good-quality rustless pins – alternatively, needles are often used instead of pins as they never leave marks in even the most delicate fabrics; basting thread; a large darning needle, chalk pencil or dressmaker's tracing paper for transferring designs; two pairs of scissors, one for cutting fabrics, one for cutting threads; templates (see below); a frame – ideally a proper quilting frame should be used, but if you do not want to go to the expense of buying one, or the trouble of making one, then an ordinary, embroidery frame can be used, including the Swiss or tambour frame for small pieces of work. It is possible to work small items in the hand with care, but results are rarely as satisfactory as if the fabrics are held properly stretched and taut throughout working. If you are quilting by machine then, obviously, it will not be possible to use a frame.

PLANNING A DESIGN

The first step in any quilting project is to plan your design. This is marked out on the right side of the upper layer of fabric, and the ideal method to use is to mark out the pattern with the tip of a darning needle – this will leave a faint crease line on the fabric which can be used as a stitching guide.

Alternatively, the design can be marked out in chalk – or perhaps key points, such as the centre and the mid-points of each side, marked in chalk, with the rest needle-marked. Dressmaker's carbon paper can also be used provided you are certain the lines of the marking will be completely covered by stitching when the design is complete.

'Plain' quilting consists simply of even, regular lines across the entire area of work, thus forming diamonds, squares, or sometimes octagons. Such patterns are often known as backgrounds or fillings, and can be used as border patterns for a big design, with a more decorative pattern motif in the centre.

The important thing to remember when planning a quilting design, and combining several different pattern motifs, is that the pattern should fill the entire area of fabric. Also, the primary purpose of quilting is to hold the filling securely in place – you should never therefore have unquilted areas of more than about two square inches, otherwise the filling will tend to get displaced.

It is also important to spend time marking out your design accurately – little is worse than an uneven or non-symmetrical quilting pattern. As the edges of your fabric may not necessarily be straight, the first point to establish is the central point then measure out from this, taking care to keep straight lines even. If you use a diamond patterning as a background, and this is interrupted in the centre by a decorative pattern motif, then make sure that the diagonals on one side of the work match up with those on the other.

TEMPLATES

As with patchwork, these are an essential aid to uniform and accurate patterns. Various quilting templates are manufactured in metal and plastic and should be available from any good needlecraft supply shop. But it is perfectly easy to construct your own set of templates from stiff card. As you are likely to want a fair number of different pattern shapes, it is probably a good idea to buy one or two basic shapes, such as circle, diamond, star and rose motifs, then construct a number of others yourself.

In most cases the template gives a basic outline, which can be varied by using different arrangements of stitching lines inside the shape.

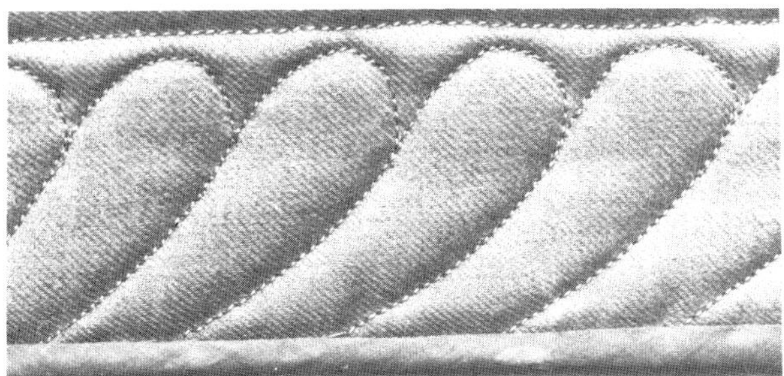

One small template can often be used to create a larger motif – for instance, the small motif shown above can be used to build up various forms of the traditional feather pattern. Several traditional template shapes are shown on page 270.

SEWING YOUR FABRIC

Once your design is clearly and accurately marked out, the next step is to combine the three-layered 'sandwich': the top fabric, the padding and the under fabric or lining. Pin the three layers carefully in position, and baste together – it is important, especially if you are not using a frame, that basting is done firmly and thoroughly. Begin by machine stitching right round outer edges so the layers will not move during stitching, then hand or machine baste across work, horizontally, vertically and diagonally so the entire surface of the work is well covered with lines of basting.

A choice of three stitches is available for the stitching of the design: chain, back or running. Chain stitch is rarely used nowadays, although the effect of working a design from the back in chain stitch can be most attractive.

Running stitch is reasonably quick and easy to do, but it is important to keep stitches and spaces absolutely uniform in length. Back stitch is by the far the firmest stitch as it forms an unbroken outline along the line of the design. If, for instance, you are using an ironed-on transfer design, then you must use back stitch if you are to cover all lines of the transfer. Whichever stitch you choose you must keep to this same stitch throughout the design.

Begin stitching in the centre of your design and gradually work outwards. If you try to work from the top down your fabric will be inclined to pucker or pull out of shape. Work each stitch individually with a positive stabbing movement to make sure stitches go through all three layers of fabric, and remain regular throughout.

If you have a quilting attachment on your sewing machine then stitching can be done by machine – follow the instructions in your machine manual.

FINISHING METHODS

When your design is completely stitched, remove all basting threads. Edges can now be neatened either by turning in the raw edges of outer and under layers and slipstitching them together, or the edges can be encased in seam binding or bias strips of matching fabric. If wished, a cord can be enclosed in the binding to give a firm outer edge – this is popular for bedcovers.

If you intend to stitch two or more pieces of quilted fabric together – to make a jacket or skirt, for instance – then leave fairly wide unquilted edges on the separate pieces. Stitch together in the usual way, using these unquilted edges as turnings. Trim away any excess padding in the turnings. If any of the lines of the quilting design do not go far enough into the seams then add a few more stitches to them.

ITALIAN QUILTING

This form of quilting, which is also sometimes known as corded quilting, is worked with only two layers of fabric, and no filling. The design is stitched in double outline, and then a thick cord or length of thick wool is threaded through this double outline so the design stands out in relief.

Work quilting from the wrong side, then cut a small hole in one channel of the design. Thread cord or wool on to a large blunt-pointed needle and carefully take this through the channel. Be careful not to catch the fabric in as you thread. Rug wool makes a good padding, or several thicknesses of tapestry wool; cotton cord is also suitable. Whichever type of cord or yarn you choose, it is important that it gives a good round padding to your design.

Although cord or wool should normally be chosen to match the fabric colour, an interesting effect can be achieved by using a contrasting colour of cord – with delicate fabrics in particular, the contrast colour will just shine faintly through the corded areas giving a new dimension to your design.

At corners of the design bring needle and cord out to the surface (on the wrong side), allow cord to form a small loop, then take it back into the next channel (see diagram below).

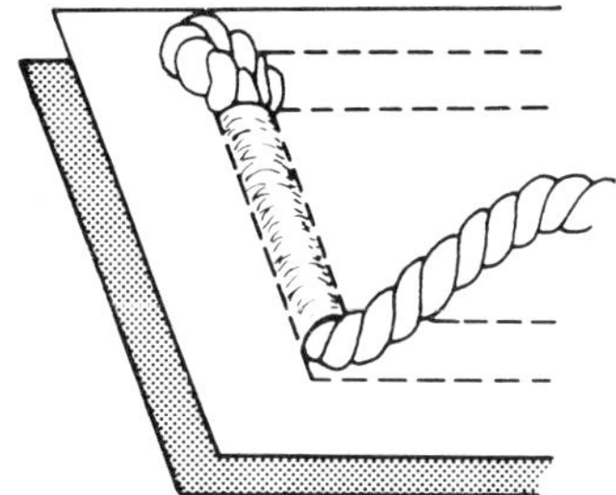

TRAPUNTO QUILTING

This, like Italian quilting, is worked with only two layers of fabric, but in this technique areas of the design are stitched with a single line of stitching, and then these areas are padded with a suitable wadding or filling.

Above: *18-century sample of quilting on linen.*

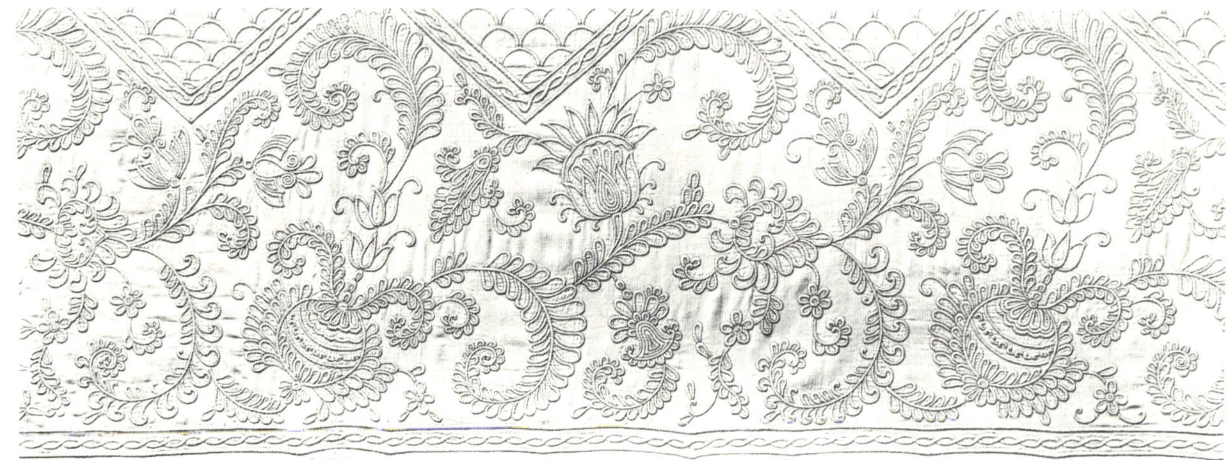

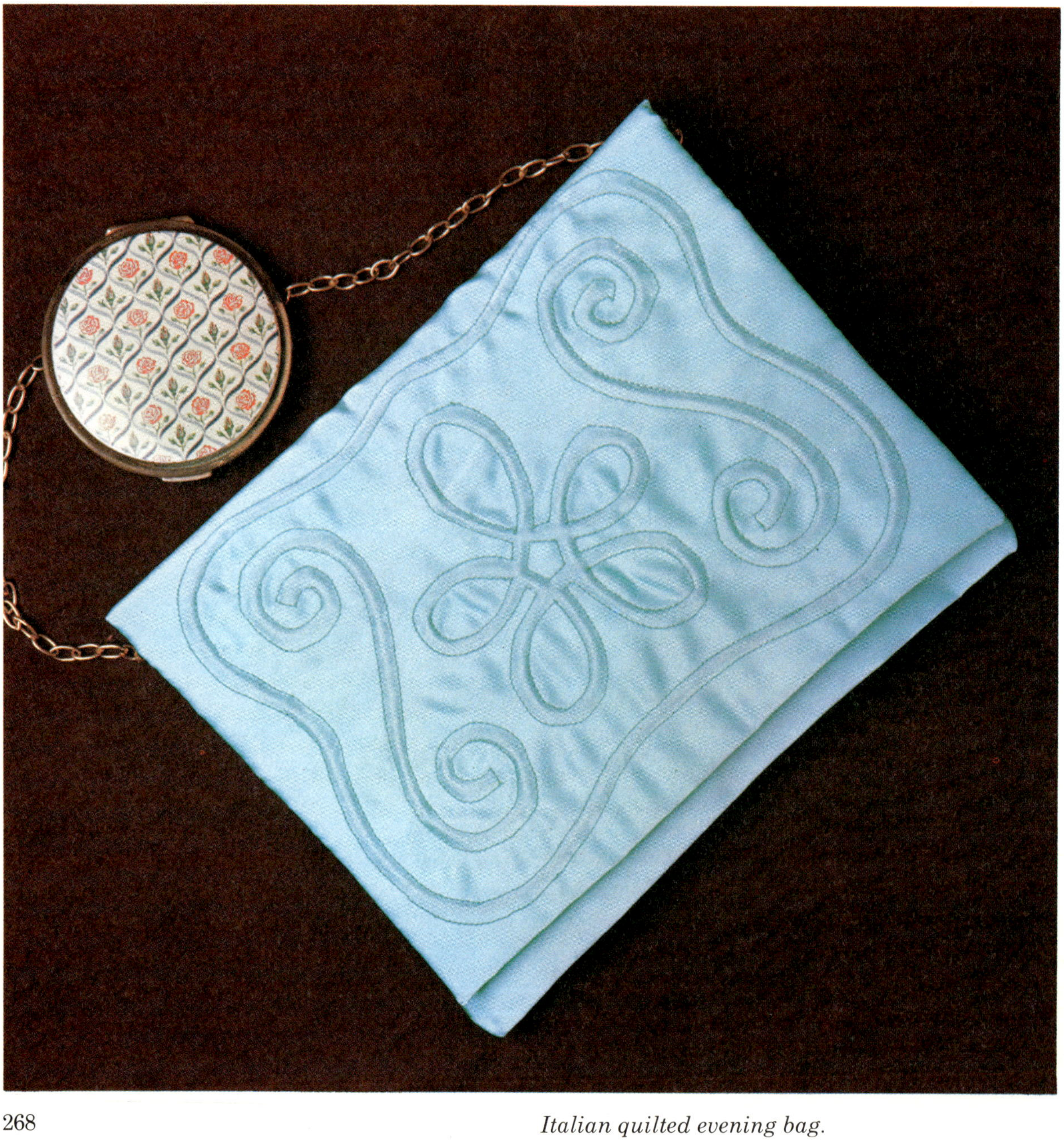

Italian quilted evening bag.

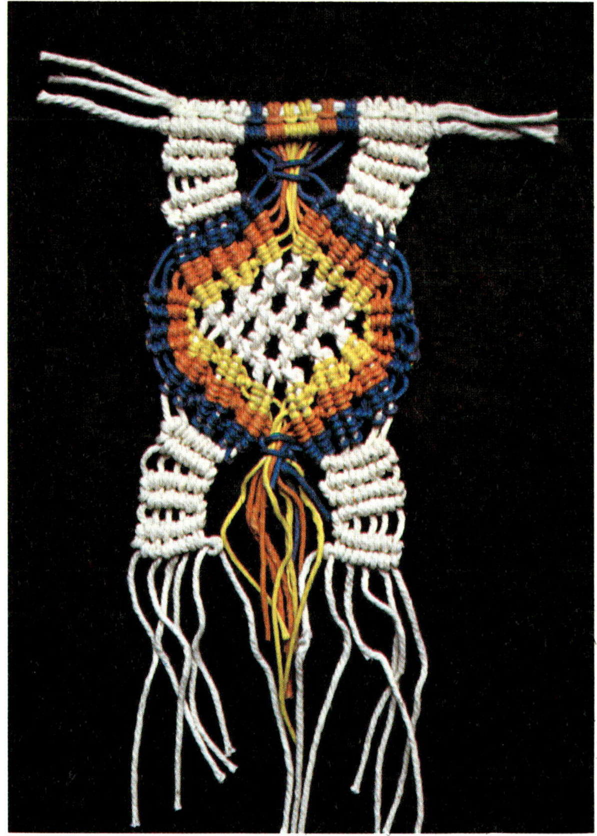

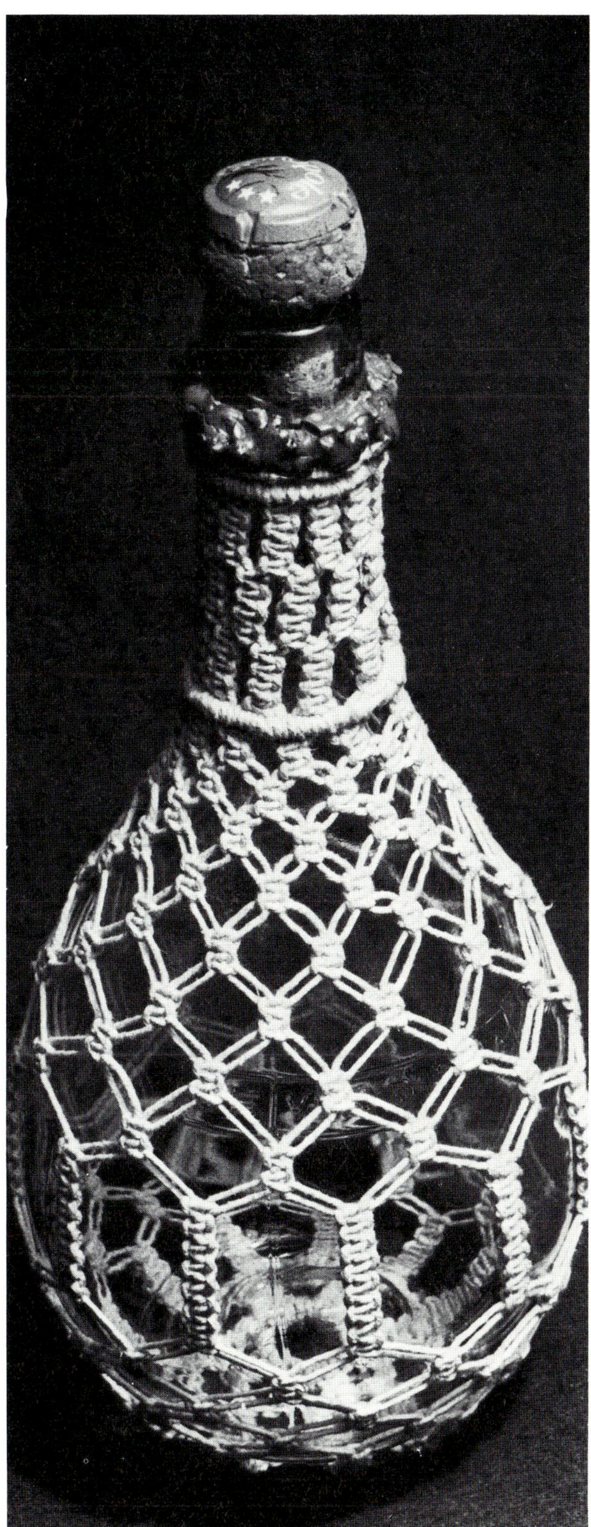

See Section Five—Macramé

Above, left: *macramé bag worked in a chunky synthetic yarn (see page 284).* **Left:** *sample of multicolour work in macramé, showing how cording takes colour from one part of the design to another.* **Above:** *bottle holder knotted in string in a pattern based on flat knots.*

QUILTING PATTERNS

All these patterns can be used in different groupings, and with different stitching arrangements within each motif. Each drawing shows the template outline in solid line; the dotted lines indicate suggested arrangements for stitching.

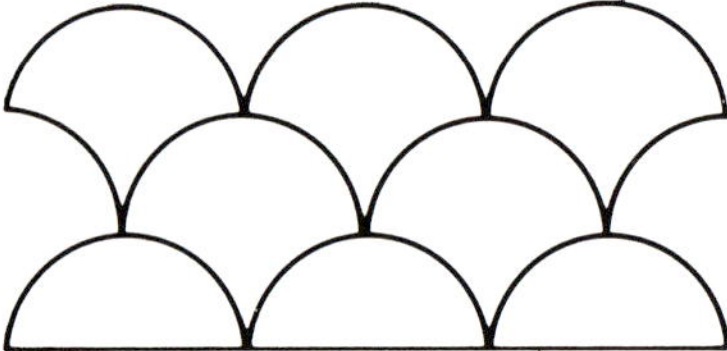

The scale – similar to the scale pattern used in patchwork.

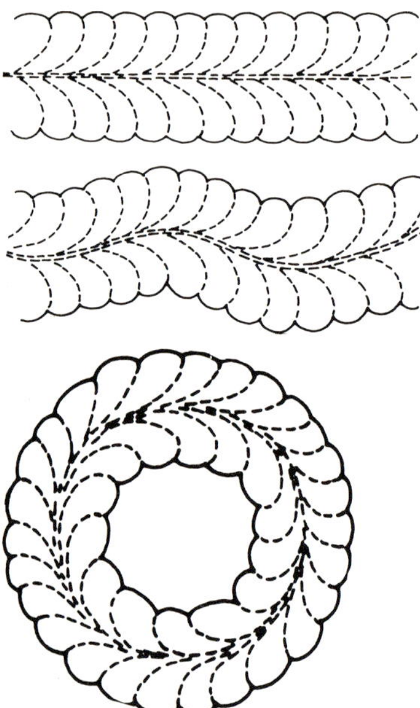

Feather – used in groups to build up complete feather patterns. Straight feather; running feather; feather circle.

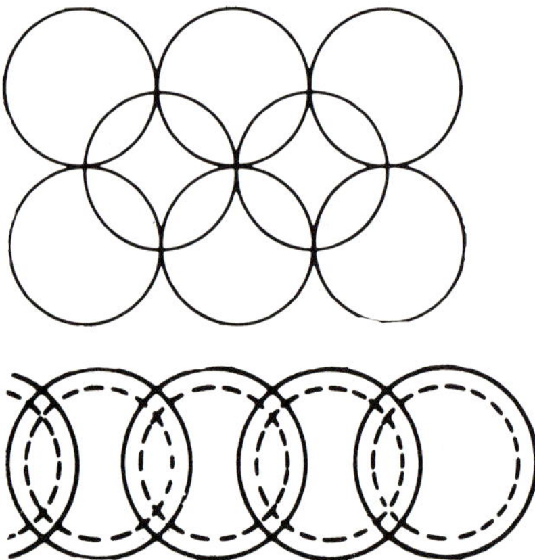

Wine glass – showing different arrangements and fillings.

Rose – showing two different fillings.

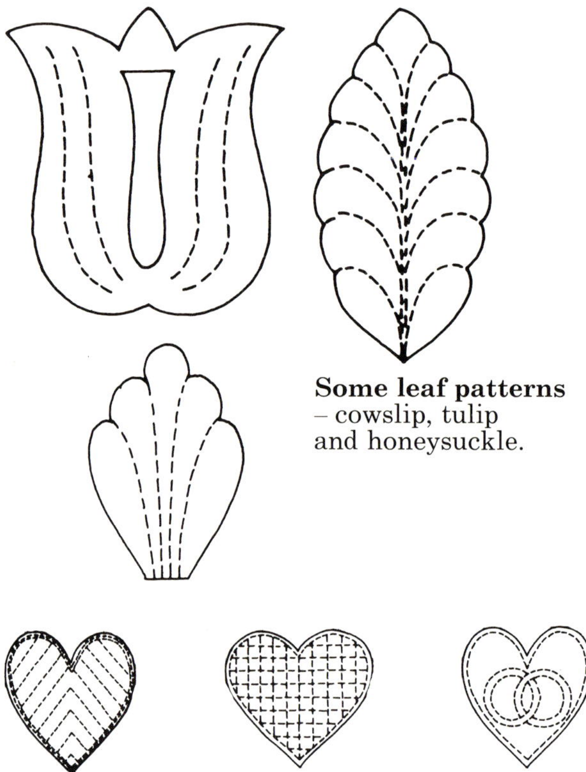

Some leaf patterns – cowslip, tulip and honeysuckle.

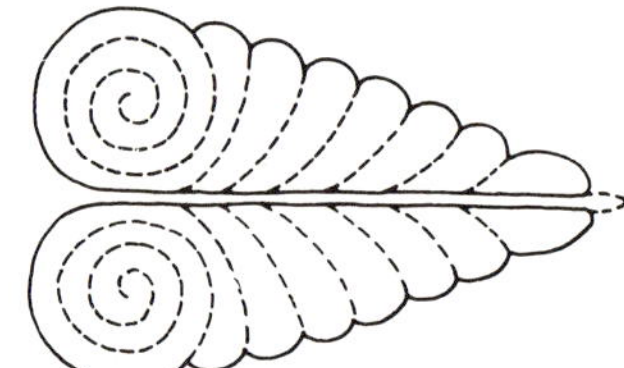

Heart – showing different fillings.

Scissors – the same template used twice, the second time in reverse, to give a pair of scissors.

Some background fillings – square diamonds, double diamonds, Victoria diamonds.

A PATTERN

Child's reversible jacket

illustrated in colour on page 265

MATERIALS

$\frac{7}{8}$ yd. soft wool fabric, 36 in. wide, in first colour (red), and $\frac{7}{8}$ yd. of a similar fabric in second colour (blue). $\frac{7}{8}$ yd. Courtelle wadding (or similar synthetic wadding). One packet bias binding tape, $\frac{1}{2}$ in. wide, to match one of fabrics.

MEASUREMENTS

The jacket is fairly loose-fitting, so should comfortably fit chest size 26–28 in.; length at centre back 16 in.

TO MAKE YOUR PATTERN

The diagram, right, gives the pattern pieces you will need for the jacket: one square on the diagram equals 1 in. Mark out a large sheet of strong brown or white paper into 1-in. squares, then copy the pattern pieces as given in the miniature diagram on to your full-size grid. Each of the squares on the miniature diagram represents one square on your paper. Copy the outlines and positions of lines, curves and angles in relation to the squares as accurately as possible. Cut out the two pattern pieces.

TO MAKE

Using your paper pattern, cut out jacket back and front pieces from both fabrics, and from the Courtelle wadding. In every case cut from double thickness fabric or wadding, placing centre back of back section to fold of fabric, as indicated on diagram.

The feather template is given below in actual size. Using this as a guide, make your own template in stiff card. Mark a vertical row of feathering down centre front opening of jacket on left and right fronts. Begin at lower edge and mark in first feather motif, then place template immediately above this first motif, so lower line of template fits exactly on top line of first motif, and with straight edge still lining up with front edges of jacket. Mark in motif, and continue in this way. At neckline edge of jacket, use only enough of the motif to fill space available. The rest of the jacket will be quilted with lines of vertical stitching, spaced $\frac{3}{4}$ in. apart. Carefully mark lines over remaining surface of fronts and back, beginning first line on fronts $\frac{1}{8}$ in. from feathering, and then spacing other lines at $\frac{3}{4}$-in. intervals.

Sandwich wadding between corresponding shapes of fabric, having one layer in first colour, and one in second. Baste firmly together (see page 267), then work quilting either by machine (see note below), or with firm back stitches. Leave $\frac{1}{2}$ in. unstitched at shoulder and side edges.

TO COMPLETE

Place jacket fronts and back together, with red sides facing. With $\frac{1}{2}$-in. turnings, stitch shoulder and side seams, only stitching red fabric. Trim turnings, and trim away wadding from seams. Turn in $\frac{1}{2}$-in. seam allowances on sides and shoulders on blue fabric, and slipstitch neatly. Make stitches as small and invisible as possible. Bind armholes, neck, centre front opening and lower edge of jacket with bias binding.

Note. This design was quilted by machine, with blue thread used in the sewing machine spool for underneath stitching, and scarlet thread for the top stitching, to match the two fabric colours used.

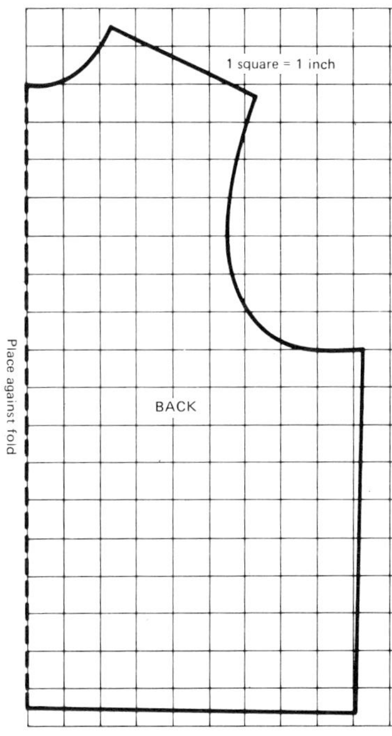

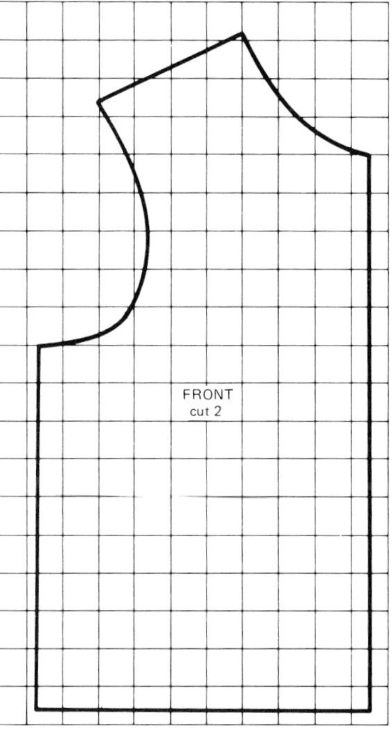

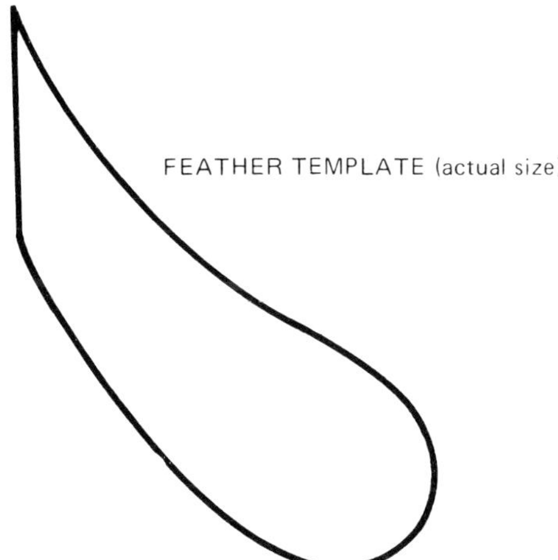

FEATHER TEMPLATE (actual size)

Chains of flat knots worked in assorted yarns, strings and cords. (See also page 269.)

Macramé is one of the newest old crafts to be revived in recent years. The basis of the craft is simply tying knots in lengths of string, rope, cord or other yarn, and by arranging knots in a decorative pattern to build up a fabric – fashion accessories, belts, bags, jewellery and dress trimmings, can be quickly and effectively made in this way, and also decorations for the home – wall hangings, cushion covers, lampshades, tablecloths, curtains, No hooks, tools, needles or other implements are necessary, so within minutes of learning to tie the two basic knots it is possible for even a child to make a simple belt, or a bag. Once a complete knowledge of knotting techniques has been acquired, and an understanding of the permutations of the basic knots, there is virtually no limit to the designs it is possible to create – just by tying knots.

Part 1—General

EQUIPMENT

Of all crafts, macramé requires the absolute minimum of equipment: all that is needed is a ball of string, a pair of scissors – and your hands. There are however various other 'aids' which will help your work along.

Yarns

Traditionally macramé has always been worked in string, or a strong linen thread, and this type of 'hard' yarn certainly gives the most satisfactory results. However it is possible to produce attractive fashion garments, for instance, using ordinary knitting yarns, in natural or synthetic fibres. Rug wool is particularly good, as it is more 'stable' than some of the finer knitting wools. Also because it is thick, knotting grows quickly. Any type of cotton yarn works well, especially piping cord, and all forms of cords, natural or synthetic. The 'harder' the yarn, the crisper will be the finished knotted fabric. Novelty yarns, such as Goldfingering, mixtures, metal threads and other similar, special-effect yarns, can also be effectively used. It is worth spending time browsing round shops and stores which sell all sorts of yarns – marine stores, for instance, often yield fascinating treasures – so do hardware departments, gardening stores, art and craft shops, and even theatrical supply stores. Part of the enjoyment of macramé work is seeking out and discovering new materials.

Pins

These are essential to control your work and to anchor it to a working surface. Ideally, use 'T' pins, or the rustless, glass-headed variety.

Working surface

Although it is possible to knot small pieces of work on your knee, you will find working a great deal more comfortable if you anchor your knotting to a rigid surface. For flat pieces of work, a working board can be easily made from a piece of soft wood (any wood which will easily take pins), or a hard wood padded with foam plastic or towelling. Cork makes a good working sur-face. A tape measure glued across the top and down one side edge of your board gives a useful, at-a-glance guide to measurements, and if you also rule out your surface into 1-in. squares this will help you keep the lines of your design straight and regular.

If you are working 'in the round', then a three-dimensional working base should be used – ideally this should be as near to the finished shape and size of the design you are making as possible as shaping will be achieved by easing knots over the surface. Cut a block of wood to the approximate size and shape required, and then pad it with foam plastic or towelling. If you are making a hat, then a wig stand gives an excellent working base.

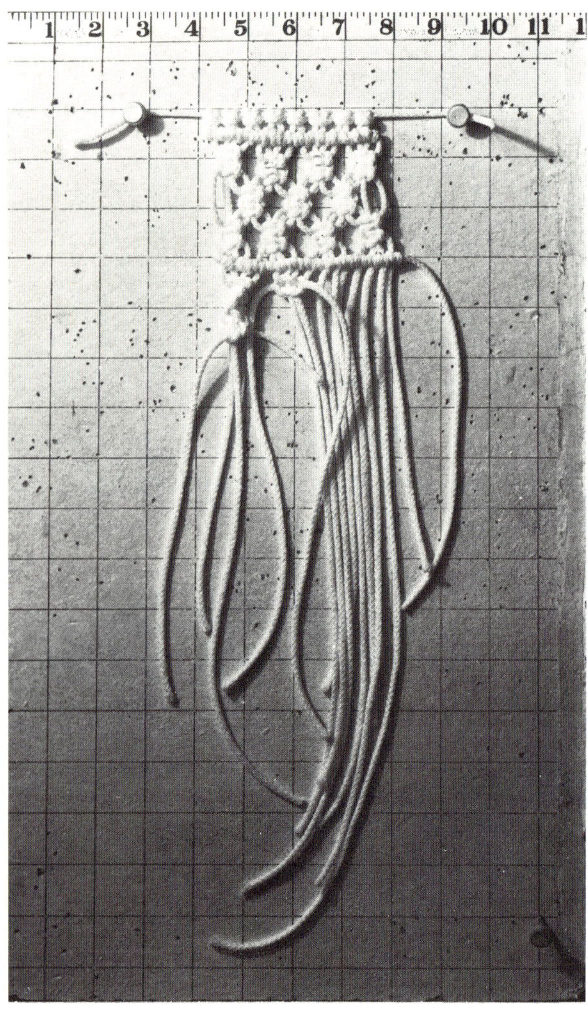

Also useful

A selection of beads, buttons and other oddments which can be incorporated in your knotting, glue and transparent self-adhesive tape for securing cord ends, drawing pins, tape measure, needle and sewing thread for making up items, or stitching cord ends to back of work.

STARTING WORK

Measuring and cutting cords

Probably the most tedious part of macramé work is the initial preparation required, before you can begin the exciting business of knotting. Contrary to most other crafts where you can launch almost straight away into creative work, and attend to making-up and neatening details afterwards, with macramé almost all the 'ground work' must be carried out at the beginning. If the details are carefully and accurately attended to first, then knotting should proceed easily and smoothly through to the finished design.

It is, for instance, difficult – and sometimes even impossible – to join on a new length of cord in mid-knotting should one length fall short. For this reason yarn has to be cut into lengths long enough to take you right through your chosen pattern. Estimating what length this should be is not always easy, as some knotting patterns use up more cord than others. As a very approximate guide however, a reasonable estimate is to cut each cord length to eight times the length you want the finished design to be. If a fringe is wanted, this measurement should then be added. For example, if you wish to make a bag to measure 12 in. deep, with a plain (unknotted) fringe of 4 in., then cords should be cut to 8 ft. 4 in. (eight times twelve, plus four). This method applies when cords are 'set on' (see below) doubled to give two working cords (the usual method). Occasionally however a pattern may instruct you to set on cords singly – in this case they need only be cut to four times the finished length required.

As you become familiar with knotting patterns and techniques you will be able to assess which knots use up a lot of cord, and which use only a little, and cut your cords accordingly. Naturally one does not wish to waste expensive yarn unnecessarily, but in the early stages it is advisable to over-estimate your needs rather than risk running short and so spoiling an attractive design.

If you have to cut a large number of cords for a particular design, it is worth measuring out the length you will be cutting against a table edge or similar surface, and marking this area. It is then a simple matter to measure out your cord lengths against the markers. To keep cords orderly and prevent tangling, group cords as you cut them into batches of ten each and tie them loosely together. This will also help to keep count of the number of cords you have cut.

Setting on cords

With your cords cut to size the next step is to mount them ready for knotting to begin. This process is usually referred to as **'setting on'**, and cords may be either set on to another length of yarn (known as a **holding cord**), or they may be set on to a metal or wooden bar or ring (for instance for a wall hanging), or on to the bar of a buckle for a belt.

To set on to a holding cord, cut a length of yarn the width of your design plus 6 in. Tie a knot near one end by taking the string over and round itself, and through the loop formed. Pull knot tight. This is an **overhand knot**. Tie a similar knot near the other end of the cord, then pin the

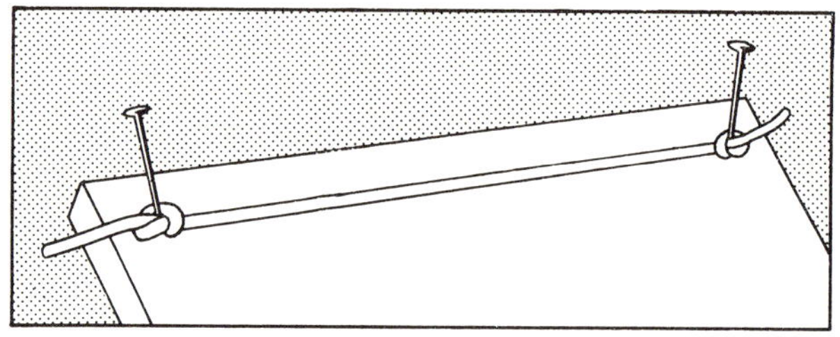

cord to your working surface, near the top, and stretching the cord as tautly as possible. Insert pins through the overhand knots.

Now you are ready to set on your cut cords: to do this, take each cord in turn, double it and insert the looped end under the holding cord from top to bottom. Take the loose ends of the doubled cord, pull them over the holding cord and down through the loop. Draw tight. Repeat with every cord until all are set on to the holding

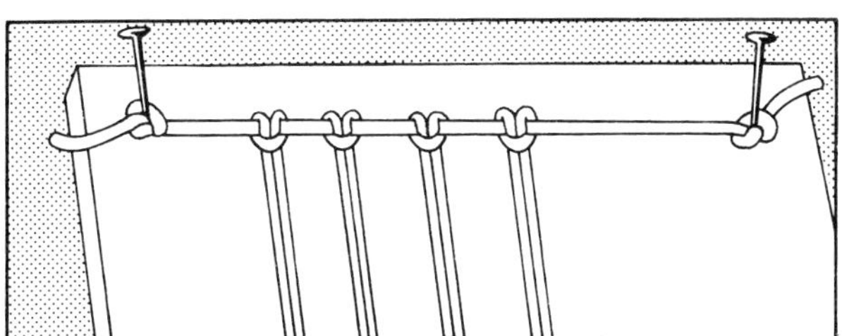

cord. Position each doubled set-on cord close to the previous one. Each individual cord length is now referred to as a knotting or working cord – there should be double the number of knotting cords, as the number of cords you cut. For instance, if you cut ten cords, now they are set on you will have twenty working or knotting cords.

THE KNOTS

Half hitch

This may be worked from the left or from the right. In its simplest form, you need only 2 knotting cords. To work the knot from the left, hold cord 2 taut, and take cord 1 across cord 2, then under it from right to left, and down through the loop formed. Draw tight, this is one half hitch (A). Continue to repeat the knot to form a chain. As cord 1 forms the knot, it is known as a **knotting cord**; cord 2 is the **knot-bearing cord.**

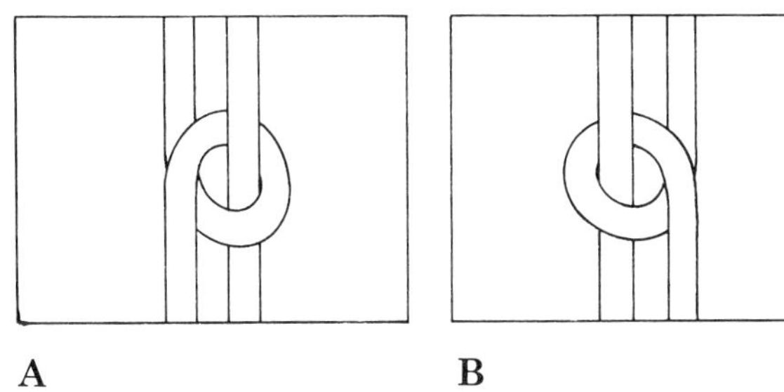

A   B

To tie a half hitch from the right, the procedure is reversed. Cord 1 becomes the knotbearing cord and it is held taut, while cord 2 is the knotting cord and is taken across cord 1, then up under it from left to right and down through loop (diagram B).

Reversed double half hitch

This knot can be used to create attractive braids. It consists of one half hitch worked in the normal way followed by a half hitch worked in reverse – i.e. take knotting cord under the knotbearing cord, round and over it and through the loop formed. A reversed double half hitch may be worked from the left or from the right.

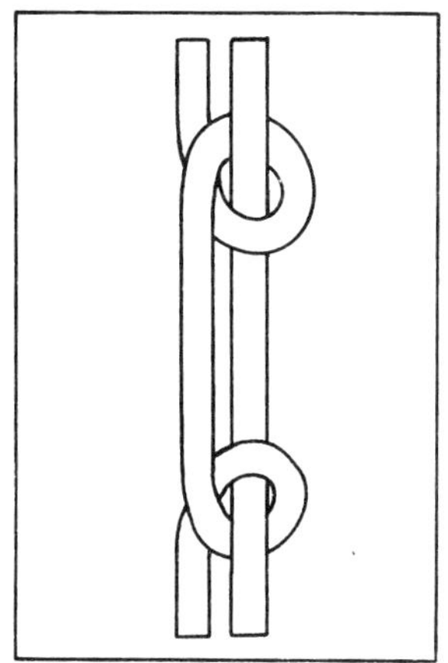

Flat knot

This knot is the basis for most macramé fabrics, or if the knot is worked in a continuous chain the result is a strong, hardwearing braid which can be used for a handbag handle, for a belt, or even for a dog lead. In its simplest form, a minimum of 4 cords are needed. In this case 2 cords (the 2 outside ones) are knotting cords; the 2 centre cords are knotbearers. It is important at all times that the centre knotbearing cords are kept as taut as possible, as this is the secret of tying an even, regularly-shaped flat knot. The knot is tied in 2 stages: begin by taking cord 1 under cords 2 and 3 and over cord 4. Now bring cord 4 over 2 and 3 and under 1. Pull gently into place. This is the first stage of the knot, and is known as the **half knot.**

Complete the flat knot by bringing cord 1 back under cords 3 and 2 and over 4. Bring cord 4 over 2 and 3 and under 1. Pull gently into place below first half knot.

Multiend flat knot

This is merely a flat knot worked with multiple thicknesses of string. It can be worked with single knotting cords as in the basic flat knot, and all the extra cords used to give a multiple knotbearing centre; or cords may be divided evenly to give multiple knotting cords, and multiple knotbearing cords; or you may have only 2 knotbearing centre cords as in the basic knot, and the remaining cords divided evenly to give 2 equal groups of multiple knotting cords.

Cording

This is an important macramé technique. It can be worked horizontally, vertically or diagonally, and used to shape edges, to create solid fabrics or open-work lacy patterns, and once the technique has been fully mastered it can also be used to 'draw' figures. A row of horizontal cording worked immediately after cords have been set on gives a good firm start to knotting, and similarly a row of horizontal cording can be worked at the end of a design to bring it to a neat conclusion. In a design which used different panels of pattern a dividing row of cording between each panel introduces a pleasing element of order (see sampler wall hanging, page 278). Cording is based on the half hitch, and each complete knot in cording, whether it is worked horizontally, vertically or diagonally, consists of two half hitches worked closely together. The complete knot is known as a double half hitch.

Horizontal cording

The knotbearing cord in cording is called a **leader cord** and this may be either one of the set-on cords or it may be a separate cord. To work cording with a separate leader, cut a new cord similar in length to each of your set-on cords. Tie an overhand knot near one end of the leader cord and pin it through the knot to your working surface, positioning it just below holding cord edge and to the left of the first set-on cord. Stretch leader tautly across working cords, then beginning with set-on cord on far left,

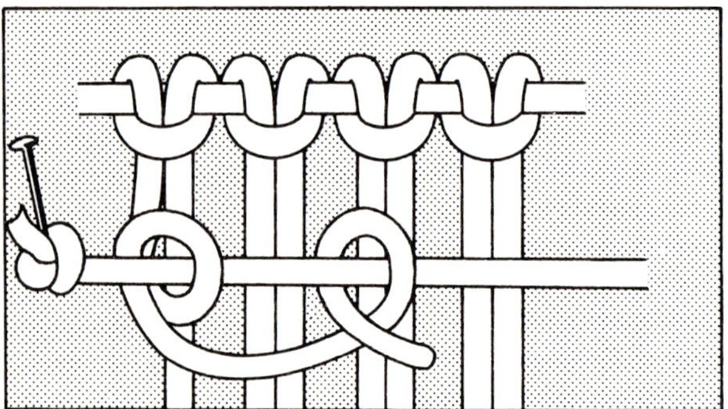

bring it up in front of leader, then down behind it and bring end through to the left of loop formed round leader. Repeat this process exactly: this completes one double half hitch. Continue in this way along row of set-on cords, tying a double half hitch with each cord in turn round leader. Draw each knot tightly and push it close to the previous one.

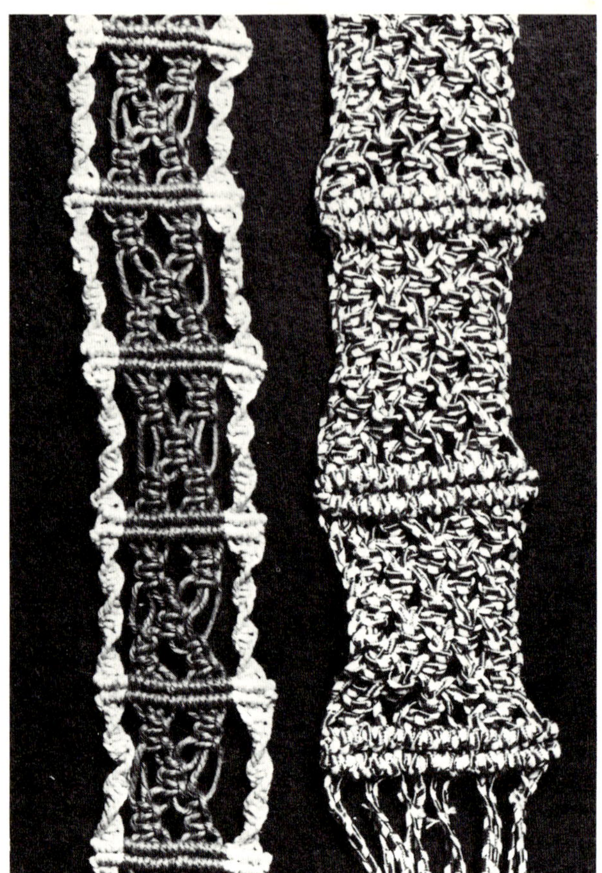

Two braids – flat knot patterns separated by rows of cording.

To work a second row of horizontal cording immediately below the first, place a pin in your working surface to the right of the last knot in the first row, then bring leader round the pin and stretch it tautly across work as before, but this time from right to left. Work double half

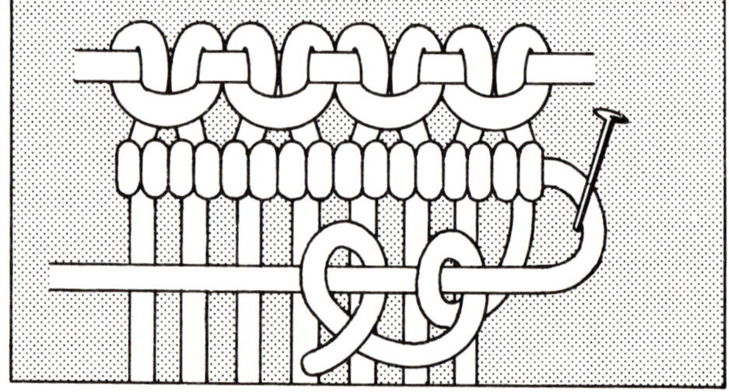

hitches across row over leader, working this time from right to left. Now each half hitch will be tied by bringing working cord up and over leader, then down behind it and the end brought through to the right of the loop formed.

Diagonal cording

This is worked in a similar way to horizontal cording, but leader cord is placed across work at an angle, according to where you wish the line of cording to appear.

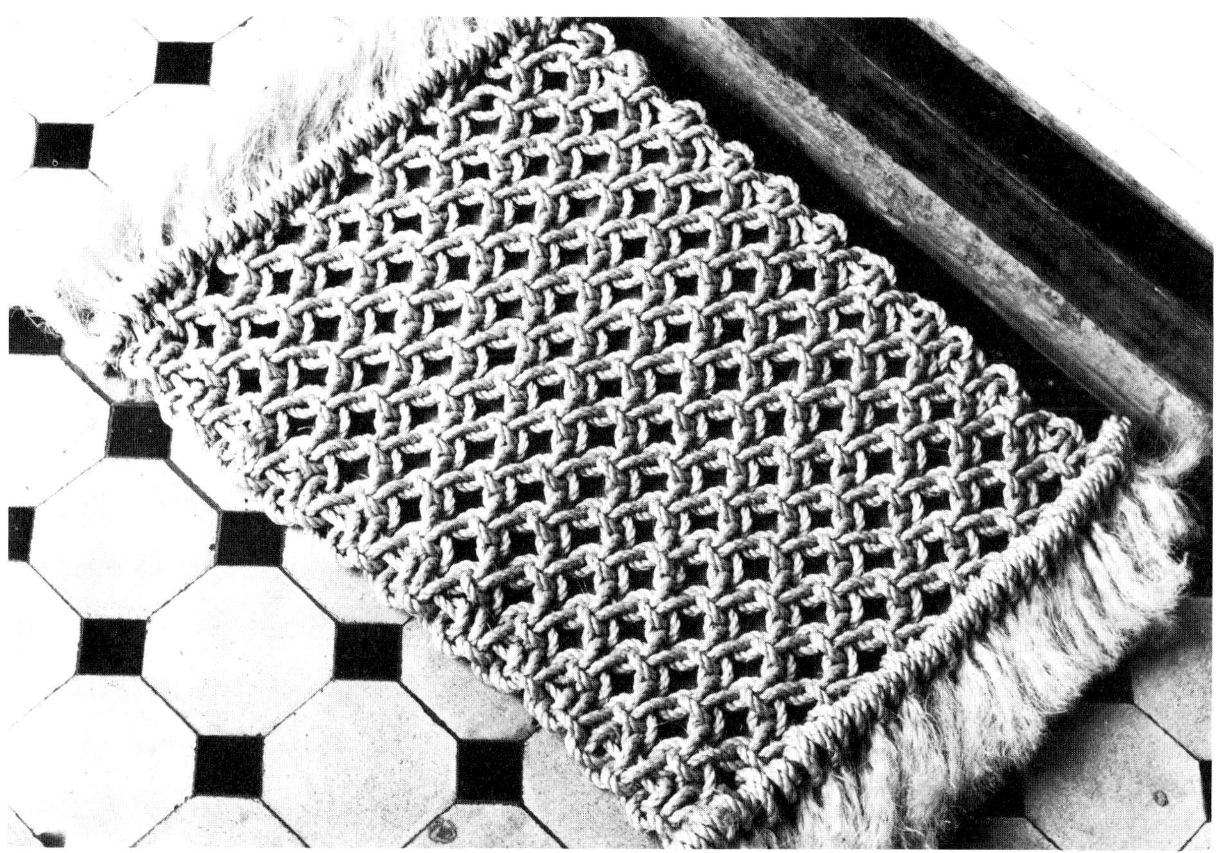

Above: door mat worked in sisal string, in
alternate flat knots.

Below: bag knotted in plastic twine, with a
band of leaf motifs.

*Sampler wall hanging – panels of different
knotting patterns are separated by rows of
horizontal cording.*

Necklace worked in fine string with china beads.

Vertical cording

In this cording technique, all the knots are tied with one cord, and each set-on cord in turn becomes the knotbearer (or leader). Attach a separate cord, as for horizontal cording, to the left of working cords. Take this cord under the first set-on cord and then bring it in front of set-on cord from right to left, round behind it from left to right and bring end through to the right of work above loop formed. Repeat process exactly: this completes one vertical double half hitch. Take knotting cord under second set-on cord and repeat knotting process as for first cord. Continue in this way across row.

To work a second row of vertical cording, reverse knotting cord's direction round a pin, and continue working double half hitches across row as before, but this time from right to left. Always take the knotting cord **under** the knot-bearing cord before beginning to tie each knot.

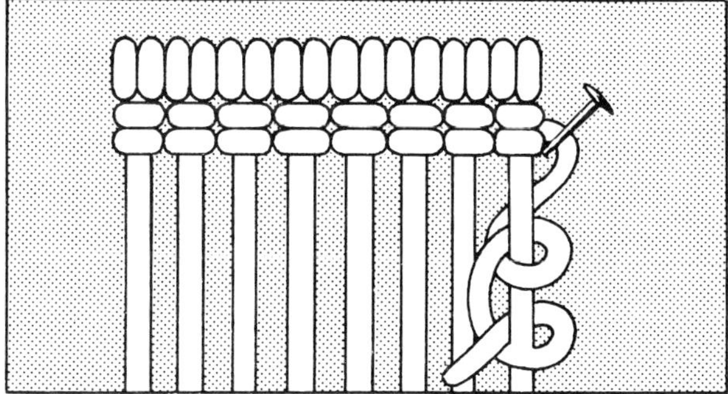

KNOT PATTERNS
Solomon's bar

This is simply a continuous chain of flat knots.

Alternative half hitch chain

To work a single alternate half hitch chain, work with 2 knotting cords, tying a half hitch first from the left, and then from the right. Continue in this way, alternating the direction of each knot.

The double alternate half hitch chain is worked in a similar way as for the single alternate half hitch chain, but double knotting cords are used.

Banister bar

If the half knot (the first half of the flat knot) is tied continuously an attractive spiral is produced, known traditionally as a banister bar. After every fourth half knot the spiral will twist right round on itself. Allow it to do this then continue tying knots with the cords in their new positions.

Alternate flat knot pattern

This is probably the most frequently used pattern in all macramé work, and is the most suitable pattern for making a fabric. If knots are tied tightly and close together a dense fabric is produced; if they are tied loosely and space left between knots and rows a lacy, open-work fabric is created. The total of knotting cords should always be a multiple of four. The pattern is worked as follows:

1st row: tie a flat knot with each group of 4 cords to end of row.

2nd row: leave first 2 cords unworked, then tie a flat knot with each group of 4 cords to last 2 cords in row; leave these unworked.

These two rows are repeated throughout until work is length required.

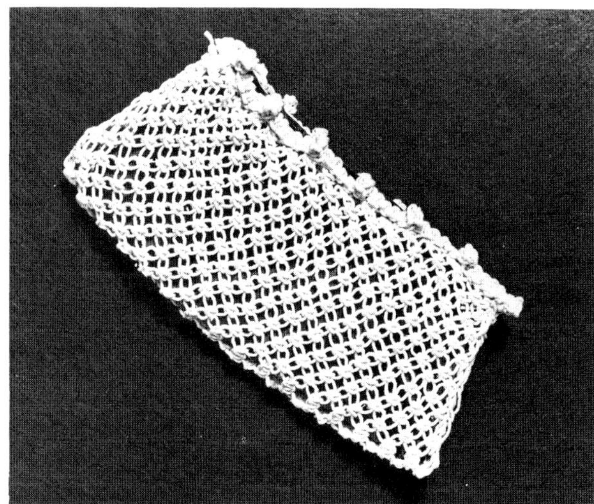

Purse worked in the alternate flat knot pattern.

The alternate flat knot pattern may be varied by having two knots in every row (instead of single ones), or by having one row of three knots, followed by two rows of single knots, and then a row of three knots again, maintaining the alternate sequence all the time. Many other variations are possible.

Tatted bar braid variation

Work with 8 cords as follows:
1st row: work a reversed double half hitch from the left with cord 1 over cords 2 and 3; take cord 5 under cord 4 and use it to tie a reversed double half hitch from the right over cords 2 and 3. Tie a reversed double half hitch from the right with cord 8 over cords 6 and 7, then tie a reversed double half hitch from the left with cord 4 over cords 6 and 7.
Next row: tie a reversed double half hitch from the left with cord 1 over cords 2 and 3, bring cord 4 under cord 5 and use it to tie a reversed double half hitch from the right over cords 2 and 3. Tie a reversed double half hitch from the right with cord 8 over cords 6 and 7. Tie a reversed double half hitch from the left with cord 5 over cords 6 and 7. Repeat these two rows until braid is length required.

Leaf pattern

This is another traditional pattern which occurs frequently in all types of macramé work. It is based on cording, and may be worked with cords in groups of 6 or 8, although 8 is the more traditional number.

The top curve of the leaf is formed by using cord 1 as leader and positioning it into the curve shape, then working cording over it with each knotting cord in turn. To complete the lower curve of the leaf, cord 2 becomes leader and is positioned to form the curve. Cording is then worked over it with each knotting cord in turn, including the leader from previous row — this closes the leaf at its tip. Leaves may be arranged to lie from left to right, or right to left, or a pleasing pattern created by working rows of leaves alternating the direction of each row (see sample shown here).

FINISHING WORK

The simplest and often the most effective finish to a piece of macramé work is a fringe. The fringe may merely be trimmed evenly and left plain, or if wished a further knotting pattern may be worked on the fringe cords. Overhand knots tied in individual cords of a fringe can look attractive, so can coil knots, which are worked as follows: form a large loop at the point where you wish the coil to appear. At the point where the loop crosses wind cord several times round itself. Gently pull both ends of the cord and the winds will form themselves into a coil.

Cords can be 'collected' into groups at the end of work with a collecting knot: arrange cords in groups as required, then take cord on far right of group, form a loop in it and take the cord across the front of the group from right to left, round the back and through the loop. Draw tight. The knot may be worked several times if wished to give a stronger finish.

If an unfringed, smooth edge is wanted at the end of work, it is best to finish design with a row

Half knot spirals, cording diamonds and flat knots are used in each panel of this knotted lampshade.

of horizontal cording. Trim cord ends to about $\frac{1}{2}$ in. from this row of cording, then unpin work from surface, turn it over and press ends to back of work. They can be held in place with a spot of glue, a strip of self-adhesive transparent tape, or by working a row of running stitches across them with needle and fine sewing thread.

COLOUR WORK

A simple colour pattern may be achieved merely by using different colours of cords, and setting them on in any arrangement wished. Cording is a useful technique for taking colour from one part of the work to another, as the colour of a leader cord is always hidden. When it is wished for the colour to reappear select a different leader, and let first leader become a knotting cord.

Cavandoli work

This is a particular form of colour knotting which was devised in Italy in fairly recent years. The finished effect is similar to a solid woven fabric — when worked in fine yarn, it can in fact be easily mistaken for tapestry work.

The work is carried out entirely in close horizontal and vertical cording. The background is worked in horizontal cording, the design, in a contrast colour, is picked out in vertical cording thus all the set-on cords are in the same colour, and only the leader cord is in the contrast shade. Designs can be 'plotted' on graph paper for this technique, each square on the graph representing one double half hitch knot (horizontal or vertical).

Part 2—
THE PATTERNS

Buckled belt
MATERIALS. 1 ball of mediumweight parcel string. A 3-in. buckle.

MEASUREMENTS. Finished belt measures approximately 36 in. long, 2 in. wide, but can be made to any length as required.

TENSION. 5 double half hitches (horizontal cording) measure 1 in.

PREPARATION. Cut 6 cords, each 8 yd. Take one of these cords and pin it by its midway point to working surface so it forms an inverted 'V' shape from the midway point. Set on one cord to the centre tip of the inverted 'V' holding cord, setting on cord with double half hitches (cording) instead of usual method. Arrange knots so one double half hitch falls either side of tip of 'V'. Now set on remaining cords in a similar way (i.e. with double half hitches), two on either side of this centre cord. The holding cords now drop down to become knotting cords, so you have a total of 12 working cords.

TO MAKE
* Tie a single flat knot with cords 5, 6, 7 and 8.
Working in alternate flat knot pattern, tie a flat knot with cords 3, 4, 5 and 6, and then with cords 7, 8, 9 and 10.

Tie a flat knot with cords 5, 6, 7 and 8. (This completes a diamond of alternate flat knot pattern.)
** With cord on far left as leader slanting down to the right, work diagonal cording over it with first 5 cords.
With cord on far right as leader slanting down to the left, work diagonal cording over it with remaining 5 cords.
Now link the 2 leaders by knotting a double half hitch with right-hand leader over left-hand leader.
Tie a single flat knot with 4 cords now lying on far left of work. In a similar way tie a single flat knot with the 4 cords at far right.
Leader from left-hand side of work now continues across work and 5 cords at right-hand side are knotted over it. In a similar way leader from right-hand side becomes leader on the left, and the 5 left-hand cords are knotted over it.
Tie a single flat knot first with 4 cords in centre of work, then with the 2 left-hand cords from this knot together with 2 cords on its left, and finally with the 2 left-hand cords from second knot together with 2 cords on far left of work (one of these cords will be the leader from previous row of diagonal cording).
Complete right-hand side of work with single flat knots to correspond.
Now take 2 cords lying in centre of work, and with left-hand

cord as leader slanting down to the right, work a double half
hitch (cording) over it with cord on the right.
This right-hand cord now continues as leader slanting down
to the left and diagonal cording is worked over it with the 5
cords on left-hand side. In a similar way left-hand cord
continues as leader slanting down to the right and cording is
worked over it with cords on right-hand side. **
Tie a multiend flat knot with 10 cords in centre of work (i.e. all
cords except leaders from previous rows of diagonal cording).
Have triple knotting cords; 4 centre knotbearing cords.
Reverse directions of leaders from previous rows of cording,
then repeat from ** to **. ***
Repeat from * to *** until belt is 36 in. (or length required).
When belt is long enough, finish with a row of flat knots
straight across work (to give a level edge to finished work).

TO COMPLETE
Unpin work from working surface. Turn it over then lay buckle
on top of cords so bar of buckle is close to the last row of
knots worked. Now work a double half hitch over the buckle
bar with each cord in turn. Trim cord ends neatly, and if
necessary secure with a spot of fabric glue to back of knotting.

Ribbon-trimmed hat

MATERIALS. 2 balls mediumweight parcel string. 1½ yd.
ribbon binding, 1 in. wide.

MEASUREMENTS. Total depth of hat, including brim, is
approximately 9 in.

TENSION. Chain of 2 flat knots measures ½ in.

PREPARATION. (*Note. As this design is worked 'in the
round', a flat working surface is not suitable. The ideal working
base is a wig stand, preferably padded with a thin layer of
foam plastic, as this will give an accurate guide to shaping.*)
Cut 12 cords, each 2 yd. Cut a holding cord of about 6 in.
Set on 11 of the cords to the holding cord in the usual way,
then tie the ends of the holding cord together in a single knot.
Set on remaining cord to holding cord over this knot. Pull
knot tight, so a small circle is formed with set-on cords evenly
spaced around it. Do not draw circle too tightly, but leave it
open with a diameter of about 1 in. Trim ends of holding cord,
and tuck them into set-on edge of cords nearest, so they are
hidden. Further cords are set on as work progresses to give
increased width.

TO MAKE
Work a 2-row band of alternate flat knot pattern, with 2 knots
in each row.
Cut a separate leader, about 12 in. Lay this round work close
to last knots worked, then work horizontal cording over it
with each cord in turn. Between each group of 4 cords, set
on to the leader cord 2 new cords, each cut to 2 yd. Set cords
on with double half hitches, so completed row looks like a
continuous row of horizontal cording. Tie ends of leader cord
together, and tuck in ends to half hitches nearest to hide them.
You should now have a total of 48 working cords.
Place work on wig stand, or whatever working base you are
using, and proceed with main crown section of hat as follows:
1st patt. band: work half knot spirals with each group of
4 cords. Work 7 knots in each spiral, and allow spirals to turn
right round on themselves after the 4th knot.
Work a 2nd row of half knot spirals in alternate sequence from
first.
As you knot, ease distance between rows and knots to achieve
correct shaping.
Cording row: cut a separate leader, about 20 in. In a similar
way as before, work cording over this leader with each cord
in turn, introducing 36 new cords, each cut to 5 ft., evenly
round row. Tie ends of leader cord and conceal, as before.

2nd patt. band: work 2 rows of alternate flat knot pattern,
with single knots in each row. Continue in alternate flat knot
pattern for another 4 rows, but this time have 2 knots in each
row. Continue to ease distance between knots and rows to
give the correct shaping.
Cording row: cut a separate leader, about 30 in. In a similar
way as before, work cording over this leader with each cord in
turn, introducing 24 new cords, each cut to 1 yd., evenly
round row. Tie ends of leader cord and conceal, as before.
This completes crown section of hat.
Work brim section, as follows:
Continue in the alternate flat knot pattern, with 2 knots in
each row. Work 7 rows in all (or more for a deeper brim).
Again adjust and ease knots and spaces between rows to give
shaping of brim. Towards the end, knots and rows should be
drawn tighter to give an upward-curving brim.

TO COMPLETE
Lay a separate leader round cords and work cording over it
with each cord in turn to neaten edge. Tie ends of leader cord
and conceal, as before.
Cut ribbon into two lengths: one at 2 ft., the other at 2½ ft.
Use longer length to bind outside edges of brim. Thread other
length through flat knot chains immediately above cording
row on lower edge of crown section. Cross ends of ribbon
over each other and secure with a few neat stitches.

Sampler bag
illustrated opposite

MATERIALS. 3 balls of mediumweight parcel string. ¾ yd.
lining material, 36 in. wide (optional).

MEASUREMENTS. Finished bag measures approximately
12 in. wide, 11 in. deep.

TENSION. Chain of 2 flat knots measures $\frac{1}{2}$ in.

PREPARATION. Each side of the bag is made alike.
For each side therefore cut 36 cords, each 8 ft. Set these on to a holding cord, of about 18 in.

TO MAKE MAIN SECTION (make 2 pieces alike)
With cord on far left as leader, work a row of horizontal cording across all cords.

1st pattern panel. Work spirals of half knots with each group of 4 cords. Work 12 half knots in each spiral, and allow spiral to twist round on itself after every 4th knot.
1st divider row: with cord on far left as leader, work a row of horizontal cording across all cords.

2nd pattern panel. Divide cords into groups of 8 cords. Work on first group of 8 cords:
With cord 8 as leader slanting down to the left work diagonal cording over it with cords 7, 6, 5, 4, 3, 2 and 1.
Now slant cord 7 down to the left and work a second row of diagonal cording immediately below the first, knotting over it cords 6, 5, 4, 3, 2, 1 and 8 (leader from previous row). Work a third row of diagonal cording this time using cord 6 as leader and knotting all cords over it, including cord 7 (leader from previous row.)
Repeat this three-row band of diagonal cording with each group of 8 cords across row.
2nd divider row: as first divider row.

3rd pattern panel. With first 4 cords work a chain of 5 flat knots. With last 4 cords in row work a similar chain of 5 flat knots. Now divide remaining cords into groups of 16. Work on first group of 16 cords:
With cord 8 as leader slanting down to the left, work diagonal cording over it with cords 7, 6, 5, 4, 3, 2 and 1.
With cord 9 as leader slanting down to the right, work diagonal cording over it with cords 10, 11, 12, 13, 14, 15 and 16.
Now tie a multiend flat knot with cords 4, 5, 6, 7, 10, 11, 12 and 13 (i.e. the 8 cords now lying in centre of group). Have double knotting cords, 4 centre knotbearing cords.
Reverse direction of cord 8 round a pin, and using it as leader slanting down to the right, work cording over it with cords 1, 2, 3, 4, 5, 6 and 7.
In a similar way reverse direction of cord 9 round a pin, and use it as leader slanting down to the left to work diagonal cording with all cords on right-hand side of motif.
Repeat this motif with each group of 16 cords across row.
3rd divider row: as first divider row.

4th pattern panel. As first pattern panel.
4th divider row: as first divider row.

5th pattern panel. Work on centre 24 cords first:
Work in alternate flat knot pattern, tying $1\frac{1}{2}$ flat knots in each row (i.e. one complete flat knot plus a half knot).
First row will have 6 chains of knots in it.
2nd row: leave first 2 cords unworked; work 5 chains of knots; leave final 2 cords unworked.
3rd row: leave first 4 cords unworked; work 4 chains of knots; leave final 4 cords unworked.
Continue in this way, working one knot fewer in each row, and dropping 2 cords from each end of row each time, until the row is worked with only one chain in it. This should have formed a 'V' pattern of alternate flat knots.
Now divide remaining cords in this pattern panel into groups of 8 each (three groups on either side of centre flat-knot panel just worked). Work on first group of 8 cords:
Work a four-row band of diagonal cording slanting down to the right, using cord on far left as leader for each row. At the end of each row the leader for that row will drop down to become a knotting cord in following row.

After fourth row of cording has been worked reverse direction of last leader used round a pin, and work a similar four-row band of diagonal cording this time slanting down to the left. Use cord on far right of group as leader for each row.
Repeat this pattern sequence with each group of 8 cords across row.
5th divider row: as first divider row.
6th pattern panel. Work 4 rows of alternate flat knot pattern, with 2 knots in each row.
Finish with a row of horizontal cording across all cords, using cord on far left as leader.

TO MAKE HANDLE

Cut 6 cords, each 8 yd. plus 8 times the length of finished handle required. Set these on to a holding cord, about 6 in. Work in alternate flat knot pattern, with 2 knots to each row until work is 3 ft., plus length of handle required.

Finish with a row of horizontal cording across all cords, using cord on far left as leader.

TO COMPLETE

Trim cords at lower end of each main section to within ½ in. of knotting.

Trim leader cords for each main section and also handle to within ½ in. of knotting. Press these ends to wrong side of work, and secure with a few neat overcasting stitches. Trim cords at end of handle to about 1 in. Place this edge to the set-on edge and stitch neatly together with overcasting stitches, keeping cord ends at back of work. Place both main sections together, wrong sides facing. Place handle in position, so its stitched short edges line up with top edge of, main sections, and it forms a gusset going down one side. along lower edge and up other side. Stitch neatly in place. Make up lining if wished, and insert into bag, wrong sides together. Oversew in place round top edges.

Blue bag

illustrated in colour on page 269

MATERIALS. 2 hanks Twilley's '747' Orlon Sayelle (alternatively, rug wool can be used, or even a thick knitting yarn. If a knitting yarn is used, however, it may be necessary to set on more threads than given here in order to achieve the correct finished width of bag). A piece of lining fabric, approx. 13 in. by 25 in.

MEASUREMENTS. Finished bag measures approximately 12 in. square, excluding fringe, with a 36-in. handle.

TENSION. 1 flat knot in '747' Orlon Sayelle measures approximately 1¼ in. across.

PREPARATION. For each side of bag: cut 12 cords, each 3 yd. Set them on to a holding cord of about 40 in., positioning cords centrally on the holding cord. You now have 24 working ends. **For handle:** cut 4 cords, 2 at 7 yd. 1 ft., 2 at 3 yd.

TO MAKE BAG (make 2 pieces alike)
***1st row:** tie flat knots with each group of 4 cords (6 flat knots altogether).
2nd row: leave first 2 cords unworked; tie flat knots with each group of 4 cords to last 2 cords; leave these unworked (5 knots).**

Repeat from * to ** until 10 rows of flat knots have been worked altogether, or to length required. (*Note. Do not tie knots too close together, but space them out so you get a lacy effect.*)

Make second section to match.

Now place both bag sections together, wrong sides facing, and tie multiend flat knots across lower edge, combining 4 cords from each side in every knot; tie each knot with double thickness knotting cords, 4 central knotbearing cords.

TO MAKE HANDLE

Lay 4 cut cords side by side on your working surface so 2 shorter cords are in the middle. Tie an overhand knot about 10 in. down from the ends.

Begin knotting immediately below the overhand knot and work a continuous chain of flat knots for 5 ft., or to length required. When chain is long enough, tie an overhand knot close to last knot.

TO COMPLETE

Position one end of handle down one side of bag, so overhand knot lines up with lower edge of bag. Thread each holding cord from top edges of bag on to a large-eyed darning needle and use to stitch bag to handle on each side.

In a similar way, stitch other end of handle down other side of bag. Fold lining material in half, right sides together, and stitch side seams together, taking ½ in. turnings. Trim and clip seams, turn right side out and place in bag so wrong sides are together. Turn in ½-in. hem round top edge and slipstitch in place to inside of bag.

Trim fringe to approximately 10 in. or length required.

Lace-up beaded belt

MATERIALS. 1 ball mediumweight parcel string (dyed, if wished). Approx. 53 china beads.

MEASUREMENTS. Width of belt approx. 3½ in.; length is adjustable to fit size of waist for which belt is being made.

TENSION. Chain of 2 flat knots measures ½ in.

PREPARATION. Cut 16 cords, each measuring 8 times the finished length of belt raquired. Set these on to a holding cord of about 8 in.

TO MAKE

1st pattern panel. 1st row: work chains of 2 flat knots with each group of 4 cords to end of row.
2nd row: thread a china bead on to first 2 cords; work a chain of 2 flat knots with next 4 cords; (thread a bead on to next 4 cords; work a chain of 2 flat knots with next 4 cords) 3 times; thread a bead on to last 2 cords.
3rd row: as first row.
Divider row: with cord on far left as leader work a row of horizontal cording across all cords.

2nd pattern panel: work 3 rows of alternate flat knot pattern, with 2 knots in each row.
Next row: as 2nd row of first pattern panel.
Work another 3 rows of alternate flat knot pattern, 2 knots in each row.

Divider row: as previous divider row.

3rd pattern panel: as first pattern panel.
Divider row: as previous divider row.

4th pattern panel: work an alternate 4-row pattern of half knot spirals, with 7 knots in each spiral.
(*Note. If it is wished to increase or decrease the size of finished belt, add or subtract half the extra measurement here — i.e. work an extra row of spirals, or one fewer.*)
Divider row: as previous divider row.

5th pattern panel: as 2nd pattern panel.
Work divider row as before.
6th pattern panel: as 4th pattern panel but only work 2 rows of half knot spirals.
Work divider row as before.
7th pattern panel: as 2nd pattern panel.
Work divider row as before.

8th pattern panel: as 4th pattern panel, adding (or subtracting) the remaining extra measurement, if required, to adjust the size of belt here.
Divider row as before.
9th pattern panel: as first pattern panel.
Divider row as before.
10th pattern panel: as 2nd pattern panel.
Divider row as before.
11th pattern panel: as first pattern panel.
Work divider row to finish.

TO COMPLETE

Trim cord ends to about $\frac{1}{2}$ in. Press to wrong side of work, and secure with a neat row of running stitches. Work a crochet chain about 46 in. long, with 4 beads threaded on each end of the chain, to lace through front edges of belt to fasten. Alternatively a single alternate half hitch chain can be worked. Tie an overhand knot at beginning and end of chain to keep beads in position.

FINISHING TOUCHES

The right trimming can often add further interest to any piece of work — knitting, crochet, embroidery, macrame or sewing. Here are a few ideas for simple, easy-to-make trimmings, plus hints on keeping your needlework looking as good as new for as long as possible.

TRIMMINGS

Tassels

Cut a piece of cardboard the desired length of tassel. Wrap yarn around cardboard, tie a thread through upper end, cut through lower end. Wrap thread around upper part several times to hold tassel together.

Fringes

Yarn fringe. Cut a length of heavy paper the desired width of fringe plus $\frac{1}{2}$ in. and as long as the part to which the fringe will be attached. Fasten the yarn to the paper and wrap it around the paper, laying the strands touching each other but not overlapping. Machine stitch across one long side about $\frac{1}{2}$ in. from the edge. Cut through the strands on the opposite side. Tear away the lower part of the paper. Turn under and top-stitch the edge of the garment to the top of the fringe. Remove remaining paper.

Knotted fringe. Narrowly hem the edge to which fringe will be attached. Thread a large darning needle with 2 or more strands of the yarn. Turn under the edge to which the fringe is to be attached. Working from right to left, bring needle up through turned edge of fabric. Take stitches about $\frac{1}{4}$ in. apart, leaving loops of the desired length between stitches. When a sufficient number of loops have been made, cut them and knot the yarn of each stitch. Trim lower ends evenly.

Pompons

Method 1. Cut a large number of long strands of yarn and secure the ends. At intervals, tie a thread tightly around the strands. Cut through the yarn between these threads. Roll between the palms of your hands to shape a ball and trim evenly.

Method 2. Cut 2 circular pieces of cardboard the same size as required for finished pompon. Place together and cut a hole through the centre; the larger the hole the thicker the finished pompon will be. Wind yarn evenly around cardboard passing through the hole each time until cardboard is covered. Continue to wind yarn round until hole is almost completely full. Break off yarn and cut through yarn and outer rim of cardboard. Tie yarn around centre between cards to secure and slip cardboard discs off. Shake well and trim if necessary.

AFTER-CARE

Knitting and crochet

Washing. Never allow a knitted or crocheted garment to get too dirty. Careful washing does not damage any fabric but when a garment is very soiled, normal use of washing agents will not remove all the dirt without rubbing and it is this rubbing which causes damage to the fibres. Make sure the washing agent, whether it is soap, soap flakes, soap powder or a detergent, is thoroughly dissolved in hot water, and then add cold water to reduce the temperature before placing the knitted garment in the solution. Always make sure that enough washing water is prepared to cover the garment completed.

Never boil any knitted or crocheted garment. The water temperature should be about 40 deg. C. (104 deg. F.), just hot enough for your hand. Do not use any form of bleach.

Allow the washing agent to remove the dirt. Do not rub the fabric. Gently ease the fabric in the washing water, but do not lift the garment in and out of the water as this causes stretching. All fabrics are more easily harmed or distorted when wet than in a dry state.

Take the garment from the washing water and gently squeeze to remove as much of the water as possible. Rinse the garment in at least three changes of warm water. The third rinsing water should be quite clear after rinsing the garment in it. If it is not it means that there is still some soap or detergent in the garment and another rinse is needed until the water is absolutely clear. Gently squeeze the garment on removing it from the final rinse and roll it in a clean dry white towel without twisting. This will absorb most of the excess moisture.

Spread the garment out flat on a clean towel and ease it into the correct shape and size. Allow it to dry slowly in the shade or in an airing cupboard.

Embroidery

Embroideries should be pressed as you go along as well as when you are finished a design. Damp thoroughly and place face downwards on top of a thick pad of material so threads will not be crushed. Choose iron setting according to fabric, and press well. Embroideries should be washed in warm water and soap powder. Always squeeze the article in the soapy water, then rinse well. Iron on wrong side when still slightly damp.

Needlepoint tapestry

A piece of embroidery worked on canvas must always be dry cleaned as the use of water would soften the canvas.

ACKNOWLEDGEMENTS

The author and editor acknowledge with thanks the help given with the preparation of this book by the following:

J. & P. Coats Ltd, 155 St. Vincent St., Glasgow C.2.
Emu Wools Ltd., Low Street Mills, Keighley, Yorks.
John C. Horsfall and Sons Ltd. (Hayfield Wools), Hayfield Mills, Glusburn, Nr. Keighley, Yorks.
Lister and Co. Ltd., Providence Mills, Wakefield, Yorks.
Martin Mahony and Bros. Ltd., Blarney, Co. Cork.
Patons and Baldwins, P.O. Box 22, Darlington, Co. Durham.
Robin Wools Ltd., Bradford, Yorks.
Sirdar Ltd., Bective Mills, Stamford, Lincs.
Wendy and Peter Pan Knitting Wools, Carter & Parker Ltd., Gordon Mills, Guiseley, Yorks.
Abel Morrall Ltd. (Aero knitting needles, crochet hooks, Twinpins and other products).
H. G. Twilley Ltd., Roman Mills, Stamford, Lincs.
Victoria and Albert Museum, London—for permission to reproduce photograph on page 268 (black and white). Crown copyright.
Barbara Snook—for samples and designs illustrated on pages 184, 192 (couching and flat), 206, 210, 211, 217 (yellow sample), 222, 236, 237, 262.
Kate Pountney—for patchwork, appliqué and quilting designs illustrated on pages 229, 253, 257, 261, 264, 265.
Joan Lodge—for samples and designs illustrated on pages 185, 217 (duck), 228, 229 (canvas work belt), 260.
Mrs. F. M. Blake—for smocking samples illustrated on pages 248, 249.
Wm. Briggs and Co. Ltd.—Penelope designs illustrated on page 196.
Simplicity Patterns Ltd.—for photographs on pages 25 and 28.
The Singer Company (UK) Ltd., Consumer Products Division—for machine embroidery sample illustrated on page 192.
Brolac—for colour illustration on page 17.
The trustees of Michelham Priory, Sussex—who permitted the use of the Priory as a background for photography in the knitting, crochet and sewing sections.
The photographs on pages 125, 128, 132, 152 were taken at the Westerham Riding Stables, Westerham, Kent.
The photographs on pages 133, 157, 176, 177 and 181 were taken outside The Merry Harriers coaching inn, Cowbeech, E. Sussex.